28810

DATE DUE

DEC 1976			
DUE APR 2 8 1981			
DUE JUL 1 1982			

j

Information Technology
in a Democracy

Harvard Studies in Technology and Society

The volumes in this series present the results of studies conducted at the Harvard University Program on Technology and Society. The Program was established in 1964 by a grant from the International Business Machines Corporation to undertake an inquiry in depth into the effects of technological change on the economy, on public policies, and on the character of the society, as well as into the reciprocal effects of social progress on the nature, dimensions, and direction of scientific and technological developments.

Volumes in the Series

Information Technology in a Democracy

EDITED BY ALAN F. WESTIN

Harvard University Press
Cambridge, Massachusetts
1971

Preface

This collection grows out of a larger study on the use of information technology by American government, on which I have been working since 1967 under the auspices of the Harvard Program on Technology and Society. The Program has done all the nurturing things that an intellectually oriented center can do for scholars, such as supplying stipends, research assistance, travel funds, and secretarial aid. But the deepest value to me has been the climate of argumentative inquiry provided through continuous discussions with the Program's Director, Emmanuel G. Mesthene, its Associate Director, Juergen Schmandt, and the Head of the Program's Information Center, Irene Taviss. My evolving ideas on information technology have been presented also at informal meetings with scholars working in the Program; this has saved me from committing more than my fair share of mistakes, and leaves me in the debt of Harvey Brooks, David Landes, Seymour Lipset, John Meyer, Anthony Oettinger, and Richard Rosenbloom.

In collecting and preparing the materials on which this reader is based, I was greatly aided by Ellen Schroeder and Mary O'Melveny, who served as research assistants on the larger project. For reading the next-to-last version of this collection and helping me reorganize it "one last time," I am grateful to Julie Heilman. Typing aid in the final stages of the manuscript was provided by Katie Sullivan, last-minute searches of periodicals by Marjory Karukin, and work on galleys by Lorene Cox, Rita Harris, and Gladys Cooper. For great help in the final editing process, I am indebted to Stanley Dry, the Harvard Program's Associate for Publications.

In assembling this book, I have chosen pieces of writing that seemed to me to exemplify the main currents of opinion in each area being treated. This has often meant having to select one or two pieces from among many excellent statements of a particular position, relegating the parallel commentaries to the bibliography. Each piece has been edited to minimize repetition of factual, technical, or political discussions within this collection. Rather than have the book continually spattered with dots to indicate such deletions, I have obtained permission from most of the individual authors to omit such editorial stigmata. Each such author received a copy of the selection as it had been edited and gave permission for its use in that form. A few authors wished the omissions specifically noted, and, of course, this has been done with their selections.

Alan F. Westin

New York
September 1970

Contents

II. "Control Technology" in a Democracy: The Broad Socio-Political Debate   147

III. The Information Function in Organizational Decision-Making   237

IV. Emerging Information Systems: The Policy Debates   287

A. Databanks

B. Management Science Techniques

Information Technology
in a Democracy

The new [management science] techniques . . . are beginning to be recognized as the greatest advance in the art of government since the introduction nearly a hundred years ago of a civil service based on competence.

Max Ways, "The Road to 1977,"
Fortune Magazine (*1967*)

[This] marks the beginning of a new era—the really *scientific era. Up to now, everything has been haphazard . . . [Now] there are to be forty interlocking committees sitting every day and they've got a wonderful gadget . . . by which the findings of each committee print themselves off in their own little compartment on the Analytical Notice-Board every half hour. Then, that report slides itself into the right position where it's connected up by little arrows with all the relevant parts of the other reports. A glance at the Board shows you the policy of the whole Institute actually taking shape under your own eyes. There'll be a staff of at least twenty experts at the top of the building working this Notice-Board in a room rather like the Tube control rooms. It's a marvelous gadget. The different kinds of business all come out in the Board in different coloured lights. It must have cost half a million. They call it a Pragmatometer.*

C. S. Lewis, That Hideous Strength: A
Modern Fairy-Tale for Grown Ups (*1946*)

ALAN F. WESTIN

Prologue: Of Technological Visions and Democratic Politics

The dream that a new technology might liberate man from both the tyranny of nature and the fruits of his own folly is as old as Western civilization. With the printing press men thought the spread of literacy would dispel the ignorance, prejudice, and terror of life. It was felt that the steam engine and the factory system would at last give man the capacity to produce enough so that populations would no longer be hungry, unclothed, and ill housed; on this foundation, wars and revolutions would no longer plague mankind. When the aerial balloon was invented, leading statesmen saw this as the end to national wars; each side would observe the other and there would be no surprise or advantage in border maneuvers. The telegraph and radio were hailed as instruments that would bind all peoples into a connected network. After the explosions at Hiroshima and Nagasaki, we "knew" wars would be unthinkable in the future.

Now we have entered the electronic age. Between 1950 and 1970, computers revolutionized data processing, mathematical calculations, and physical control systems. From this foundation of real achievement, voices rose again to suggest that computers and communication systems might serve as the agents to bring society into an entirely new phase. Information about social reality could now be made so rich and detailed, policy options could be so clearly defined, the probable outcomes of alternative measures could be so accurately predicted, and the feedback mechanisms from society would be so effective that man could at last bring his full intelligence to bear on resolving the central problems of society.

1

But there is another theme that is also as old as Western civilization: the fear that man might seize more knowledge than he was meant to have, or than he is able to control. Our theology, myths, and folk wisdom reverberate with this warning, from the expulsion of Adam for tasting the apple of knowledge to the sorcerer's apprentice who almost drowned when he tried the magic that was reserved for the Master. In real life today, it is not paranoid to worry whether atomic weapons may lead to the destruction of all life on earth, or whether man may so contaminate his environment through the offshoots of his technology that life will become unbearable amid its luxuries.

It was in the 1960's that writings about the computer began to echo this tradition. In both popular and intellectual circles, alarms were sounded about the future of privacy in an age of computer databanks, over the dehumanization created when computerized transactions replace face-to-face relations, and about the possible rise of technological elites with insufficient fidelity to democratic processes. As the 1960's came to an end, one foreboding emerged that drew all the others together and carried the popular concern to its "ultimate" end. Rather than try to express this in analytical terms, let me use the format of science fiction to present its basic fears and prophecy.

The setting of my story is the United States in the early years of the twenty-first century; the year 2020 would be about right. The leading character, Cosmo Pragmos, is a master program-caseworker in the Bureau of Life Simulations. As the story opens, Pragmos' latest assignment has him composing a narrative of how things developed as they did during the last quarter of the twentieth century. What is bothering him is whether he should attribute the progress of those years primarily to the breakthroughs in computer technology during the late 1970's (fourth-generation machines and their laser communication network) or to human decisions prompted by the great social upheavals of the 1980's.

As he had learned in his youth, in his courses on "Prescientific History," social disturbances had been on the increase in the United States since the 1960's. But the use of tactical nuclear weapons by the Federal Peace Corps to quell the Black Guerilla Forces in Chicago in 1980 clearly marked a new level of confrontation. The two-year national boycott of public schools in 1982–1984 added to the tension. Little comfort came from the report of the Surgeon General in 1982 that 70% of those under 40 were using "hard" drugs an average of 2.4 times per week. The mutiny of the Los Angeles police draftees and the movement of Miami, Florida, to become a federated republic within the United States typified what was happening in cities all over the country.

Pragmos remembered that no system-wide response was made to these and other social dislocations until the F.S.S.M.M. (the Fold, Staple, Spindle, and Mutilate Movement) managed to insinuate their own subroutines into the Northeastern Computer Information Network, precipitating the disastrous information wipe-out of July 1987.

The National Internal Security Council had immediately convened a secret conference of governmental and civic leaders at National Databank Headquarters in Philadelphia. The opening presentation by Daniel Ring, the President's Social Science Advisor, reminded the conferees that the basic pattern of prescientific America had been set exactly 200 years before in this very city, at a similar closed meeting of national leaders concerned over the drift of events in the newly independent American states. The time had come, said Dr. Ring, to reshape American government once again.

Council Chairman Robert F. Kennedy III then introduced a position paper produced jointly by a consortium of not-for-profit research organizations in the nation, including the CRAND Corporation (Computerized Research and Normative Development), DemoInfo Inc., and Perfect Systems Ltd. The paper drew three powerful but simple conclusions from its review of the American situation in 1987:

1. Man's technological capacities were still outstripping his social and political skills, creating an "anti-technology backlash" that was paralyzing serious efforts to "get on top" of social problems.
2. Information-technology and scientific decision-making — the paramount tools of the computer age — could never fully benefit society as long as the irrationalities and dislocations of popular politics were continued.
3. The potential for solution was clearly present, because repairing the information wipe-out would mean replacing all the data about the past from the underground micro-image vaults in Langley, Virginia, and resetting the programs that controlled the collection, evaluation, and distribution of public information about the present. Thus the power to define and shape social reality for the entire population lay in the hands of those who would be resetting the data systems. If they could agree upon a concerted policy and give up their usual partisan bickering, a fundamental reform of the political and social system was clearly possible.

A conference member from the Inter-University Consortium of Research Centers remarked that playing around with records and falsifying news sounded perilously close to Orwell's *1984* to him. But a CRAND Corporation spokesman reminded the conference that the Ministry of Truth in Orwell's novel, with its continuous "rectification" of the printed page, was a crude system designed to bolster an openly totalitarian dictatorship. By contrast, this conference was proposing to preserve democratic society. The only way to do that was by resolving the conflict between expert planning and popular participation that was making it impossible to heal the divisions and eliminate the causes of social conflict in American society.

The implications of the Consortium's studies proved to be tremendously persuasive to the Philadelphia Conference; from social analysis they moved rapidly to social action. By unanimous agreement they created a National Systems Design Commission which encompassed all the influential groups in the national establishment — industry, the military, the knowledge communities, labor unions, the planners, professional associations, the Union of Ethnic and Minority Interests, and government leaders from local, state, and national agencies. A special post as System Ombudsman was filled by the Chairman of the American Civil Liberties Union.

What the NSDC produced was a "two-track information design" for American society. One track, called *reallife,* routed actual information about social events to committees of highly skilled systems analysts and public administrators. The other information channel, called *simtrack,* contained a mixture of real and manufactured data. This was the one fed into the public channels of communication.

By 1989, the two tracks were set in place. Policies on key economic and political affairs were handled on *reallife* while *simtrack* programs were designed to explain and produce ratifications of *reallife* decisions. Elections for public office were still exciting, hard-fought contests involving 100 million American voters in the deeply satisfying turmoil of democracy. But they were really pseudoevents; all the policy issues, personality clashes, and campaign events were designed on *simtrack,* which now emanated from the secret Bureau of Political Simulations in Johnson City, Texas. To help smooth this transition, all legal restrictions on drug use were abolished, as were the remaining censorship laws on Total-Vision, and the compulsory education statutes.

With its virtually unlimited data-storage capacities and vast programmer resources, the NSDC created a Bureau of Life Simulations to program the personal careers of all those not part of the *reallife* system. This monumental step was followed in the 1990's with an expansion of *simtrack* from political events into a new third channel, called *lifetrack*. Educators, lawyers, artists, sportsmen, service workers, housewives, engineers, and everyone else had the major encounters of their lives planned by program caseworkers, who had access to each individual's Life Dossier.

The caseworker made sure that each life was made challenging but never so difficult that the individual could not achieve feelings of competence and purpose. Such *lifetrack* programs were written on the basis of a new psychology known as simulation-response, which replaced the earlier stimulus-response concepts of the prescientific age.

As a first rate program-caseworker Pragmos regarded simulated processes as thoroughly logical and socially beneficial. Social problems had simply outgrown the traditional participative processes and the three-track information system was the most cost-effective, benefit-maximizing way to deal with them. The solution of the Men of '87 — to place popular politics outside the "loop" of real decision-making rather than eliminate it — had met the ultimate test. It worked. Certainly some policies and projects failed. The F.S.S.M.M. persisted in isolated spots around the country, and there were rumors that they were being financed by the Union of Asian Communist Republics. But Pragmos knew how much better things were than they had been in the middle decades of the twentieth century, and he believed strongly, as did all his colleagues, in the basic ethic of the scientific age — *optimize*.

This was the situation in 2020 when Pragmos was assigned a new life-simulation case — a young professor of prescientific history. To program this man's encounters, Pragmos had to read works of history, philosophy, and political science from the eighteenth, nineteenth, and twentieth centuries. As he pored over these chronicles of life and thought in a strange, unprogrammed society, with its fascinating pattern of disorderly and accidental creativity, he began to wonder whether programming personal lives and making social decisions scientifically was — he had difficulty coming up with the right words — a "good thing."

At first the thought was casual. Master program-caseworkers were expected to question their tasks from time to time. It gave them the opportunity to reflect on and then recognize even more clearly the advantages of social programming over social chaos. But this time Pragmos could not get it out of his mind. Just what was it that was supposed to be so harmful in a free balance of individual choice and social order?

As Pragmos read further (Marx, Kant, Croce, Dewey) and even branched into fiction (Zamyatin's *We* and Karp's *One*), he became more and more taken with these colorful times. Finally, he decided he had to

5

take positive action. He began preparing in his spare time a report and analysis of what seemed to be missing under the three-track information system. He was not yet sure where he would submit the report, but he felt that if his ideas were well developed, they would be sure to receive a fair hearing in the Bureau.

Then, while he was working on another case, his mind wandered for an instant and he punched an incorrect set of numbers into his console. He was about to abort the instruction, when a message flashed on the viewing screen:

> LIFE-SIMULATION ACCOUNT No. 71-33-4450 (Cosmo Pragmos) Instructions for February 2020.
> He will continue this month his concern over the programming of personal lives and political decisions. Readings will include John Stuart Mill, *On Liberty*; Almond and Verba, *The Civic Culture*; and Paul Goodman, *Growing Up Absurd*. He will complete "Simulated Civilization and Its Discontents," and begin final consideration of the proper body to receive it. . . .

This ends my story.[1] Readers familiar with computers will note quickly that Pragmos' shock of recognition could have been avoided through better system design. His console should have been programmed to reject his own life account, even if that number were put in accidentally.

But the more intriguing question — its "lady or tiger" aspect — is: "Who was Pragmos' program-caseworker?" The most obvious answer is someone in a higher bureau. But my story also suggests the possibility that by the early twenty-first century, the computers realized (calculated) that the human beings who managed them, for all their technical expertise and optimizing neutrality, were constantly distorting the decision-making process with human biases and the desire to perpetuate their own elite status. The capacity of computers to learn from experience, to create their own programs, and even to achieve and improve upon the goals of the original programmers has already been predicted.[2] Just as my story assumes it was technologically possible for the political elites to operate a multiple-track information system successfully after 1987, so, too, it

1. Some time ago, I read a science fiction story that utilized the programmed programmer device. I have not been able to locate the original story, and have thus constructed my own account to lead up to that moment. I register here my apologies to the author for not being able to cite his contribution.

2. See, for example, Marvin L. Minsky, "Artificial Intelligence," in *Information* (San Francisco and New York: W. H. Freeman, 1966); Herman Kahn and Anthony J. Wiener, *The Year 2000: A Framework for Speculation on the Next Thirty-three Years* (New York: Macmillan, 1967), pp. 88–98, 351–352.

contemplates that the computers were able to take over from the techno-logical elite a few decades later, making even the *reallife* track a simulation.

My "2020 Vision" is obviously a cautionary tale, in the tradition of negative utopias. It parallels the delightful book by Olof Johannesson, *The Tale of the Big Computer*.[3] In Johannesson's story, computers are relied on more and more to record and regulate the complexity of economic, social, and political life in the later twentieth century. Then a power shortage develops through a combination of human carelessness and a struggle for advantage among the computer scientists. The computers came to a standstill, and with them, all productive and life-sustaining activities. A human society that had ceased to trouble itself with the knowledge of how the computers worked was unable to repair the computer systems. It took a long time for the age of the "Great Disaster" to end, but man returned to his starting point and the computers were slowly put back into operation. As they moved into high speed again, the computer program and analysis components calculated that they could no longer afford to depend on human tenders; they developed a completely self-generating and self-maintaining system within the computer networks. Toward the end of the novel, the question is posed in the computer units whether mankind serves any useful function and should be preserved. There is concern that man is a "security risk," capable of attempting an uprising against the communication networks or the power sources. But these risks have been so minimized that the decision is made to keep man. Just as man kept a limited number of horses even after the invention of the internal-combustion engine enabled man to dispense with horsepower, the data machines wish to keep man out of an affection for the earlier symbiotic relation of man and machine that produced the data machine civilization.

Similar tales of take-over by computers have appeared recently in a wide variety of cultural forms, such as Stanley Kubrick's science fiction movie, "2001: A Space Odyssey," John Barth's satiric novel of society as a college campus (*Giles Goat-Boy*),[4] and Burt Cole's account of computer-detected deviations (*The Funco File*).[5] In all of them, there is first the novelist's assumption that computer systems can accomplish these feats of information storage and program response, followed by a belief

3. New York: Coward-McCann, 1968.
4. New York: Doubleday, 1966.
5. New York: Doubleday, 1969.

that the more malevolent human groups of society will take charge of the computers, and then, that the computers will capture the whole system.

These works are obviously attempting to focus society's attention on where electronic technology might take us if we do not develop instruments of legal, political, and cultural control. In a sense, such literature is a counterweight to the flood of writing about the year 2000 that arose in the mid-1960's,[6] in which visions of new social competence were so often predicated on improvements in computer technology and the widespread use of information systems for scientific decision-making.

But are we really dealing with 2020, or even 1987? The basic ingredients for moving toward technological information systems are already here — powerful computers, complex communication systems, and a variety of "management science" techniques for decision-making through data analysis and systems theory. Sometimes singly and sometimes in multifaceted programs, these techniques are spreading rapidly throughout the governmental and private-organization sectors of American society. More and more, government officials beset by the complexity of current social problems and the difficulties of achieving success with traditional decision-making techniques are beginning to consider the new information technology, listening to systems developers and social scientists who paint alluring visions of this approach as the way to save a democratic society from *data-over-load* and *decision-impasse*.

Even at this early stage, when the technology is admittedly imperfect and the organizational patterns for such an approach are highly experimental, the use of information-technology components in public decision-making has stirred important debate. Is information technology delivering — or can it ever deliver — its promised benefits? Do such systems represent an inevitable centralizing and tightening of corporate and elite power in American society? Could the systems be used to redistribute and equalize power if the electorate so demands? What effects is the arrival of such systems having or will it have on such things as the structural aspects of public agencies, the relations of executive agency decision-making to the organs of criticism and review, and the classic political and constitutional arrangements for conducting government in the United States? Do such systems lead to dehumanization of and dependence by the clients under their jurisdiction? Could information technology be designed to

6. See Kahn and Wiener, *The Year 2000*; "Toward the Year 2000: Work in Progress," *Daedalus*, vol. 96, no. 3 (Summer 1967).

increase individual and group participation in the decision-making processes that affect them?

It was to explore these questions that the Harvard Program on Technology and Society invited me in 1967 to do research into the effects of information technology on decision-making by government agencies. In my book on *Privacy and Freedom,* which had been completed earlier in 1967, I had speculated that computers and complex communications systems, when linked with various organizational and social trends in contemporary American life, might be moving us into a new era in the relationship of information-production to organizational decision-making.[7] My concern in *Privacy and Freedom* had been with the effects of surveillance technologies on individual civil liberties, particularly the citizen's right to privacy and his guarantees of due process of law, and I had limited my analysis of computerization to that issue. But at a weekend conference that the Harvard Program had sponsored in 1967 to discuss technology and civil liberties, I had joined some of the social scientists present in raising the larger question of the effects that computerization might have on democratic political practices. It was this issue that the Harvard Program encouraged me to pursue, as part of its studies in "Technology and the Polity."

I began work by refreshing my reading in my own field of political science, especially in the materials on public administration and intergovernmental relations. From there, I waded into the swamp of multidisciplinary literature on organizational behavior, decision-making, and information technology. I also began writing to a wide variety of government agencies that had announced their adoption of advanced computer systems or computer-based management science techniques, asking for copies of their system plans, progress reports, and policy documents.

After working through these source materials, I wrote a long essay in February of 1968 on "Information Technology and Democratic Government." The paper defined a "public technological information system" as one in which "a government agency accumulates large-scale pools of data (with a heavily behavioral focus), manipulates these by computer hardware and software, and applies the output to the production and use of systems-analysis in the decision-making process of the agency on issues of public policy." The essay described the basic nature of public decision-making in modern society, set out a simple classification scheme to represent the factors that shape public decision-making in any

7. Alan F. Westin, *Privacy and Freedom* (New York: Atheneum, 1967).

society, and sketched lightly the ways in which changes in those factors in American society during the 1950's and 1960's seemed to be altering some "classic" American patterns of public decision-making. The essay then described in detail the two main "routes toward information technology" that had appeared thus far: the creation of computerized databanks for use by government agencies and the adoption of various management science techniques such as program budgeting and systems analysis.

The essay then set out a series of fundamental questions that these trends raised about the future of public decision-making, much along the lines of those posed earlier in this introduction. At this point in the essay I had to note that there were no adequate empirical materials on which to attempt fact-based answers to those leading questions. Government databanks and scientific management systems were in such early stages of development in 1967; their effects were still so soft and tentative, especially in the civilian sector to which my inquiry was limited; and their future courses of growth and trauma were still so uncertain that anyone who attempted to reach judgments about the basic questions in early 1968 would be making an ideological rather than an empirical response.

After this paper was read and discussed at the Harvard Program, it was agreed that the Program would sponsor a small research project which would collect materials on the progress of information technology in the late 1960's and prepare several publications that would try to present what the first fifteen years of computerization had meant for the decision-making processes of American government. The plan called for the production of two books.

The first — this volume — was to be an edited collection of original and secondary materials about government use of information technology. As the reader can now see for himself, the volume includes descriptions of information technology systems by the agency spokesmen and consultants who have created them, providing readers with the operating assumptions, systems objectives, and stages of development as the managers of these systems see these happenings. Then, this trend is put in a context of broad sociopolitical debate over the role of electronic technology in the "post-industrial society," through ideological analyses that range from hard-conservative through technocratic and on to the region of the cultural left.

From there, the collection moves into some pinpointed essays by social scientists on the role of information and information-handling in organizations per se, public and private. This is followed by a full-dress debate over the specifics of computerized databanks and management science techniques as this debate began to emerge in the late 1960's. Material from my 1968 essay has also been included, along with an extensive bibliography. The value of publishing such a collection, it was felt, would be its presentation of the issues in and debates over information technology in American government as these matters were perceived in the 1960's. In that sense, it is a documentary portrait of the issue and an intellectual history of our responses to it so far.

Meanwhile, a second volume would be undertaken during 1968–1970 based on empirical case studies of several government agencies and jurisdictions that were installing information-technology systems and had gone far enough with these to test their effects on the organizational forms and decision-making patterns of the agency. This volume will set out a series of factual assumptions and theoretical hypotheses about decision-making in American government in the pre-computer era (essentially 1945–1960), survey the movement of information technology into government operations during the 1960's, and use the case studies to illustrate what seem to be the typical and revealing results of this adoption on our governmental processes and institutions. This volume is now being completed.

I. Descriptions of the Developing Systems by Their Advocates

Introduction

For Part I, I have chosen selections by the managers and advocates of technological information systems. These illustrate with their own writings the claims that are being made for the new techniques and the steps being taken toward installation of these techniques in government agencies. The selections are divided into what I see as the two major "routes" along which government agencies are moving steadily toward full-dress technological information systems: (1) the creation of computerized databanks and (2) the adoption of management science techniques. Each of these routes deserves a preliminary discussion here.

The Databank Route to Technological Information Systems

The most common classification of databanks, popularized during the National Data Center debates of 1966–67, distinguishes between "statistical" and "intelligence" systems. A statistical system is one organized to receive or collect data on individuals or groups in order to study systematic variations in the characteristics of groups. The purpose of the system is to conduct research and policy-planning studies. Though it requires identification of data by the individuals in the sample populations in order to associate new data with older holdings and to conduct longitudinal studies, data on individual persons are not the intended output of a statistical system. Furthermore, it is not intended to serve as a means of regulating or prosecuting individuals.

An intelligence system is one in which the data are deliberately organized into "person" files or dossiers to furnish reports about specific individuals. It is precisely to centralize data about individuals now held by scattered sources within government (and perhaps by private data holders as well) that the intelligence system is created. Intelligence systems can be used for research and policy studies, but their primary purposes are administrative (personnel management, licensing, payroll, etc.); regulatory (taxation, welfare, zoning, etc.); or punitive (police and law enforcement, national security, etc.).

This twofold classification separates databanks according to their basic purpose and the directness of their regulatory effect on particular individuals. While these categories have value for considering the different policies that might be set for protecting privacy and providing due process in administering the two types of databanks, I think this is not the most useful way to consider databanks in the decision-making process. "Intelligence" is a word that carries too many investigative, law enforcement, and loyalty-security connotations, and the databanks developing in education, transportation, welfare, or urban management ought not to be saddled with such an emotionally charged term. In addition, "intelligence" is too gross a category, and can be separated into several operating categories with greater profit to analysis.

In the typology that follows, five types of current government databanks are identified, based on a combination of their location within the organizational structure of the executive branch and the central purpose of the databank. Figure 1 illustrates the way these relate to the political executive of a city, county or state.

Type 1, the *Statistical Databank for Policy Studies,* is an independent agency that collects information for research and policy-planning; it has no operating responsibilities to administer, regulate, or prosecute. It may be available to several or all agencies and departments for statistical services and special reports, or it may be used solely by the political executive (mayor, governor, etc.) or his principal administrative agency (budget bureau, controller's office, etc.).

An example of Type 1 is Detroit, Michigan's "Physical and Social Data Bank," described in one of the selections in Part I.[1] Though developed primarily to plan and study the city's urban renewal projects — Detroit spent $200 million in this area in the past decade — the databanks are available to any city department.

City officials report that the databank has "proved to be an immensely

1. Harold Black and Edward Shaw, "Detroit's Data Banks," *Datamation* (March 1967), pp. 25–27.

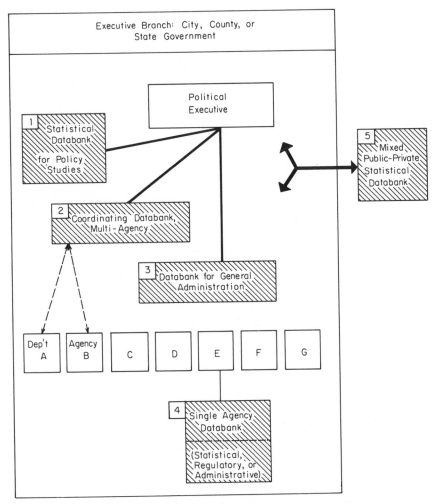

Fig. 1. Five types of databanks involved in public decision-making

useful tool." It was used in writing the city's application for a federal Demonstration Cities Act grant; by the city board of education, which "can use the crime and truancy data to see if more emphasis might be put on school-oriented after-hours activities (such as athletics, special vocational training, teen club programs, and the like)," and by the neighborhood rehabilitation program, which needs to know the "attitudes, motivations, and social characteristics" of the people with whom it works.

Detroit officials stated in early 1967 that "the age of computers has ushered in a new age of urban planning." Their description of progress was published in March of 1967; four months later, however, the city went up in flames, urban renewal projects and all.

Another example of the policy studies databank is the "District of Columbia Real Property Data Bank." The basic unit of record is a lot or parcel, identified by address, lot and block number, census tract, police and voting precinct, school district, etc., and containing such information about the property as its size, land use, zoning, taxes, improvements, assessments, etc. Albert Mindlin, the Chief Statistician for the District of Columbia, has reported as follows on the uses of the bank:

> Examples of the uses that have been made of the D.C. real property databank are site acquisition studies by School, Highway and Fire Departments; sampling frame by Urban Renewal and Health Departments for such things as blight, sanitation control, and neighborhood health center studies; manpower distribution programming of housing and other inspectors, and of policemen; civil defense community shelter programs; numerous economic studies by various organizations both public and private; zoning vs. actual land use studies; address, city block, census tract and other directories; and as a base for mechanization of agency files. The bank provided the principal data base of the community renewal program. In the absence of the bank most of these projects would have been more costly, far less satisfactory, and many of them would have been impossible.[2]

Type 2, the *Coordinating Databank,* is an agency formed to collect and store information from various departments and agencies, usually at more than one level of government, and to perform various information analysis and data-dissemination functions for the participating agencies. Like the statistical databank, the coordinating databank is not created to operate substantive programs but to serve as an "information handler" for the "line agencies."

A leading example of Type 2 is the New York State Identification and Intelligence System (NYSIIS), also described by its director in a selection in Part I. NYSIIS was developed by a gubernatorial study group in 1963 and created by legislative act in 1965 as an independent state agency to facilitate "information sharing" among the 3600 criminal justice agencies in New York State. The director of NYSIIS, Dr. Robert R. J. Gallati, describes the system as follows:

---

2. Albert Mindlin, "Confidentiality and Local Data Systems," Conference on Small Area Statistics, American Statistical Association, December 27, 1967. Census Tract Papers Series GE-40, No. 4, U.S. Bureau of the Census.

NYSIIS as independent agency in the Executive Department, is specifically empowered to collect, coordinate, store, process, retrieve and disseminate information relevant to the investigation and prosecution of crime and the administration of criminal justice. As a state information service only, it has no other operational functions; therefore it will not be in competition with any existing criminal justice agency. The system and its Director have no powers, duties or facilities to arrest, prosecute, confine or supervise.

NYSIIS is bringing to more than 3,600 agencies of criminal justice in the State the latest techniques of automation, electronic data processing and related technology. It provides a data base of shared information to serve the information needs of the six major functional areas of criminal justice. Thus, by serving *all* officials and agencies concerned with criminal justice, a unitary concept — whether they be police, district attorneys, courts, or authorities in probation, correction, and parole — a common information pool will enable achievement of common goals. For separate purposes involved, each agency needs to know the same things: Who the defendant is, what he did, and his relevant background.[3]

California has developed a similar statewide criminal justice information system and already has state coordinating databanks in the motor vehicle[4] and educational fields.[5] Florida's State Department of Education has installed a coordinating data system called SPEDE (System for Processing Educational Data Electronically) which it describes as a "statewide total pupil information system." [6]

Type 3, the *Databank for General Administration,* is the technologically minded public administrator's dream, the "total management information system" that has all the operating agencies at a governmental level "on line" in "real time," with the data generated available for system-oriented decision-making. So far, the pioneers with this concept have been county governments, with cities also involved in developmental efforts.

In Alameda County, California, whose one million population includes Oakland and Berkeley, an administrative databank was begun

3. Robert R. J. Gallati, "Computerized Information Against Crime," *State Government* (Spring 1967), p. 108.

4. Montijo, R. E., Jr., "California DMV Goes On-Line," *Datamation* (May 1967), pp. 31–36.

5. Grossman, A., "The California Educational Information System," *Datamation* (March 1967), pp. 32–37.

6. L. Everett Yarbrough, "The Florida Project: A System for Processing Educational Data Electronically," *Journal of Educational Data Processing,* vol. 3, no. 2 (Spring 1966); *System for Processing Educational Data Electronically* (Tallahassee, Fla.: State Department of Education, 1966); *Activities Summary of Information Systems* (Tallahassee, Fla.: State Department of Education, 1966).

in 1965 with the initiation of a "People Information System." [7] In 1967, this contained files on 200,000 individual county residents. The goal of the system was to "print out what the computer knows" about John Jones when he applied for "social services like welfare, hospitals, health, and probation" or if he was the subject of an inquiry by any of the 93 law enforcement agencies in the Greater San Francisco Bay area. Alameda County's director of data processing in 1967 described his plans to expand the system to "embrace other county people files." The long-range goal was to link an expanded "People Information System" with a "Property Information System" and an "Administrative Services System." [8]

The city of Los Angeles has an even more ambitious system under way, the Los Angeles Municipal Information System (LAMIS).[9] Initiated in 1963 as an eight-year, three-phase project, LAMIS is presently a Data Service Bureau with "200 analysts, programmers, systems specialists, operators and clerical personnel . . ." Phase I, planning, was completed in late 1964; Phase II, installation and implementation of an IBM 360 computer and supporting programs, has proceeded since December 1965; Phase III, reconceptualization and redesign of the various applications and subsystems into a coordinated municipal information system, is "to be completed by 1972." Current applications, beyond payroll, city-contractor transactions, and inventory control, include developing a "management system" for sanitation functions, an automated library system, and putting harbor management "on-line," with "a comprehensive data base serving all City departments" as the goal.

Santa Clara County, California's LOGIC system, one of the most advanced Type 3 databanks, is described in Part I in a selection based on the system brochure currently distributed by the County.

The Type 4 databank, *the Single Agency Databank,* is one maintained within a particular department or agency in the executive branch, for statistical, regulatory, or administrative purposes. The United States Secret Service has developed a computerized databank of potentially dangerous persons or groups who might attempt to assassinate the President.[10] The Federal Bureau of Investigation has created a National Crime Information Center to store data on wanted persons, stolen cars,

7. Gordon Milliman, "Alameda County's 'People Information System,' " *Datamation* (March 1967), pp. 28–31.

8. Ibid., p. 31.

9. Takuji Tamaru, "Prospects in Municipal Information Systems: The Example of Los Angeles," *Computers and Automation* (January 1968), pp. 15–18.

10. See Congressional *Record,* Nov. 10, 1969, pp. 13982–13984.

and certain types of stolen property. Local and state law enforcement agencies feed in reports of crimes and can make inquiries about suspicious persons, vehicles, or property in their jurisdictions.[11] The NCIC will be expanded to cover "additional criminal information" in the future, but the direction in which the system will grow has not been made public.

The California Department of Motor Vehicles has developed the Automated Management Information System (AMIS), which stores files on the individual's driver's license, vehicle registration, legal files on his history of moving violations or court convictions, accident reports, and other related motor vehicle data.[12] This information is provided to drivers and to insurance companies for a nominal fee; it also creates instantaneous access to the information for management decision-making purposes. Included in the AMIS system is an automated databank in Sacramento with a large storage capacity and an on-line system linking DMV field officials with courts, law enforcement agencies, and as many as 1,400 terminals.

Type 5, the *Mixed, Public-Private Statistical Databank*, is a system in which data from public agencies and private groups are given to a nongovernmental organization which produces statistical studies of public programs. One example, also represented by a selection in Part I, is the United Planning Organization, a private corporation financed by federal funds to conduct anti-poverty programs in the District of Columbia. UPO has created a Social Data Bank to examine social problems affecting the poor and to study the impact of D.C. anti-poverty programs, under a grant from the U.S. Department of Health, Education, and Welfare.[13]

The District of Columbia government has authorized release of approximately 81,000 individual records to the databank, primarily from education, police, and welfare agencies in the District. To protect the confidentiality of the data, UPO has created a trust, controlled by three independent trustees, to oversee the databank to insure that no information about specific individuals is ever issued by the trust or released to government agencies. Mixed public-private databanks may well develop in the next few years in the medical field, where the creation of regional health information centers will depend on creating an "acceptable" agency out-

11. "N.C.I.C. Progress Report," *F.B.I. Law Enforcement Bulletin* (September 1967), p. 107.
12. R. E. Montijo, "California DMV Goes On-Line," *Datamation* (May 1967), pp. 31–36.
13. "UPO Votes to Collect Wide Data on the Poor," *Washington Post,* January 17, 1968.

side the regular governmental structure to receive and use health data from private as well as public sources.

As this brief catalog illustrates, various types of computerized data-banks are appearing throughout the governmental and semi-governmental structure at every level of American government. The selections presented in Part I provide a "managers' eye" view of them.

The Management Science Route
to Technological Information Systems

As used here, "management science" techniques refer to methods designed to improve the planning and decision-making process of middle or top management in large organizations. They should not be confused with the "scientific management" concepts associated with Frederick Taylor and his disciples, which had production-efficiency rather than decision-making as their focus. The two principal management science techniques operating in the 1960's have been program budgeting (P.P.B.S. — the Planning, Programming, and Budgeting System), and the related analytical perspectives known as system analysis and operations research.

The institution of P.P.B.S. in the Defense Department in the early 1960's and the high regard in which it was held by the White House in the middle 1960's led President Johnson to issue a series of directives instructing all federal departments and agencies to adopt P.P.B.S. procedures.[14] The President's first directive, in 1965, described P.P.B.S. as a "very new and very revolutionary system" that would enable federal officials to do five things:

(1) Identify our national goals with precision and on a continuing basis.
(2) Choose among those goals the ones that are most urgent.
(3) Search for alternative means of reaching those goals most effectively at the least cost.
(4) Inform ourselves not merely on next year's costs but on the second, and third, and subsequent years' costs of our program.
(5) Measure the performance of our programs to insure a dollar's worth of service for each dollar spent.[15]

Progress toward general federal use of P.P.B.S. during the Johnson

14. These directives are reprinted in *Planning-Programming-Budgeting, Official Documents*, prepared by the Subcommittee on National Security and International Operations of the Committee on Government Operations, U.S. Senate, 90th Cong., 1st Sess. 1967, pp. 1–6.
15. Ibid., p. 1.

Administration was somewhat uneven, however. Late in 1966, a memorandum from the President to heads of departments and agencies noted that "too many agencies . . . have been slow in establishing effective planning-programming-and-budgeting systems. And, even when established, they have often not been used in making top management decisions. It is my desire that every agency of the Federal Government have such a system, and use it effectively."[16] The President stressed that heads of agencies would have to bear down on these objectives if they were to be successfully implemented; to show the depth of his "desire," the President indicated that he would have the Budget Director sit down with each agency head in the next few months and review his P.P.B. system, then prepare a quarterly report to the President on "the progress of your implementation of my directive." This would then be in the forefront of the President's thinking, he added, when he made up his own budget and "legislative decisions" for the period ahead.

The President gave P.P.B.S. additional momentum when he called on Congress in his 1967 Budget message[17] and in a special message on "The Quality of American Government"[18] to authorize requested appropriations for P.P.B.S. staffs for the various federal agencies. In addition, the Bureau of the Budget drew up guidelines for applying P.P.B.S. to federal agencies, and called on each agency to submit program categories under which it was organizing its P.P.B.S. analysis.[19] A listing of these program category responses in March of 1967 showed that some agencies, such as OEO, Agriculture, Defense, Interior, and HEW, had taken the direction seriously and had turned out the desired list of labels.[20] Some agencies, such as Justice and Transportation, reported "no program categories yet," and the State Department responded that "the Program structure adopted last spring did not prove satisfactory. Work on a new program structure is stopped pending development of an interagency foreign affairs programming system." The Agency for International Development submitted the following brief response that suggested AID officials might not be completely enraptured with P.P.B.S.:

> The program categories for AID are the individual countries. The subcategories are the major economic sectors, i.e., Agriculture, Health, Industry and Education. The subcategories vary from country to country.

16. Ibid., p. 3.
17. Ibid., p. 4.
18. Ibid., p. 6.
19. Ibid., pp. 9–17.
20. Ibid., pp. 18–34.

The combination of the spread of P.P.B.S. in 1965–1967 and its potential impact on established relations (both within executive agencies and in executive-Congressional relations), led to a series of generally critical hearings on P.P.B.S. during 1967, before Senator Henry M. Jackson's Subcommittee on National Security and International Operations.[21] The hearings reviewed the record of P.P.B.S. in the Department of Defense (calling Dr. Alain C. Enthoven, Assistant Secretary of Defense for Systems Analysis), heard Budget Director Charles L. Schultze on the state of P.P.B.S. in the federal establishment, and published a series of memoranda and articles by social scientists raising doubts about the values of P.P.B.S., especially when extended to "politicized areas" such as foreign affairs and social welfare. Several selections from these hearings are included in this volume, with the "proponents' " view of Alain Enthoven in Part I. In addition, a rising flurry of articles and papers on P.P.B.S. in Washington began to appear during 1966–1967 in the social science literature,[22] raising many of the questions that will be explored in selections from 1966–1970 in Part IV of this volume.

Though it has been less orderly and centralized, a comparable trend toward experimentation with program budgeting and systems analysis appeared strongly at the state and local governmental levels during the 1960's. Often, this represented a response to federal incentives. Federal funds for planning studies were available (and sometimes conducting such studies was made a prerequisite for securing program grants) under major grant-in-aid legislation such as the Federal Law Enforcement Assistance Act, the 1961 Housing Act, the 1962 Federal Highway Act, and the Urban Mass Transit Act of 1964, to mention only a few.

However, some states and localities moved on their own toward management science techniques, often by commissioning private corporations or consulting firms to conduct the basic studies. New York City, after creating a relatively inactive Operations Research Council at the start

21. *Planning-Programming-Budgeting*, Hearings before the Subcommittee on National Security and International Operations of the Committee on Government Operations, U.S. Senate, 90th Cong., 1st Sess., Parts I & II, Selected Comment (1967).

22. See, among others, Virginia Held, "P.P.B.S. Comes to Washington," *Public Interest* (Summer 1966), pp. 102–115; "Defense Systems Resources in the Civil Sector," A Report from the Denver Research Institute to the U.S. Arms Control and Disarmament Agency (U.S. Government Printing Office, 1967); Philip M. Boffey, "Systems Analysis: No Panacea for Nations' Domestic Problems," *Science* 158 (November 24, 1967): 1028–1030; "Planning-Programming-Budgeting Symposium," *Public Administration Review* 26 (December 1966): 243–310; Frederick C. Mosher, "P.P.B.S.: Two Questions," Letter to the Editor, ibid. 27 (March 1967); Yehezkel Dror, "Policy Analysts: A New Professional Role in Government Service," ibid. (September 1967): 197–203; Harold L. Wilensky, *Organizational Intelligence* (New York: Basic Books, 1967), pp. 184–191.

of the Lindsay Administration, signed a contract in 1967 with the RAND Corporation to do a systems study of four major city departments — police, fire, health, and welfare — the goal being application of cost-benefit formulae to reorganization of these city functions. A selection in Part I describes some of these activities. San Francisco commissioned the consulting firm of Arthur D. Little to do a simulation model of the city housing market, for urban planning purposes, with partial financing from the then U.S. Housing and Home Finance Agency.[23] Similar models have been done for Baltimore, Boston, Pittsburgh, and other cities.[24] In 1966, during a congressional hearing on data processing, the System Development Corporation listed a long series of such systems and databank work for state and local governments; these included projects for the Los Angeles and New York City police departments, Youth Opportunities Board of Greater Los Angeles, New York State Identification and Intelligence System, State of Oregon Information System, and San Francisco Bay Area Transportation Commission.[25] Selections describing the activities of SDC and of a leading aerospace firm doing such work, TRW Systems, are included in Part I.

The most innovative state in drawing on private industry to apply systems analysis to state government problems has been California, a trend explained in no small degree by the fact that most of the nation's aerospace corporations are located in California. The story of Governor Pat Brown's commissioning of four such studies (transportation, North American Aviation; waste disposal, Aerojet-General; crime, Space-General; and information, Lockheed) is included in a selection here.

State and local officials interested in applying management science techniques have sought special aid from both private foundations and Congress to finance such efforts. The Council of State Governments, International City Managers Association, National Association of Counties, National Governors Conference, National League of Cities, and U.S. Conference of Mayors — virtually the entire state and local governmental establishment — have joined in a test demonstration of P.P.B.S. for state and local governments. This is financed by a Ford Foundation grant to the State-Local-Finances Project of George Washington University, and

23. See Harry B. Wolfe and Martin L. Ernst, "Simulation Models and Urban Planning," in *Operations Research for Public Systems*, ed. Philip M. Morse (Cambridge: MIT Press, 1967), pp. 49–82.

24. See the *Journal of the American Institute of Planners*, May 1965.

25. Testimony of Dr. Thomas C. Rowan, Vice President, System Development Corporation, "Government Electronic Data Processing Systems," *Hearings before the Subcommittee on Census and Statistics of the Committee on Post Office and Civil Service*, House of Representatives, 89th Cong., 2d Sess., 1966, pp. 231–236.

is using five states, five cities, and five counties for the test. A selection on the results thus far is included in this section.

Support for financing or aiding such state and local efforts to utilize management science methods mounted steadily in Congress during the 1960's and continues in the early 1970's. Bills have been introduced to allow particular federal departments such as Commerce and Labor to support state and local experiments with systems approaches. Rep. Bradford Morse of Massachusetts secured 50 sponsors in the House and 15 in the Senate during the late 1960's for a bill to create a National Commission on Public Management to study the use of "systems techniques" for "non-defense, non-space problems," and to develop programs to use these techniques in specific areas.[26]

Senator Edward Kennedy of Massachusetts introduced a bill to create a computerized information system on federal programs for state and local governments that he foresees as a means of applying systems analysis to the federal-state-local grants-in-aid process.[27] Senator Edward Muskie of Maine, Chairman of the Senate Subcommittee on Intergovernmental Relations, has held hearings on P.P.B.S. by state and local governments and has declared such techniques "a way to . . . creative federalism." Senator Gaylord Nelson of Wisconsin has submitted legislation to give states grants-in-aid for systems analysis.[28]

Support for both databanks and management science measures has continued during the Nixon Administration's first years. For example, the Department of Health, Education and Welfare funded four states to develop "social information systems" for administering individual welfare and medical assistance.[29] The U.S. Office of Education funded a project to create a "Model Total Management Information System" for local school districts.[30] The Department of Justice, under the Law Enforcement Assistance Act, funded ten states to develop databanks of summary criminal history files.[31] And the Department of Housing and

26. See the speech of Rep. F. Bradford Morse (Mass.), "Congress Views the Application of the Systems Approach to Public Problems," reviewing various pro-systems measures in Congress, reprinted in *Congressional Record*, Daily Edition, February 8, 1968, p. 643.

27. Senator Kennedy's explanatory statement is reprinted in Robert O. MacBride, *The Automated State: Computer Systems as a New Force in Society* (Philadelphia: Chilton Book Co., 1967), Appendix 4.

28. See the Senator's foreword in "Criteria for Evaluation in Planning State and Local Programs," A Study Submitted to the Subcommittee on Intergovernmental Relations of the Committee on Government Operations, U.S. Senate, 90th Cong., 1st Sess., 1967, p. iii.

29. "Computer Systems for Welfare," *Public Automation* (December 1969), p. 5.

30. Press Release, U.S.O.E., August 6, 1969.

31. *Public Automation* (September 1969), p. 4.

Urban Development has awarded contracts to two middle-sized municipalities to develop comprehensive municipal information systems; HUD also gave contracts in the same program to four municipalities to create databank "sub-systems" for public safety, public finance, human resources, and physical development.[32]

Significant support for such programs has also continued within Congress during the Nixon Administration. In a lengthy report on "Systems Technology Applied to Social and Community Problems," issued in 1969, the Subcommittee on Employment, Manpower, and Poverty of the Senate Committee on Labor and Public Welfare described approvingly the continuing spread of systems analysis and program budgeting techniques throughout the federal executive agencies and state and local government.[33] The report also listed various activities of Congress promoting this trend and called for their acceleration.

Enough has probably been said in this introduction to show the extensive movement of computerized databanks and management science techniques through major sectors of American local and national government during the 1960's. Though this essay has identified these two "routes" as separate trends, it should be noted that they are usually interlocking phenomena. The technicians and promoters involved in each of the two approaches usually come from a similar technologically oriented and modernized-management outlook. Furthermore, each "route" tends to lead into the other. Creation of a computerized databank usually requires development of a "systems approach" to conceptualize the area and operations on which data are to be more "systematically" collected. Once the data from a computerized reporting system begin to flow in, there is a natural tendency to utilize these expensive and voluminous outputs to achieve the supposed benefits of simulation, operations research, program budgeting, and related management science techniques.

Similarly, the adoption of systems analysis, operations research, and program budgeting by government agencies often creates heavy demands for "better data" — more of it, and more regularly gathered, collated, processed, and distributed. This may result in "one-time" data collections (sometimes called "static databanks"), but if the agency is heavily committed to management science approaches, it is almost inevitable that some kind of computerized databank will be called for, if budgets permit.

32. *Datamation* (November 1969), p. 383.
33. "Systems Technology Applied to Social and Community Problems," Report Prepared for the Subcommittee on Employment, Manpower, and Poverty, of the Committee on Labor and Public Welfare, U.S. Senate, 91st Cong., 1st Sess., June 1969.

Thus the two "routes" toward technological information systems tend to be mutually stimulating.

With these patterns in mind, we can now sample the descriptions of the emerging technological information systems by their managers and advocates. A word about the particular selections that have been chosen may be helpful.

Under the "Databank Route," the first selection describes Detroit's social databank — described earlier in a municipal project designed to provide statistical data for city agencies and the Mayor's office to use in policy-planning and in the preparation of project proposals to federal and state funding agencies. The second selection describes the Santa Clara County total information system, a system that is used for administering programs and evaluating their performance, as well as for planning and statistical analysis. The third selection describes the New York State Identification and Intelligence System, a statewide computer databank covering criminal justice agencies at the city, county, and state levels.

Finally, the article on the United Planning Organization's social databank portrays a databank set up by a mixed public-private, anti-poverty agency in Washington, D.C. With both government agency and private agency data in its hands, the UPO is attempting evaluative studies outside the official government setting.

The selections describing the "Management Science Route" are grouped under three subsections: (1) Planning, Programming, and Budgeting Systems (PPB); (2) Systems Analysis and Operations Research; and (3) the Corporate Consultants.

PPB has already stimulated a flood of literature. There are half a dozen books on PPB theory by its proponents and practitioners, presentations of early experience with PPB in specific government agencies, and extensive criticisms of PPB. Since we are interested in PPB not as a system per se, but as a force moving public agencies toward larger technological information systems, these selections discuss favorably the uses of PPB in a representative set of areas — in Vietnam, in New York State, and in several cities such as Philadelphia and New York. There is also an article describing an experiment with program budgeting in the U.S. State Department that sees PPB as a means of more effectively managing our foreign affairs.

The selections on systems analysis and operations research are grouped together on the assumption that the differences between these two approaches are less significant than the common methodologies and perspectives they share. The first two selections describe systems analysis used for defining better fire protection for East Lansing, Michigan, and for making weapons-system decisions in the Pentagon. The Morse and Ramo selections provide more theoretical justifications, but each also gives concrete examples of areas in which the authors believe the new techniques have proved useful, or could so prove if they were adopted. Finally, there is a selection arguing that legislatures as well as executives and executive agencies need to use systems analysis, not only to keep pace with modern developments but also to preserve effective separation of powers in the computer age.

The subsection on corporate consultants reproduces the published brochures of two companies competing in the market for contracts to perform systems analysis, operations research, or databank projects for civilian agencies. TRW (Thompson-Ramo-Wooldridge) Systems illustrates the space and defense contractor moving into the civil-sector market. SDC (System Development Corporation) is a parallel example, but representing what was at that time the leading "not-for-profit" corporation in this field. The article by Genensky describes the RAND Corporation's "mother contract" to work with New York City on several key areas of urban life, while former Governor Edmund Brown's article relates the story of California's experiment in hiring four major aerospace companies to do systems analysis of basic social issues and to suggest innovative ways for government to attack social problems.

Though the selections in Part I are broad descriptions by those who have embraced the new techniques, later parts of the book contain selections that analyze their use critically. For example, in Part IV, Hoos reviews California's experience with systems analysis in its welfare programs; Schelling argues against using PPB in the State Department; and the University of Denver Research Institute casts a cool eye on the outcome of the California aerospace contracts.

For those seeking further examples of these routes in use today, the Bibliography contains extensive listings organized under the headings used in Part I.

HAROLD BLACK AND EDWARD SHAW

Detroit's Social Data Bank

City government is big business. Like business, a city government is complex and diversified; it deals annually with huge sums of money, and every day its administrators have to make hundreds of decisions. And, like businessmen, city administrators must have at their disposal enough information (and the right kind of information) to make their decisions quickly, effectively, and meaningfully. While it is true that a city does not deal predominantly in the currency of profit and loss, it does deal in something of equal importance and sensitivity: the health and well-being of its people, the vitality of its economy, and the physical integrity of its buildings. So effective decision making is as crucial to city administrators as it is to businessmen or management personnel.

The need for data, for facts and figures and analyses, in the city of Detroit is felt nowhere more keenly than in the city's urban renewal program. In the last decade Detroit has spent or committed more than $200 million in renewal work, and the projects and programs for which this money was spent have affected the lives of over four million people. In the decades to come, even more will be spent, and much more will be done to make Detroit a safe, decent, and beautiful city in which to live and work.

From Harold Black and Edward Shaw, "Detroit's Data Banks," *Datamation* 13 (March 1967); 25–27. Reprinted with permission from *Datamation*®, March, published and copyrighted 1967 by F. D. Thompson Publications, Inc., 35 Mason St., Greenwich, Conn. 06830.

Mr. Black is now in private planning practice and is working toward his Ph.D. in Urban and Regional Planning at the University of Michigan. Mr. Shaw is in public relations work in San Francisco.

In order to carry on its renewal programs effectively — in order to maximize all the available funds, manpower, and know-how — Detroit will have to gather a good bit of data about its people and its buildings. Information about mobility, income, employment, health, substandard housing, obsolescent structures, crime rates, and much more will have to be compiled continually over the years. In addition, of course, systems will have to be developed to sort, analyze, and store this data, and to retrieve just the right information for any given problem or study.

The problem of data collection and processing is not new to Detroit, for over the last few years the city has carried on a number of studies, surveys, and research programs that have involved huge masses of data. In order to solve the problem of organizing and storing this information, we have devised what we call the physical and social data banks. These two data processing and storage systems are precisely what their names imply: repositories for the physical and social data gathered by the city over the last few years.

The hardware we have been using in our dp [data processing] systems consists primarily of the IBM 7040 installation at the Wayne State University computing center.

The physical data bank was designed by a users' group composed primarily of planners and economists in the city government. Since, when we began, we were not particularly sophisticated in our understanding and application of dp techniques, the data system that came out of the initial design has tended to be somewhat inadequate. Our editing procedures, for example, were quite rudimentary, and, as a result, we are faced now with gaps in the data file and, in some cases, with "dirty data." Nonetheless, the physical data bank has proved to be a tremendous improvement over anything we had before, and it has been one of the most useful planning tools we have ever been able to use. And we did, moreover, learn a valuable lesson about data processing from our experiences with it.

The physical data bank contains such information as the condition of the city's residential, commercial, and industrial buildings; property assessment figures; age characteristics of various structures; type of structure; the estimated costs of various kinds of physical treatment of residential structures (e.g., conservation, redevelopment and code enforcement); population characteristics and occupancy patterns; and many other kinds of data. The information in this bank is collected from census material, local surveys and studies, and our board of assessors' records (Detroit, for example, rated most of its residential areas, structure-by-structure, on a seven-point scale ranging from "sound" to "extremely dilapidated" in order to get an idea of the extent of residential blight in the city).

Most of the data in the physical data bank is now two to six years old, and the bank must soon be updated, improved, and expanded. But it has already served us well. The blight ratings have been especially useful in helping us to make decisions about such things as where clearance projects might be started, where rehabilitation might prove most effective, what our city's overall housing resource is, and so on. Moreover, since so much of our physical data is so readily at hand (and so easily manipulated), Detroit has enjoyed something of a head start in applying for federal grant-in-aid programs. Many of the grant applications require a great deal of physical information, in a number of different forms, and with our computerized data processing systems we have been able to come up with the necessary data in short order.

Soon the assessors' office will have its records on tape. This will make it possible to update our physical data bank annually at a modest cost.

When we decided to extend our dp approach in urban planning to the realm of social data, we called in professionals in the field. We hired the firm of Touche, Ross, Bailey and Smart in the initial design stages of the social data bank. Their personnel, in cooperation with a group of city people, made a careful study of all the possible sources of social data, what kind of information might prove most helpful, and what sort of edp [electronic data-processing] system might best suit our needs. When the appropriate data sources had been identified, individual forms and reporting procedures were designed for each kind of raw data. A systems flow was developed that spelled out the individual steps that were to be taken from the point of data collection to the eventual merging of the data in the computer. While the various computer programs were being written at Wayne State University, our consultants acted in a management capacity. When the system became operational, their job was finished, and we took over the social data bank completely.

The social data bank is a little over a year old. It is designed to bring together various social statistics (which are gathered on a monthly basis from a number of public and private service organizations), and to provide statistical summaries of this information. The bank was originally designed to report and store information according to city planning areas, but the geographical base has now been changed to the census tract.

The data stored in this bank includes statistics on crime rates, welfare, births and deaths, school truancy and dropout rates, the occurrence of venereal diseases and tuberculosis, and other information. Printouts are obtained quarterly, although data on any given census tract can be retrieved whenever it is needed.

Detroit's social data bank, while still only in its formative, rudimentary stage, has already proved to be an immensely useful tool. Although it has been used until now primarily as a descriptive aid, we have been able to greatly expand and improve our renewal programming because of the flexibility and data resource the social data bank gives us.

Recently, the bank has been particularly significant to the various city departments who are engaged in writing Detroit's application for a grant under the new Demonstration Cities Act of 1966. This new federal program calls for a massive, coordinated, concentrated attack on *all* the problems of certain areas within each of the participating cities. This means, very simply, that we must design programs for both social and physical improvement. It means we must improve the quality of life in our city, as well as the physical environment. This kind of in-depth, total planning must be based on information, for we cannot improve a neighborhood's social vitality if we do not know what that neighborhood's social problems are and how its people live.

We have been able to get much of this information from our social data bank. We don't know everything we would like to, of course, but we do know a good deal more than, for example, the census data could tell us. We can get a good, general idea of the social well-being of any area in the city by retrieving the requisite data from the social data bank.

In addition, the bank has been extremely useful to other agencies in Detroit, such as the board of education and United Community Services, all of whom can use the bank to determine (generally, at least) which areas need the most help and which kinds of programs might be most successful in various sections of the city.

Specific city programs have already benefitted from the social data bank. In our neighborhood rehabilitation effort, for example, we have been able to judge with some degree of confidence what areas might respond favorably. For it is clear that if one can get some idea of the comparative social well-being of various neighborhoods, he can make some estimation of which of those areas might be more amenable to improvement. Renewal involves people (and their social behavior) as well as buildings; it involves the attitudes, motivations, and social characteristics (migration patterns, income, education, etc.) of the people, and all these things are extremely important factors in any improvement effort.

We know, of course, that the social data bank must be improved a good deal before it can become a truly effective analytical or problem-solving tool. At this point, we really haven't the knowledge or the experience with social data processing to make the best possible use either of the data or the dp system we are using.

As a first step, we hope to bring in experts (sociologists, epidemologists, systems analysts) who can analyze the existing data and draw meaningful conclusions from it. It may well be that we have already collected truly significant data — that we have already captured on tape some important trends — and that we simply have to submit what we have gathered to the scrutiny of professional data analysts. Such experts may be able to tell us that, in time, even the data we have (and are collecting) will be able to indicate whether an area is getting "better" or "worse" in terms of social variables. We may find that with the proper manipulation we can develop a "social stability scale," based on various combinations of social statistics.

We might discover, on the other hand, that we may not be tapping the best data sources. We might wish to expand or limit the data we collect, to change the time or geographical base of our data collection, or devise trend-deriving programs based on social data combined with other information. In time, we may even be able to devise an "early warning system" which could alert us to a neighborhood drifting into instability or social decline.

Whatever the future holds for the social data bank, we know at least that we have happily discovered what might be called a new "dimension" to urban planning. We know that the equipment, the knowledge, and the technical know-how is available to gather and use social data in a meaningful, fruitful way. We know, too, that we have a lot to learn in this field, but we are dedicated now to the task of learning much more as quickly as we can. We feel that, in a very real sense, the age of computers has ushered in a new age of urban planning.

SANTA CLARA COUNTY, CALIFORNIA

The "Logic" Information System

Santa Clara County is now implementing its computer operated total information system — LOGIC. Welfare, Medical Center, Juvenile Probation, Adult Probation, and Health Department employees today are able to ask a computer to identify and display to them, in seconds, information on any one of 180,000 individuals or 60,000 case files.

The part of the total information system currently implemented consists of ten inquiry terminals at these five departments which are tied by telephone lines to a computer located at the Civic Center. The computer automatically controls information data files for County departments and transmits this information to the inquiry terminals at the various departments upon request.

The network of remote terminals now makes available to each department, upon command, the computer's ability to search massive files and perform complex calculations in split seconds.

The entire total information system, upon completion in several years, will eliminate the necessity and cost of duplicate files of information now common among departments. Information will be collected once only, and then made available to other departments. The information to be maintained in computer files is the same as is now maintained in filing cabinets and card indexes in every County department.

Now in its first stages, LOGIC, as the Santa Clara County information system is termed, will make possible more efficient governmental services,

Reprinted from a publication release of the Data Processing Center, General Services Agency, San Jose, County of Santa Clara, California, August 1969.

in spite of increased volumes of work. Each terminal costs about $200 a month, yet one Welfare Department clerk at a terminal can now provide more service with much greater accuracy than several clerks working with hand-operated files.

For the other departments — Medical Center, Health, and the Probation Departments — this first stage means a sharing of information and the prompt, accurate identification of persons eligible for Welfare services.

Inquiry Terminals. An Inquiry Terminal is an electro-mechanical device that may be located some distance from a computer operated file, yet provide the means for obtaining file information. The terminal operator keys in a request to the computer over ordinary telephone lines. The computer instantly retrieves the information from its memory and sends a response over the same lines to be displayed on the terminal. The data provided by terminal is the same as that formerly transmitted by printed form or voice telephone communication. These inquiry terminals are located in the Identification Collection and Case Processing Office of the Welfare Department, as well as the Identification and Billing Office of the Medical Center. Additional terminals are located in the Health and Probation Departments.

Information Available. The information system makes available upon inquiry the following data:

1. Person Identification Information
   Name
   Birth date and State
   Sex
   Social Security number
   First four characters of address (for identification only)
   Other names (AKA's for the person)
   County departments which have information on the person
2. Welfare Person Information
   Case name
   Case serial number
   Family budget unit
   Discontinued flag
   Close date
   Medical eligibility
   Person number
   Aid type
   District

3. Welfare Case Information
   All persons in a case
   Case name, number, district and family budget unit
   Close date
   Last contract date
   Payee address

Departments Participating. The participating departments are able to identify persons and look at current Welfare person and case information from inquiry terminals located in their offices.

How Information Is Used. The principal use of the information system at the Welfare Department is to identify persons requesting aid or services. The system provides the means for prompt identification and direction of persons to the concerned social worker, as well as directing clerks to the proper case folder.

If an inquiry is made and a person is new to Welfare, then that information can also be added directly to the LOGIC computer files through the terminal in the department. A number is assigned which will become the case number if an application is completed. The added information is then immediately available to serve subsequent requests for information from any location.

Social workers in the future will use the inquiry terminal to determine whether a person is known to other County departments or agencies, and to retrieve information held by other departments. This exchange of information between departments will most effectively reduce costs.

The operator of a computer terminal can also answer telephone requests for Welfare information from doctors, schools, pharmacists, etc., more promptly and accurately than ever before possible.

It is also now possible for the Welfare Department to update the computer information file from the terminal in order to record last contact date and any newly acquired information such as birth date or social security number. All information thus added is immediately available to departments making subsequent inquiries.

The other participating departments use the system to identify persons and their Welfare case, determine the responsible social worker if known to Welfare, and to determine eligibility for State and Federal medical aid.

It is important to note that the Santa Clara County system is a responsive operation. An inquiry is triggered by a citizen appearing and requesting a public service.

Information Security Provisions. LOGIC permits each County department to define for the Data Processing Center which departments may have access to their information and at what level. These criteria may be changed at any time to satisfy changes in law and policy.

Access is controlled independently at several levels. For example, the Welfare Department must authorize in writing the following:

1. What department may know a person is on Welfare?
2. What department may have Welfare information such as aid, worker, etc., on a person?
3. What departments may change or update Welfare information?

The LOGIC information system provides the means for County departments, such as Welfare, to carefully control access to their own information.

It will continue to be the responsibility of each department to guarantee that information terminals are used by authorized persons, and that these persons be completely familiar with policy on information released. These policy conditions are now in effect and will continue with use of the computer based information system. It is submitted that data maintained in a computer file system is more secure than the same data being kept in filing cabinets or other commonly used office storage equipment.

Sources of the Information. The information stored and made available by LOGIC is as accurate and complete as provided by the user departments.

The information file developed for the Welfare Department was derived initially from the hand operated card files in the Department.

Information is also updated internally by the computer from changes and additions to present Welfare computer files that serve the payment process, and changes and additions entered at the terminal as contact is made with persons. The number of manual entries at the terminal will be far less than formerly required for the hand operated card file since a large number of these changes are derived directly from existing computer programs.

General Comments. The pressure of population growth and the massive increase in the volume of public information and records has forced government and business to develop methods for the more effective processing, storing, and handling of information.

The Santa Clara County total information system will, over the next several years, provide County departments with direct access to a computerized pool of information.

As the volume of this data increases, a valuable County resource in the form of an information system is realized. This system will reduce the cost of governmental services by allowing the collection of information once only, and then making it available to other departments upon inquiry. The duplication of effort now necessary by many departments is eliminated.

The Santa Clara County total information system is simply the organized pooling by all County departments of all commonly used information. Each department and function will mutually benefit from the work and support of all others. The result will be increased efficiency and better County services for less cost.

Concerning individual privacy and computer information systems, it seems just and inevitable in a democratic society that citizens be afforded some basic rights concerning personal information which is being maintained. Legislation should provide every citizen with the right to obtain a printed copy of any computer file which contains personal information. The citizen should also have the right to obtain a list of the organizations or individuals that have made inquiry into any such personal information file. Further, the government agency or private organization maintaining such files should assume legal responsibility for the accuracy of information being maintained about private citizens.

ROBERT R. J. GALLATI

The New York State Identification and Intelligence System

New York State took a major step toward the control of crime in 1965 when, at the request of Governor Nelson A. Rockefeller, and after an exhaustive feasibility study, the Legislature created the New York State Identification and Intelligence System (NYSIIS), the nation's first statewide criminal justice information system.

In its findings the Legislature declared that "the sound administration of criminal justice importantly depends on the effective collection, assimilation, and retrieval of available information and its dissemination to appropriate agencies of Government"; that such information should be shared among government agencies concerned with "the detection, apprehension, prosecution, sentencing, confinement and rehabilitation of criminal offenders. . . ." and that "through the use of electronic data processing and related procedures, a system should be established to provide a central data facility by which relevant information can be coordinated and made readily available whenever and wherever required in the investigation and prosecution of crime and the administration of criminal justice."

NYSIIS was thereupon charged with the responsibility of facilitating information sharing between and among agencies through the implementation of modern technology. The ultimate objective of the New York State Identification and Intelligence System is to assist in the improvement of criminal justice through development and establishment

This essay was written at the invitation of the editor.
Mr. Gallati is Director of the New York State Identification and Intelligence System.

of a computer-based information sharing system, implementation of improved operational techniques, and development of a broad program of research in the area of criminal justice.

The concept of NYSIIS rests on the following basic principles of the unitary nature of criminal justice: all criminal justice agencies need to participate in and share a joint data bank; the submission of information thereto should be primarily voluntary; NYSIIS is to be a service agency only, with no powers, duties or facilities to arrest, prosecute, confine or supervise; security and privacy considerations must permeate the system and involve central and remote NYSIIS operations; new dimensions of science and technology can be applied to provide greater effectiveness in filing methodology and the utility of processed data; and criminological research will be supported by a vast resource of empirical data readily available for variable searching to test theses, hypotheses, theories and pilot projects, thereby enabling criminal justice administration to evaluate its own procedures, practices and operations.

As part of the mandate to implement improved operational techniques the State Bureau of Identification was transferred from the Department of Correction to NYSIIS in April 1966. Various procedural changes were immediately implemented in order to provide more rapid responses to requests from the agencies of criminal justice serviced by the Bureau of Identification. These changes aimed at providing orderly transition from the manual system of the Bureau of Identification to a computerized system. Among the more significant improvements were: initiation of the nation's first statewide criminal justice facsimile transceiver network for rapid transmission of arrest fingerprints to NYSIIS and the rapid return of summary criminal history responses; initiation of a twenty-four-hour daily service in the Bureau of Identification to assist criminal justice agencies on a round-the-clock basis; and reorganization, realignment and streamlining of internal procedures and work flow. Through the establishment of the State-funded facsimile system and computerization of several components of the identification function in the Bureau of Identification, criminal justice agencies in New York State now have, for the first time, the capability of transmitting fingerprints to NYSIIS and receiving a detailed summary case history in less than three hours (a process which formerly required 7 to 10 days).

The criminal records of more than 600,000 persons have been converted to computer readable form so that these records, enriched with additional relevant data, may now be produced directly by the NYSIIS Burroughs B-5500 computer and transmitted by facsimile device to the police, sheriffs, prosecutors, criminal courts, probation, correction and parole authorities as requested. Among many significant breakthroughs achieved by NYSIIS' research and systems studies is the fantastic capability of searching incoming sets of fingerprints by computer against a base file of 1.6 million fingerprint classifications in no more than 25 seconds. Likewise, NYSIIS has developed an operational wanted system which enables criminal justice agencies anywhere in the State to check rapidly on suspects, missing persons, amnesiacs, etc., against both the statewide NYSIIS file and the nationwide files of the FBI's computerized National Crime Information Center (NCIC). Concomitantly, after extensive research and study of personal privacy considerations, NYSIIS initiated a pilot organized crime intelligence capability which is being used as a model by the United States Department of Justice for its own about-to-be computerized organized crime files.

Indeed, the innovative thrust of the NYSIIS commitment has guided the conceptualization of many facets of federal involvement toward a more scientific and rational system of criminal justice administration. Funding from the Law Enforcement Assistance Administration (LEAA) has been received for original research in automatic license plate scanning to apprehend automobile thieves, for psychological and anthropometrical studies to define the elements of an effective computerized personal appearance data base, and for in-depth evaluation of the economic impact of organized crime. Most recently LEAA launched a multi-million dollar project to encourage the development of criminal justice information systems similar to NYSIIS in every state; NYSIIS has received a substantial grant to participate in this endeavor.

It is anticipated that many additional activities will be financially assisted by LEAA under the Safe Streets Act, since NYSIIS was cited by the National Crime Commission as a prototype.

NYSIIS is being constructed in a series of stages or "building blocks" to provide for a phased and integrated program of development toward a total information system for criminal justice. Each newly implemented module, despite its intrinsic merit, has ultimate value only if it contributes to hoisting criminal justice out of its present pre-scientific stage. A large portion of the ills associated with law enforcement and criminal justice in this nation is due to cultural lag in embracing the scientific method. Inadequacies, irrationalities, often over-compensated by what is sometimes charitably referred to as excessive zeal, will persist so long as we must await the dawning of the age of science in criminal justice. If we wish to be scientific, it is obvious that we must have information —

lots and lots of data about oodles and oodles of persons and things. This information needs to be translated from an undifferentiated mass into correlated, coherent, classified, retrievable, relevant data (knowledge) so that it may be applied to the testing of theories, hypotheses and proposals and may be readily available for decision-making, evaluation of programs and stimulation of additional probes and wise questioning of every accepted practice and procedure.

Thus, the future development of NYSIIS is a challenge to the pursuit of excellence in planning, as indeed was the special kind of vision which originally planned NYSIIS as we know it today. We are engaged in three levels of planning at this time. In the immediate future our already announced plans are to add, consistent with cost/effectiveness criteria, computerized analytical capabilities for: the identification of persons and things, such as, personal appearance, fraudulent check, modus operandi, latent fingerprint, and automatic license plate scanning. We also plan to continue our thrust toward completing the automation of the fingerprint identification function by computerizing the name search function and automating the image retrieval of filed fingerprints for final verification of identity. In terms of extending the service of NYSIIS to an ever-widening circle of users, we plan to extend the content of the computerized summary case history files to include additional data specially relevant to the needs of the rehabilitative agencies and to newly realized utilization of NYSIIS services for all criminal justice agencies.

As we thrust beyond the course charted to an intermediate level of planning, we intend to catalogue unmet needs and recognize emerging needs. These requirements will be the subject of research and analysis to determine priorities, utility, feasibility and cost/effectiveness within the framework of the NYSIIS commitment. In the intermediate range we anticipate the development of additional computerized analytical capabilities such as: voice prints, partial license plate searching, ballistic firearms identification, handwriting analysis, laundry and dry cleaning files and criminalistic research, possibly in our own research laboratory. In addition, we expect to perform variable search techniques on the computer to develop pattern analyses of criminal activity, predict trends, evaluate criminal justice processes and procedures, produce organized crime estimates and engage in criminological research.

Finally, we will focus upon true long-range planning which will include the study of many possible facets of development which have not yet been delineated, for example: interstate exchange of offender and statistical data, criminal law analysis, juvenile records, crime complaints, and recidivism and disposition analysis. Also new methods of communication will be planned to provide complete services for criminal justice, including closed circuit TV, toll-free telephone "dial-up" system, and facsimile linkage with the FBI Identification Division. The possibilities are limited only by the scope of man's ingenuity and the continued successful implementation of each step of the NYSIIS contribution to the prevention and control of crime.

The story of NYSIIS is a saga of challenge, change, growth and problem solving response. Five years ago we were six people; now we are six hundred. Five years ago we shared one small room; today we are building our own ten-story structure. Five years ago there were no statewide criminal justice information systems; in 1969, the NYSIIS prototype is being proliferated with the support of federal grants. Five years ago I stated truthfully that while our nation was spending 16 billion dollars a year for research in the arts of war, hardly a penny was being spent on research in criminal justice; the 1969–1970 federal budget provides more than 200 million dollars for law enforcement research, planning and development. NYSIIS was conceived in the astute perception of an impending crisis in crime and came to be at a time when it was most needed to reduce hysteria and point the way toward the achievement of domestic tranquility in a context of scrupulous regard for constitutional guarantees — civil liberty, privacy and personal freedom.

In the course of achieving change and growth, there were many problems that needed to be met and overcome. First, there was the historical autonomy of the various functional branches of criminal justice with their precious individual record systems totally uncoordinated even within the functional area itself. Second, there was the widespread belief that suspicion existed between criminal justice agencies and that there could be no common meeting ground between the police, and, for example, the probation and parole people — indeed, it was predicted that within law enforcement itself there could be no happy marriage of state police, sheriff and municipal police records because of alleged longstanding antagonisms. Third, there was the fear of this great unknown monster — the computer; a fear that persisted not only among the identification employees at NYSIIS, but also among the heads of some user agencies who anticipated their own obsolescence. Fourth, there was a lack of understanding on the part of some legislators of the development role of NYSIIS and the need for research in all the dark alleys of pre-scientific criminal justice. Fifth, there was the need to transfer important functions from already existing agencies to the newly established NYSIIS, with all the inevitable wrenching human upset involved. Sixth, there was the nagging anxiety among a few police types that a "civilian" agency should not be trusted with police records.

Most of these problems have been resolved through the leadership, vision and support of Governor Rockefeller. Much of the suspicion and distrust that may have existed among criminal justice agencies and between operating agencies and NYSIIS was dissipated by frequent meetings over the years of the Advisory Committee which was composed of outstanding statewide representatives of all the functional agencies of criminal justice including: State and New York City Departments of Correction; Division of Parole; State Police; Judicial Conference; State Association of Chiefs of Police; State Sheriffs Association; State and New York City Probation; New York City Police Department; and New York State District Attorneys Association.

The wholesome relationship which currently exists among the various criminal justice agencies and between our NYSIIS staff and the criminal justice environment in which it operates was subjected to the acid test during the past year when an Organized Crime Intelligence Pilot Project was conducted. Twelve agencies, including state police, sheriffs, municipal police, district attorneys, special commissioners and parole authorities, were requested to participate in this experimental program involving the turning over of sensitive data from state and local files to our System; every one of the twelve cooperated in the Pilot Project. Our analysts were virtually given carte blanche in the acquisition of files and extensive data was collected and collated, demonstrating the effectiveness of our proposed Organized Crime Intelligence Module.

The problems of the present and the future are largely extensions or variations of the problems of the past. Our preeminent concern from the very beginning for security and privacy led us to seek out the continuing expert guidance of specialists in constitutional law and civil liberties; we have no fears for the future in this regard, for we expect to steer a forthright course which will enhance privacy and freedom as, concomitantly, the quality of criminal justice performance is improved. There are some who do not comprehend the importance of maintaining NYSIIS as an independent agency, for they fail to understand the meaning of a criminal justice information system. Recently a recommendation was made to transfer NYSIIS to the State Police, while at the same time, another recommendation favored transferring NYSIIS to the State Department of Correction. This inconsistency illustrates an unfortunate conceptual bewilderment which must be overcome if we would preserve inviolate the independence of a staff agency which must serve all equally without special bias toward any particular functional branch, and without even the suspicion of self-interest. Neanderthals among the police who will never trust "civilians" are fortunately few and becoming fast extinct; they can hardly expect to survive in the era of criminal justice information systems, which, of their very nature, posit the unitary principle of criminal justice. Virtually all police officers support NYSIIS; indeed, a recent survey indicated that police chiefs thought a statewide criminal justice information system was "absolutely essential" for the control of crime. The New York State Association of Chiefs of Police passed a special resolution at their 1969 Conference commending NYSIIS and the International Association of Chiefs of Police awarded NYSIIS its coveted "Certificate of Achievement."

In conclusion, I would like to predict that the NYSIIS concept will prevail not only in New York State, but throughout the nation. We were first to break new ground, and much that is new, important and vital in this area today began with the working out of the grand dream, the special vision of Governor Rockefeller who said:

> We pioneered the New York State Identification and Intelligence System because we want to give every policeman, every sheriff, every district attorney, every criminal court, every probation, parole and correction officer in this State the best possible support in carrying out a job that is second to none in importance.

As we walk on the moon and reach for the stars in outer space, we see the wave of the future for tranquility on earth in the NYSIIS story.

EDWARD M. BROOKS

The United Planning Organization's Social Databank

The evaluation of the efforts of UPO and other public and private agencies to deal with social problems is expected to:

1. Generate continuous and updated information regarding the incidence and distribution of social problems in the city
2. Isolate and identify problem areas
3. Develop broad indices of social change
4. Generate substantive information on the responsiveness and utility of public institutions and agencies
5. Develop substantive information regarding the impact of UPO's programs on the target population
6. Determine the impact of UPO upon the policies of public agencies and institutions
7. Systematically relate the activities of various agencies in order to predict the probable impact of changes in any of them upon the operation of the total system with respect to its consequences for the target population

In order to implement an evaluative research program, it is necessary to have systematic information regarding not only the programs and operations of UPO, but also the operations of the various agencies, on the one hand, and the status of the target population, on the other. Perhaps the problem can best be stated negatively.

If it were the case that UPO (1) had only one objective (e.g., eliminating illegitimacy), (2) did only one thing to accomplish this objective

This essay was written at the invitation of the editor, and supported by Department of Health, Education, and Welfare grant HEW 7:JD 67013.
Mr. Brooks is Director, Research Division, United Planning Organization.

(e.g., passed out free birth control pills), (3) reached all of the target population, (4) was the only force affecting the rate of illegitimacy, and (5) had a static population with no in- or out-migration — then evaluation would only need to ascertain periodically the rate of illegitimacy in the city in order to assess effectiveness.

As it happens, none of the five conditions prevails. UPO has many objectives, does many things (some of which are conflicting), reaches an *unknown part* of the city's disadvantaged, is only one (relatively minor) force affecting change, and has a fluid target population with an unknown rate of in- and out-migration.

I. *Some of the more prominent objectives* of the United Planning Organization are:

1. Institutional change
2. Amelioration of poverty through direct services
3. Organization of the poor
4. Mobilization of the poor around issues
5. Reduction of delinquency

II. *Most UPO programs attempt to achieve more than one of the above objectives.* If the Research Division is to evaluate UPO programs it must have ongoing measures reflecting all five of the above objectives. This, in turn, clearly requires systematic information about the major variables in the community with which UPO is involved — including information about the clients of UPO's programs, the intended target population, the agencies that deal with both, and the interrelationships that exist among these groups and institutions.

III. *UPO also does many things* to achieve the various objectives of the agency, including:

1. Persuasion to bring about institutional change
2. Community organization
3. Operation of delinquency prevention programs
4. Operation of rehabilitation programs
5. Operation of direct service programs

Here again, evaluation of these efforts requires systematic and comprehensive information.

IV. *UPO does not involve all of the poor and disadvantaged* in the city of Washington, and the ratio of program participants to target population remains unknown. No serious evaluation can occur until we have first ascertained (1) the proportion of the poor that are participants of UPO's programs, and (2) the extent to which UPO program participants are representative of various groups or segments of the poor. To achieve this, it is necessary to obtain the identity and characteristics of *all* members of various groups in UPO's target population — e.g., all people on AFDC, all school dropouts, all people arrested, all people convicted, all people seeking employment, all people in public housing, etc. The United Planning Organization should not remain ignorant of the extent to which it is, and is not, representing and involving its ostensible target population — and this determination requires population parameters based on agency data that have not heretofore been available.

V. The United Planning Organization is *only one of the many forces* that impinge upon and affect the target population. Among the other significant variables are:

1. The job market
2. Congressional appropriations
3. The cost of living (e.g., what are the consequences for UPO's target population of an across-the-board Federal pay raise)
4. Policy changes in any of the agencies dealing with the target population
5. The availability of low-cost housing (especially as affected by increases in public housing, on the one hand, and the encroachment of high-rise apartments in previously low-cost areas)

All of these, and many other, variables significantly affect the quality of life among UPO's target population. While everyone agrees this is true, no one today can assess the impact of a change in the value of any one of the above variables upon the total system.

Here again, the need obviously demands systematic data about both the clients and the target population of UPO, the agencies that deal with them, and the interrelationships among them.

VI. *There is an unknown amount of in- and out-migration in the target population* of UPO. This fact has a general and specific implication for UPO. On the general level it means that the United Planning Organization is unaware of the extent to which it deals with a new set of poor each year as opposed to dealing with the same population year in and year out. On the specific level, it must be recognized that to the extent that UPO is successful in moving people out of poverty, it will also move them out of the target population. As a consequence, the evaluation of UPO programs must be in terms of what happens to particular *people* through time rather than what happens to particular *areas* — since the latter will underestimate the extent of program success.

The Utility of the Databank for Evaluative Research

If the Research Division is to evaluate social problems and the agencies that deal with them, then an integrated data system is essential. This stems from the fact that such an evaluative effort requires:

1. Identification of social problems
2. Identification of the people those problems affect
3. Determination of the institutional and agency inadequacies that create and maintain the problem
4. Specification of the corrective policy or program adopted by UPO to ameliorate the institutional deficiency (or, in the case of direct service programs, the condition of the affected population)
5. Evaluation of the impact of the corrective program adopted by UPO upon the target agency (or, in the case of direct services, upon the affected population)
6. Determination of the ultimate consequences, for the target population, of any changes that take place in the target agencies

In order to achieve the capacity to implement such an evaluative program it is necessary to develop broad indices of social malaise, agency practices, and UPO operations. In order to systematically relate and control for (1) the many objectives and approaches adopted, (2) the fact that only an unknown part of the target population is involved, (3) the extraneous factors that affect the outcome, and (4) the mobility of the population — it is necessary to have data, linked to individuals and derived from a variety of agencies involved with these problems. To develop an evaluative capacity, these data must be collected systematically and routinely through time in order to permit an assessment of the significant changes that take place and link these changes to:

1. The individuals affected
2. The actual (as opposed to the assumed) consequences for these people
3. The agency and institutional policy changes that brought about these changes
4. The catalytic agent that brought about the institutional policy change
5. The implications of the new state of affairs for policy and planning in the United Planning Organization

The development of such a comprehensive evaluative model will enable the United Planning Organization to isolate and identify problem areas with much greater precision — and to evaluate its efforts in rectifying the existing problems.

This, then, defines the utility of the databank for an evaluative research program. In effect, information derived from a variety of sources — both within and without UPO — will be collected and stored cumulatively in the databank, such that all data relating to any individual, irrespective of their source, are stored at that individual's location. With this approach it will be possible largely to control the five factors mentioned in the preceding paragraph, assess the incidence and location of social problems, and determine any changes that take place in those problems as a consequence of various forces — including those initiated by UPO.

In addition to the concern that has been expressed regarding the potential abuse of the confidentiality of data stored in the proposed data bank, a number of other arguments have been put forth in opposition to the development of this system.

It has been suggested that if UPO embarks upon such a massive statistical effort, it will be the bellwether of a trend toward increasing bureaucratization and a further step in the direction of becoming "another old-line conservative welfare agency." In fact, the opposite is the case. One of the striking characteristics of "old-line conservative welfare agencies" is the lack of adequate information about their clients and the forces that determine the quality of their lives. Typically, such agencies have caseworkers who fill out intake forms at the initiation of the case action and then process the clients through their mills — only to lose sight of them at the termination of that particular process. It was one of the major objectives of the United Planning Organization to deal with just this myopic condition existing in the old-line agencies today. It is not enough simply to know that X number of people are on the AFDC rolls, or in NCHA housing, or are arrested by the police department during a given time period. To use this information intelligently it is necessary to understand the interrelationships among, and long-term consequences of, these agency operations. This, in turn, requires longitudinal and cumulative information on individuals derived from the involved agencies.

It is quite impossible to obtain longitudinal information on the entire target population of the United Planning Organization — simply because we cannot identify and locate everybody who is poor, much less obtain information from them periodically about relevant aspects of their lives. Furthermore, even if it were possible, the acquisition of data exclusively related to the target population would provide very little information about the agencies UPO is attempting to change. The most effective approach, therefore, is to obtain information from as many relevant agencies as possible regarding the identification, characteristics and problems of the clients, together with the actions of these agencies and the consequences of those actions. The development of such a body of data will not only provide UPO with substantially more knowledge about major groupings within its target population but, more importantly, will provide the analytical tools for evaluating social problems and mounting appropriate efforts to deal with them.

It should also be noted that we are now [in the late 1960's] in the "bad statistical years" inasmuch as the 1960 census data are now . . . old and it will be [several] years before new data are available. It will, therefore, be particularly advantageous during the next [few] years to have as many broad indices of social problems, and as much current information regarding their geographic distribution, as possible.

Finally, by relating the elements of data obtained from agencies to the developed data systems regarding UPO participants, it will be possible to determine the extent to which program participants are representative of major components of the target population.

The Development of Safeguards to Insure the Confidentiality of Information Stored in the Databank

The most strenuous objections to the development of the databank have been voiced by those concerned about the potential abuse of the information in such a way as to harm the individuals to whom the data refer. This is indeed a potentially serious problem and one which requires close examination.

There are, it would appear, two types of potential abuses. First of all, it might be the case that in processing (collecting, transposing, coding and keypunching) information, someone might filch a *particular* item of information and use it to blackmail or disparage the reputation of the individual in question. This is the less serious of the two potential forms of abuse. In the first place, the problem is more general than the issue of the databank, since it is not related to the unique characteristics of the bank — i.e., the accumulation of diverse sets of data in a single place with respect to individuals — but is rather one that occurs in any situation in which potentially damaging information is processed about individuals.

The other potential abuse, however, is more serious because it *does* exploit the bank's unique characteristic. This problem has to do with the possibility that someone in the Research Division might (either intentionally or inadvertently) breach the confidentiality of the stored information, either on an individual basis or by wholesale sellout to some other agency or interested party.

The issue here is not so much a question of what data are going to be collected, or in what form, but is rather a question of the principles and philosophy that govern the usage of that information.

It will be worthwhile, in this regard, to indicate the difference between two types of databanks. On the one hand, there is the dossier databank, such as the FBI maintains, which has as its major purpose the development of information about individuals to be used on an individual-by-individual basis. On the other hand, there are statistical databanks, such as we are developing, which have as their major purpose the development of information about individuals *to be used to generate aggregate information in which the identity of the individual is lost.*

Notwithstanding our concern regarding the use of data on an individual-by-individual basis, the fact remains that the acquisition of the data creates the possibility for its abuse — and there are many who doubt the wisdom of running this risk.

It is essential, even in the development of a statistical databank, that we *collect* information about individuals — simply because it is the linkage of information to individuals that permits the aggregation of elements from different data sets in a meaningful fashion. The whole point of the development of the databank is to determine the relationship between diverse variables in a manner that will permit analysis of trends, problems, agency operations, and so forth. A number becomes meaningful only when it is related to something — and the more things it can be related to, the more meaning it acquires.

This is the purpose of the databank — not to develop information about individuals to be used as such, but to develop the capacity to relate information collected from various data sets on the basis of their linkage to individuals — thereby permitting an analysis of the relationships among various groups that are of interest to UPO.

As noted above, however, the accumulation of data about an individual, collected for whatever purpose, creates by its very existence the possibility of misuse. It is this possibility that we must minimize. Fortunately, the fact that the Division has no interest in utilizing information about individuals, except in the developmental process, permits the development of safeguards to minimize the possibility of misuse by the Research Division staff.

During the course of our thinking about this problem we have developed a number of alternative methods for reducing or eliminating the possibility of abuse by the Division.

In closing, we would like to observe that the real issue is not whether or not a databank is going to be developed, but whether or not UPO will exercise some control over how the data will be used.

We suspect that if UPO is seriously interested in "throwing an anchor to the windward" with respect to the increasing trend toward the cavalier and irresponsible proliferation of data heretofore considered confidential, then the wisest course of action would be to develop as sophisticated and efficient a databank as possible in order to be in a position to bargain for legislative safeguards as a prerequisite to turning that databank over to the city.

ALAIN ENTHOVEN

PPB and Vietnam

Because it illustrates the strengths and limitations of PPBS, I think it is useful to discuss the question: "How has PPB been relevant or useful in Vietnam?"

Does PPBS play a significant role in the really crucial decisions concerning Vietnam? Did we make the right decision in going into Vietnam in the first place? Did we go in the right way, at the right time, and on the right scale? How many forces should we deploy there next year? How can we do substantially better next year than we did last year? How can we achieve a just settlement? These are really crucial questions. The Planning-Programming-Budgeting System will not help in answering them. Nobody claims that it will.

Moreover, PPBS does not affect the tactical decisions. Should we deploy one of our divisions into the Delta? Should we assault this hill or make that sweep? Should we devote more of our men to offensive action against main forces or use them in pacification? The Planning-Programming-Budgeting System will not answer these questions. Nobody claims that it will.

Should the South Vietnamese Government negotiate with the NLF? Under what conditions should we negotiate with the Government of

Reprinted from the Statement of Alain Enthoven before the United States Congress, Subcommittee on National Security and International Operations, Committee on Government Operations, United States Senate, *Hearings: Planning-Programming-Budgeting*, 90th Congress, 1st Session, Part 2, September 27, 1967.

At the time of his statement, Mr. Enthoven was the Assistant Secretary of Defense (Systems Analysis).

North Vietnam? Where? How? On what terms? The Planning-Programming-Budgeting System will not help in answering these questions. Nobody claims that it will.

Thus, PPBS is definitely not a panacea. There are obvious limits to what any management system can accomplish. Still, the contributions of PPBS to our effort in Vietnam have been important and worthwhile. First, we entered the war with balanced forces ready to fight. The forces were deployed as needed without personnel or matériel shortages.

Second, the forces that we deployed were qualitatively much better than they were a few years earlier. The Air Mobile Division was ready when it was needed.

As a part of the Vietnam buildup, we have added about 500,000 men to the Army and about 100,000 men to the Marine Corps to strengthen our land forces. As a result of our experience in PPBS, it has been possible to do a much more orderly, effective job of planning these increases. As an extension of PPBS, we have a Vietnam deployment planning system for coordinating the force planning, the budgeting, the personnel planning, and the procurement. When the Secretary of Defense decided to add a division to the Army, our experience in PPBS helped us to do a better job of determining what we should recommend be added to the financial plan, to the manpower plan, etc. And, these increases could be made in a more balanced and synchronized way.

Insofar as there is conflict in our political system between the experts and the politicians, I believe that PPBS is on the side of the politicians. I would like to make four points to illustrate my belief.

First, one main purpose of PPBS is to translate the financial budgets from detailed listings of objects of expenditure, whose purpose is not set forth for the generalist, into mission-oriented categories, whose broad purposes are set forth. Thus, PPBS has translated the Defense budget from procurement, operating expenses, manpower, construction lists, etc., into a breakdown by Strategic Retaliatory Forces, Continental Air and Missile Defense Forces, General Purposes Forces, Research and Development, etc. We have additional breakdowns under these headings by output-oriented weapon systems.

Second, PPBS is a response to requests from the Congress, particularly from the Senate Government Operations Committee and from the House Appropriations Committee. This committee has been especially clear on this point. In 1961 it stated that budgets should be prepared "in such a way as to make them most useful in establishing priorities, in forward planning, in choosing between programs, and in measuring expenditures against meaningful performance yardsticks."

Third, PPBS is not a substitute for debate. It is a way of making the relevant factors, issues, assumptions, and uncertainties explicit so that a constructive, useful debate can be held. Then the significant points of agreement and disagreement can be identified and their importance assessed in a systematic way. In fact, I believe that effective systems analysis requires stimulation and testing by debate, and that one of the most important contributions that systems analysis has made to the operation of the Department of Defense has been to provide ground rules and procedures for making the debate on strategy and requirements more factual, informed, and relevant.

Fourth, [the Jackson subcommittee's] *Initial Memorandum* states: "The experience to date does not suggest that the Department of Defense is likely to place before Congressional committees the analyses of costs and benefits of competing policies and programs on which the Department based its own choices." That is not true. Secretary McNamara has clearly and explicitly displayed the major alternatives considered and an evaluation of them in his testimony to the Congress on major issues.

I don't want to "oversell" PPBS or "undersell" it. I do think, however, when one looks at the record of PPBS in the Defense Department since 1961, that a large part of the enthusiasm for the system is justified.

First, since 1961, we have developed a Planning-Programming-Budgeting System in the Department of Defense that: (1) starts with a review of strategy and military needs, develops a program to meet them, and derives an annual budget without regard to predetermined financial limits; (2) is based on a financial plan that identifies Defense spending by the major military missions subdivided into meaningful "output-oriented" program elements; (3) projects forces eight years into the future, costs at least five years (and to completion for major systems); and (4) focuses attention on explicit measures of effectiveness. For the very reasons that the Congress called for these reforms, I believe that they enable us to manage the Department of Defense better.

Second, open and explicit analysis, reviewed and commented on by all interested parties, is fundamental to the working of PPBS in the Pentagon. No major force issues are decided by the Secretary of Defense on the basis of analysis by any one office or department alone. The analyses underlying the Secretary's decisions are circulated for comment and review by all interested parties, and their comments go directly to him. The procedures are designed so that the Secretary will hear all sides, so that no one has a monopoly on the information going to the Secretary. This open and explicit approach is our best protection against persistent error; it makes it virtually impossible for any group to rig the analysis without that point being made clear to the Secretary. It ensures that all assumptions are made explicit and that all opinions are considered.

Third, systems analysis is an integral part of PPBS. Systems analysis is not synonymous with the application of mathematical techniques or computers. Systems analysis is not a substitute for judgment; it is an aid to judgment.

"Cost-effectiveness" analysis does not lead to an over-emphasis on cost. It does not stifle innovation; on the contrary, it helps it. It does not always lead to buying the cheapest system; there are numerous examples to the contrary. "Cost-effectiveness" analysis does not lead to an over-emphasis on factors that can be reduced to numbers; on the contrary, good systems analysis frees the decision maker to concentrate on the intangibles and uncertainties.

Fourth, PPBS has not led to a single set of assumptions dominating military strategy; it has not led to a single, rigid military strategy; it has not eliminated flexibility; and it has not over-centralized the Defense decision-making process. On the contrary, PPBS in the Department of Defense has been associated with a change from the inflexible strategy of "massive retaliation" to a strategy of "flexible response." Moreover, it has been associated with large increases in our military strength to give us the balanced, ready forces we need to support this strategy.

Fifth, the potential of PPBS is great in clarifying debate over program issues, in stimulating and recognizing new solutions to problems, and in helping the Government to spend money wisely. Within the limits of what any improvement in management can do, I believe that PPBS has the potential to be a most important innovation in government management.

DANIEL J. ALESCH

PPB in New York State

In New York there is a high level of commitment to the planning/
programming/budgeting system. The process is used by government officials to make more effective decisions; it is definitely not an esoteric
experiment. The system is supervised jointly by the Division of Budget
and the Office of Planning Coordination. Both agencies are within the
executive department; the director of each office reports directly to the
governor.

Two elements of the New York program work toward institutionalizing
the system. First, the annual PPB cycle is geared closely to the preparation
of the annual executive budget. Second, the agency planning required for
the PPB submission is made a part of the overall state plan.

In June each agency submits a PPB report to the central agencies team.
The reports cover a five-year period and are updated annually. The first-
year portion of the submission must closely approximate the next budget
request by the agency. Each agency submission includes sections devoted
to influencing factors, functional needs, governmental and private roles,
departmental roles, program plans and targets, personnel requirements,
fiscal requirements, and program research.

The budget and planning staff members analyze the agency reports

From Daniel J. Alesch, "Government in Evolution: A Real World Focus for State
Planning," *Public Administration Review* 28 (May–June 1968): 264–267. Copyright ©
1968 by American Society for Public Administration.
Mr. Alesch, formerly with the New York State Office of Planning Coordination, is
with the RAND Corporation, Santa Monica, California.

and confer on any problems with the agencies. Adjustments are then reflected in the November budget requests of the agencies.

The personnel from the Division of Budget focus their analyses on management and control on an agency-by-agency basis. The planning coordination staff members focus their analyses on the external impact of governmental activities and on their contribution toward total state development. The planners focus on functional topic and geographic analyses rather than on individual agencies.

Benefits

Two years of developing and using the system in New York have yielded substantial benefits. Viewed in terms of their contribution to systematic and comprehensive state planning, these include:

First, PPBS has been an incentive for advance planning in the line agencies. A primary objective of New York's state development planning program is to develop professional expertise in the agencies to prepare decentralized components of the plan. These components are centrally evaluated and coordinated. Rapid progress has been made toward systematic line planning. Comprehensive planning is becoming institutionalized and the agencies, having participated in the preparation of plans, support their implementation.

Second, PPBS has already resulted in considerably more interagency communication and data sharing than existed previously. By viewing government's activities functionally, contact points between programs of separate agencies are clearly identified and their relationships clarified. A realistic, useful communication network is growing to ensure reciprocal recognition and provision for the needs of central service agencies and operating units.

Third, the system has provided a logical and practical means for plan implementation. The primary control over agency activities is the annual executive budget. Budget examiners evaluate agency requests in terms of that agency's plan. The agency plan is evaluated in terms of its contribution to overall goals and its harmony with policy constraints. The result is that the incremental activities which are systematically implemented contribute to planned goal attainment. PPBS is a workable, realistic means to integrate planning and budgeting.

Problems

Even with the benefits of PPBS there are problems and points of friction. There is a critical shortage of people familiar with the techniques and the objectives of the system. There is also the problem that often comes with change: some people and agencies feel that a new system will reduce their power and prerogatives.

Perhaps more basic and more difficult to cure is the problem that both civil service regulations and bureaucratic hardening of the arteries resist shifting persons from areas of low priority, or from programs which no longer contribute significantly to goals, to high-priority areas as pointed out in PPB analyses.

There are operational problems in establishing standard quantifiers of work units and goals and evaluating progress toward goal attainment. There is a massive problem of evaluating the submissions of agencies in comparison to one another in a short period of time. A special operational problem arises when a number of governmental functions are either funded from earmarked sources or when activities have been delegated to special, autonomous authorities. While PPB brings effective focus on the general fund of the annual budget, this only bears on a portion of state level action and expenditures. Mechanisms must be devised so that the activities of authorities are brought within the scope of PPB.

There are also political problems arising from PPB. The legislature must approve the annual budget. If the finance committees do not know the projected needs in functional areas and the long-term plans designed to meet those needs, they cannot make as intelligent recommendations as they might. On the other hand, there are legislators who tend not to look beyond the next election. If PPB submissions were generally available to the entire legislature, and consequently to the public, agencies might very well tend to conceal their true and frank expressions of probable future requirements. The problem of involvement of the legislature in the process of planning/programming/budgeting requires careful consideration at the highest levels of government and in the universities.

Prognosis

Given the benefits to be derived from PPB and the problems involved in its implementation, what is the prognosis for the system? Planning/programming/budgeting is a means to an end. It is intended to enable government officials to make improved decisions on resources allocation to attain public goals. As such, it is beginning to replace other mechanisms which have been devised and widely used. As our understanding of process improves and as our technical capabilities expand, the dialectic will continue and a new point of synthesis will be reached. At that time, PPB may be replaced with another mechanism.

SELMA MUSHKIN

PPB in Cities

City activity on PPB systems started in New York City, Philadelphia, and the ten local governments that joined together, with five states, in a cooperative intergovernmental demonstration of the application of PPB that came to be known as the "5-5-5 Project." The five cities — Dayton, Denver, Detroit, New Haven, and San Diego — participated in this demonstration, along with five counties — Dade (Florida), Davidson (Tennessee), Los Angeles (California), Nassau (New York), and Wayne (Michigan). The five counties are heavily urban, and two of them were the then only existing metropolitanwide governments in the nation, namely, Miami-Dade and Nashville-Davidson.

City adaptations to PPB were likely to be major. In addition to adjustments for staff deficiency, lack of training resources, and inadequacies of a research base from which to draw, cities faced uniquely city problems. At this time experience is still insufficient to permit full identification of the range of differences in a PPB system for federal agencies and for the cities. Some simple facts about city government point to extensive adaptations of PPB.

Cities are whole systems, not agencies. Cities, furthermore, are at both the receiving and doing ends of intergovernmental relations. To plan their programs, they depend on federal and state fund offerings and meet concomitant restraints, both on types and levels of services and on ad-

From Selma Mushkin, "PPB in Cities," *Public Administration Review* 29 (March–April 1969): 167–178. Copyright © 1969 by American Society for Public Administration. Miss Mushkin is senior project manager at the Urban Institute, Washington, D.C.

ministrative arrangements, imposed by federal law or state statute. Within this complex pattern, the cities as immediate agents for joint intergovernmental action bring together the national, state, and local efforts and face the problem of estimating composite federal-state-city program effects, not in aggregate terms, but in the specifics of impact on the people who live and work in the city.

Thus, the task of program analysis in the cities is harder than it is in other governments. It is made harder by the particularity of the city, by the directness of the relationship between those charged with policy responsibility and the residents, and by the combined task of spending and taxing when revenue resources are severely constrained by authorized taxing and borrowing capacity. The transfer of PPB technology to the cities involves a broadening and a deepening of the PPB process and the addition of tax policy decisions. It requires detailed small-area data and in a sense more complex analysis without the safeguards in an averaging out of large numbers.

New York City's Tall "Unstructured" System

In the spring of 1966, under the direction of Mayor John V. Lindsay, officials began to explore the possibilities and potential of a PPB system for New York City. Work effectively got underway with the recruitment of Fred O'R. Hayes as the city's budget director, who stated in testifying before the Joint Economic Committee of the U.S. Congress:

> The approach adopted has deliberately been opportunistic rather than systematic and comprehensive. . . . One reason for this approach was the conviction that massive effort to classify expenditures by program category, to articulate and quantify program objectives, and to establish the mechanism of this program plan, all on a government-wide basis, would literally suffocate the basic concept of PPBS as a means of rational choice among alternatives. But more important, our strategy was based on a recognition of realities — the strengths and weaknesses, the constraints and limitations inherent in the existing pattern of municipal government.[1]

While the federal agencies and most states were placing initial emphasis on the development of a program structure that would identify expenditures by objective, New York City put its initial emphasis on analysis of programs that permitted Mayor Lindsay to report in an interview in

1. Testimony of Frederick O'Reilly Hayes, Hearings before the Subcommittee on Economy in Government, Joint Economic Committee, 90th Congress, 1st Sess., pp. 95–99.

September 1967, ". . . we've saved money and improved services by bringing modern research techniques to bear on the sometimes rigid and musty routines of government."

New York City's commitment to PPB is relatively large. The resources allocated probably approach those of all other city governments combined. Within a year of the initial tentative explorations, an organization had been established to spearhead the PPB effort. A separate and new division on program planning was established within the city's Bureau of the Budget. An intensive recruitment campaign was underway to strengthen the capacity for analytical work. Other organizational steps were also taken. A Policy Planning Council was established, which included the mayor, deputy mayor, city administrator, budget director, and chairman of the city Planning Commission. And ad hoc task forces drawing on experts in and out of city government were put to work on a range of analytical activity. Several areas were identified for initial emphasis and to unleash innovation in encrusted city services. These included public order, housing, fire, health, waste, and pollution control.

Among the first payoffs of the work were: (1) the introduction of a rehabilitation program for alcoholics, which freed police from their traditional apprehension of alcoholics; (2) the institution of a 24-hour arraignment system in Manhattan to eliminate unnecessary bail and detention; (3) development of a foundation of both fact and concept for exploring cost-effectiveness of health services in the city with particular emphasis on changing requirements for public hospital services with the introduction of Medicare, Medicaid, and the population trends in the city; (4) a study of tax abatement as a method of encouraging housing construction and rehabilitation; (5) a method for predicting probable levels and instance in terms of geographic area and time of fires, false alarms, and emergencies; and (6) changes in policy of motor vehicle usage and replacements.

The first analytical efforts on police attracted The RAND Corporation to offer its resources to the city government, thus initiating a partnership of city and RAND. The first joint undertaking was designed to further the work started in public order, health services, fire, and housing. Experienced analytical capacity began to be devoted to city problems. And, given the range, size, and depth of the New York City problems, even a strengthened partnership in research on urban problems between the city and The RAND Corporation is under consideration.

Budget documents of New York City for the past two years evidence

65

the progress made by the city toward improving the information for decision making and also for public and legislative debate.[2] The steps toward PPB implementation, however, were not taken in isolation; they were part of a range of activities to improve city government. To build analysis into government as a routine, New York City has moved to the development of program structures and to training of departmental personnel. This next step aims at regular comprehensive program submissions, including systematic collection and analysis of program output, impact indicators, and cost data.

PPB in the City of Brotherly Love

Philadelphia started down a path toward PPB implementation that contrasts sharply with that of New York City. Whereas New York's PPB was initiated in the office of the mayor and moves forward with his active involvement and support, Philadelphia's PPB was originated by the professionals in government and furthered largely through their cooperation at central and agency levels with the agreement, but not day-by-day participation, of the mayor. A gradual development of the system was sought step by step with a buildup of staff capability through periodic training and orientation. The first products were structural — the development of an output-oriented classification of programs, subprograms, elements, and subelements. Orientation programs were designed as a "kick-off" to gain a common understanding of PPB among central and staff agency personnel, and to inform heads of departments. The Philadelphia orientation program, the first organized for local officials, achieved a common basis for cooperative agency action and paved the way for a tentative first cut at classification of programs and subsequent revision. To assure that the structures developed by the agencies would have an overall rational relationship to each other, general agreement on a broad basic program framework in the entire city government was reached initially between the Department of Finance, which housed the central staff for the PPB effort, and operating agency personnel.

From its beginnings in December 1966, the Philadelphia PPB system was grounded in agency cooperation. No special organizational unit was set up, but the development of the system was sparked by the Budget Division and Cost Analysis Section in the City's Finance Department.

2. City of New York, Budget Message of the Mayor to the Board of Estimates and the City Council for FY 1967–68, April 15, 1967.

Training and orientation of staffs and of department heads laid the foundation. The program structuring work was cemented in the subsequent year's budget request when the 1968 budget recommended to the City Council by the mayor contained the program structure as developed. Furthermore, basic accounting and data processing systems were revised in accord with the program structure so that, beginning with the calendar year 1968, accumulated cost data by program would become available.

Whereas New York City started with analysis of program and turned subsequently to institutionalization of the analytical work by developing an overall structure, Philadelphia, with a program structure as its first order of implementation, subsequently initiated program analysis. Analysis was undertaken on a hesitant trial basis on the venereal disease control program in the Health Department. Subsequently, the analytical effort was broadened, with emphasis on selectivity and long-run development. To accomplish the program analysis, committees have been established, made up of top-level program executives with authority to make program decisions, and staffed from the finance department, the managing director's office, and the planning commission, as well as the departments and agencies. These program analysis committees are charged with preparing the informational materials for decisions made by the mayor and his cabinet. Director of Finance Edward J. Martin, in issuing the memorandum in the spring of 1968, noted:

> This Program Analysis will be a pioneering effort and will undoubtedly encounter difficulties. However, there is no group more capable of accomplishing this task than the personnel of the City of Philadelphia; and if we all make our contribution, we can blaze the trail for other cities to follow in the solution of major urban problems.
>
> The City of Philadelphia, like all major American Cities, is faced with serious problems which are crying for strong positive leadership in the development of effective solutions. Those who share in the responsibility for the management of the City government are faced with an opportunity to make a major contribution to a brighter future for our City.
>
> Instead of our previous disjointed, departmentalized efforts to solve major problems by pecking at the edges of them, we must marshal all of our capabilities and resources into a broad-scale frontal attack on those problems. We must clarify our thinking, apply our broad knowledge and experience to systematic and thorough analysis of our problems, and determine how we can obtain the

greatest possible effectiveness in the allocation of our resources to achieve the solutions to those problems. Our attention must be focused on our program outputs, not our departmental inputs.[3]

The combined New York City-Philadelphia experience suggests that both the structural and analytical aspects of PPB are clearly important in improving the information for policy choice. The structural component is the framework for organizing information about public products and displaying for legislative and executive policy officials the allocation of financial resources among program purposes. It is the basis for showing the implicit fund allocation for years beyond the budget period. Systematic comparisons through analysis of costs and effectiveness of alternative ways to attain a program purpose is the essential staff support of those charged with responsibility for choosing.

Initial emphasis of the ten local jurisdictions participating in the cooperative pilot demonstration "5-5-5 Project" of integrated PPB systems lies somewhere between that of New York City and Philadelphia.

3. Memorandum from Edward J. Martin, Director of Finance, City of Philadelphia, to All Offices, Departments, Commissions and List Attached, February 8, 1968.

JOHN DIEBOLD

Program Budgeting
for the State Department

Two recent Presidential directives provide the framework for testing the application of the newest tools of information technology to the conduct of foreign affairs. If such tools are effectively applied and gain wider acceptance they could radically affect the management and even the substance of international relations.

On October 12, 1965, the President "directed the introduction of an integrated programming-planning-budgeting system [P.P.B.S.] in the executive branch," including the State Department. . . .

The second directive was issued on March 4, 1966, when the President "directed the Secretary of State . . . to assume authority and responsibility for the overall direction, coordination and supervision of interdepartmental activities of the United States Government overseas." Within certain limitations, the Secretary now has the charter to become the manager of our foreign affairs rather than merely the coordinator.

The success with which the Secretary manages the State Department will depend to a major extent on his ability to meet its requirements for information and communications. These are now so complex that the question is no longer whether technology should be applied to meet them, but how. The success of such technology within the Department depends critically on three factors: (1) sound analysis at the highest level

From John Diebold, "Computers, Program Management and Foreign Affairs," *Foreign Affairs* 45 (October 1966): 125–134. Reprinted by special permission from *Foreign Affairs*, October 1966. Copyright © 1966 by the Council on Foreign Relations, Inc., New York.

Mr. Diebold is President of The Diebold Group, Inc., management consultants.

of the information needs of the Department; (2) the effective application of information technology to these needs, rather than simply the mechanization of the current inadequate information systems; and (3) the communication of the information thus collected to those who need and must act upon it.

To those who conduct our foreign affairs, as to the manager of a private enterprise, information technology poses not only questions of application but also challenges of change. For the application of technology not only changes the method by which an operation is performed, but frequently changes *what* is performed. . . .

The choices of instruments for decision and action are widening. The old obstacles to judgment and service are receding and are in the process of taking on new and, at this time, unpredictable shapes. It is my judgment, however, that as the new technology becomes applied to foreign affairs, reliance on personal judgment and personal and national moral standards will increase — not decrease. As the horizons of factual ignorance and misinformation fade, the decision-maker will be presented with vast new areas of choice.

If, for example, information systems are perfected by technology, what will be the role of the Ambassador? He could have available instantly all of the information and analysis available to the Secretary of State but might still lack the latter's overall view of national priorities and interests. Two or three hundred years ago, when it required days, weeks, months or, in some cases, years for an Ambassador to reach his assignment or to communicate with his sovereign, he was indeed plenipotentiary. There was no choice. He knew more than anyone at home about conditions in his assigned country, and orders regarding the most fundamental and long-term actions could not, in most cases, reach him in time to be relevant. Over the past one hundred years, with the coming of the telegraph, the wireless, the express train and the jet, the role of the Ambassador has diminished, at least in terms of his power to act. At home the number of people who know as much about his mission as he does has increased. As a matter of fact, the Ambassador's home office has at its disposal sources of information and analytical talents to which he has no access.

Now, however, the situation is changing again. If we so decide, the Ambassador will be able to have all the information relevant to his assignment. He could once more be designated in fact plenipotentiary if this were the wish of his superiors. On the other hand, as his home office will be able to be in even closer touch with his mission than before, the need to rely on the judgment of the man-on-the-spot could diminish even further. When the leaders of nations can confer for hours, face to face, on closed-circuit television, will the Ambassador's role become even more limited to that of an information-gatherer, pulse-taker and "holder of hands"? It is interesting to speculate on the kind of summitry we will have when such technologies really become effective.

Thus, the areas of choice between effective courses of action widen. Who makes the decisions? Who is the instrument of response? Other examples, perhaps more portentous in nature, will appear later. But even in the case of the Ambassador, the implications for foreign-affairs management are not to be dismissed lightly. If some sort of middle course is chosen, let us say by making the power of the Ambassador dependent on the sensitivity of his post or on his personal abilities, serious consequences to the prestige of our envoys could result. The fact that this problem has been developing for some time does not diminish its implications for the future. For, as the distance between alternative policies lengthens, deliberate or unconscious inconsistencies become more obvious and more fraught with consequence.

Sir Winston Churchill, in discussing the process of making strategic wartime decisions, wrote: "Success depends on sound deductions from a mass of intelligence, often specialized and highly technical, on every aspect of the enemy's national life, and much of this information has to be gathered in peace-time." How much simpler the decision-making process might have been for him had it been possible then, as it is becoming increasingly so now, to centralize such information technologically.

In the State Department in Washington, some 2,000 telegrams are processed every day and an average of 70 copies is made of each. The resultant 140,000 pieces of paper daily are filed both centrally and in various user files. The Central Foreign Policy file alone grows at the rate of 600 cubic feet (400 file drawers) a year. The Intelligence staff has 200 professional employees who read and try to analyze some 100,000 documents monthly. Most of this information is filed to meet the personal requirements of those in charge of various bureaus and offices. Its existence is not known or useful to others. Senior officers must wade through stacks of telegrams and airgrams to get a few bits of significant information. The new or most important information is mixed with the old or trivial. In an emergency situation the central filing system is ignored

71

almost entirely and a crisis team of experts on that particular situation or country is called together to offer its analysis and advice.

Richard Barrett, Director of the Office of Management Planning in the State Department, [has said,] "Secretary McNamara, in introducing P.P.B.S. in the Defense Department, had a definite managerial concept and strategy in mind. State is trying to formulate a managerial strategy at the same time as it is trying to develop a system to support that strategy." The question is, in the absence of a management strategy, will the computer — now an integral part of the P.P.B.S. system — be used merely to decorate and speed up already obsolete processes? Will information technology simply be applied to existing information-gathering processes? Will more information be gathered only to become useless because the persons who need it do not get it, or get it at the wrong time? P.P.B.S., which is principally concerned with planning and budgeting, is only a small part of this dilemma. The problem becomes more complex and urgent, say, in the implementation of policy or crisis management.

But those who plan carefully may be able to learn much from business experience with the application of advanced information technologies. . . .

The lessons have been and still are learned by business the hard way: mounting costs for useless data, duplication of functions and personnel, large-scale errors in business operations and decisions. The key problem resides in the inability or unwillingness of management to ask itself what it really wants from technology. What kind of information is needed by which persons at what times? What is the relation of the costs of this information to the benefits derived? More and more such questions are being formulated with insight and imagination and, as a result, the latest technological capabilities have made possible not only a change in the methods but also in the substance of business operations.

Today one can no longer think of just the computer. One must think in the more comprehensive terms of information technology or information systems. . . .

The key questions that have to be answered in order to build these systems and make them work usefully are: (1) Who needs the information? (2) What kind of information must be made available, in what detail, and how currently? (3) Must the system be complex enough to allow for machine guidance of the questioner if the question is unclear or unanswerable in the form presented?

In other words, what do we want from our technology? As our commercial systems are beginning to demonstrate, we can get what we want.

In the management of foreign affairs, information technology gives us usefully the chance to review what we are doing as well as what we want to do. I shall try to show that it will affect not only who makes the decisions or who is the instrument of response, as in the case of the Ambassador, but that for this and even more complex questions it will also change what the decisions are about. Further, it will determine whether decisions or conscious responses in particular instances are necessary at all, or are built into the system automatically.

The question of what we want raises, in turn, numerous questions which must be solved organizationally. Who will make the initial and continuing decisions on the data to be fed into the information system? How is data to be weighted for analysis and summary conclusions? Should more than one system be set up — for example, one for the State Department and one for the Central Intelligence Agency? Who should have access to the information from one or more systems? Should there be a switching center which controls who gets what?

However, I shall not concern myself here with these organizational questions. The answers to them will depend in large part on how we envisage the total impact of information technology on the substance of foreign-affairs management. The form we want the conduct of international relations to take — and we still have the weight in the world to shape that, if we assume the leadership — will have a profound effect on what the world looks like.

When Hitler embarked on the direct course leading to World War II, beginning with the announcement that Germany would rearm and culminating with the occupations of the Rhineland, Austria, the Sudetenland and Czechoslovakia, three principal arguments were made by those who counseled against intervention: (1) Hitler could not threaten Europe because Germany did not possess the means for all-out war and, therefore, he should be permitted to assert claims which might be legitimate; (2) Hitler already possessed enough power to make intervention too costly; and (3) Hitler, after he achieved Germany's immediate demands, would live in peace with his neighbors.

The first two arguments were based on information which was inadequate. The third argument was based on an inadequate appraisal of the man and of the psychological forces in Germany which supported him. The proper use of the kind of information and communications technologies now or soon to be available to us could have placed in perspective the first two arguments. Vast quantities of intelligence, most of it not secret but only undigested, on production, manpower, foreign trade, resources and technological probabilities could have provided the Allies at any stage with an accurate picture of German versus Allied capabilities. The imponderables would have remained — questions about who would side with whom, about Hitler, the man, and the psychology of his nation — but even these could have been subjected to analysis aided by information technology. This is not to assert that history would necessarily have been changed; information can still be ignored or misused, and those who make policy are influenced by many factors, some of them essentially irrational. But technology cuts down the area of the unknown, narrows the basis for rational decision.

Many treaties are based on promises to do or not to do things which the partner cannot know about. This is so especially with nonaggression or disarmament treaties and their corollaries. If the ability to collect and process vast quantities of data, ranging from atmospheric samples to economic and transportation statistics, can give any one nation an increasingly accurate picture of trends and unusual activities in other nations, will the universal realization that others can divine a break in faith make such treaties obsolete? This could make the response of one nation to certain actions by others automatic, perhaps pre-programmed through simulation. Such "gaming" on the part of many competing powers could give them such an improved view of the possible consequences of their actions as to save them from many hazardous international experiments. Perhaps, in a crude way, this already is happening. The nuclear test-ban treaty might be considered just a formalized acknowledgement of mutually perceived facts. Can the use of information systems which are increasingly becoming more responsive and accurate push forward this kind of acknowledgements into broader areas of arms control and, someday, even make certain kinds of treaties obsolete?

Undoubtedly, information systems for the conduct of foreign affairs will have to include major techniques for the forecasting of technological and socio-economic change. In order to prepare for the consequences of economic development in the emerging nations, and in the international exploitation of ocean, sub-arctic and extraterrestrial resources, substantial revisions in international law and economic policy obviously are going to be required. Information technology could be applied immediately to the collection of relevant socio-economic data both on the emerging nations and on newly developing resource areas, and eventually could relate them meaningfully to alternative courses of action — what kinds of investments should be made and by whom, what should be the distribution of costs and benefits, etc. On this basis of information, the substance of the decisions in these fields could be altered fundamentally. National and international concern could be concentrated on real issues and realistic alternatives.

In the same decade that the new technology has emerged, the number of countries with which the United States conducts relations has more than doubled, the number of departments and agencies involved in foreign affairs has vastly increased and our sources of information have taken a quantum jump. The very process of decision-making has become infinitely complicated. Under these circumstances, the challenge of conducting our foreign affairs intelligently, of grounding policy on the best possible information, is a challenge to modern management and its use of organizational systems and technological tools. Is modern management now being applied to the conduct of United States foreign affairs? I think that a beginning has been made. Perhaps in this beginning we may also find that our statesmen — not the technicians, but those who must decide what is to be demanded of the technicians — have begun to think about what they want. For, once again, this is the central question: What do we want from our technology? If we know, we can get it.

G. MICHAEL CONLISK

Systems Analysis in East Lansing

East Lansing's task was to find an alternate approach to selecting fire station locations over and above the traditional time and distance application. The city established a city team to formulate the problem and then proceeded into the application of systems analysis.

Finding an alternate approach was particularly important in East Lansing since the city is contracted to provide fire protection to Michigan State University. Much of the land owned by the University is agricultural and lies a considerable distance south of the city's present fire station locations with the result that a longer time period may be involved in traveling south to these large holdings of University land. However, no serious building program for the southern portion of the campus has been proposed in any of the planning by the University.

Consequently, it seemed logical to consider a variance of the time and distance approach balanced against the probability of fires that might originate from a particular area. Obviously, high-rise dormitories had a more serious fire potential than the agricultural acreage to the south. It was based on this premise — that other criteria beside the given time and distance should be considered as the determining factor for the location of future fire stations — that the original study application was made.

We first tried to determine the probabilities of fires based on a study of the history of fires which had occurred within the city during the last

From G. Michael Conlisk, "Systems Analysis — How It Works in East Lansing," *Public Management* 51 (February 1969): 6–8. Copyright © 1969 by International City Management Association.

Mr. Conlisk is Planning Director of East Lansing, Michigan.

76

10 years. To do this it was necessary to determine occupancy type; type, height, and fire rating of structure; age of building; cause of fire; and number of people endangered. These data were collected from fire records to determine discernible trends as to the probabilities of fires that could occur in the future. We expected that this approach would give us an insight into the type of point system that could be used — along with the traditional time and distance factor — in determining station locations.

Next a weighting factor was established for each element considered important in determining fire probability. One of the early determinations was that the "people endangered" would be one of the most heavily weighted factors of the program. In other words it was expected, and eventually proven, that the concentration of people is one of the most dangerous elements affecting the probability of fires. Therefore, "people endangered" became the most critical factor in the entire formulation of the weighted system to be used in determining future station locations. Consequently we had, in outline form, the following type of progression:

• First, determine from historical records what had occurred — a method of trying to determine probabilities of fire based on actual review of past fires.

• Second, project this probability into the future and apply it to the anticipated environment for the year 1980. This would be done in the form of a weighting function applied to the most important elements. As mentioned, population is one of the most important. Building height, age, and floor area; construction type; and fire rating of materials involved in construction were all elements considered in the total rating formula.

• Third, determine the time and distance of a given location from any selected fire station site. This time and distance relationship was established over the city's entire street network system. A distance and estimate of the time required to travel that distance, based on calibrated speeds across that distance, were all put into the computer program.

The computer program was constructed so that the weighted function could be evaluated for each structure within a block, and the block (or group of blocks) could be associated with a node in the network. The value calculated by the weighted function was then multiplied by the travel time calculated from the trial fire location to determine the relative danger of a given area.

The end result of this approach produced a ranking of selected locations, in order of importance, based on a total number of points to all other blocks within the structure of the city. Thus, from a number of selected sites, we were able to determine which location would most effectively respond to the most critical degree of danger probability within the city network.

In order to make the program simultaneously responsive to several probable stations it was necessary to select an area by sectors so that several sites could be proposed and tested for each sector. In this way each location could be scrutinized both for its coverage within its sector and also for its interrelationship with other sectors.

In the future, a computer program could conceivably be used to establish a range of points which would show the probability of "under coverage" — where it would be impractical or unsafe to establish only one station. At the present moment, however, we are doing this on a judgment basis.

Although the analysis is not yet complete, information to date indicates a relocation of the city's existing No. 1 fire station. These indications shift the No. 1 station further north to cover the anticipated growth of the northern area while remaining responsive to existing structures in the south. The results also indicate retaining the No. 2 station, presently covering the campus area, but shifting its response area to the north. The probability of a third station, to be located on campus in proximity of the proposed new medical center and high-rise dormitory area, is also shown.

Based on our point systems and travel times our study now indicates that three stations can provide sufficient coverage of the city instead of the four stations proposed several years ago. This would mean a considerable material savings to the city. At the same time, triangular coverage for the city would evolve, which proves to be most satisfactory in terms of both time-distance and the weighted point system. It appears that with some modifications based on circumstances in a given city, East Lansing's established computer program could be effectively applied to many small cities throughout the country.

Although the program is obviously going to be effective and produce a saving to the city, it seems only fair to point out some of the drawbacks which became readily apparent to the city team. The most obvious was the lack of national data which would have provided fire probability information by housing and occupancy types. A study is presently underway by the National Bureau of Standards that will yield results in terms of this type of statistical approach to fire probability.

From the city's brief experience with the systems process we would argue that there are two distinct roles to be played. First, there is the problem expert — the person or persons most familiar with the objectives of the study. In a city this might be the mayor, manager, planner, any other department head, or combination. The second role must be filled by the program expert — the person who, because of his technical ability, will construct the system model.

Coordination between these elements is needed from the very beginning of the formulation of methodology and construction of the project model. The two kinds of experts must work closely through all stages, i.e., coding, data collection, testing, processing, and final evaluation. It is conceivable that if the problem expert does not understand the coding formulas or processing techniques he might not be able to interpret the data. This is the role of the coordinator.

It is interesting to note the many side effects this program established. These same effects would be readily established in any city applying a systems analysis computer program to an urban problem. It was anticipated from the beginning that if a data bank was established for each property within East Lansing — and an attempt made to determine how parcels of land were to be developed in the future — the data bank should be used for other purposes than just the location of fire stations. In addition to locational questions, problems of increased density and its effect on sewer plant and line capacities, school locations and populations, park locations and acreage needs for the resulting parks could eventually be fed into the program.

Some of the more obvious locational studies might be the routing of garbage pickups, determination of traffic generators as they affect various local and major streets in a community, and the location of other city buildings such as libraries and the city hall.

Since such a multiplicity of information is necessary we suggest that any city considering the use of computer application to a given problem consider simultaneously solving other community problems and needs. Eventually this can lead to a review of exactly what data is necessary or helpful in making a decision on a given problem. Thus, the data bank required for one problem should be constructed so the data may be utilized for a variety of studies.

Furthermore, a city team, composed of various departments cooperating to compare data and suggest studies, will find the exchange beneficial right at the beginning. One of the unvarnished truths of computer analysis is that it forces specific identification of objectives and facts to be applied to the program. It is this very exactness that forces consideration

79

of alternate effects on a given problem rather than gradual development of the problem and the typical belated attempts to solve it after it is created.

One brief example is the possibility of determining the capacity of a new sanitary treatment plant. If the city's population projections include areas outside the boundaries of the city and a vague assumption is made concerning that area's population density, the exactness of the computer's data needs will force attention to that vagueness.

It will become necessary to find out exactly what is proposed by the governing unit so that the design of the plant can be prepared accordingly. At the same time the effects of that redesign or additional cost brought about by increased densities in the outlying area will be identified and the resulting cost assigned to the given area projecting those densities. This same approach could be utilized for water plant capacities, school populations, and other problems that have an interrelationship or overlapping governmental units.

Seemingly, the most beneficial results of the systems analysis approach have been the exchange and understanding between departments of mutual problems and the possible approaches to solving those problems. It has stirred the imagination of several department heads concerning the use of the data bank and studies resulting from such use. We feel the program will become a continuing process, and application of systems analysis to existing and future problems of the community will become a reality.

ALAIN ENTHOVEN

Systems Analysis in the Pentagon

Hardly a week goes by that I don't read some fantastic description of systems analysis in the Pentagon. The more I read about it in the public press, the more I get the feeling I must not be doing it. According to some accounts, the essence of systems analysis is the application of computers and fancy mathematics to reduce all issues to numbers, with lots of attention to cost and none to effectiveness, and with a complete lack of interest in military judgment or anyone else's judgment. If I believed that even a small fraction of such descriptions were accurate, I would recommend to Secretary McNamara and Deputy Secretary Nitze that they fire me; I am sure that if they believed I was trying to replace their judgment with a computer, they would not wait for my recommendation.

In fact, systems analysis is just one name for an approach to problems of decision making that good management has always practiced. The essence of systems analysis is not mysterious, nor particularly complicated, nor entirely new, nor of special value only to Defense planning. Rather, it is a reasoned approach to highly complicated problems of choice characterized by much uncertainty; it provides room for very differing values and judgments; and it seeks alternative ways of doing the job. It is neither a panacea nor a Pandora's box.

Reprinted from the Statement of Alain Enthoven before the United States Congress, Subcommittee on National Security and International Operations, Committee on Government Operations, United States Senate, *Hearings: Planning-Programming-Budgeting*, 90th Congress, 1st Session, Part 2, September 27, 1967.
At the time of his statement, Mr. Enthoven was the Assistant Secretary of Defense (Systems Analysis).

Decisions must be made by responsible officials on the basis of fact and judgment. Systems analysis is an effort to define the issues and alternatives clearly and to provide responsible officials with a full, accurate, and meaningful summary of as many as possible of the relevant facts so that they can exercise well-informed judgment; it is not a substitute for judgment.

You might object, "But you're merely describing disciplined, orderly thought; why call it 'systems analysis'?" Most labels are imperfect; this one is no exception. We use the phrase "systems analysis" to emphasize two aspects of this kind of thinking.

First, every decision should be viewed in some meaningful context. In most cases, decisions deal with elements that are parts of a larger system. Good decisions must recognize that each element is one of a number of components that work together to serve a larger purpose. The strategic bomber, the airfield, the pilot, the fuel, and the spare parts are all parts of a weapon *system*. One cannot make sense out of airfield requirements without looking at the objectives the bomber is intended to achieve. For some purposes, it is necessary to look at the airfield construction program as such; there would be no sense in building a new bomber base if a perfectly good transport base were being vacated a few miles away. Systems analysis emphasizes the airfield as a part of the weapon system. Similarly, to make sense of strategic bomber requirements, you need to look at other strategic offensive weapons, such as missiles.

One of the foundations of systems analysis in the Department of Defense is the concept of "open and explicit analysis."

An analysis is "open and explicit" if it is presented in such a way that the objectives and alternatives are clearly defined, and all of the assumptions, factors, calculations, and judgments are laid bare so that all interested parties can see exactly how the conclusions were derived, how information they provided was used, and how the various assumptions influenced the results. We do not achieve this in every case, but this is the objective, and important issues are almost always approached this way.

In cases of substantial disagreement, it is much better to join your adversary in a joint analysis than to restate without change last year's arguments for last year's frozen position. Joint analyses often narrow the differences, and sometimes lead to agreement, by helping the adversaries to persuade each other of the merits of their arguments and by identifying new alternatives that are mutually more satisfactory.

The open and explicit approach is fundamental to systems analysis as it operates in the decision-making process of the Department of Defense. Open and explicit analysis is our best protection against persistent error. Also, the open and explicit approach makes it very difficult, if not virtually impossible, for any group to rig or manipulate the results.

Systems analysis usually includes some calculations. Where appropriate, it includes the application of modern methods of quantitative analysis, including economic theory, mathematical statistics, mathematical operations research, and various techniques known as decision theory. However, systems analysis is not synonymous with the application of these mathematical techniques, and much of the most important systems analysis work in the Department of Defense does not use them.

Systems analysis is not an attempt to measure the unmeasurable. But one of the opportunities that systems analysis offers for creative work is seeking ways of giving valid measurement to things previously thought to be unmeasurable. A good systems analyst does not leave considerations that cannot be quantified out of the analysis. Inevitably such considerations will be left out of the *calculations,* but a good analyst will and does list and describe such factors.

Systems analysis is definitely not synonymous with the application of computers. We sometimes use computers, we also use pencils, paper, slide rules, telephones, etc. The computer aspect has been grossly overplayed in many discussions of systems analysis. The use or misuse of computers is too minor an aspect of this subject to be relevant to the serious concerns of this committee.

Some of the main tools of systems analysis come from economics. Where appropriate, we approach problems of choice by defining the objectives, identifying alternative ways of achieving the objectives, and identifying the alternative that yields the greatest effectiveness for any given cost, or what amounts to the same thing, that yields a specific degree of effectiveness for the least cost. In other words, the main idea is to find the alternative that yields the greatest military effectiveness from the resources available.

Systems analysis includes a critical evaluation of the objectives. It recognizes that most ends are, in fact, means to still broader objectives. For example, an ability to destroy a particular target is not likely to be an end in itself; it is a means to some more basic end such as deterrence. Therefore, a good systems analyst will seek to determine whether or not the pursuit of certain intermediate objectives is the best way of pursuing the broader ends.

Thus, systems analysis is often associated with "cost-effectiveness" or "cost-benefit" analysis. The term "cost-effectiveness" analysis is often misunderstood.

Every weapon system we buy has both benefits and costs associated with it. You cannot get "effectiveness" without paying a "cost." Each program uses up resources that could otherwise be put to some other useful purpose. Sensible decisions on the use of these resources must depend on the costs incurred in relation to the military effectiveness obtained. "Cost-effectiveness" analysis is nothing more than an attempt to identify the alternatives that yield the most effectiveness in relation to the money spent and other costs incurred.

I certainly agree that we cannot afford to buy less than the military forces we really need, and that we must not let defense spending be constrained by arbitrary financial limits that are unrelated to military needs. But it is simply naïve to assert, as some people do, that the cost we pay for our military power is irrelevant. Our experience with the war in Southeast Asia each day demonstrates the opposite conclusion. We are in the midst of a great national debate over whether the objectives we are fighting for are worth the cost. Whatever the merits of the particular arguments, it is clear that the cost is relevant if for no other reason than that it affects popular support for the war effort.

Cost in any program merely represents "effectiveness foregone elsewhere." The reason that the Secretary of Defense cares about the cost as well as the effectiveness of proposed weapon systems is because he recognizes that the dollars used to support a particular program represent resources that could possibly be used to greater benefit elsewhere. Cost and effectiveness must be related to achieve national policy goals, just as the front and rear sights of a rifle must both be used to hit the target. The position of the rear sight matters only in relation to the front sight. Likewise, the cost of a program matters only in relation to the military effectiveness provided, and vice versa.

Does "cost-effectiveness" analysis stifle innovation? On the contrary, such analysis has given the proponents of good ideas a better way of making their case and of getting prompt and favorable decisions. Systems such as the Minuteman II, Minuteman III, and Poseidon strategic missile systems are examples of cases where very good ideas were identified early and sold on the basis of "cost-effectiveness" analysis. Also, by helping to cut back programs that are based on poor ideas, "cost-effectiveness analysis" helps to leave more resources available for the most effective programs.

Does "cost-effectiveness" analysis always lead to a preference for the cheapest system on a unit cost basis? The record shows it does not. Many systems that were justified on the basis of "cost-effectiveness" analysis cost more per unit than their predecessors, but the margin of extra effectiveness per unit is worth the extra cost.

PHILIP M. MORSE

Putting Operations Research to Work

Operations research or management science or systems analysis proceeds by analyzing the quantitative aspects of the human activity, the operation; by developing mathematical models which represent some of the inter-relations between these aspects; and by using the model to predict the reaction of the operation to various possible changes in external or internal influences. These predictions are then available to the manager of the operation, to assist him in choosing between alternative policies and plans.

Operations research was first applied to military problems, where it was so successful in working out the interrelations between one's own tactics and those of the enemy, that most armed forces now have operations research teams reporting to their top staffs and carrying on continuing analysis of military plans and operation. Tactical and, eventually, strategic decisions could be made more quickly and with greater insight into the consequences.

In the past twenty years operations research has been applied with increasing success to industrial and commercial operations. The successes at first were in the relatively simple portions of the operation, such things as the behavior of inventory in the face of the variability of supply and

Reprinted from *Operations Research for Public Systems,* edited by Philip M. Morse and Laura W. Bacon, by permission of The M.I.T. Press, Cambridge, Massachusetts. Copyright © 1967 by The M.I.T. Press.

Mr. Morse is Professor of Physics and Director of the Operations Research Center, Massachusetts Institute of Technology.

demand, and the scheduling of production in such a way as to utilize most effectively the machinery on hand.

With increased knowledge of the workings of the simpler elements and with the resulting increased cooperation and trust of industrial management in their operations research staffs, broader problems of system integration and long-range planning are now being solved. The locations of new factories and warehouses are worked out to minimize transport costs and to maximize accessibility to markets. Data on the elements of the operation are often kept in accessible form on computers so that the implications of various production or marketing plans can be worked out quickly, to assist management in deciding between alternative policies under consideration.

It should be emphasized that the procedures of operations research are not expected to provide all the bases for managerial decisions; the operations research staff is not expected to take over the administrative function. In most cases there are human aspects of politics or morale which cannot yet be quantified and which the manager must supply from his experience. Sometimes these human factors tend to modify the quantitative aspects and occasionally to negate their implications. Nevertheless, the process of quantifying what can be so expressed helps to clarify the nature of the decision to be made; the manager then knows how much it will cost to let the human aspects overrule the purely quantitative implications. For this to work effectively, the operations research team must be in close touch with top administration; each half of the partnership must have trust in the other's competence and integrity.

The operations research team [may act] as a sort of feedback control for the administration, finding out what is actually going on and comparing it with what management believes is or should be going on, so that management can issue orders to rectify the discrepancy in behavior or else can revise their plans and estimates to conform more closely to actuality.

When dealing with large and complex systems, the operations research group often involves the assistance of a high-speed computing machine. In many cases the operation is too complicated to be able to be expressed in a system of equations which can be solved with paper and pencil. In these cases a computer can often be programmed to simulate the operation's behavior, with all the important interrelations and variabilities represented by computer actions. Rather than being a mathematical model, the simulation is a computer model of the system's behavior; it can be adjusted to fit the actual operation to as detailed a degree or to as rough an approximation as seems desirable and feasible. Instead of trying out a new plan of operation with the real flesh-and-blood system, the plan can be tried out on the simulation; it is usually much quicker, and certainly there is less at stake if the plan is a failure.

Operations research has only recently been applied to the problems of public affairs. The delay is not surprising, for public operations are usually more complex and involve more purely human aspects than do industrial or military operations. Only recently have the techniques of operations research been capable of handling such problems. Also, it has taken longer for the public administrator to realize that operations research could help him in his administrative task. Since operations research does not advance in the absence of close cooperation with the administrator, such a lack of desire for help has meant that no progress has been possible.

Operations Research is an experimental science; its mathematical model of an operation must be based on quantitative observation of that operation. For this reason the O.R. man must have close contact with the participants in the operation, from manager to laborer, particularly at the beginning of the study. He must arrange it so that each echelon in the organization will treat him as a friend and helper rather than as a spy to be fobbed off with partial answers. In this way he can begin to learn from the manager the policy requirements and the management problems in meeting the requirements and, from the lower echelons, the degree of understanding of the orders which reach them and the operational problems arising from their execution.

Early in the investigation the O.R. worker must begin to formulate quantitative *measures of effectiveness* for the operation.

In larger systems, particularly those in the public sector, the measures are not so easy to formulate and there may be several mutually contradictory ones. For instance, should automobile traffic through a network be regulated to minimize the time per trip or to maximize the trips per accident? Should the drug dispensary of a hospital be operated to maximize the speed of supply or to minimize the number of mistakes? In cases such as this, alternative solutions are often required, with the several measures calculated for each solution, so that management can see quantitatively how much one measure is worsened when another one is improved.

The operations research worker is usually trying to help the administrator to reach as wise a decision as possible, not to devise as accurate a model as he can. Frequently, the decision must be made next month, not five years from now, so the amount of data collection and the accuracy of the calculations must be cut to fit the time schedule. A highly accurate finding presented a month after the administrative decision has been made is worth precisely zero to the administrator. Hence, an estimated value of some measure of effectiveness which may be 50 per cent in error is far better than no estimate.

Furthermore, this may be accurate enough anyway. In fact, too great a concentration on accuracy at first may bring out so many minor details that the major effects may be missed.

Data that are collected without specific purpose are usually of little future use. In starting a new problem, after the preliminary discussions with participants at all levels and after the initial observation of the activity, the O.R. worker next needs to begin to formulate his model of the operation, to postulate what the important factors are and how they depend on each other. His first data-gathering, then, must be to check out the model, to see whether his guesses are correct; it need only be extensive enough and accurate enough to show that he is on the right track. If the assumed model does not check out, he must try another; if it does appear to be right, then his next data-gathering and analysis should be to improve the model and to estimate the variability of the various components.

Like any other model, the computer model will not predict correct results unless it corresponds to the actual operation in all important respects. Often, the complexity of the programming induces the analyst to feel that complexity can substitute for realism. The temptation is to insert a sub-routine because the operational element "ought to behave" in such-and-such a way, without checking to see whether it does.

Unless realism is built into the details of the program and unless the whole simulation is checked for normal behavior, the computer model is only a complicated and impressive way of making an unverified guess. With appropriate safeguards, however, the machine simulation is a technique of operational experiment which is rapidly gaining in scope and usefulness.

The payoff for the research lies in the action of the administrator; in a very real sense, the results depend on the partnership of effort between the administrator and his O.R. team. In general, this partnership works most smoothly if the administrator has his own team which is continually studying the system he controls and is anticipating the decisions he will have to be making in the near future. This is now the case in military staffs and in many industries; perhaps it will eventually be the case in the public domain. But at present there are few public administrators who have their own O.R. teams. The question therefore arises, how can work be started, how can the public administrator organize or find a team to give him the sort of assistance we have been describing?

[A consulting O.R. team] is not easy to collect. It must include specialists in many disciplines — mathematicians, economists, engineers, social scientists, computer programmers, and others — and these people must have experience in working together. Unless the unit of government is very large, it is difficult to assemble such a group to work exclusively for the single unit; even as large a city as Boston or San Francisco would find it hard, perhaps impossible, to have such a group working for itself alone.

The pattern of operations research in the field of public service is one of calling in the expert team, whether it be a private consulting firm or a group supported by the central government, to do the majority of the work.

But just because the city or other public-service administration has come to rely on an expert consulting team to carry out the details of the initial study doesn't mean that there is nothing for the administration to do. The administrator and his staff have certain duties and actions with respect to the study and its implementation which they *must* carry out, or the whole procedure will produce no result and the cost of the study will have been wasted.

The minimal amount of participation required of the administrator and his staff is threefold: first, the management of the company or city must conclude that they have problems which need O.R. analysis; second, the administrative staff must be sufficiently convinced of the importance of the analysis to be willing to assist in the gathering of data; and third, both management and its staff must be willing to listen to the results of the analysis and, if they agree with the findings, to act in accord with the recommendations.

It often takes a fair amount of work and thought to formulate the problem, to determine that some part of the system's operation or some aspect of the plans for future operation would be improved by an operations research analysis. If the city or other public service is large enough to afford it, there can be an officer of the administration, a sort of science advisor to the mayor or to the director, who knows enough about the workings of the system and also knows enough about the techniques of operations research to be able to locate the places where such analysis can help. He often will not have the time or the special knowledge to do the analysis, to solve the problem, but he can call attention to the problem and suggest that help is needed to solve it. Even if there is not a specially delegated "science advisor," there often is a member of the administrative staff with enough technical experience to be able to formulate the problem and to recommend that a study be carried out to solve it.

It will seldom be the case that all the talents required to make the analysis are already present in the administrative staff. Present practice is to call in a consulting group, either a commercial consulting firm or a governmentally supported group available to many parts of the government, or a group in a university organized to carry on such consulting work.

But a consulting group of this sort cannot solve the problems of the city or the agency by themselves; they need to be called in and they must be assisted. Someone in the organization has to decide that there is a problem and that its solution is important enough to be worth spending some money to get it solved. And after the group has been called in, they cannot do the job by themselves. Many people in the agency or city staff must help in gathering the data needed for the analysis, and several members of the staff must become partners in the analysis so that they can inform the consulting team about details of the system's operations and, more important, so that they can understand the details of the team's analysis and conclusions.

If the city or agency has only a written report to show for the money it has paid a consulting team, the chances are that the report will not be effectively utilized and that the money has been wasted. A report is not a successful solution of an operational problem. The true success, the implementation of the recommendations, is much more likely if, in addition to the report, a few members of the administrative staff have worked closely with the consulting team so that they understand the main outlines of the analysis and the reasons for the conclusions.

A plan or a recommendation for action is not worth much until it is put into practice. And the putting into practice usually requires much ingenuity and a thorough understanding of what is important and what is peripheral. Special difficulties always come up during implementation; they may indicate minor omissions in the plan which can be corrected with little modification of the whole, or they may be signs that there is some basic error. Unless there is understanding of the analysis, a plan which is basically sound may be discarded because of a minor discrepancy.

As soon as the public administrator has decided on the need for a

large-scale operations research study to be made by a consulting organization, he should at the same time plan to organize a small group in his
own staff to monitor the implementation of the study. It also means that
the best way — indeed perhaps the only way — to start building this
"in-house" group is to assign one or two appropriate members of one's
own staff to work closely with the consulting group. After this specialized
training, these staff members will automatically be the nucleus of one's
own operations research team, capable of following the plan, of modify-
ing it if necessary, and of calling for further detailed study if required
later.

This "in-house" group may later be expanded if the work increases
and may, if circumstances permit, become an expert group which can
carry out further studies on its own initiative.

SIMON RAMO

The Systems Approach to Social Problems

There is little doubt that the most widespread and pressing domestic problem facing us today is the condition of our cities and our lives within them.

Because 70 per cent of our people are living on 2 per cent of the land — and others are moving from farms and other rural areas onto that 2 per cent at the rate of 600,000 annually — this problem is intensifying at an alarming rate. And, as it does, our people are demanding, with growing impatience, that something be done to reduce the discomforts and health hazards of urban living. Our people are beginning to see and sense that somehow there is a solution — or at least a vast improvement — available through advanced technology.

After all, a society which can assure astronauts a clean environment as far away as the moon surely could keep the air of its cities on earth clean; a technology that can produce a supersonic transport to fly passengers from the center of one continent to the center of another in a few hours certainly ought to be able to arrange a far quicker trip for those passengers than is now possible from the airport to the center of town; and computers which can handle vast amounts of sophisticated data certainly ought to be useful in increasing the efficiency of our inadequate educational, medical, and administrative systems, which depend so much on the gathering and flow of information.

From Simon Ramo, "The Systems Approach: Automated Common Sense," *Nation's Cities* 6 (March 1968): 14–19. Copyright © 1968 by *Nation's Cities*.

Mr. Ramo, a scientist and engineer, is Vice Chairman of the Board and Chairman of the Policy Committee, TRW, Inc.

Gradually, over the last decade or two, a powerful methodology has been developing: the systems approach. This methodology, this systematic approach to problem solving, is the successful application of science to military and space systems.

In the systems approach, concentration is on the design of the whole, as distinct from the design and production of the parts. It is an approach that insists upon looking at the problem in its entirety, taking into account all the facets, and seeking to understand how they interact with one another and how the best solution will bring these factors into proper relationship.

Essentially, the systems approach relates technology to the need; indeed, it starts by insisting on a clear understanding of exactly what the problem is, the goals that will lead to a solution, and the criteria for evaluating alternative avenues. As the end result, the approach seeks to work out a detailed description of a combination of men and machines with such concomitant flow of matériel, assignment of function, and pattern of information flow that the whole system represents a compatible and most satisfactory ensemble for achieving the performance desired. Using computers and other sophisticated tools of information analysis, the systems approach makes possible the consideration of vast amounts of data and requirements. It also recognizes the need for carefully worked out compromises, for tradeoffs among competing factors (such as time and cost), for simulation and modeling to make possible the prediction of actual performance long before the entire system is brought into being. And it makes feasible the assessment and selection of the best approach from all the many conceivable ones.

Boil away all the complex language and you find that the systems approach is really automated common sense — a highly methodized use of creative logic to analyze a problem, the whole problem and everything related to it, then picking the best way to solve the problem.

The systems approach is not really a new concept. The word "systems" is certainly not unfamiliar to us. We have known it in "telephone systems," "electrical power and distribution systems," "transportation systems," even "military weapon systems."

When the Sphinx was built, and the Roman roads and the London Bridge and the Panama Canal and the New York subways constructed, there had to be in every instance a part of the citizenry whose professional job it was to relate the existing technology to the problem, the available resources, the time constraints, and the economics — in short, to consider the problem in relation to the society it must serve.

What makes the systems approach now appear new? What makes it justified and significant to talk about it now as a "mobilizing" technology that is ready for application to the big civil systems problems of our times? It is partly because of the great acceleration of the development of the specific tools of systems engineering in recent years. Most of this has resulted from the need for a deep application of this kind of methodology to the highly complex and costly defense and space programs. In these programs, techniques of great importance have been developed to improve the systems engineering discipline.

There are now large-scale electronic computers that make possible the handling of the information basic to good, quantitative, tradeoff analyses and mathematical modeling. There are now, as well, a substantial number of professionals who are well seasoned in interdisciplinary problems, who know how to relate the many facets of one technology to another and to relate these in turn to all the non-technical factors that characterize practical problems.

Solutions to such immensely complex problems as putting a man on the moon or renovating New York City must satisfy, and require the cooperation of, many semi-autonomous groups not accustomed to working tightly together. What is needed is an interacting arrangement of people and things, of matériel and information flow for which there is little precedence. New concepts, new machinery, new apparatus, novel functions for people, and untried interconnections among them are needed so that the whole complex of sub-elements will constitute together a system which represents a considerable deviation from the present method of doing things.

Economists confidently predict that within less than a decade we shall substantially exceed a $1 trillion Gross National Product. This means that during the decade of the '70s the gross value of all of our products and services will be $10 trillion, give or take a few billion. Fully 10 per cent of that total, $1 trillion, will represent effort in just those fields that we have mentioned above under the title "civil systems" — transportation, urban development, water and air pollution control, and new medical and educational facilities. The true worth to our society of this trillion dollars can be altered greatly depending upon whether or not the effort is properly chosen, well organized, and efficiently operated.

The proper application of science and technology to the fullest — and this is what the systems approach seeks to effect — can greatly influence this value. The costs of applying the systems approach will be a small part of the greater worth that its successful application should bring.

To see how such powerful leverage might occur, let us try now to examine a bit more closely the nature of this mobilizing methodology we call the systems approach.

Clearly the highway transportation system is more than the automobile itself. It is roads and spare parts supply, gasoline production and distribution, traffic lights, traffic laws, drivers' licensing systems, casualty insurance, and much more. Without all these sub-systems, the overall system could not operate. But our nation's transportation system never was thought out and designed as an integrated system. It just grew and it has all the ills resulting from our failure to design it and operate it as a well-integrated system from its very inception. Hence, our automobiles are not suited for the kind of city driving for which most of them are used. Cars that are capable of doing more than 100 miles per hour are allowed to do 60 or 70 on most of the highways of the nation, where they are constantly subjected to the kind of massive traffic congestion that wastes millions upon millions of man-hours each day, that creates nervous driving habits that place lives in jeopardy, that pollutes much of the air we breathe.

The air transportation system similarly is much more than the airplane. It is baggage, and getting to the airport, and radar, and maintenance crews, and ticket agents, and food preparation, and national hook-ups of electronic reservation-making equipment, and automobile parking. Here again, it has not in the past been given the kind of high-quality, complete, integrated, overall systems engineering approach which the importance and complexity of the system and the payoff to be realized by so doing clearly justifies. But more than with personal automobile transportation, it has been recognized by the leaders of the industry as a systems problem. However, it is a difficult and nearly impossible organizational job to get government, technological industry, and airline companies together to deal with the problem as a system. The technological, sociological, and economic factors are puzzling, costly to analyze, and no one organization has overall responsibility. Thus the airport systems deliberations to date have been most often below that level of quality and detailed attention needed to make the expenditures and resources assigned to air transportation more than only partially effective.

Perhaps, in the end, the systems approach will be most essential because it encourages and makes possible action. In a natural and logical way, follow-on implementation is a major systems objective. Starting with the acquisition of all of the data and facts, the systems effort describes the performance and the costs, the equipment, matériel, information flow patterns, the people required to work at prescribed tasks. It shows how the proposed system integrates with the other existing operations of society. Accordingly, the systems approach, when applied, answers a good many questions for everyone who is involved in decision making.

It is easier by far, after system analysis of a problem, for all concerned to make decisions.

The systems approach is a first step in answering the question of how much money is needed, for example. It helps to articulate the goals that might be only crudely understood otherwise. It helps set priorities, suggest solutions, and propose organization. All this sets the stage for subsequent decision-making which might, in the absence of a systems approach, be endlessly delayed. Of course, if systems work is done competently, it is inherent in it that it is logical and quantitative as much as is truly possible, and it provides comparisons. You know what you will get for what you pay.

This, then, is the systems approach. Now it is technology for the use of science and technology, a technique of mobilizing science for society. How will this fare in the coming decades? Will it be applied and will it greatly alter the balance between technological advance and lagging social maturity? The answer is probably that it is going to be applied very rapidly on an increasingly larger scale, but probably 10 years will pass before we can confidently say that the battle has been joined — the contest between the great need for the application of technology to the area of social engineering problems and the full application of science and technology to try to solve these problems. After that, it may take another couple of decades, with strong utilization of the systems approach, to get on top of these problems so that we can then say an even more important thing: Science and technology are now being used to the fullest on behalf of society.

Perhaps the chief reason why it will take this long is not that the public, the Congress, the city and state governments, the people of influence in industry and in science and technology will fail to appreciate adequately the value of a good systems approach. Rather, it will take time because all of us must first mature in our appreciation of the way our society can control approaches to such problems.

The more important bottleneck, however, will be the shortage of really good systems engineers. We do have today groups of people in industry, in government, in some of our foundations, universities, and private consulting groups with competence in systems techniques and with great interest to enter the systems field. We also have embryonic systems teams.

97

But not enough of them. The work is difficult; the requirements extremely exacting. The combination of common sense, creative talent, and technological sophistication is a very rare thing indeed.

Thus, while society today is not using science and technology to the fullest, we are suggesting that within a decade or two science will seek to do just that. And it is interesting that we also are forced to predict that the moment it does so, society will find that science and technology will still be a limiting factor to social progress. Nonetheless, that will be our golden age.

ROBERT L. CHARTRAND

Congress Needs the Systems Approach

The demands upon the Congressman of today are legion. He must be a veritable Everyman, cognizant of several dozen major and minor issues of key significance to the nation as a whole, his party, the political unit which he represents, and the various elements of his constituency. He must master and work within the intricacies of a framework founded nearly 200 years ago, and yet be attuned to the personalities and procedures of the present. His handling of information must be well timed, highly selective, and reflect the constraints of protocol and pragmatism. In commenting upon this distinctive milieu, Dr. Charles R. Dechert points out that:

> . . . the Congress as a corporate body within the governmental structure is essentially an information processing and decision system, characterized by an extremely complex internal network of channels and filters, with some flux in membership and communications nodes.[1]

As the population of the United States increases, and the problems which accompany this growth are reflected in legislation, it may be useful

From Robert L. Chartrand, "Congress Seeks a Systems Approach," *Datamation* 14 (May 1968): 46–49. Reprinted with permisison from *Datamation*®, May, published and copyrighted 1968 by F. D. Thompson Publications, Inc., 35 Mason St., Greenwich, Conn. 06830.

Mr. Chartrand is the information sciences specialist for the Legislative Reference Service of the Library of Congress.

1. Charles R. Dechert, "Availability of Information for Congressional Operations," in *Congress: The First Branch of Government* (Washington: American Enterprise Institute for Public Policy Research, 1966), p. 168.

to recall the mounting pressures upon the individual Congressman. For example, in the days of our nation's beginning, a member of the House of Representatives would be elected by a constituency averaging 33,000 persons; today's Representative comes from a district averaging 460,000 constituents. The volume of legislation which must be dealt with is of awe-inspiring proportions: during the first session of the 90th Congress (1967), more than 20,000 public and private bills and resolutions were introduced in the two chambers.

Each Congressman serves as a member of several committees and sub-committees, spending hours considering agenda items and hearing testimony. In addition, he is called to the chamber floor for quorum calls, yea and nay calls, and division, teller, and voice votes by the hundred.

The contemporary Congressman has every incentive to discover new ways to function more effectively. He and his limited staff are hard pressed to collect, filter, assimilate, and recall the pertinent information which will help answer a given problem. The dilemma of the overworked Congressional staff is not easily solved, for in addition to supporting the member in legislative matters, there is a heavy load of constituent-related work. Correspondence from constituents may run as high as several thousands of letters a day. The office staff also must screen large numbers of telephone calls and play host to many visitors.

So numerous are the requests for information that the Congressional office must utilize all possible resources. In many instances, requests will be relayed to the appropriate executive branch agency; on other occasions, support will be obtained from the Legislative Reference Service of the Library of Congress, or perhaps some group from the private sector (e.g., universities or lobbyist organizations). With all of these pressures upon them, many Congressmen are commencing to examine seriously the potential of the systems approach in handling some of their legislative and administrative problems.

Within the past two years, there has been discernible interest on the part of Congressional members in the application of information technology to various aspects of legislative functioning. Consideration of this approach was addressed by the Joint Committee on the Organization of the Congress, under the leadership of Senator A. S. Mike Monroney and Representative Ray J. Madden. A number of specific recommendations designed to modernize the organization, operations, and support capabilities of the Congress was prepared. Among these, as embodied in the Legislative Reorganization Act which has passed the Senate and now is being considered by the House of Representatives, is a provision for the creation of a computer facility to support the Congress.

Other sections related to the use of systems technology established the responsibility for the continuing study of adp for Congress with the proposed Joint Committee on Congressional Operations, and called for the development of a standardized information and data processing system for budgetary and fiscal data for use by all federal agencies.

In addition to the provisions found in the Legislative Reorganization Act, a series of bills have been introduced by a bipartisan group of House members calling for the establishment of an adp facility which would support exclusively the Congress. Representative Robert McClory, who introduced the first bill for such a facility late in the 89th Congress, repeatedly has urged his colleagues to consider realistically the need for improved information handling by Congressional elements.

Congressional awareness of its information problems has led some of the members to discuss common problems with outside groups, such as the American Political Science Association, and to request surveys and studies of the information problem. In a report prepared for general distribution to the Congress entitled "Automatic Data Processing for the Congress," several priority applications where adp could be useful were identified and discussed;[2] Fig. 1 presents a listing of the candidate task areas. In some instances, the Congress as a whole might benefit; in other cases, the functioning committee or individual Congressman would be the chief beneficiary. Included for consideration were: a current schedule of committee hearings and meetings, summary information on issues up for vote, an automated index-catalog of Congressional documents, histories of committee action, the content and status of pending legislation, and an adp-oriented Selective Dissemination of Information (SDI) system to retrieve key subject matter information and materials which would be responsive to the requirements of the member or committee.

Initial steps now are being taken to provide enhanced support to the Congress. The Legislative Reference Service has designed a computer-centered system which allows entering identifying and synoptic information on bills and resolutions introduced in both chambers of the Congress via keyboard terminals to a remote computer. Also, selected bibliographic data are being placed on magnetic tape for the future generation of lists of selected references.

2. Robert L. Chartrand, "Automatic Data Processing for the Congress," U.S. Congress, Joint Committee on the Organization of the Congress, Hearings before the Joint Committee, Part 15, Appendix (89th Cong., 2nd Sess., 1966), pp. 2313–2317.

Legislative Functioning:

Status of pending legislation
Current schedule of committee and subcommittee activity
Authorization and appropriations data
Topical research information and statistical data
Computer-oriented index of Congressional documents
Pre-vote information on major issues
Post-vote analytical information
Information on federal contract awards

Administrative Functioning:

Histories of committee and subcommittee activity
Lobbyist activity information
Constituent interest file
Constituent correspondence file
Congressional payroll accounts
Current Congressional telephone book

Fig. 1. Candidate applications for Congressional use of ADP and the systems approach

Information technology today is able to allow the operational implementation of certain needed improvements. The decision as to when and where systems technology is to be applied resides, appropriately, with the Congress itself.

The United States Congress has moved to position itself to address better the many problems now facing our civilization. Age-old questions are being asked, but with a new urgency. On what projects should we spend federal funds? How much needs to be spent? What should be the scheduling for these expenditures? The society which for the past generation has empowered its representatives to place overwhelming emphasis on defense, space, and nuclear energy developmental projects now is demanding that increased attention be given to the new series of problems which touch the daily lives of all citizens.

Organizations and establishments in the private and public sectors have begun to review their ability to meet the new challenges. Realistic plans for urban renewal and expansion, environmental pollution control, precision design of transportation networks, and other problems are achievable only after intensive, imaginative planning.

Among the first members of the Congress to consider the possible advantages of using the systems approach in the new problem areas was Senator Gaylord Nelson. In his Scientific Manpower Utilization Act, he stressed the need to mobilize the scientific and engineering manpower of the nation and to employ systems analysis and engineering in support of these scarce skilled groups. Senator Nelson also called upon state and local governments and private enterprise to apply their resources to the fight against these specters of disaster:

> Nothing short of a massive effort by industry and government at every level will solve this problem. This can be done only after a total analysis of the problem and development of an overall program of action.[3]

The need to forge a strong business-government action group also is championed by Representative F. Bradford Morse. Both in the 89th and 90th Congresses he has served as spokesman for a group of nearly 50 House Republicans calling for the establishment of a National Commission on Public Management. Similar legislation has been introduced in the upper chamber by Senator Hugh Scott and more than a dozen colleagues. The Morse-Scott approach concentrates upon the need for further study of the applicability of systems technology to civil problems. Representative Morse believes that:

> We are on the threshold of an entirely new approach to the solution of these public problems. Long-standing relationships between government and business will, of necessity, have to be exerted through the evolution, testing, and full utilization of more forceful, imaginative techniques and devices.[4]

As the result of discussions among Senator Nelson, Senator Scott, and Representative Morse, efforts are underway to merge the grants-in-aid approach of Senator Nelson — wherein a state office or university receives funds for the development of a pilot project — with the Morse-Scott proposal.

Other Congressional activity reflects the alternative ways in which systems technology may be applied, including the use of systems analysis and PPBS techniques in organizing federal research and operational efforts in pollution abatement. Another development involved the projected study of how adp and systems procedures might be applied to the admin-

---

3. U.S. Congress, Senate, Committee on Labor and Public Welfare, Special Subcommittee on the Utilization of Scientific Manpower, *Hearings* before the Special Subcommittee (89th Cong., 1st Sess., November 18, 1965), p. 16.

4. F. Bradford Morse, "Private Responsibility for Public Management," *Harvard Business Review* 45 (March/April 1967): 7.

istration of the courts of the United States; this was contained in the Federal Judicial Center legislation. Thus, the areas in which Congress is beginning to see the desirability of including direct provision or recommended consideration for the use of systems tools and techniques are increasing in number.

The solution to many of our problems will not be reached without a considerable struggle, and we must scrutinize most thoroughly how our national resources are to be distributed between the defense-space-nuclear power programs and the new areas demanding attention. President Kennedy's concern over the existing imbalance in spending and manpower prompted him to caution the nation that:

> . . . in the course of meeting specific challenges so brilliantly, we have paid a price by sharply limiting the scarce scientific and engineering resources available to the civilian sector of the economy.[5]

Positive corrective action is taking place within the legislative branch as the policy makers there, together with the leadership of the executive branch, strive to apply the nation's resources to the problems of the age.

5. *Economic Report of the President* (Washington: GPO, 1963), p. xxv.

System Development Corporation

SDC's Public Systems Divisions helps its customers — federal, state and local government organizations and other public-serving institutions such as universities, libraries and hospitals — to solve problems: information problems, operating problems, communication, education, health, transportation, safety, documentation and planning problems.

All of SDC's resources — almost 2000 professional staff members, one of the most comprehensive arrays of computers in the country, facilities at eight widely dispersed major business areas in the U.S. — are at PSD's disposal, making the help the division provides unusually effective.

The background PSD brings to a job is unique. System Development Corporation, as the name implies, understands systems, techniques for analyzing systems, ways of building good systems and ways of improving old ones. SDC began as far back as 11 years ago to apply techniques that have come to the forefront only recently — systems analysis, computer programming, mathematical modeling, operations research, simulation, cost-effectiveness analysis, system training.

The Public Systems Division focuses these skills and more than 1000 man-years of directly applicable experience on the problems facing its customers. PSD services range from information processing assistance through planning support to analysis, design, development, implementa-

From a brochure, "SDC Public Systems," issued in 1968 by System Development Corporation, Santa Monica, California. Copyright © 1968 by System Development Corporation.

tion, installation and maintenance of systems — including training of people to work with them. Providing these services are 200 professionals and a complement of support people.

Each professional is an expert in his field, be it information science, linguistics, engineering, telecommunications, urban and regional planning, transportation, economics, training, mathematics, sociology, library science, statistics, psychology, education, marine sciences, law enforcement, civil emergencies, information management or health. And all are used to working together, attacking problems as an interdisciplinary team.

Since 1960 SDC's public systems work has spanned 325 contracts with more than 25 federal agencies, 16 universities and numerous other public organizations. PSD personnel have worked in 75-plus cities, all 50 states, Puerto Rico, the Virgin Islands, Canada, Vietnam and Thailand.

In anticipation of growing needs in the public sector, PSD conducts advanced research and development, building tools for dealing with complex social, economic and organizational situations. This program is augmented by a large-scale corporate R&D effort in the behavioral, mathematical, information and computer sciences.

The people in SDC's Public Systems Division understand public agencies and public programs. The following sampling of accomplishments indicates what they offer within their main fields of concern.

Information Management

The Public Systems Division makes system science and computer capabilities available to the needs of public-serving organizations. SDC developments in on-line, interactive computer use, general-purpose data management systems and natural-language processing make the computer a flexible, responsive tool for the government program manager, the transportation planner, the medical researcher, the computer-assisted instructor, the professional programmer in an agency's data processing shop, and a multitude of others who need effective, customized solutions to their data handling needs.

Time-Shared Data Management

SDC's Time-Shared Data Management System (TS/DMS) is a versatile computer system easily used by the manager, the researcher, the planner, the decision-maker. TS/DMS makes all the advantages of immediate, English-based dialogue programs available to the user, helping him store, sort, examine, rearrange and understand the significance of information vital to his task.

TS/DMS operates as part of SDC's time-sharing system, one of the first general-purpose time-sharing systems operating on the IBM 360 computer. Time-sharing enables many people to use one computer simultaneously, sharing cost as well as time, and get such rapid responses to their instructions that each feels like the only user.

Since the TS/DMS program is written in a relatively machine-independent programming language, it is not limited to users of the System/360 computers; it may be implemented on other computers comparable to those in the 360 family.

Public Systems Division personnel are using parts of TS/DMS in designing specialized computer-based information systems for law enforcement, instructional management and library support. Many of the computer-based tools to be described later are adaptable for use with TS/DMS.

For Simpler Data Management Needs

SDC's MADAM (Moderately Advanced Data Management) program offers many of the advantages of TS/DMS to users who need the aid of a computer only from time to time for data management jobs that are not extraordinarily large or complex.

The program operates on IBM 360 computers. MADAM services can be run on the user's machine or at SDC computer centers. MADAM is an easy to use program that allows a nonprogrammer to build a file of data, store it in the computer, search it, update it, abstract it, rearrange it, copy it or combine parts of one file with parts of others.

Government Operations

For more than eleven years, SDC has been providing government agencies with effective ways of managing and monitoring programs. In the process, Public Systems Division personnel have become familiar with government operations and problems and have developed an exceptional understanding of what information is needed and appropriate at each level of administration.

The systems they have designed range from manual reporting systems to be operated by poverty-area residents to flexible computer-based information retrieval systems.

Office of Economic Opportunity

For the Office of Economic Opportunity, SDC developed a complete manpower management information system, using as target environments three Opportunities Industrialization Centers (OIC) and two other manpower projects. More than a record-keeping mechanism, the system actually facilitates day-to-day operations and can be handled by nonprofessional workers recruited from the local community.

The development of this system was based on information gathered during a study of the pilot OIC in Philadelphia. This self-help program sponsored by the black community had been set up to provide remedial skill training, job development and placement. The SDC study reviewed and analyzed the operational structure of OIC, made recommendations for improving that operation and structure and examined the applicability of using OIC as a model for other programs.

From data gathered during the study, a model was constructed and generalized to make it applicable to other cities. The system is in operational use today.

Department of Housing and Urban Development

In 1966, SDC began working with the recently formed Department of Housing and Urban Development to create an effective integrated management system, responsive to the needs of its Secretary and preserving useful components of the several systems brought to HUD by its formerly autonomous component agencies. PSD personnel completed a thorough study of the existing systems and made recommendations for and assisted with interim system improvements. PSD has been developing a centralized management system for HUD reports, including information retrieval system design.

Department of Agriculture

The Federal Extension Service of the Department of Agriculture cooperates with state and county governments to help the public interpret and apply the latest agricultural technology developed through research by land-grant universities, the Department of Agriculture and other sources. SDC has developed an information retrieval system to support the Federal Extension Service at all levels. Designed specifically for use by persons with no computer background, the system enables each user to obtain reports tailored to his specifications.

U.S. Agency for International Development

PSD has people in Vietnam working with the U.S. Agency for International Development. They are examining and documenting current USAID/Vietnam policies and procedures; identifying functional and information systems to determine the adequacy of the information provided and the reliability of the data flow; determining the quality of data required for an automatic data processing system; designing EDP systems to satisfy functional and management informaiton requirements; and operating the computer installation to fulfill the required applications. Results of their work are being used in such areas as the commodity import program, logistics, economic policy, public health, public safety and management reporting.

Job Corps

At the request of the Office of Economic Opportunity's Job Corps Task Force, SDC has developed and operated an information system that provides Job Corps Headquarters with rapid access to a data base of enrollees, rejects and staff. SDC has also analyzed and evaluated the arithmetic screening test for Job Corps applicants, performed a system analysis of the reporting requirements of Job Corps Centers and developed a system for accurate recording of enrollee identification data.

Urban and Regional Information Systems

SDC joined the current assault on urban problems because of its special competence in the analysis, design, development and implementation of information systems. As one of the first organizations to employ the system approach to the critical information needs of agencies responsible for urban and regional planning and development, SDC has acquired a thorough understanding of the tasks and problems confronting such agencies.

Dominion Bureau of Statistics

The Canadian Dominion Bureau of Statistics (DBS) is the central agency responsible for all Canadian government statistical data acquisition and processing. The scope of its operations is extremely broad, ranging from the population census to analyses of foreign trade. DBS has initiated a procurement and development program to convert its data processing activities to a large-scale third-generation computer system. PSD personnel have assisted DBS in planning for this conversion and are providing consultation in such areas as organization, training and standards for technical operation of the new installation.

Department of the Interior, Topographic Division, Geological Survey

A pioneering analysis in the development of planning, programming and budgeting was carried out by SDC for the National Topographic Program. SDC determined the relative utility of existing maps and the potential utility of new ones. Quantitative models, based on utilities of existing and anticipated new maps, were developed to perform these determinations.

Other Planning and Information Systems

SDC's numerous other clients for state, regional and local planning and information systems include Marin County (California); the cities of New York, Charlotte (North Carolina) and Los Angeles; the states of New York and Oregon; the Puerto Rico Economic Development Administration; and several dozen more.

Education

Our system of education is faced with increasing demands for excellence in the context of a growing set of social problems. Today's technology shows great promise for helping to meet these conflicting demands. For some time, SDC has been developing some of the most advanced tools available to aid teachers, counselors and school administrators. Studies by Public Systems Division personnel have produced new perspectives on present and future education problems and methods for solving them.

Department of Labor

The Concentrated Employment Program, launched in April 1967 by the Department of Labor in collaboration with the C͡ice of Economic

Opportunity, is designed to help disadvantaged persons prepare for and obtain steady, decent-paying jobs. SDC is furnishing broad support to this program in its goal of bringing together individual manpower programs in slum areas and weaving them into a single process.

Under five separate contracts PSD personnel are evaluating the overall effectiveness of the program in six major cities throughout the country; evaluating new CEPS in an additional six cities; determining why persons drop out of the program by identifying characteristics of CEP dropouts, the scope and magnitude of the problem, and when during the program dropouts occur; providing guidelines and assistance in the implementation of local CEP information systems; and training CEP personnel in meeting federal reporting requirements. In addition, a CEP Planning Source Book was designed by the corporation to aid directors and planning staffs.

In a related area SDC is helping the Department of Labor with its analysis of the JOBS (Job Opportunities in the Business Sector) program. A joint venture of the Labor Department, private employers and the National Alliance of Businessmen, JOBS is a program that involves the business community in efforts to employ disadvantaged ghetto residents.

Appalachia

SDC's involvement with Appalachia began in 1964, when the corporation provided consultation to the Area Redevelopment Administration of the Department of Commerce. Following the development of a system and a model for a regional development organization — the Appalachia Regional Commission — SDC prepared an initial statement of information requirements for review and monitoring; drew up recommendations for the structure, organization and administration of the commission; and assisted in working out details of commission interface with federal, state and local governmental jurisdictions.

State of California

SDC served as consultant to the state of California in the evaluation of contracts with four aerospace companies to apply advanced system science and technology to problems of crime and delinquency, transportation, waste management and information systems.

The corporation assisted the State of California Governor's Office in implementing a personnel data retrieval system on SDC's time-sharing system, utilizing remote teletype input/output terminals in Sacramento. The Department of Corrections has also used the system to study the potential of on-line access to its personnel data base.

Public Systems Division personnel have provided system analysis, system design and data processing consultation to the Department of General Services and to other departments, organizations and committees in state government.

Computer-Aided Tools for Education

For the Southwest Regional Laboratory for Educational Research and Development, SDC has developed a first version of a computer-based instructional management system (IMS). The system gives a teacher information about pupil performance on which to base decisions concerning pacing of groups, assignment of children to ability groups and assignment of remedial instructional materials. Public Systems Division personnel are continuing to improve the IMS data processing system and the diagnostic and prescriptive materials it uses.

SPLAN (School Budget Planning) is a time-shared, interactive system developed by SDC for the Southwest Regional Laboratory. A school administrator can use SPLAN to gain quick insight into fiscal and personnel information concerning his district and to evaluate the effects of proposed changes on his district's budget.

PLANIT is an SDC-developed computer language that enables lesson designers and teachers to construct computer-based lessons and administer them to students in the form of computer-aided instruction. Neither lesson designer nor student needs any previous experience in computer use. PLANIT has been used for the development of lessons ranging from first-grade reading to college-level statistics. The National Science Foundation has asked SDC to reprogram PLANIT for a medium-sized third generation computer to make the language more widely available.

Educational Information Systems

SDC has designed and developed information management systems and data processing facilities for New York's statewide system of educational data centers; the Orange, New Jersey, Educational Resource Center; the school systems of Rockland County, New York, and the Province of Quebec; and a number of colleges and universities, including Montclair State College, New Jersey, the Claremont Colleges in California, the

University of New Mexico, and Gallaudet College, the world's only institution of higher learning for the deaf.

The most comprehensive undertaking was the design and computer programming of an information system for the Washington, D.C., public schools. The system assists administrators, principals and teachers in processing records of student attendance, supply distribution, personnel assignment and other administrative operations. Following a survey of computer facilities and services available within the capital, SDC determined the administrative and economic feasibility of the system. The PSD study team provided an implementation plan and defined the necessary data to assist administrators in evaluating and monitoring the school system's programs. SDC then developed coding specifications for personnel, student and fiscal subsystems of the management information system; produced and checked out the programs; provided user manuals and assisted with the installation of the system and the training of user personnel.

Under the sponsorship of the American Council on Education and the College Entrance Examination Board, SDC conducted a nationwide study of computer uses in colleges and universities. The final report of this study was published as a book in May 1967 by ACE — *Computers on Campus: A Report to the President on Their Use and Management.*

Educational Research

For the state of California, SDC has analyzed the content of three different approaches (television, programmed instruction and teacher-conducted instruction) to teaching Spanish, developed criterion tests and attitude-measuring instruments, and conducted the final data analyses in a statewide evaluation of foreign language instruction in elementary schools.

Under a National Science Foundation grant, PSD has developed a time-shared system for teaching statistical methods to college students. The system has been used experimentally at California's San Fernando Valley State College and UCLA.

In another use of time-sharing, Public Systems Division personnel, under joint USOE and SDC sponsorship, have designed and are developing an interactive system that enables a school counselor to shift to the computer the burden of data handling, freeing him to pursue the uniquely human aspects of counseling.

For the U.S. Office of Education, SDC has programmed a computer model of an innovative high school. This model made it possible to test the effects of various kinds of instructional innovations via computer simulation.

The corporation has developed and demonstrated, for the Ford Foundation Fund for the Advancement of Education, procedures for adapting instructional materials and teaching techniques to the needs of culturally disadvantaged children. Out of this work came new techniques for a "tutorial community" — a systematic approach to improve the teaching of Mexican-American school children.

Library and Documentation Systems

SDC has developed some of the most advanced techniques available for managing the documentary fallout of the "knowledge explosion."

Public Systems Division personnel have produced significant advances in the understanding of abstracting and indexing techniques and in the development of computer-based systems for library processes and for information retrieval and dissemination.

Health

In 1958 SDC began its first corporate-sponsored research project — Project MEDIC. Project MEDIC started with a model of a nationwide system for medical data processing and concluded with on-the-spot work with physicians, surgeons, medical researchers and hospital administrators.

Since then, SDC has continued to provide support to the medical profession. Efforts have included medical record keeping, hospital simulation, statistical analysis of patient data, personnel and accounting systems, and design of hospital information systems.

Regional Medical Programs

The Public Systems Division has important commitments to several of the Regional Medical Programs funded by the National Institutes of Health to combat heart disease, cancer, stroke and related diseases.

For the Mountain States program, SDC is helping to design and develop data gathering and processing instruments for surveying health needs and facilities in a four-state region. The Western Interstate Commission for Higher Education — contracting agency for the Mountain

States RMP — has also retained SDC for statistical analysis of health survey data.

For the Colorado-Wyoming RMP, SDC is developing community profiles — detailed representations of health care facilities and institutions in the area. PSD personnel are also developing a cardiac registry for California and a tumor registry for the Northlands RMP.

SDC is working with the South Dakota Health Research Institute, under a contract with the U.S. Public Health Service, to develop a computer-based health information system for the state. The system will encompass physicians' offices, hospitals, medical schools, libraries and other health resource agencies. It will interface with other systems and agencies to provide and receive vital information relating to epidemiology, drug usage, hospital usage and delivery of medical care.

Medicaid Support

The Health Services Administration of New York City has called on SDC to perform a study that would help the city prepare for federally sponsored Medicare and Medicaid programs. The study produced a clear picture of these programs and recommended specific improvements in organizational and information processing capabilities.

SDC is assisting New York City's Department of Welfare in the development and installation of a computer-based system for enrolling medically indigent persons in Medicaid and for processing claims from physicians, dentists and other medical vendors for services provided to the enrollees.

In addition, SDC has developed and delivered to the New York Department of Health a computer program system to generate and maintain a registry of physicians, dentists and other medical vendors eligible to participate in the program; to issue certificates of participation to these vendors; and to supply statistical information on vendor characteristics.

Metropolitan Health Care

In cooperation with the Health Research Council of New York City, SDC conducted an intensive system analysis of the relationships among public and private agencies involved in providing health services within the city. The PSD team studied the structure and roles of municipal health care organizations, health needs of the divergent communities within the city, and environmental health variables. The final report

115

described the problems facing the city's health care system and outlined a comprehensive approach to improving it.

The focus of another SDC study was the neighborhood health care center, where people can come for comprehensive health care without having to leave their own neighborhoods. A work plan for districting such centers was developed by the SDC team.

Hospital Information Processing Systems

SDC has participated in developing a system that will provide New Jersey Hospital Association members with a data processing capability on a cooperative basis. First priority has been given to automating business functions. Upon completion of the business capabilities, efforts will focus on problems related to patient care and information sharing among the member hospitals. Eventually, the system is planned to provide each of the 147 member hospitals access to a central computer on a time-shared basis.

Other selected hospital projects include developing an integrated health record system for the Gouverneur Health and Hospital Center in New York City; and applying electronic data processing to accounting, payroll and personnel functions at New Jersey's Hackensack Hospital.

Environmental Health

SDC established a comprehensive environmental health program in 1966. PSD personnel developed a planning paper on cooperative organization in the environmental health field for the European Organization for Economic Cooperation and Development; performed an on-line analysis of air quality data for the Continental Research Institute; and are developing a system for the Toxicology Information Program of the National Library of Medicine for the acquisition of expert knowledge from authorities in the fields of drugs, environmental health, occupational health and pesticides. SDC is also conducting a six-city study of driving patterns to help define realistic test cycles for the evaluation of automobile exhaust control devices.

Administration of Justice

SDC is making prominent contributions to the ability of justice agencies to determine, maintain and manage growing volumes of essential information. Research and development in cooperation with local government police departments, state correctional and administration of justice agencies, federal customs officials and international police assistance programs have demonstrated the utility of computer-based information and intelligence systems as aids in the administration of justice.

Los Angeles Police Department Information System

SDC and Los Angeles Police Department personnel, with contract funds from the Office of Law Enforcement Assistance, Department of Justice, are jointly developing a prototype information system that will provide for the rapid and efficient processing of crime and related reports, wants and warrants, and field interviews. In addition, the system will give an investigating officer the capability to search the computer's memory for crime reports relating to his investigation.

New York State Identication and Intelligence System (NYSIIS)

SDC was engaged in a joint effort with the state of New York to design and develop a computer-based identification and intelligence system. When fully implemented, the system will allow information sharing among the many agencies involved in administering criminal justice in the state, including police, prosecutors, criminal courts, probation, correction and parole. It will provide rapid processing, storage and retrieval of summary criminal history, latent fingerprints, personal appearance, fraudulent checks and other data presently provided by the Division of Identification of the New York State Department of Corrections. The size of the information file will approach several billion characters.

Institute for the Study of Crime and Delinquency

Development of a computer-based information system for the California Youth and Adult Corrections Agency was carried out with assistance from SDC under a contract from the Institute for the Study of Crime and Delinquency in Sacramento. The Public Systems Division provided system analysis and design support to improve the agency's casework decision-making by making information more readily available through the use of data processing techniques. This study featured computer-assisted analysis of the information requirements of the decisions under study.

117

Norwalk Crime Study

For the city administration of Norwalk, California, the corporation has conducted a study to define the current crime situation in the city and to evaluate alternative methods of law enforcement. The SDC team analyzed data compiled daily by the Norwalk Sheriff's Office, evaluated present procedures with alternative techniques and provided estimates of costs required to achieve various levels of effectiveness within each crime or service category recommended.

Federal Customs Information System

SDC has designed, produced and delivered an electronic data processing system to the Customs Section, Civil Division, United States Department of Justice. The system aids the department in litigation concerning disputes with importers over duties levied on imported goods. When fully implemented, the system will contain information on approximately 150,000 cases. Data on a case will include a description of its status at any time during the process of going from initial protest through trial to final decision.

United States Agency for International Development (USAID)

The feasibility, practicability and desirability of introducing data processing techniques to both the Vietnam and Thailand National Police Departments were determined by PSD personnel. Under contract to the State Department's Agency for International Development, system analysts studied Vietnam's National Police and a system for crime records and criminal statistics within the Thailand National Police Department.

Civil Emergency Operations

SDC's ability to prepare organizations to cope with large-scale emergencies — from hurricanes to nuclear attack — is unique.

SDC's analytical and experimental research studies contributed to the formulation, by the Office of Civil Defense, of more effective emergency operations management systems and procedures. The Public Systems Division has trained and exercised fire, police and civil defense personnel from more than 30 cities and has assisted OCD as well as state and local governments in developing operating procedures and suggesting configurations for emergency operating centers.

Civil Emergency System Design

An SDC-developed Increased Readiness Information System has been implemented at OCD national headquarters, 8 OCD regional offices, 49 states and approximately 750 local governments. The system supports civil defense authorities at all levels of government by providing essential readiness information either directly to decision-makers or indirectly as support intelligence to agencies or Presidential decision-making groups. In the event of an imminent disaster, authorities will immediately know which state and local governments have taken readiness actions, the measures taken and the changes in the national readiness posture that have resulted.

A manual system that processes and disseminates emergency operational information to all potential users was designed and developed by PSD personnel for the Office of Civil Defense/Office of Emergency Planning Federal Regional Centers (FRCS). The FRCS coordinate and direct federal response to a nuclear attack. SDC is now designing and developing a similar reporting system among federal, state and local levels.

Disaster System Research

The question of how people would react to an attack on this country is vital to civil defense planning. To be assured that current warning systems are functional, SDC conducted an intensive study of public reaction following a false alarm that occurred in Concord, California, in July 1965.

Recognizing the importance of internal communications in Emergency Operating Centers — particularly at the local level — the Office of Civil Defense contracted with SDC and another organization to study intra-EOC communications and operations. Two analyses on each of two selected EOC systems were performed for comparative purposes.

PSD is performing for OCD a series of in-depth field investigations of industrial disasters, and then producing evaluations of emergency operations in each disaster area. These analyses will pinpoint the effectiveness of emergency operations planning, the operations of mutual aid associations, prior individual and group training, and the coordination between industry and local civil defense organizations.

SDC is studying the pattern of adoption of an OCD program that calls for incorporation of fallout protection in new construction. Using a theoretical model of the process for comparison, the actual flow of program information, interaction of individuals affected and decisions to adopt or not to adopt the technique of fallout protection are being analyzed.

Emergency Operations Training

SDC developed an Emergency Operations Simulation Training (EOST) Program for OCD and has prepared university extension personnel to implement it. The simulation techniques developed by SDC are used to train local governments in combatting disaster by integrating civil command and control in a community emergency operations center.

A wide-ranging evaluation of the OCD Adult Education Program and its impact on the civilian population is being conducted by PSD personnel. Analysis of the program has been carried out in six states, using an analytical model and survey techniques specially developed for the study at SDC.

SDC studied state and local civil defense training in order to develop model training plans. The final report to OCD analyzed the emergency tasks of each state and local agency, specified training and personnel requirements and described training methods.

Emergency Operations Research Center

A prime tool in SDC's civil emergencies work is the Emergency Operations Research Center — a laboratory, a staff and a method. The method, called operations simulation, basically consists of pitting management organizations such as a city government, a police or fire department, or a civil defense group against an accurately simulated emergency.

The EORC includes flexible areas for use by members of participating organizations, observation areas from which the organization's responses can be monitored, a communications center that links the participants with the simulated outside world, and a simulation room from which EORC staff members representing outside agencies and resources communicate developments to the decision-makers and respond to their directives.

The EORC staff has also devised "portable laboratories," including display, monitoring and other necessary equipment, making it possible for an organization to receive training in its normal surroundings.

Transportation

Since 1960, SDC has been working on important aspects of transportation, from air traffic control through highway design to ocean navigation aids. SDC-developed mathematical modeling and computer simulation techniques make possible thorough and economical analysis, evaluation and design of transportation systems, as well as realistic prediction of future transportation patterns and needs. Corporate system analysis and computer programming capabilities are also being applied to transportation research and planning.

Traffic Simulation

For some time, SDC has been using computer simulation to increase understanding of automotive traffic flow. For the U.S. Department of Transportation, a continuing project — modeling of traffic flow within a freeway diamond interchange — has produced new techniques of general applicability, including computer algorithms describing the movement of vehicles, a data collection system that uses aerial photography and semiautomatic film readers, and statistical techniques for determining whether a model is behaving realistically as compared to an actual interchange.

The Public Systems Division used some of these techniques in a study for the California Division of Highways to evaluate the quality of peakhour traffic flow through an interchange on Interstate Highway 8 in San Diego. The interchange was modified to relieve congestion; and SDC collected data before, during and after the modification. SDC's final report analyzed the value of the modification.

In another project for the Department of Transportation, SDC is studying and validating existing theories for multi-lane, unidirectional, unimpeded traffic flow and developing and evaluating alternative models where gaps in the theories exist. As a part of this study, a PSD team is collecting and analyzing data and developing mathematical descriptions of weaving and merging patterns of drivers upstream of a freeway exit ramp, to develop criteria for on- and off-ramp spacing and locations.

In the important area of smog control, SDC is experimenting with techniques for predicting where the heaviest traffic — and therefore the heaviest smog concentrations — will be over a number of years. Through mathematical modeling, such predictions can be formed from data on projected population and business shifts, freeway routes and other pertinent factors.

Skylounge

For the Los Angeles Department of Airports, PSD has studied the economic and technical feasibility of Skylounge — a system proposed as a means of speeding transportation between airport and civic center. Basically, the proposed system consisted of mobile "lounges" that would take passengers and baggage to a central heliport, then to be picked up by crane helicopters and carried some 15 miles to the airport.

One product of the Skylounge study was a mathematical model that compares the total trip time between any two locations within a city for different modes of travel. This enables planners to determine the relative merits of various modes of transportation for specified trips.

Survey of Driver Patterns

SDC is analyzing 200 Los Angeles drivers' patterns in the first phase of a study for the National Center for Air Pollution Control to develop composite average driving patterns for testing smog control devices. Instruments that measure rate of acceleration and deceleration, speed and distances traveled and indicate the number of stops, elapsed time, trip frequency and time of day were installed in volunteers' cars. A stylus, activated by the driver, indicates type of route being traveled, i.e., freeway or surface street. Data collected are being analyzed, and profiles of average and extreme driving patterns will be developed. The same survey is being conducted in five other cities.

Bay Area Transportation Study Commission

The Bay Area Transportation Study Commission (BATSC), created by the California Legislature in 1963, is conducting a comprehensive transportation study and preparing a master regional transportation plan for the San Francisco Bay Area. SDC consultants are providing wide-ranging assistance to BATSC.

This support has included the design and implementation of an information management system primarily based on three SDC-developed general-purpose program systems: the MADAM (Moderately Advanced

Data Management) file processing system; DATADOX, which provides quick reference to and easy maintenance of complex information files; and SPAN (Statistical Processing and Analysis), a large-scale data management, file processing, graphic display and statistical analysis system.

Transportation Information Systems

SDC is developing a large-scale computer-based system to support the National Highway Safety Bureau's National Highway Accident and Injury Analysis Center's operating and research activities. SDC's initial task was to evolve a method for efficiently collecting data from state files in a form that could be easily automated. A PSD team is continuing the system analysis which will culminate in a detailed design and implementation plan.

In a related undertaking, SDC has been helping the U.S. Department of Transportation create a traffic data base to provide means of gathering, maintaining and interpreting statistics affecting highway safety.

Marine Systems

Advances in the important field of marine sciences can only be made if needed data get to the scientists and engineers who use it. With the broadening of ocean-related activities, data acquisition becomes more complex and costly, and data as a commodity must be shared by a larger complex of users. Because of SDC's broad experience with techniques for the collection, management and use of data, the corporation is exceptionally well equipped to handle this problem and contribute to the advancement of marine sciences.

National Data Program for the Marine Environment

SDC is assisting the National Council on Marine Resources in the development of a national data system for the expanding field of marine science. The prime goal of the project is to provide a 10-year technical development plan for marine data management.

The current phase includes planning a national data program in support of users of the marine environment — federal agencies, states, private institutions, universities and the general public. The plan will provide for the orderly collection, transmission, processing, storage and dissemination of data from the national marine science programs.

123

In the six-part study, PSD personnel are analyzing the data needs of those concerned with the marine environment, studying the handling of marine data, evaluating data functions, planning data program implementation, designing a national data planning system and synthesizing the data programs.

Phase I of this project — a preliminary system analysis — was previously completed by PSD, and the results were incorporated in a final report submitted to the Council in December 1967.

Marine Data Management

Public Systems Division personnel have been developing specialized data management techniques in support of the data needs of the marine community. As a result of these developments, marine users can work with SDC's time-sharing system on-line to interrogate various sample data bases on oceanographic stations, ships of the world and marine pollution. A special display program permits the user to construct graphic displays — such as a graph of salinity versus temperature of a segment of the ocean. The National Oceanographic Data Center, through a remote tele-terminal in Washington, D.C., has been a user of SDC's time-sharing system. Corporate personnel also assisted the Center with the review of a plan to develop a data processing system to organize and process the huge volume of oceanographic data flowing into NODC.

Telecommunications

SDC's Public Systems Division is building a strong capability in the increasingly important technology of telecommunications. The corporation's several engineering laboratories and related computer support areas as well as its 88 professional engineers, with their 1300 man-years of experience in making and testing experimental and special-purpose hardware, are available to support Public Systems Division's expert team in telecommunications.

Office of Telecommunications Management

For the Office of Telecommunications Management in the Executive Office of the President, PSD is determining the impact of grant-in-aid and other federal assistance programs upon the development of telecommunications in the United States. The objective of this contract is to define the present federal, state and industry roles in the development of nation-wide and statewide telecommunications to support normal and emergency activities. PSD analysts are surveying the many federal assistance programs, correlating the acquired information into significant categories and identifying the policy factors that can bear on the development of telecommunications systems to carry out the programs. Based on this analysis, the Director of Telecommunications Management can determine to what extent the assistance programs are influencing the systematic growth of telecommunications systems at the federal and state levels.

Illinois Telecommunications Commission

A directly related study will provide the Illinois Telecommunications Commission with systematic, comprehensive information on the current telecommunications capacity of the state government, a projection of 1975 needs, and alternative approaches by which the state can meet such needs. All telephone installations, computer networks, teleprinter services, radio systems and educational television and radio systems are included in the study. The alternative system designs consider all technological, legal, regulatory, cost and organizational factors that would affect the state in the coming years. The Commission will use the study results to recommend future telecommunications policy and systems to the state legislature.

TRW (Thompson-Ramo-Wooldridge) Systems

Social and economic forces in our society are generating complex problems in such areas as transportation, urban development, land use, medical care, and many other large-scale public activities. In their search for solutions to these problems, the cities, states, and nations are drawing upon the management/technical groups that have developed complex systems on missile and space programs and are today working on public programs.

For more than a decade, TRW has been successfully involved in the planning and development of complex systems; and the company's management/technical staff has a unique combination of skills in both software and hardware. On many of today's civil systems programs, TRW is applying its capabilities in systems engineering, using the most advanced digital computer programs, and its detailed knowledge of space-age hardware.

High Speed Ground Transportation: Northeast Corridor

Under contract with the U.S. Department of Transportation, TRW is performing detailed engineering studies of transportation requirements for the Northeast Corridor — the highly congested region between Washington, D.C., and Boston. The studies involve all types of vehicles and

This self-description is from a brochure of the TRW Systems Group, *Systems Technology in the Service of Society*, in use during 1969. Copyright © 1969 by TRW, Inc.

concepts which can be used in a safe and convenient High Speed Ground Transportation network.

TRW applies systems engineering methodology and techniques to compare, evaluate, synthesize, and design transportation systems, including: continuous capacity, multimodal, auto ferry, tube-inherent, rolling-sliding, tracked-levitated, automated-highway, and others. Using computer programs and system analysis, TRW is weighing such factors as vehicle configurations, route selections, terminal locations, and system costs to attain the ultimate transportation goals of:

- Low door-to-door travel time
- High reliability (predictability of arrival time)
- Maximum safety, comfort, and convenience
- Service flexibility
- Compatibility with surroundings (minimum noise, pollution, etc.)
- Growth potential

Urban Transportation Planning Studies

TRW is applying its resources, talent, and techniques accumulated for the nation's military and space programs to the planning, evaluation, modeling, and simulation of urban transportation problems.

Modern urban centers, operating with limited funds and manpower, must make maximum use of their resources to provide efficient transportation systems. Modern systems engineering and its tools — the high speed digital computer and advanced programming techniques — can help in the proper apportionment of resources by integrating transportation systems, social influences, engineering and economic resources, land availability, people and goods load requirements, and general city development.

Vehicle Inspection Systems for Highway Safety

Adoption of the Highway Safety Act of 1966 has raised the problem of mass automobile safety inspection programs to be administered by the various states. Checking for the road-worthy condition of every vehicle is a monumental and complex undertaking which requires the use of modern automated techniques and systems planning.

Under contract with the U.S. Department of Transportation, TRW is studying the vehicle safety inspection problem and is developing a mathematical cost model which will serve as a practical working tool in setting up inspection programs.

TRW's capabilities in the transportation field include:

- Analysis and design of optimum transportation systems
- Use of systems analysis to solve problems of traffic control and congestion, including automatic control systems
- Systems support and design for the development of airline ground facilities
- Design of computer systems for all aspects of air and surface transportation
- Application to transportation systems of command and control techniques developed by TRW on space and missile programs

FDIC Information System

The Federal Deposit Insurance Corporation, created by Congress in 1933, now provides protection for more than 150 million deposit accounts in approximately 14,000 insured banks. Management of this complex network requires timely and accurate information from many sources. The FDIC also processes large amounts of data in connection with its research activities, operations management, and support of bank examiners.

TRW was selected by the FDIC to participate in the study and design of a Management Information System for handling its many data activities. TRW's responsibility is the application of modern computer technology to banking problems.

TRW's capabilities in information systems include:

- Analysis of data requirements and procedures
- Design and development of on-line data management systems
- Design and development of large digital computing and data reduction centers to support scientific and engineering efforts
- Development of associated software systems for management systems, program planning and control, parts acquisition data systems, numeric integration, statistics, etc.
- Design and development of general-purpose software systems for information storage and retrieval

Water Resources

Twenty-five per cent of the earth's total supply of fresh water exists in the form of ground water which is within the first two miles of the earth's surface. We must have a complete knowledge of the ground water storage and motion so that we can effectively manage water supplies to meet increasing industrial needs and soaring populations.

TRW is studying the coordinated use of water supplies in the Bunker Hill Water Basin of San Bernardino, California. The study involves:

- Development of a mathematical model representing ground and surface flow within the basin
- Construction of computer programs for the model
- Use of the computer to estimate costs for various options for future operation

Land Use Information System

Many local, state, and federal agencies collect data about land and how it is used because they are concerned with such things as taxes, water resources, transportation, urban development, and many other facets of community life. In the collection of this information, there is much duplication of effort, and it is often difficult for one agency to profit from the data collected by another. The information specialists at TRW, who have been involved in data collection and management for more than ten years, are developing land-use information systems to help solve these problems. TRW makes inventories of the data gathered by different agencies, examines the data for duplication, seeks useful new patterns in the assembled data, and determines the most effective system for the interchange of data among various users.

For the California Office of Planning, TRW developed a regional land-use information system to serve as a pilot demonstration for a statewide system. Portions of Santa Clara County were used to demonstrate how automatic data processing techniques can handle vast amounts of information for administrative and planning purposes.

TRW's capabilities in Urban/Regional Planning include:

- Application of systems engineering to technological problems of the cities, e.g., construction, transportation, communications, planning
- Use of modern computers in the solution of urban problems, e.g., financial control, planning, data storage and retrieval, simulation
- Creation of new cities, including planning, realization, and management

Security System for Corrections Facility

TRW is assisting the California Department of Corrections in solving the problem of prison security through the use of modern electronic devices that can detect prisoners in unauthorized areas. TRW engineers are studying detection techniques for use in the security prison being built in Vacaville, California. This new facility will house 1,250 inmates and will consist of a rectangular array of buildings surrounded by a 4,800-foot chain-link fence.

Using its background of military security system design, TRW is considering various kinds of transmitting devices, cameras, and other sensors as part of an integrated detection system. TRW's tasks are to:

- Determine the requirements and constraints of the facility
- Survey and study available detection techniques
- Evaluate alternate detection systems
- Recommend one or more systems for development and testing

Command and Control Systems for Law Enforcement

Large metropolitan police departments, faced with increasing crime and outbreaks of violence, are seeking more efficient methods for deploying and controlling their motorized units. To assist in this effort, TRW is studying the use of advanced computerized systems similar to those used by the military for command and control of tactical forces. This approach would permit the use of a centralized console displaying the location and direction of every police unit. Thus, immediate decisions could be made for the most effective deployment of police to meet emergency situations. A computer-based information system could also be employed to supply data to police in the field; for example, an officer could obtain direct data concerning a suspect's criminal record or "wanted" status.

TRW is working with the Los Angeles Police Department to develop plans for a computerized command and control system. This type of system is adaptable to various enforcement agencies, fire departments, and organizations involved in the management of large-scale mobile activities.

TRW's capabilities in the Public Safety field include:

- Development of communication, command, and control systems for public safety tactical operations, employing modern, automated methods for quick response and optimum dispersement of forces
- Engineering analysis to support the planning and design of new cost-effective prison facilities

S. M. GENENSKY

The RAND Projects in New York City

Back in August 1967, RAND was approached by the City of New York to initiate a research program aimed at assisting New York City's Police Department with some of its short- and long-term problems. During subsequent discussions with City officials, and in particular with the office of the City's budget director, Frederick O'R. Hayes, it became clear that both RAND and the City were excited about initiating a broad program of research aimed at attacking and hopefully making significant contributions toward solving a wide variety of problems faced by the City. Since September 1967, members of RAND's research staff, as well as representatives of its management, have been conferring with representatives of several administrative units of the City regarding what those units do, what they perceive as problem areas, what they think RAND might do for them, what RAND thinks it might do for them, etc. Thus far those discussions have led to the generation and signing of "a mother contract," that is, a contract that lays down the general ground rules for the RAND –New York City relationship; and to the writing and signing of specific but rather broad agreements covering research that RAND is to carry on in behalf of the New York City Fire Department, Health Services Administration, Housing Development Administration, and Police Department. Negotiations are in progress with other administrative units of the

From S. M. Genensky, "Some Comments on Urban Research," presented at the IEEE Meeting at the Space Technology Laboratories, Los Angeles, California, March 19, 1968, and issued as RAND Report P-3827, April 1968. Copyright © 1968 by RAND Corporation.

Mr. Genensky is a staff member of the RAND Corporation.

131

City, and it is hoped that these will lead to additional research efforts. Needless to say, the fact that these negotiations are still in progress makes it inadvisable, at this time, for me to single out what those efforts might be.

Before I embark on a brief discussion of some of the specific things that RAND is doing or is planning to try to do for the City of New York, it is important to point out again that RAND was invited to assist the City by officials of that City, and to point out also that the government of New York City recognizes that the City has problems, that those problems must be solved, that the City must try to solve them, but that it cannot solve some of them itself, and that, therefore, it needs outside help to try to accomplish the job. Furthermore, both RAND and the City recognize that RAND does not regard its efforts for the City to be isolated pieces of research which, when completed, will terminate RAND's relationship with the City and its adventure into urban research. On the contrary, both RAND and the City regard RAND's efforts in and on behalf of the City as being the beginning of a multi-year effort by RAND to carry on research in and between the numerous problem areas which, by both conventional and unconventional usage, are regarded as facets of urban research. To carry on this very ambitious and hopefully commendable task, it will be necessary for RAND to obtain additional, very broadly based funding, including perhaps support from one or more foundations and from the Federal Government. Therefore, in the course of my discussion of RAND's work for the City's Fire Department, Health Services Administration, Housing Development Administration, and Police Department, please keep in mind that RAND does not regard these efforts as being isolated "one-shot" affairs, but rather as being the first steps toward the achievement of a broad, challenging program of urban research whose life is measured in decades and not months or years.

Our agreement with the City and its Fire Department calls for research on six general topics, namely (1) planning-programming-budgeting, (2) incidence of fires, false alarms and emergencies, (3) departmental effectiveness and efficiency, (4) communications, (5) potential applications of new technological developments, and (6) existing data sources. To date, emphasis has been placed upon communications, potential applications of new technological developments, and an examination of data sources.

Like all the other efforts for New York City, those for the Fire Department have been going on for only about two months, so it is not reasonable to expect that any definite conclusions have been reached as yet.

General and specific impressions are legion, but most of them must remain unstated until more information is collected and evaluated.

Our agreement with the City and its Health Services Administration (HSA) calls initially for the development of a planning-programming-budgeting (PPB) system. For those of you who are not familiar with planning-programming-budgeting, let me explain that it is an approach or technique by which an organization is analyzed on a functional basis. The functions which the organization performed N_1, N_2, N_3, etc., years ago are determined, the functions that the organization currently performs are ascertained, and various sets of functions that the organization might perform at one or more dates in the future are postulated. The costs of carrying on each of the functions performed N_1, N_2, N_3, etc., years ago are determined, as well as those of carrying on the current functions. On the basis of this functional cost history, projections or estimates are made of the cost of each of the alternative sets of functions that might be performed at various dates in the future. Using these cost-estimates, managers and executives hopefully can make more rational decisions regarding what courses of action the organization ought to follow over the next five, ten, etc., years.

Advising the Health Services Administration on the development of a PPB system will give RAND an excellent opportunity to learn a great deal about HSA's functional structure and its formal and informal operational procedures. With this information our research staff and management will be in a better position to make a more intelligent estimate of what RAND ought next to do for HSA. Hopefully, the PPB exercise will also help HSA's management to understand their organization better, and to decide what it would like RAND to do for it in the future.

Incidentally, New York City's Health Services Administration is one of several super-administrative units created by the Lindsay Administration in the hope of providing New Yorkers with more efficient services. It includes the Department of Hospitals, the Health Department, which runs clinics in the City, the Community Mental Health Board, and the Office of the Chief Medical Examiner.

RAND's agreement with the City and the Housing Development Administration (HDA) calls for (1) advising HDA on the development of a PPB system, (2) making a cost analysis of the publicly assisted housing program, (3) investigating the circumstances resulting in under-maintenance and abandonment of privately owned rental property, (4) examining various long-range housing strategies, and (5) exploring the usefulness of making a housing market analysis. Currently, work is progressing on a PPB system, and data are being gathered preparatory to beginning work on item (3).

The Housing Development Administration includes the Departments of Development, Rent and Housing Maintenance, Relocation and Management Services, and Buildings.

For its work with the City and the Police Department, RAND has agreed to: (1) advise the Department on the development of a PPB system, (2) search for methods of measuring effectiveness, (3) examine the scale and nature of future police services, (4) analyze the recruitment, selection, and training of Department personnel, and (5) examine communications.

I take special pride in our effort for the City's Police Department because I had the pleasure of initially bringing together many of the people at RAND who are working on police problems. For roughly 10 months prior to the signing of the contract with the City, I met with these people, and we discussed the Report of the President's Crime Commission, including several of its supplementary volumes, listened to real and alleged experts on various phases of law enforcement and the administration of justice, took part in national meetings related to public order and technology, and conferred and visited with the Los Angeles Police Department and the Los Angeles District Attorney's Office. Thus, when the New York City Police effort came into being, we were ready for it, and what we initially may have lacked in experience, we made up for in enthusiasm.

I would now like to turn away from what RAND is doing for the City of New York and, instead, direct my focus upon a more general but, in my opinion, a more important matter, namely, a discussion of some of the advantages and disadvantages of embarking on urban research.

On the positive side of the ledger, I believe we all would include the fact that our cities offer the researcher an opportunity to attempt to solve a wide variety of important, fascinating, challenging, and frequently very difficult problems — problems which the nation must cope with if it is to avoid partial or even total urban disaster. Among these problems I would include finding and implementing ways to reduce racial tension, control population growth, reduce air and water pollution, improve health services and housing, and reduce the incidence of crimes of violence perpetrated against persons and property. Note that I not only call for finding ways to solve problems (in the physical scientist's conception of a solution) but also for finding ways to *implement solutions*. The latter requires that researchers work closely with various community leaders so that research findings can be converted into programs that can be implemented in the sense, say, of being sold to, and financed by, a city council, state legislature, or federal agency.

Urban problems also have advantages for the researcher who has spent years working on military problems, in that they offer him a chance to attack a new and hopefully refreshing set of problems. He may be able to apply some of what he has learned in the past to those problems, and from them he may learn much that might later apply to his future work, be it military or civil. I do not wish to convey the idea that I believe one must choose to work either on military or urban problems but not on both. On the contrary, I believe it is possible to work on both types of problems concurrently. However, I readily admit that a researcher's success in doing this depends upon his ability to partition his time, the willingness of management to support him, and the availability of funds to support a divided effort.

On the other side of the ledger several factors come immediately to mind. First of all, urban masters may turn out to be more insistent upon getting rapid results than military masters. This may arise from the fact that local officials are under much more pressure to show results than military officers or their civilian superiors. Local officials, for example, must face re-election every two or four years, and this probably is more nerve-racking than worrying about a military promotion or a reappointment due to a possible change in national administration. Regardless what the cause or causes may be, this thirst for rapid results has a high probability of precluding the possibility of carrying on genuine research, particularly research requiring a long-term financial commitment, and regarding which it is understood that the probability of arriving at a solution in the short run is fairly low, and although higher in the long run, is still far from certain.

Another matter that may plague the researcher is the fact that he will be working in, as it were, a large transparent fish bowl. He will be exposed to the constant scrutiny of not only the elected and appointed city officials but also the press, business, labor, and the clergy, etc. While I do not believe that this exposure is inherently bad, I must admit that I fear some of it might lead to harassment and unfair criticism, and this in turn could also seriously damage the possibility of pursuing a worthwhile research effort.

Potential abuse may arise from many causes. Among them I would include a misconception of what is involved in carrying on scientific research, a misunderstanding of what the research is intended to accomplish, a misunderstanding of the motivations of the people trying to carry on the research, and, unfortunately, even an attempt to embarrass the party in power.

When I think of the possible abuses that may accrue as a result of continuous and, in particular, premature public exposure of urban research programs, I am almost tempted to conclude that there may be a distinct advantage to working in a classified environment. In such an environment the researcher can wander up blind alleys, can make judgments, which, while appearing to be reasonable at the time, may look far less profound at a later date, and he can try various approaches to solving problems with comparative freedom from the fear of being subjected to premature, misinformed, or even malicious criticism. However, I have a strong personal conviction, perhaps stemming from my professional training, that there is something inherently better about carrying on research in an open environment than in a classified environment. Therefore, I believe we should be willing to take our chances with the unpleasant possibilities that might accrue from premature public exposure and misguided criticism. I nevertheless recommend that persons involved in urban research, particularly research financed with local funds, be very careful not to discuss such things as untested ideas, contemplated experiments, confidential data, and tentative conclusions with people whose discretion they cannot absolutely trust.

With regard to confidential or, in Defense Department parlance, classified material, it should be noted that the urban researcher can expect to encounter such material, and must be prepared to guard it just as carefully as he would classified material. Now, unfortunately, even if he takes every reasonable precaution with such material, including locking it in a safe each night and discussing it only with persons he knows he can trust, the material could still cause him considerable grief because it could be subpoenaed by a court. Thus, suppose you had won the confidence of the "Kibosh City" Police Department, and its chief gave you access to sensitive data regarding the activities of the local chapter of the crime syndicate. Suppose that this information indicated that certain allegedly respectable people in town might be implicated in the syndicate's operations, but this information was not sufficient to prove a case in court against them or members of the syndicate. Further, suppose that these data were given to you with the specific understanding that you would under no circumstances reveal that you had them, where you got them, or what the data contained. I now ask you what you would do if a court suspected you had the information and issued an order directing you to turn it over to the court. Fortunately, the chance of such a dilemma arising is probably quite slim because most government officials would be very reluctant to put you or themselves or their agency in such an awkward position.

Other problems that arise in trying to carry on urban research are those of divided authority and multiple-source funding. One finds, for example, some communities in which the jurisdiction over the city streets falls under the city government, but the bridges and tunnels leading into and out of the city fall under an independent body, and the highways leading from those bridges and tunnels to outlying communities or connecting the bridges and tunnels within the city fall under the authority of the state. Now if the city, the bridge and tunnel commission, and the state are not working in close accord with one another, which is probably more the rule than the exception, one will usually have difficulty obtaining funding for an integrated study of the city's traffic problems. Oh! you may get support for, say, a study of traffic problems on city streets, or vehicular flow across a particular bridge, or the need for widening state highway 10-A, but those are not studies of the city's overall traffic problems.

As for multiple-source funding, consider the fact that many local welfare programs, as well as many local health services, are financed by money contributed by the federal government, the state government, and the city government. Therefore, it is not surprising to encounter a dilemma as to whether a particular research program should be supported with federal, state, or locally derived funds, or some combination thereof. Resolving problems of this type can be frustrating if not downright exasperating. In most cases patience, tact, and a little luck will go a long way toward saving the day.

Urban and military research have one important thing in common, which is that the success of both depends, in large measure, upon the ability of the researcher to win the confidence of middle- as well as upper-level management. This is easy to say but not always so simple to accomplish. It requires that every researcher dealing with middle-level personnel must be discreet, tactful, understanding, patient, etc. Finding enough competent people with all these other characteristics is very hard and sometimes impossible, so care must be taken to avoid, as much as possible, direct contact between middle-level personnel and members of one's staff who lack these necessary characteristics. In addition, one must constantly be prepared to repair the damage that will inevitably occur as a result of an unforeseen volatile or otherwise nondiplomatic encounter.

When the shoe is on the other foot and key personnel of the city's middle-level management are uncooperative, deceptive, or otherwise prove to be a headache, the problem may be much more serious. If the city's top-level personnel cannot or are not willing to help resolve the difficulty, it might be impossible to continue some or all of the research for the department or agency whose personnel are causing the difficulty. Chances are, however, that some kind of tolerable compromise can be reached, particularly if high city officials want the research pursued, believe the city needs the help, and recognize that the consulting research team has a good chance of doing the job and doing it well.

I hope this brief discussion of RAND's urban research and the advantages and disadvantages of urban research in general are of some value to you. Personally, I believe that carrying on genuine research in the urban sphere is going to be very tough, particularly if that research is not supported, at least in part, by foundations or federal agencies. But even if those sources of funding are not forthcoming, I believe that the need to solve the problems faced by our cities is so great and important to the survival of a healthy, free society that I would vote in favor of making the attempt in any event.

EDMUND BROWN

California Hires the Aerospace Companies

Can the same systems development skills that put John Glenn into orbit be used to cut the time a commuter must spend between home and office?

Can the kind of "new dimension" thinking that found a way to get a moon-probe off the launching pad also find a way to get able-bodied men off the welfare rolls?

In California, we are finding out. And the preliminary answer is an emphatic YES.

Some months ago, I asked the leaders of California's great aerospace industry to put their systems engineers to work on four insistent problems facing this fastest-growing of all states — transportation, waste disposal, crime, and information collection and control.

These aerospace studies arose from a concern not only for the quality of the life we lead today but for the kind of world we will pass on to our children. And this concern arises from the pressures which our tremendous population growth places on schools, highways, public utilities — on every public and private institution in California — to expand without destroying the very natural beauty which is the primary cause of our growth.

By the end of this century — just thirty-five short years away — there will be 150 million more Americans than there are today. Where there is one house today, there will be two. Where there is one hospital, one

From Edmund Brown, "Aerospace Studies for the Problems of Men," *State Government* 39 (Winter 1966): 2–7. Copyright © 1966 by *State Government*.
Edmund Brown, the former Governor of California, is now in private law practice.

school, two will be needed. Five times as much electricity as we generate today will be required. There will be 240 million cars — more than three times as many as we have on our roads now.

But California has been riding the wave of the future longer than any other state. We grow enough each year to create a city the size of New Orleans; every five years by nearly enough to fill a city the size of Chicago. This means we must hire and train 2,500 new policemen every year. We must build classrooms for 200,000 new students every year. We spend nearly $1 billion a year on roads for some 10 million cars and trucks and for the 676,000 new ones we buy every year.

California is the largest agricultural state in the nation, but it is also one of the most urbanized. Nearly 90 per cent of our people live in or near cities. We import and export more goods in foreign trade than any other state.

About one-third of our manufacturing is space- and defense-oriented. As such, it is subject to policies set nearly 3,000 miles from us, and these policies can change on very short notice, as we have discovered in recent years with the phaseout of the Skybolt air-to-ground missile two years ago and the dropping of the M-1 hydrogen engine this year.

Shortly after Skybolt, I assembled a panel of leading executives from the aerospace and electronics companies to meet regularly with me and members of my staff. Over a period of time, two facts kept cropping up in those discussions.

First, fully one-half of all engineers and scientists trained in space research and development live and work in California.

Second, these men shared a talent that might well be applied to development of systems to solve nearly any problem presented to them. And when we began thinking in terms of the public sector — of the many unmet needs of the community — we began to realize that we had a precious and unused resource.

These were men who had been trained to think in totally new dimensions, to solve problems and create systems for carrying out missions unique in human history.

As our discussions continued, we kept coming back to the same question: Can the techniques of the engineers and scientists of the space age be applied to some of the perplexing social and governmental problems here at home?

About a year ago, the members of my aerospace panel said they thought the answer was yes, and we signed $100,000 contracts with four different firms.

140

North American Aviation was asked whether systems engineering could help us plan and build a transportation complex that would meet our needs for the next fifty years.

Aerojet-General was asked to investigate our methods of waste disposal, which cost California taxpayers $300 million each year and which each year leave the air dirtier, the water fouler, the land more littered.

Space-General was asked to study crime. We spend $600 million a year fighting crime. We have passed laws that keep violent offenders in prison longer; enacted the nation's best narcotics laws; tightened controls on firearms; and raised training standards for police officers. But the crime rate here, as in other states, continues to rise.

Finally, Lockheed was asked to develop a better system for information — a system that would permit one police department to get information about a suspect as fast as an airline clerk can find out whether there's a vacant seat on a plane 3,000 miles away, for example.

In every case, the reports said systems engineering is a feasible approach to the problems at hand. In some cases, the engineers said it was the *only* workable approach.

The Transportations Study

North American made it clear, for one thing, that while we must keep building freeways, the freeway is not the long-run answer to our problem.

Its report inventoried vehicles already in existence or on the drawing board that must be considered in the long-range design of a transportation system. The list included trains moving at the speed of jet airliners in underground tubes. It included pipelines to move produce from our agricultural valleys to our cities in a fraction of the time it now takes. It included virtually accident-free electronic highways, automatically guiding and spacing individual vehicles — vehicles, they said, which would not make smog.

But North American said that the first step toward putting such hardware to work on a large scale must be a planning device — a series of sub-models that would simulate California in memory banks of computers.

With this planning tool, state engineers could compare the cost and effectiveness of all available modes of transportation as well as completely new modes. They could tell how one highway route would affect the economy of a major city as opposed to another route or another form of transportation entirely. They would be able to see the consequences of construction without ever putting down a foot of concrete. And if one route proved to be wrong, they could start over again without having to tear out several miles of six-lane freeway.

The importance of making the right choice the first time, among alternative modes of transportation over the next fifty years, is contained in just two figures: The demand for transportation for goods will increase 700 per cent. The demand for transportation for people will go up 500 per cent.

The planning device which North American recommends would cost some $10 million — about what we spend today on a single mile of urban freeway. It could be delivered fifty-two months after work began on it.

There is one other point that is emphasized in North American's study: The planning device would make no decisions. Only the officials responsible for building transportation systems could do that. We would pose the problems. The computers would offer up alternatives. But we would make the final judgment as to the best system.

Waste Management

Aerojet-General's waste management system also gave us a new look at the dimensions of the growth that lies ahead.

Their systems analysts figure that by 1990, the cost of handling waste in California will rise from $300 million a year to $1 billion. The indirect cost of pollution of air and water — the damage to health, property, and the state's natural beauty — will by then run about $6 billion a year.

That is what waste will cost California if we do nothing more than expand and extend the present methods of waste disposal. And even with the expenditure of $1 billion a year, the quality of our environment, the purity of air and water, will continue to deteriorate.

On the other hand, Aerojet tells us that if we start now to plan and build a coordinated waste management system, we can cut the losses from damage by 75 per cent. The direct cost of handling waste would go up by 50 per cent. But the net would leave us several billion dollars ahead.

Again, they inventoried some of the elements that a waste management system of the future might contain.

But the Aerojet report made it clear that hardware is not the biggest problem in waste management — it is attitude. Waste and pollution must be dealt with as a single problem instead of as separate problems of garbage disposal, sewage, industrial pollution. And they tell us that we must first decide how clear we want our water, how clear we want our air, how well we want to dispose of waste, before a true system can be designed. As one scientist put it: "They didn't come to us and say 'Design Gemini. We'll figure out later how to use it.' "

The Aerojet program would take ten years to complete and would provide an integrated waste management system. As with the North American study, the first step would be to assemble a statistical model so that various alternatives could be tested.

Crime

Space-General analyzed the ways in which state and local government in California are now spending some $600 million a year in crime prevention and criminal control, and its report produced several specific recommendations for action.

It advised development of advanced data processing and data transmission techniques to help police.

Space-General advised us that a feed-back to judges on the results of their decisions is almost nonexistent. If a judge could see the cumulative effect of his decisions in criminal cases, he should be able to sharpen the decisions.

And, of course, the most famous part of the report was a series of overlays with five indicators — low income; heavy concentration of segregated Negro population; high population density; high drop-out rate; and high arrest rate. This was the demonstration that a boiling point could be predicted for an area in time for preventive steps to be taken. And the area on which the report's over-lay zeroed in was the Watts area in Los Angeles.

That, of course, was a conclusion clearly attainable without the help of systems engineering. But it provided a clue to the sort of information which a sophisticated systems analysis could produce in much less obvious cases.

An Information System

Finally, there is the information report in which Lockheed proposed a system that would save city, county, and state government in California $415 million a year in paperwork. The Lockheed engineers found that electronic data processing is coming into use at all levels of government here. Since the transition is taking place, Lockheed recommended tying it all together into a master information system with a central information index. This way, a small water district could ask for and receive information from the State Department of Water Resources simply by dialing for it.

If the small district did not know where the information was on file, it could find out by going to a central information index, which would have a record of the nature and location of all records in the state.

As the Lockheed report put it: "Machines would talk to machines throughout the length and breadth of the state, from Sacramento state offices to each and every local office."

Lockheed also calculated the alternative to such a system. Its engineers estimate that we have 75 miles of filing cabinets in government service today. By 1990, at the rate we are going, we would have nearly 400 miles of filing cabinets.

There is one final aspect of the Lockheed report worth noting. The engineers would code it so that the memory banks would refuse to talk to any machine not authorized to ask for the information.

In California, we have been so encouraged by the first studies that we are planning to call for bids on a fifth — a survey of our social welfare programs. The nature and causes of poverty and dependency have changed since the 1930's, when most of our welfare programs were started. But the programs themselves have changed very little in response to new social and economic conditions. To the degree that they are out of touch with reality, they are ineffective. We want to know how to cut the costs of dependency by helping people avoid poverty. We want to know how to cut through the paperwork curtain that separates a social worker from the people who need his help. We hope to get the beginning of the answers to these and other questions from this new study.

As a Governor, I do not expect magic cures from the systems approach. Nor do I anticipate abdicating my responsibility for public policy to a bank of computers. Our pilot studies have been very clear on this point. The models — the computer simulators — can give us factual comparisons of the results we can expect from various approaches to problems. But, to reemphasize a fundamental, they cannot make decisions. What the systems engineers can do is to construct a set of facts without bias or prejudgment of the results.

Frank Lehan of Space-General Corporation calls systems engineers "the grand skeptics." Says Mr. Lehan: "We have to be shown everything; we don't take anything for granted. We are oriented toward the cold mathematical scientific engineering approach."

And it may well be that this "cold mathematical" approach is the only way we can afford the compassionate goals of our society during the crucial decade just ahead.

Ironically, it is the heavy federal investment in space and defense systems at the expense of the public sector that has led to the present major backlog of public needs.

From 1953 to 1963, federal expenditures rose more slowly than the gross national product. During the same years, state and local outlay rose at double the rate of the gross national product, from $28 billion to $65 billion.

As a matter of fact, federal spending in areas outside space and defense has actually declined in the past twenty years. And what has happened to costs at the state and local level?

Education — up 155 per cent.
Highways — up 123 per cent.
Sewage and sanitation — up 140 per cent.

By 1970, the Brookings Institution estimates that state and local expenses will total $103 billion, and income — at present tax levels — will be $88 billion, a gap of $15 billion to be closed in four short years.

And yet, even with this huge deficit, large areas of the public sector are starving. Highway construction lags behind actual need. Pollution clouds air and water. Blight breeds slums faster than they can be torn down.

A recent study by the United States Office of Education shows that 23 million Americans have never finished the eighth grade. Eight million more haven't had enough education to fill out an employment form.

Aerospace Studies for All?

We have been struggling with these problems in the individual states, but in a mobile nation such as ours, very few problems can be said to be truly local in character. Each of the aerospace studies California has produced could as easily be applied to any of the other forty-nine states. Air and water pollution do not respect state boundaries. Nor does education in these days, when a family may move halfway across the continent between school sessions.

One other factor — cost — makes these studies more national than local in scope. No state can afford to carry the burden of a fully engineered system in very many problem areas. And even more which could do so should not be asked to, since the studies will be useful in nearly all of the states.

Systems engineering is not an inexpensive way to solve problems. The State of California paid $100,000 for each of its four studies. I am advised that this same amount in the Apollo project bought no more than a calculation of the velocity Apollo (sic) will need to escape the gravity of earth. I think it should be noted also that all four companies made substantial investments of their own funds in our projects.

But while the short-term cost of systems development is high, our studies indicate tremendous long-term savings, along the line suggested in my summary of findings above.

As a matter of national policy, the federal government has invested some $22 billion over the last nine years in the race for space. The scientists of the space industry have demonstrated that their talents can serve causes other than space. I submit that the engineering needs in other fields where the broad public welfare is at stake are as urgent as those in space.

When I appeared before the U.S. Senate Subcommittee Studying Aerospace Techniques in July, 1965, I said that over the centuries men have stumbled on new minerals and new techniques and then hunted for a way to use them.

Our new aerospace studies make it clear that we have progressed to a point where we can reverse that process. We can now decide what must be done to cope with a problem facing men, and design a system to do it. That is an exciting turning point in man's history.

II. "Control Technology" in a Democracy: The Broad Socio-Political Debate

Introduction

So far, our focus has been on the adoption of computerized databanks and management science techniques by government agencies, which we have characterized as two related routes moving government toward technological information systems. Before we move from the self-descriptions of the proponents to some specific debate over the effects of these new systems on the American governmental process, some broad socio-political analysis of technology and democracy is needed to set the larger stage.

Commentary on technology and democracy during the 1960's mirrored almost exactly the transition of American social thought from the liberal confidence and optimism of the early Kennedy era to the deep political cleavages and national confrontations of 1968–1970. In the early to mid-1960's, three groups exercised a virtual monopoly on the dialogue.

First, there were technical spokesmen and their popularizers. Primarily, these writers explored the benefits and promises of electronic technology. Some commentators predicted that computer systems would inevitably rationalize and reorganize the American political system in the 1970's and 1980's, and that the process could already be seen to be beginning in the late 1960's. Robert O. MacBride's book, *The Automated State: Computer Systems as a New Force in Society* (1967), illustrates this stream of commentary. Much of this literature can fairly be called "technocratic" writing, in which the capacity of new tools to transform human and political affairs is treated as a virtually irresistible force. The essay by Harold Sackman on "A Public Philosophy for Real Time Information

Systems," reprinted in Part II of this volume, represents one of the more thoughtful statements of this "peaceful transformation" theme.

A second group that dominated discussions in the early to mid-1960's were what can be called the "affirmative-minded" intellectuals. Historians, political scientists, sociologists, philosophers, and social psychologists in this group drew up predictive balance sheets positing the social gains from the new technology and some of the negative consequences that would also follow. The issue of how determinative the new electronic technologies would be on American (and world) society was a frequent theme in these inquiries. Some social scientists, such as Zbigniew Brzezinski in the selection included here, portrayed "technetronic society" as the wave of the future, sweeping before it those groups and movements which failed to see the direction of the wave and which might try feebly to oppose it. Other commentators took more tentative readings of the technology-society relationship, as in the essay by Emmanuel Mesthene that opens Part II, attempting to locate the arrival of current technologies on a longer continuum of history. The essay by Harold Lasswell illustrates the effort to identify the major effects on democratic society that "data-richness" might bring to human and political affairs, again with a stress on the positive aspects of this development.

The third group sharing the monopoly of discussion in the early to mid-1960's were the "culture critics." In an American tradition as old as the Republic, spokesmen for various brands of "garden" society attacked the arrival of yet another "machine" to despoil the "natural" environment of man. Here, commentaries ran a gamut from liberal humanists in the tradition of Lewis Mumford, Jacques Ellul, and Jules Henry (represented here by the selections from Erich Fromm and W. H. Ferry) to spokesmen for the conservative-traditionalist position (reflected here in the selection from Robert Strausz-Hupé).

As the last third of the 1960's arrived, however, "technetronic determinism" and the use of information technology by government came under attack from several new quarters. The reformist liberals, increasingly angered by the Vietnam War and American racial policies, began to mount a direct challenge to these trends. Arthur Mendel's article, written originally in the premier organ of American rationalist reform, the *New Republic,* portrays the "great refusal" of technetronic society by segments of American youth and liberalism. Similarly, Congressman Cornelius Gallagher's concern over "computing power" represents a warning from a liberal Democrat who presided over some of the most publicized hearings in Congress on the social effects of computers and information systems.

By the close of the 1960's, the New Left began to treat information technology as a specific phenomenon. A lengthy article by John McDermott in the *New York Review of Books* in 1969 took up this issue, under the title of "Technology: The Opiate of the Intellectuals." McDermott treats computers and information systems as a weapon with which the industrial-military complex and its political allies are tightening their hold over subject populations of the young, the poor, and the black and trying to execute more effectively their war policies abroad. The "laissez-faire" ideology of capitalists in the eighteenth and nineteenth centuries is now being replaced, says McDermott, by a demand for "laissez-innover" in the 1960's and 1970's. McDermott also embraces the "New Mandarin" theme voiced earlier by Noam Chomsky, that the extensive cooperation of social and physical scientists in the Kennedy and Johnson government programs represents a violation of the intellectual's "duty" to criticize and oppose the Establishment policies pursued in the 1960's. Unfortunately, the McDermott essay represents the only New Left treatment I know which deals even partially with information technology per se, and I was not able to secure permission to excerpt it for this volume. Interested readers can consult it in the July 31, 1969, issue of *New York Review of Books,* or in a longer book version that is scheduled to appear shortly.

Interestingly, I have not found any treatment of information technology in the writings of the American radical-right. They may simply take it for granted that computer technology is tightening the hold of a "pro-communist conspiracy" in business, government, and the intellectual community. Or, they may see information technology as a minor element in the larger moral confrontation between their poles of "godless communism" and "American values." In any event, I have found no radical-right commentaries to include in this section on the larger setting of advanced technology in democratic society.

What Part II represents, then, is a debate that ranges in ideological positions from conservative right to left-liberal. Although the selections presented here were written in a broad perspective, many of the judgments about information technology systems in government made in the articles in Part IV derive from premises enunciated in this Part, and will be better understood for having the broad treatments enunciated here.

EMMANUEL G. MESTHENE

How Technology Will Shape the Future

Our age is characterized by a deliberate fostering of technological change and, in general, by the growing social role of knowledge. "Every society now lives by innovation and growth; and it is theoretical knowledge that has become the matrix of innovation." [1]

In a modern industrialized society, particularly, there are a number of pressures that conspire toward this result. First, economic pressures argue for the greater efficiency implicit in a new technology. The principal example of this is the continuing process of capital modernization in industry. Second, there are political pressures that seek the greater absolute effectiveness of a new technology, as in our latest weapons, for example. Third, we turn more and more to the promise of new technology for help in dealing with our social problems. Fourth, there is the spur to action inherent in the mere availability of a technology: space vehicles spawn moon programs. Finally, political and industrial interests engaged in developing a new technology have the vested interest and powerful means needed to urge its adoption and widespread use irrespective of social utility.

If this social drive to develop ever more new technology is taken in conjunction with the very high probability that new technology will

From Emmanuel G. Mesthene, "How Technology Will Shape the Future," *Science* 161 (July 12, 1968): 135–143. Copyright © 1968 by the American Association for the Advancement of Science.

Mr. Mesthene is Director of the Harvard University Program on Technology and Society.

1. Daniel Bell, "Notes on the Post-Industrial Society (I)," *The Public Interest* 6 (Winter 1967): 29.

result in physical, social, and value changes, we have the conditions for a world whose defining characteristic is change.

When change becomes that pervasive in the world, it must color the ways in which we understand, organize, and evaluate the world. The sheer fact of change will have an impact on our sensibilities and ideas, our institutions and practices, our politics and values. Most of these have to date developed on the assumption that stability was more characteristic of the world than change; that is, that change was but a temporary perturbation of stability or a transition to a new (and presumed better or higher) stable state. What happens to them when that fundamental metaphysical assumption is undermined?

The nature of the answer to that question is implicit in a number of trends characteristic of present-day American society.

One such is the growing social role of knowledge. Our society values the production and inculcation of knowledge more than ever before, as is evidenced by sharply rising research, development, and education expenditures over the last twenty years. There is an increasing devotion, too, to the systematic use of information in public and private decision-making, as is exemplified by the President's Council of Economic Advisers, by various scientific advisory groups in and out of government, by the growing number of research and analysis organizations, by increasing appeal to such techniques as program planning and budgeting, and by the recent concern with assembling and analyzing a set of "social indicators" to help gauge the social (on the analogy of the economic) health of the nation.

A changing society must put a relatively strong accent on knowledge in order to offset the unfamiliarity and uncertainty that change implies. Traditional ways (beliefs, institutions, procedures, attitudes) may be adequate for dealing with the existent and known. But new technology can be generated and assimilated only if there is technical knowledge about its operation and capabilities, and economic, sociological, and political knowledge about the society into which it will be introduced.

This argues, in turn, for the importance of the social sciences. It is by now reasonably well established that policy-making in many areas can be effective only if it takes account of the findings and potentialities of the natural sciences and of their associated technologies. Starting with economics, we are gradually coming to a similar recognition of the importance of the social sciences to public policy. Research and education in the social sciences are being increasingly supported by public funds, as the natural sciences have been by the military services and the National Science Foundation for the last quarter of a century. Also, both policy-makers and social scientists are seeking new mechanisms of co-operation and exploring the modifications these will require in their respective assumptions and procedures. This trend toward more applied social science is likely to be noticeable in any highly innovative society.

The scientific mores of such a society will also be influenced by the interest in applying technology that defines it. Scientific inquiry (into nature and society) is likely to be motivated by and focused on problems of the society rather than centering mainly around the unsolved puzzles of the scientific disciplines themselves. This does *not* mean, although it *can,* if vigilance against political interference is relaxed, (1) that the resulting science will be any less pure than that proceeding from dis-interested curiosity; or (2) that there cannot therefore be any science motivated by curiosity; or (3) that the advancement of scientific knowl-edge may not be dependent on there always being some. The research into the atomic structure of matter that is undertaken in the interest of developing new materials for supersonic flight is no less basic or pure than the same research undertaken in pursuit of a new and intriguing particle, even though the research strategy may be different in the two cases. Even more to the point, social research into voting behavior is not ipso facto less basic or pure because it is paid for by an aspiring candidate rather than by a foundation grant.

There is a serious question, in any event, about just how pure is pure in scientific research. One need not subscribe to such an out-and-out Marxism as Hessen's postulation of exclusively social and economic ori-gins for Newton's research interests, for example, in order to recognize "the demonstrable fact that the thematics of science in seventeenth cen-tury England were in large part determined by the social structure of the time." [2] Nor should we ignore the fashions in science, such as the strong emphasis on physics in recent years that was triggered by the military interest in physics-based technologies, or the very similar present-day passion for computers and computer science. An innovative society *means* one in which there is a strong interest in bringing the best avail-able knowledge to bear on ameliorating society's problems and on taking advantage of its opportunities. It is not surprising that scientific objec-tives and choices in that society should be in large measure determined by what those problems and opportunities are, which does not however

2. Robert K. Merton, *Social Theory and Social Structure* (Glencoe, Ill.: Free Press, 1949), p. 348. Hessen's analysis dates from 1931 and appears in *The Social and Eco-nomic Roots of Newton's Mechanics,* Science at the Crossroads series (London: Kniga, n.d.).

mean that scientific objectives are identical with or must remain tied to social objectives.

Another way in which a society of change influences its patterns of inquiry is by putting a premium on the formulation of new questions and, in general, on the synthetic aspects of knowing. Such a society is by description one that probes at scientific and intellectual frontiers, and a scientific frontier, according to the biologist C. H. Waddington, is where "we encounter problems about which we cannot yet ask sensible questions." [3] When change is prevalent, in other words, we are frequently in the position of not knowing just what we need to know. A goodly portion of the society's intellectual effort must then be devoted to formulating new research questions (or reformulating old ones in the light of changed circumstances and needs) so that inquiry can remain pertinent to the social problems that knowledge can alleviate.

Three consequences follow. First, there is a need to reexamine the knowledge already available for its meaning in the context of the new questions. This is the synthetic aspect of knowing. Second, the need to formulate new questions coupled with the problem- (as distinct from discipline-) orientation discussed above requires that answers be sought from the intersection of several disciplines. This is the impetus for current emphases on the importance of interdisciplinary or cross-disciplinary inquiry as a supplement to the academic research aimed at expanding knowledge and training scientists. Third, there is a need for further institutionalization of the function of transferring scientific knowledge to social use. This process, which began in the late nineteenth century with the creation of large central research laboratories in the chemical, electrical, and communications industries, now sees universities spawning problem- or area-oriented, institutes, which surely augur eventual organizational change, and new policy-oriented research organizations arising at the borderlines of industry, government, and universities, and in a new no-man's land between public and private.

A fundamental intellectual implication of a world of change is the greater theoretical utility of the concept of process over that of structure in sociological/cultural analysis. Equilibrium theories of various sorts imply ascription of greater reality to stable socio-cultural patterns than to social change. But as the anthropologist Evon Vogt argues:

> Change is basic in social and cultural systems . . . [E. R.] Leach is fundamentally correct when he states that "every real society is a

3. Quoted in *Graduate Faculties Newsletter* (New York: Columbia University, March 1966).

process in time." Our problem becomes one of describing, concep-
tualizing, and explaining a set of ongoing processes . . .

But none of the current approaches is satisfactory "in providing a set of
conceptual tools for the description and analysis of the *changing* social
and cultural *systems* that we observe." [4]

There is no denial of structure: "Once the processes are understood, the
structures manifested at given time-points will emerge with even greater
clarity," and Vogt goes on to distinguish between short-run "recurrent
processes" and long-range and cumulative "directional processes." The
former are the repetitive "structural dynamics" of a society. The latter
"involve alterations in the structures of social and cultural systems." [5]
It is clear that the latter, for Vogt, are more revealing of the essence of
culture and society as changing.

There are a number of respects in which technological change and
the intellectual and social changes it brings with it are likely to alter
the conditions and patterns of government. I construe government in
this connection in the broadest possible sense of the term, that is, as
governance (with a small "g") of a *polity*. Better yet, I take the word as
equivalent to govern*ing*, since the participle helps to banish both visions
of statism and connotations of public officialdom. What I seek to encompass by the term, in other words, is the social decision-making function in general, whether exemplified by small or large or public or private groups (the large/public coupling thus yielding the subcategory
of Government with a capital "G"). I include in decision-making, moreover, both the values and criteria that govern it and the institutions,
mechanisms, procedures, and information by means of which it operates.

One notes that, as in other social sectors and institutions, the changes
that technology purports for government are of a determinate sort, that
is, they have direction: they enhance the role of government in society
and (not surprisingly, given the considerations already adduced) they
enhance the role of knowledge in government.

The importance of decision-making will tend to grow relative to other
social functions (relative to production, for example, in an affluent
society), (1) partly because the frequency with which new possibilities are
created in a technologically active age will provide many opportunities for
new choices (i.e., new decisions); (2) partly because continuing alteration
of the spectrum of available choice alternatives will shorten the useful

4. Evon Z. Vogt, "On the Concepts of Structure and Process in Cultural Anthro-
pology," *American Anthropologist* 62 (1960): 1, 19, 20.
5. Ibid., pp. 20–22.

life of decisions previously made; (3) partly because decisions in areas previously thought to be unrelated are increasingly found to impinge on and alter each other; and (4) partly because the economic affluence consequent on new technology will increase the scope of deliberate public decision-making at the expense (relatively) of the largely automatic and private charting of society's course by market forces. It is characteristic of our time that the market is increasingly distrusted as a goal-setting mechanism for society, although there is of course no question of its effectiveness as a signaling and controlling device for the formulation of economic policy.

Some of the ways in which knowledge increasingly enters the fabric of government have been amply noted, both above and in what is by now becoming a fairly voluminous literature on various aspects of the relation of science and public policy. There are other ways, in addition, in which knowledge (information, technology, science) is bound to have fundamental impacts on the structures and processes of decision-making that we as yet know little about.

The newest information-handling equipments and techniques find their way quickly into the agencies of Federal and local government and into the operations of industrial organizations, for example, in the first instance because there are many jobs that they can perform more efficiently than the traditional rows of clerks. But it is notorious that adopting new means in order better to accomplish old ends very often results in the substitution of new ends (inherent in the new means) for old ones. Computers and associated intellectual tools can thus, for example, make our public decisions more informed, efficient, and rational, and less subject to lethargy, partisanship, and ignorance. Yet that possibility seems to imply a degree of expertise and sophistication of policy-making and implementing procedures that may leave the public forever ill informed, blur the lines between executive and legislature (and private bureaucracies) as all increasingly rely on the same experts and sources of information, and chase the idea of federalism into the history books close on the heels of the public-private separation.

There is in general the problem of what happens to traditional relationships between citizens and government, to such prerogatives of the individual as personal privacy, electoral consent, and access to the independent social criticism of the press, and to the ethics of and public controls over a new elite of information keepers, when economic, military, and social policies become increasingly technical, long-range, machine processed, information based, and expert dominated.

157

An exciting possibility that is, however, so dimly seen as perhaps to be illusory is that knowledge can widen the area of political consensus. There is no question here of a naive rationalism such as we associate with the eighteenth-century Enlightenment. No amount of reason will ever triumph wholly over irrationality, certainly, nor will vested interest fully yield to love of wisdom. Yet there are some political disputes and disagreements, surely, that derive from ignorance of information bearing on an issue or from lack of the means to analyze fully the probable consequences of alternative courses of action. Is it too much to expect that better knowledge may bring about greater political consensus in such cases as these? Is the democratic tenet that an informed public contributes to the commonweal pure political myth? The sociologist S. M. Lipset suggests not:

> Insofar as most organized participants in the political struggle accept the authority of experts in economics, military affairs, interpretations of the behavior of foreign nations and the like, it becomes increasingly difficult to challenge the views of opponents in moralistic "either/or" terms. Where there is some consensus among the scientific experts on specific issues, these tend to be removed as possible sources of intense controversy.[6]

Robert E. Lane of Yale has made the point more generally:

> If we employ the term "ideology" to mean a comprehensive, passionately believed, self-activating view of society, usually organized as a social movement, . . . it makes sense to think of a domain of knowledge distinguishable from a domain of ideology, despite the extent to which they may overlap. Since knowledge and ideology serve somewhat as functional equivalents in orienting a person toward the problems he must face and the policies he must select, the growth of the domain of knowledge causes it to impinge on the domain of ideology.[7]

Harvey Brooks, finally, draws a similar conclusion from consideration of the extent to which scientific criteria and techniques have found their way into the management of political affairs. He finds an

> increasing relegation of questions which used to be matters of political debate to professional cadres of technicians and experts which function almost independently of the democratic political process

6. Seymour M. Lipset, "The Changing Class Structure and Contemporary European Politics," *Daedalus* 93 (1964): 273.

7. Robert E. Lane, "The Decline of Politics and Ideology in a Knowledgeable Society," *American Sociological Review* 31 (Oct. 1966): 660.

. . . The progress which is achieved, while slower, seems more solid, more irreversible, more capable of enlisting a wide consensus.[8]

I raise this point as fundamental to the technology-polity relationship, not by way of hazarding a prediction. I ignore neither the possibility that *value* conflicts in political debate may become sharper still as factual differences are muted by better knowledge, nor the fact that decline of political ideology does not ipso facto mean a decline of political disagreement, nor the fear of some that the hippie movement, literary anti-intellectualism, and people's fears of genuine dangers implicit in continued technological advance may in fact augur an imminent retreat from rationality and an interlude — perhaps a long interlude — either of political know-nothingism reminiscent of Joseph McCarthy or of social concentration on contemplative or religious values.

Yet, there is no warrant *in principle* in a sharp separation between knowledge and political action. Like all dualisms, this one too may have had its origins in the analytic abhorrence of uncertainty. (One is reminded in this connection of the radical dualism that Descartes arrived at as a result of his determination to base his philosophy on the only certain and self-evident principle he could discover.) There certainly is painfully much in political history and political experience to render uncertain a positive correlation between knowledge and political consensus. The correlation is not necessarily absent therefore, and to find it and lead society to act on it may be the greatest challenge yet to political inquiry and political action.

To the extent that technological change expands and alters the spectrum of what man can do, it multiplies the choices that society will have to make. These choices will increasingly have to be deliberate social choices, moreover, rather than market reflections of innumerable individual consumer choices, and will therefore have to be made by political means. Since it is unlikely — despite futurists and technological forecasters — that we will soon be able to predict future opportunities (and their attendant opportunity costs) with any significant degree of reliability in detail, it becomes important to investigate the conditions of a political system (I use the term in the wide sense I assigned to "government" above) with the flexibility and value presuppositions necessary to evaluate alternatives and make choices among them as they continue to emerge.

8. Harvey Brooks, "Scientific Concepts and Cultural Change," in *Science and Culture,* ed. G. Holton (Boston: Houghton Mifflin, 1965), p. 71.

In other words, the emphasis shifts from allegiance to the known, stable, formulated, and familiar, to a *posture* of expectation of change and readiness to deal with it. It is this kind of shift, occurring across many elements of society, that is the hallmark of our age. It is what Vogt seeks to formalize in stressing processual as against structural analysis of culture and society. The mechanisms, values, attitudes, and procedures called for by a social posture of readiness will be different in kind from those characteristic of a society that sees itself as mature, "arrived," and in stable equilibrium. The most fundamental *political* task of a technological world is that of systematizing and institutionalizing the social expectation of the changes that technology will continue to bring about.

I see that task as a precondition of profiting from our accumulating knowledge of the effects of technological change. To understand those effects is an intellectual problem, but to do something about them and profit from the opportunities that technology offers is a political one. We need above all, in other words, to gauge the effects of technology on the *polity*, so that we can derive some social value from our knowledge. This, I suppose, is the twentieth-century form of the perennial ideal of wedding wisdom and government.

ZBIGNIEW BRZEZINSKI

Moving into a Technetronic Society

America is in the midst of a transition that is both unique and baffling. The uniqueness of the change is the cause for the difficulty in understanding its nature. Marxists particularly are baffled. They see hopeful signs of mounting contradictions in the internal American turmoil. Yet that turmoil does not fit classical categories: well-fed alienated youth from well-to-do-families, middle-class disaffection, Negro self-assertiveness led by brilliant clergymen or militant Moslems — none of that fits the neat categories of the established doctrine.

Marxists are not the only ones baffled; many analysts of contemporary America are equally perplexed. For our society is leaving the phase of spontaneity and is entering a more self-conscious stage; ceasing to be an industrial society, it is being shaped to an ever-increasing extent by technology and electronics, and thus becoming the first *technetronic society*. This is at least in part the cause for much of the current tensions and violence, and largely the reason why events in America of today do not fit established categories of analyses.

Spontaneity made for an almost automatic optimism about the future, about the "American miracle," about justice and happiness for all: as America developed, grew, became richer, problems that persisted or appeared would be solved. This phase is ending. The social blinders are being ripped off — and a sense of inadequacy is becoming more wide-

From Zbigniew Brzezinski, "The American Transition," *New Republic* 157 (December 23, 1967): 18–21. Copyright © 1967 by Zbigniew Brzezinski.

Mr. Brzezinski is Professor of Government and Director of the Research Institute on Communist Affairs, Columbia University.

spread. The spread of literacy, and particularly the access to college and universities of about 40 percent of the youth, has created a new stratum — one which reinforces the formerly isolated urban intellectuals — a stratum not willing to tolerate social blinders and not sharing the complacent belief in the spontaneous goodness of American social change.

Yet it is easier to know what is wrong than to indicate what ought to be done. The difficulty is not only revealed by the inability of the new social rebels to develop a concrete and meaningful program. It is magnified by the novelty of our problem. Turning to nineteenth-century ideologies is not the answer — and it is symptomatic that the "New Left" has found it most difficult to apply the available, particularly Marxist, doctrines to the new reality. Indeed, its emphasis on human rights, the evils of depersonalization, the dangers inherent in big government — so responsive to the felt psychological needs — contain strong parallels to more conservative notions about the place and sanctity of the individual in society.

In some ways, there is an analogy here between the "New Left" and the searching attitude of various disaffected groups in early nineteenth-century Europe, reacting to the first strains of the industrial age. Not fully comprehending its meaning, not quite certain where it was heading — yet sensitive to the miseries and opportunities it was bringing — many Europeans strove desperately to adapt earlier, eighteenth-century doctrines to the new reality. It was finally Marx who achieved what appeared to millions a meaningful synthesis, combining utopian idealism about the future of the industrial age with a scorching critique of its present.

The search for meaning is characteristic of the present American scene. It could portend most divisive and bitter ideological conflicts — especially as intellectual disaffection becomes linked with the increasing bitterness of the deprived Negro masses. If carried to its extreme, this could bring to America a phase of violent, intolerant, and destructive civil strife, combining ideological and racial intolerance.

However, it seems unlikely that a unifying ideology of political action, capable of mobilizing large-scale loyalty, can emerge in the manner that Marxism arose in response to the industrial era. Unlike even Western Europe or Japan — not to speak of Soviet Russia — where the consequences and the impact of the industrial process are still reshaping political, social, and economic life — in America science and technology (particularly as socially applied through communications and, increasingly, computerization, both off-springs of the industrial age) are already more important in influencing the social behavior of a society that has moved past its industrial phase. Science and technology are notoriously unsympathetic to simple, absolute formulas. In the technetronic society there may be room for pragmatic, even impatient, idealism, but hardly for doctrinal utopianism.

At the same time, it is already evident that a resolution of some of the unfinished business of the industrial era will be rendered more acute. For example, the Negro should have been integrated into U.S. society during the American Industrial Revolution. Yet that revolution came before America, even if not the Negro, was ready for full integration. If the Negro had been only an economic legacy of the pre-industrial age, perhaps he could have integrated more effectively. Today, the more advanced urban-industrial regions of America, precisely because they are moving into a new and more complex phase, requiring even more developed social skills, are finding it difficult to integrate the Negro, both a racial minority and America's only "feudal legacy." Paradoxically, it can be argued that the American South stands a better long-range chance of fully integrating the Negro: American consciousness is changing, the Negro has stirred, and the South is beginning to move into the industrial age. The odds are that it may take the Negro along with it.

Whatever the outcome, American society is the one in which the great questions of our time will be first tested through practice. Can the individual and science coexist, or will the dynamic momentum of the latter fundamentally alter the former? Can man, living in the scientific age, grow in intellectual depth and philosophical meaning, and thus in his personal liberty too? Can the institutions of political democracy be adapted to the new conditions sufficiently quickly to meet the crises, yet without debasing their democratic character?

The challenge in its essence involves the twin dangers of fragmentation and excessive control. A few examples: Symptoms of alienation and depersonalization are already easy to find. Many Americans feel "less free." This feeling seems connected with their loss of "purpose," for freedom implies choice of action, and action requires an awareness of goals. If the present transition of America to the technetronic age achieves no personally satisfying fruits, the next phase may be one of sullen withdrawal from social and political involvement, a flight from social and political responsibility through "inner-emigration." Political frustration could increase the difficulty of absorbing and internalizing rapid environmental changes, thereby prompting increasing psychic instability.

At the same time, the capacity to assert social and political control over the individual will vastly increase. It will soon be possible to assert almost continuous surveillance over every citizen and to maintain up-to-date, complete files, containing even most personal information about the health or personal behavior of the citizen, in addition to more customary data. These files will be subject to instantaneous retrieval by the authorities.

Moreover, the rapid pace of change will put a premium on anticipating events and planning for them. Power will gravitate into the hands of those who control the information and can correlate it most rapidly. Our existing post-crisis management institutions will probably be increasingly supplanted by pre-crisis management institutions, the task of which will be to identify in advance likely social crises and to develop programs to cope with them. This could encourage tendencies during the next several decades toward a technocratic dictatorship, leaving less and less room for political procedures as we now know them.

Finally, looking ahead to the end of this century, the possibility of biochemical mind-control and the genetic tinkering with man, including eventually the creation of beings that will function like men — and reason like them as well — could give rise to the most difficult questions. According to what criteria can such controls be applied? What is the distribution of power between the social and political status of artificial beings, if they begin to approach man in their performance and creative capacities? (One dares not ask, what if they begin to "outstrip man" — something not beyond the pale of possibility during the next century?)

Yet it would be highly misleading to construct a one-sided picture, a new Orwellian piece of science fiction. Many of the changes transforming American society augur well for the the future and allow at least some optimism about this society's capacity to adapt to the requirements of the metamorphic age.

Thus, in the political sphere, the increased flow of information and more efficient techniques of coordination need not necessarily prompt greater concentration of power within some ominous control agency located at the governmental apex. Paradoxically, these developments also make possible greater devolution of authority and responsibility to the lower levels of government and society. The division of power has traditionally posed the problems of inefficiency, coordination, and dispersal of authority; but today the new communications and computer techniques make possible both increased authority at the lower levels and almost instant national coordination. It is very likely that state and local government will be strengthened in the next 10 years, and many functions currently the responsibility of the federal government will be assumed by them. (It is noteworthy that the U.S. Army has so developed its control systems that it is not uncommon for sergeants to call in and coordinate massive air strikes and artillery fire — a responsibility of colonels during World War II.)

The devolution of financial responsibility to lower echelons may encourage both the flow of better talent and greater local participation in more important local decision-making. National coordination and local participation could thus be wedded by the new systems of coordination. This has already been tried successfully by some large businesses. This development would also have the desirable effect of undermining the appeal of any new integrating ideologies that may arise; for ideologies thrive only as long as there is an acute need for abstract responses to large remote problems.

It is also a hopeful sign that improved governmental performance, and its increased sensitivity to social needs, is being stimulated by the growing involvement in national affairs of what Kenneth Boulding has called the Educational and Scientific Establishment (EASE). The university at one time, during the Middle Ages, was a key social institution. Political leaders leaned heavily on it for literate confidants and privy counselors, a rare commodity in those days. Later divorced from reality, academia in recent years has made a grand reentry into the world of action.

Today, the university is the creative eye of the massive communications complex, the source of much strategic planning, domestic and international. Its engagement in the world is encouraging the appearance of a new breed of politicians-intellectuals, men who make it a point to mobilize and draw on the most expert scientific and academic advice in the development of their political programs. This, in turn, stimulates public awareness of the value of expertise — and, again in turn, greater political competition in exploiting it.

A profound change in the intellectual community itself is inherent in this development. The largely humanist-oriented, occasionally ideologically-minded intellectual dissenter, who saw his role largely in terms of proffering social critiques, is rapidly being displaced either by experts and specialists, who become involved in special governmental undertakings, or by the generalists-integrators, who become in effect house-ideologues for those in power, providing overall intellectual integration for disparate actions. A community of organization-oriented, application-minded intellectuals, relating itself more effectively to the political system than their predecessors, serves to introduce into the political system concerns broader than those likely to be generated by that system itself and perhaps more relevant than those articulated by outside critics.

There is a danger in all this, however, that ought not to be neglected. Intense involvement in applied knowledge could gradually prompt a waning of the tradition of learning for the sake of learning. The intellectual community, including the university, could become another "industry," meeting social needs as the market dictates, with the intellectuals reaching for the highest material and political rewards. Concern with power, prestige, and the good life could mean an end to the aristocratic ideal of intellectual detachment and the disinterested search for truth.

The expansion of knowledge, and the entry into socio-political life of the intellectual community, has the further effect of making education an almost continuous process. By 1980, not only will approximately two-thirds of U.S. urban dwellers be college trained, but it is almost certain that systematic "elite-training" will be standard in the political system. It will be normal for every high official both to be engaged in almost continuous absorption of new techniques and knowledge and to take periodic retraining. The adoption of compulsory elementary education was a revolution brought on by the industrial age. In the new technetronic society, it will be equally necessary to require everyone at a sufficiently responsible post to take, say, two years of retraining every ten years. (Perhaps there will even be a constitutional amendment, requiring a President-elect to spend at least a year getting himself educationally up-to-date.) Otherwise, it will not be possible either to keep up with or absorb the new knowledge.

Given diverse needs, it is likely that the educational system will undergo a fundamental change in structure. Television-computer consoles, capable of bringing most advanced education to the home, will permit extensive and continuous adult reeducation. On the more advanced levels, it is likely that government agencies and corporations will develop — and some have already begun to do so — their own advanced educational systems, shaped to their special needs. As education becomes both a continuum and even more application-oriented, its organizational framework will be redesigned to tie directly to social and political action.

It is quite possible that a society increasingly geared to learning will be able to absorb more resiliently the expected change in social and individual life. Mechanization of labor and the introduction of robots will reduce the chores that keep millions busy doing things that they dislike doing. The increasing GNP (which could reach approximately $10,000 per capita per year), linked with educational advance, could prompt among those less involved in social management and less interested in scientific development a wave of interest in the cultural and humanistic aspects of life, in addition to purely hedonistic preoccupations. But even the latter would serve as a social valve, reducing tensions and political frustration. Greater control over external environment could make for easier, less uncertain existence.

But the key to successful adaptation to the new conditions is in the effective selection, distribution, and utilization of social talent. If the industrial society can be said to have developed through a struggle for survival of the fittest, the technetronic society — in order to prosper — requires the effective mobilization of the ablest. Objective and systematic criteria for the selection of those with the greatest gifts will have to be developed and the maximum opportunity for their training and advancement provided. The new society will require enormous talents — as well as a measure of philosophical wisdom — to manage and integrate effectively the expected changes. Otherwise, the dynamic of change could chaotically dictate the patterns of social change.

Fortunately, American society is becoming more conscious not only of the principle of equal opportunity for all but of special opportunity for the singularly talented few. Never truly an aristocratic state (except for some pockets such as the South and New England), never really subject to ideological or charismatic leadership, gradually ceasing to be a plutocratic-oligarchic society, the U.S.A. is becoming something which may be labeled the "meritocratic democracy." It combines continued respect for the popular will with an increasing role in the key decision-making institutions of individuals with special intellectual and scientific attainments. The educational and social systems are making it increasingly attractive and easy for those meritocratic few to develop to the fullest their special potential. The recruitment and advancement of social talent is yet to extend to the poorest and the most underprivileged, but that too is coming. No one can tell whether this will suffice to meet the unfolding challenge, but the increasingly cultivated and programmed American society, led by a meritocratic democracy, may stand a better chance.

ARTHUR P. MENDEL

The Great Refusal of Technetronic Society

Zbigniew Brzezinski [has] heralded the imminent arrival of a "technetronic" age with the feverish excitement of Paul Revere announcing
the British. And no wonder, for the transformation to come from the
cybernetic miracle will not only be greater than that resulting from the
French and Russian revolutions, but will, he believe[s], produce "in the
next several decades a mutation potentially as basic as that experienced
through the slow process of evolution from animal to human experience."
Computers will reason as well as man and may begin to approach man
in their "creative capacities" and perhaps even "outstrip man"; human
conduct will become "more predetermined and subject to deliberate
'programming'; man will increasingly possess the capacity to determine
the sex of his children, to affect through drugs the extent of their intelligence and to modify and control their personalities"; "it will soon be
possible to assert almost continuous surveillance over every citizen," "well-
nigh total political surveillance"; experts having the knowledge necessary to anticipate and plan will replace the plutocratic elite as the latter
replaced the rural aristocracy, thereby encouraging tendencies "towards a
technocratic dictatorship"; the university consequently, will cease being
"an aloof ivory tower, the repository of irrelevant, even if respected,
wisdom," and the intellectual community will change from the abode of
the "largely humanist-oriented, occasionally ideologically-minded intel-

From Arthur P. Mendel, "Robots and Rebels," *New Republic* 160 (January 11, 1969):
16–19. Copyright © 1969 by Harrison-Blaine of New Jersey, Inc.
Mr. Mendel is Professor of Russian History at the University of Michigan.

lectual-dissenter" to that of "experts and specialists . . . who become, in effect, house ideologues for those in power."

These changes will not come in 1969. But they will come, and those who reject them are simply responding to the coming technetronic age the way peasants, Luddites, and Chartists responded when the agrarian society entered the industrial age. Or, like National Socialists, Fascists, and the Red Guard, they in other ways represent "the last spasm of the past, and thus not really revolutions, but counterrevolutions." Consequently, instead of being granted "ambivalent concessions by the authorities in power," the nay-sayers should be "suppressed quickly" in "an early confrontation." And thereafter, the authorities should "make certain that the revolutionary forces cannot later rally again under the same leadership. If that leadership cannot be physically liquidated, it can at least be expelled from the country (or area) in which the revolution is taking place. Emigrants rarely can maintain themselves as effective revolutionaries."

Assuming we take this seriously, and not as Iron Mountain fantasy, it is very serious indeed, and not only because of the author's close association with several power worlds. Its essential significance, I think, is in the character of the thought itself. When Brzezinski's artificial beings become self-conscious this is how and what they will think. Here is the ideology of the robots, the justification of their domination and — to carry further this science-fiction anthropomorphism — their totalitarian ambition "to affect directly almost all aspects of life." We are here in the world of instruments and of the fuel that keeps them going — quantifiable information, "hard data." Man's role is to help provide and process this information, keep the artificial beings healthy and further refine them, although even this seems only a temporary function since the machines not only reason better than man but threaten to outstrip him in creative capacities.

Mr. Brzezinski believes that the availability and continuing sophistication of instruments, together with the gargantuan amassing of data, means somehow that man is moving "increasingly into the phases of controlling or even creating his environment." When Brzezinski leaves the spotless computers and turns to the world of real, not artificial, beings he shows us that things are getting disastrously *out of control:* "increasingly purposeless masses" forced by these developments into "sullen withdrawal from social and political involvement"; black revolutions, our " 'feudal legacy,' " and New Left risings, our Luddites; the frantically driven technetron who pays the price of power by working longer, harder, and faster "either to keep up with others or because he thinks he can thus accomplish more"; the backward, third-world nations falling farther and farther behind until they give up trying and retreat to dictatorship and xenophobic fanaticism; the acquisition of evermore effective "chemical and biological weapons, death rays, neutron bombs, nerve gases, and a host of other devices"; and the likelihood that local wars "may occasionally erupt — resulting perhaps even in the total nuclear extinction of one or several smaller nations? — before greater international control is imposed in the wake of the universal moral shock thereby generated."

Why this direct relationship between scientific progress and human distress? It is precisely the woefully naive confusion between means and ends, between tools and values. It is a regression to primitive fetishism, a belief that the ritualistic manipulation of technical agencies by itself assures good and wards off evil. In part, it is a particularly dreadful example of that modern false-consciousness that either hypostasizes technology and its subsidiary organizations into self-perpetuating, demiurgic forces too important and too powerful to heed soft and fuzzy human values or, far worse, virtually identifies human value and welfare with the success of these agencies themselves.

Fortunately, Brzezinski is not quite perfectly one-dimensional. He is not, after all, an artificial being, and here and there his own humanity comes through to us, providing an obligato of human protest against his own grim utopia. Towards the end, for example, the humanist in him bursts forth in a final appeal, warning us that "in the developed world, the nature of man as man is threatened," and urging that "increasing attention will have to be given to giving man meaningful content — to improving the quality of life for man *as man*," that there is need for "dialogue on what it is about man's life that we wish to safeguard or to promote."

But what, I wonder, have data storage banks, push-button information retrieval, and the "objective and systematic" selection and training of technetrons to do with questions like these? After all the horrors that in our century have accompanied the spectacular achievements of science and technology, it should be obvious that answers to these existential questions will never come from sophistication of tools or from the puerile pride mastery of them has given us. This *hubris,* the aggressive, mastery-compulsion that feeds it, and the deterministic myths that rationalize it are themselves largely responsible for the very evils they self-deceptively claim to meliorate.

Notwithstanding his occasional expressions of humanist sensitivity,

Brzezinski makes abundantly clear his intention to march, chin up and full stride, into the technetronic age. And why should he not, since it is for him a familiar and congenial world. What, after all, are his technetrons but the ideological offspring of Burnham's managerial revolution, fighting a rear guard action against those forces that are slowly dismantling their dreary and anxious world. As with all earlier elites in the process of being displaced, they disguise their fears and justify their violence by appeals to some objective legitimacy, social necessity, or historical inevitability.

It is, thus, to Brzezinski himself and not his New Left opponents that the epithet "counterrevolutionary" applies. For the dramatic revolution in process in the advanced societies today is *exactly the opposite* of that which Brzezinski proclaims. It is the revolution of those who have joined in the Great Refusal against that pitiful caricature of man created by five centuries of urban, technological, and scientific progress — *homo economicus*. The essential accusation of the Great Refusal is directed against the subordination of human experience to the economic processes of the consumer society and its increasingly more absurd products, to the aggressive militarism that at least in our case has become so tightly interwoven with this society, and to the gigantic, impersonal organizations through which it all functions.

The Great Refusal may be either active or passive. It is active when the rebels insist on action that has clearly human, moral, or creative value: they may be activists in the more publicized civil rights movement, Peace Corps, community action committees, or anti-war demonstrations, or in the more private ways in which they choose careers of social service or aesthetic creativity rather than those associated with traditional success and the pursuit of power. There is a drop in engineering school enrollment. Law firms raise beginning salaries sharply to counter the decline in applicants. Scientists forego the lush military and commercial contracts. And should they willy-nilly find themselves caught in the commercial-industrial world, the rebels undermine its essential ethos, make it more mellow and humane. The Great Refusal is passive when the rebels just let go, step down from the treadmill of time and achievement into a timeless present, the residence of sensual and contemplative delight. Here, too, there are the dramatic and the more covert expressions, both the spectacular hippies and the more reticent but more important millions who are finding the time that was supposedly never there to enjoy the books, music, sports, arts and crafts, travel, open companionships, and all the other joys that economic man could only skimpily, grudgingly, and guiltily allow himself. For technetronic man much of this may be intolerable hedonism; but for "man *as man*" it is the leap to freedom that utopians envisioned and that centuries of technological achievement and human self-sacrifice have at last prepared.

As long as deprivation and scarcity characterized social existence, as long as economic progress continued to mean a struggle for securing the material basis for social existence, these opponents, as Brzezinski correctly says, were powerless and easily overcome. What Brzezinski fails to see is that the achievement of the affluent society, the victory of science and technology, the assurance of the material conditions of life comprise a qualitative change that radically alters all this. From being innocuous irritants, the opposing forces are in fact acquiring, through the very processes of the system they oppose, the power to dethrone economic man, to soften then dissolve the taut constraints, the repressions and obligations that have welded generations of mankind with other "factors of production" into our dismal social factory.

The Great Refusal is exactly the kind of revolutionary movement one would expect to emerge from the affluent society. It is precisely the Great Refusal that focuses on the "psychic" problems, the problems of leisure, of "giving man meaningful content" and "improving the quality of life for man *as man*," on the concerns that Brzezinski himself realizes are among the most compelling that men and women in the advanced societies face. And it is a revolution that draws together the generations, belying too hasty assertions about the generation gap. The young have learned many of their lessons, and have found much of their voice, from a long list of adult social critics, past and present; names like Marcuse, Goodman, DeGrazia, and Galbraith are only the most recent of a long heritage. But more important still, the rebellious youth have found varying degrees of support from their own parents, who, while too rigidly formed, too "up-tight," too well "programmed" to abandon the compulsive style themselves, nevertheless sense that their children are right in trying to do so, that the affluent society has removed the risks such autonomy used to entail, that their children need not run as scared as they did.

What can the parents say to the children who come urging love instead of hate, service instead of self-aggrandizement, beauty instead of fashion, communion instead of competition? How can they denounce those who have initiated and carried through the civil-rights movement and the anti-war demonstrations, those who have made such noble enterprises as the Peace Corps a reality, and who today strive through their free universities and in other ways to preserve liberal education, education that concerns human, existential questions rather than the further refinement of already super-sophisticated computers, the better marketing of lipstick, or the concoction of more deadly nerve-gases?

Still, if the youth have found guidance and support among the adult world, it is nonetheless true that they are the effective vanguard of the "new class" and its Great Refusal. It is in these years of late adolescence, the years between the dependency of childhood and the dependency of adult, family responsibilities, that one is psychologically ready and socially able to stand outside of one's society and the image of it in oneself and judge them both. And to this extent the rebellion is part of the familiar and repeated assault of each generation of youth against the older authorities, both a necessary step towards adult autonomy and a last defense of youthful spontaneity and diversity. However, and this, I think, is the crux of it all, the meaning of the Great Refusal and of the leading role of youth in it, this customary adolescent reluctance to give up freedom for constrained roles or critical honesty for socially required hypocrisy, now coincides with the possibilities that affluence is beginning to allow society as a whole — for the first time in human history — to preserve or regain such freedom and honesty. Youth no longer speaks only for itself: it defines an era. And, understandably, it is at the universities of the country where this definition takes form. Not only because it is here that so many of the sensitive, thoughtful, and articulate youth find themselves, but also because it is here that they learn to look critically at different societies and values, including their own, to see truth rather than social conventions, and it is here they acquire an arsenal of perennial human values with which to sustain their struggle for the good society.

One may appreciate Brzezinski's visceral preference for technetronic social management rather than all that "hedonism." That is his business. But it is difficult to understand how after two decades of close association with historical determinist thinking he can write that "a crucial consideration in judging the validity and significance of the revolutionary process is to determine whether it is historically relevant," that the New Left represents just another "last spasm of the past," "the death rattle of the historical irrelevants." What does he say when he reminds himself that this kind of thinking helped justify the bloodshed and the terror of Stalinism?

As I have argued, there is good reason to think that it is the rebels of the Great Refusal and not the technetronic servitors who speak for the future. I have in mind the increasing number of youth in universities and their growing role throughout the society; the spread among them of all sorts of cults for letting go and their leading involvement in all the movements opposed to Brzezinski's utopia; the revival among the social sciences of personalist, subjectivist approaches in opposition to the heretofore dominant behaviorists; the spread of the humanistic psychology movement; the not-so-coincidental upsurge of anthropological studies of primitive societies, religious studies in mythology, and historians' interest in aristocracies; the richly emotional qualities of contemporary art; the leisure and sexual-sensual liberation; the growing influence of the underground church; the ubiquitous sprouting of small groups of all sorts where personal communion is rediscovered. It is mainly a quiet revolution, one without the programs and leadership that Brzezinski's nineteenth-century mind considers prerequisite for an historically relevant revolution. It is not waiting for the cataclysmic confrontation that Marcuse, repeating Marx's error, seems to think necessary for this coming social transformation. It is taking place now, gradually changing the face of our society, the quality of our thought and experience, and the character of our behavior.

ROBERT STRAUSZ-HUPÉ

Technology's Uninvited Guests

During the last hundred years, the great majority of scientific dis-
coveries and the technological innovations which they sparked were
hailed as beneficial. For example, the automobile, when first introduced,
was hailed as a device of individual and social improvement — a liber-
ator from the constraints of space and time. Now, men were able to travel
to the countryside and rejoice in the beauties of nature, to commute
from suburb to city and put distance between their homes and places
of work, freed from the restrictions of more laborious or track-schedule-
bound means of locomotion. The new industry yielded immense profits
to investors and high wages to hundreds of thousands of workers. Together with its spin-offs, it provided the principal thrust toward widely
diffused prosperity based upon mass production. It took nearly a generation until we came to realize that, together with the invited guest, several
uninvited guests had joined the feast. The congestion of traffic in, and
the smog over, our cities has evoked searching public interest when these
conditions threaten to damage grievously, if not to destroy, the pattern of
civilized existence. Certainly, very little foresight has been brought to
bear upon the consequences — most of them easily foreseeable — of automotive transportation development. Now, the point is being reached
where, to an appreciable measure, this transportation system is becoming
dysfunctional. A good many of our cities have been turned into conglom-

From Robert Strausz-Hupé, "Social Values and Politics: The Uninvited Guests,"
Review of Politics 30 (January 1968): 59–78. Copyright © 1968 by the University of
Notre Dame.
Mr. Strausz-Hupé is U.S. Ambassador to Morocco.

erate ethnic ghettos; a large part of our shrinking rural environment has been converted into bedroom cities; and those architectural heirlooms which survived the first onslaught of the industrial revolution have either been razed or stand incongruously stranded amidst squalor.

Here is not the place to dwell on the countless consequences, nearly all of them unanticipated, flowing from this single technological innovation. Suffice it to say, that this one technology profoundly altered the conditions of communal life and, thus, the condition of man. All the political measures that have been taken to cope with these alterations have been taken too late. Because they were taken too late, they entailed immense financial expenses. A good many urgently needed measures have not been taken yet. In the light of past experience it is likely that these will be fraught with even more exorbitant costs.

On the basis of richly documented experience, it is likely that many other major scientific-technological innovations have engendered results as ambiguous as those produced by the scientific insights leading to the invention of the combustion engine and, by a complex sequence of technical adaptations and managerial decisions, to the establishment of the automotive industry.

It can be argued that technical innovation has always been a factor of change. Hence, so the argument continues, there is nothing abnormal in our present situation. Have science and technology not always strained the fabric of tradition? Yet, have they not produced the means needed for coping with the problems which they themselves created?

Only one among several reasons need be here adduced in order to cast doubt upon this sanguine view, namely, massive change of scale. The pace of scientific discovery and technological application have accelerated beyond any historic precedent. Virtually all peoples have now been drawn into the orbit of modern science and technology. The effect of innovation upon both the natural and the social environment is now far more massive and immediate than ever before in the history of mankind.

Three facts stand out and should give us cause for concern: *first,* biologically, man is today what he has been since prehistoric times. Certainly, his innate capacity for learning is about what it has been since the beginning of historic times. It is not possible to adduce empirical proof showing that an intelligent Greek of Pericles' times was less intelligent than an intelligent New Yorker of the Kennedy-Johnson era. Anatomically, they cannot be distinguished from one another. A comparison of the per capita cultural output of ancient Greece and modern America does not conclusively redound to the advantage of the latter. The difference between these two eras — the one and only uncontroversial difference — is the parsimony of Athenian technology versus the enormous accumulations of the tools available to us for the alteration of our environment. A favorable mutation of the human species is, for the near future, improbable. Until disproved by conclusive empirical evidence, this hypothesis must stand. As long as it stands, man will be confronted by the exponential growth of his powers over the environment and the infinitely slower development of his biological, intellectual, and moral capacities. It is quite true that men now can live longer and healthier lives than they could expect to live in ages past. It is also true that the collective knowledge of mankind has increased by leaps and bounds — though it is also true that this increase of knowledge has been achieved by ever-narrowing specialization and, to this extent, by the increasingly rigid compartmentalization of available knowledge.

The deepening concern with the incipient dissolution of science as an integrated field has engendered attempts to align the traditional disciplines within encompassing configurations such as "Gestalt" and "System." The quest for unifying principles common to the universes of the individual sciences, natural and social, has led to the postulation of a new integrative discipline, General Systems Theory.[1] The call has been heeded: within the last decade, the new discipline has burgeoned into an imposing structure, accommodating numerous substructures — specializations — devoted to the exploration of isomorphisms in various scientific fields.

A good many of the claims made for the new discipline by its disciples have been validated by experience, especially in operations research and management of complex organizations such as large corporations and cities. It is far from clear, however, that the new approach has come any closer to achieving a unitary scientific culture than did the "wholist" speculations of early nineteenth-century natural philosophy.

The founder [Bertalanffy] conceived of the new discipline as a contribution, if not *the* strategic contribution, to a "well-developed science of society and its corresponding technology" as a way out from what he deemed the "chaos and impending destruction of our present world." Meditating upon the transcendent purpose of his endeavor, he discerned the shape of those uninvited guests who might crash the party of the debutante, General Systems Theory. [Bertalanffy] wrote:

. . . It is an empirical fact that scientific achievements are put just

1. Ludwig von Bertalanffy, "General Systems Theory," *General Systems* 1 (1956): 10.

as much, or even more, to destructive as constructive use. The science of human behavior and society is not exempt from this fate. In fact, it is perhaps the greatest danger of the systems of modern totalitarianism that they are so alarmingly up to date not only in physical and biological, but also in psychological technology . . . Scientific control of society is no highway to Utopia.[2]

To this somber warning is added a more hopeful note:

The scientific understanding of human society and its law can teach us, not only what human behavior and society have in common with other organizations, but also what is their uniqueness. Here the main tenet will be: man is not only a political animal, he is, before and above all, an individual. . . . This, I believe, is the ultimate precept a theory of organization can give: not a manual for dictators of any denomination more efficiently to subjugate human beings by the scientific application of Iron Laws, but a warning that the Leviathan of organization must not swallow the individual without sealing its own inevitable doom.[3]

In brief, we are told that the new, the unifying discipline, if it cleaves to certain normative standards which are not necessarily derived from its competence, might restore the wholeness, the harmony of society and of the unique individual being. Yet, *if* misused, the new discipline might serve the ends of totalitarianism and stultify the individual. *Quis custodiet ipsos?* The all-pervasive ambiguity of the scientific-technological approach to the enduring problem of man and society remains. Although it is expected that advances in computer technology will make possible the coded storage and, hence, instant availability of knowledge, no one has yet been able to say whether or not this process will be conducive to an increase of individual intelligence, not to speak of the increased social usefulness derived from any intellectual increment.

Encouraged by the computer community, work is going forward towards organizing the profusion of information engendered by the protean output of scientific research into central storehouses of knowledge — cosmic brains, so to speak, which not only retain and order the input of data but also, upon demand, release instantly all the information relevant to specific inquiry — the multiknowledge of multiuniversity. The uninvited guest may appear at this feast, just as he has intruded himself on other occasions. Armed with cybernetic devices, we might collectively know more about everything and *individually* less about anything — except the field of our individual specialization, at least, as long as spe-

2. Ibid.
3. Ibid.

cialization outruns, as it now does, not only the development of communication channels, but also of the "receptors," that is, the willingness of the specialists to listen to anyone but themselves. For all the little we know about understanding, the quest for universality-through-cybernetics — the making of a self-steering, open-ended encyclopedia — might, one day, achieve its goal, thus postponing, *sine die,* the break between individual understanding and the collective knowledge. Again, it appears highly improbable that this approach will, within the lifetime of this generation, solve the social and political problems created by the "information explosion." On the contrary, taking our text from past experience, we are justified in assuming that the technological solutions now applied to political and social problems, posed by the proliferation of scientific and technological knowledge, will increase the already severe strains and stresses on the structure of society and individual personality.

The information-communication technologies are as ambiguous politically and socially as all other techniques. As a matter of fact, because of the great variety of their actual and potential applications, these particular techniques beckon an even larger number of uninvited guests than did the feast offered by previous innovations. As has always been the case, the foreseeable implications for the mental and physical health of the individual and the welfare of the community evoke but the slightest interest. Many billions have gone into the development and the marketing of these techniques. It is doubtful, to say the least, that more than 1/10 of one per mil of these billions has gone into the study of the likely impact of the computer-information technologies upon, for example, constitutional government, not to speak of studying the concrete measures that might have to be taken *now* to safeguard us against the unwanted fallout.

The historical environment of modern scientific-technological progress has been: (1) the last decade of the Long Peace which lasted from the defeat of Napoleon to 1914; (2) World War I; (3) the Bolshevik Revolution; (4) the West's vain attempt after World War I to create a stable world order; (5) the rise of German and Japanese totalitarianism; (6) the collapse of the free world market; (7) World War II; and (8) the Cold War. The red thread of continuity which links these right phases is the ever-increasing power of the state. The one incontestable result of two world wars and a score of lesser wars fought for the sake of freedom, national or personal, has been the strengthening of state power and the weakening of the private associations of life. In the old polities of the West, the state now takes a vastly greater share of the national product than it has ever taken in peacetime. Nearly all new states, irrespective of their formal constitutions, are dictatorships. Since 1917, communist power has expanded to one-third of the land surface and population of the globe.

Although these trends are said to be compensated for by increased "mass participation" and the diffusion of "political culture" among heretofore apolitical layers of the population, no one has as yet been able to show how, in the absence of a legitimate political opposition armed with its own means of communication, ruling political elites can be held accountable by the masses — not to speak of being turned out and replaced by another set of rulers. Of course, the "participating masses" might, if they can find a revolutionary elite of their own and possess themselves of adequate means of force, overthrow the incumbent government and, if they are so minded, even abolish the one-party state. But such revolutionary behavior cannot be mistaken for democratic process. Indeed, of late, such revolutionary behavior and its attendant disorders, frequently sanguinary, have become the norm in many countries which have discarded representative, parliamentary institutions or have failed, upon the attainment of statehood, to provide themselves with such institutions. Certainly, within the last fifty years, the cause of representative government and personal freedom has not prospered upon this earth. Certainly, too, the milieu in which the founding generation of modern science and technology attained the peak of its productivity has changed beyond recognition.

Science and technology themselves armed the forces of political and social change. Yet, no one can now say how, in the long run, science and technology will accommodate themselves to the new environment which they helped to create. It is now argued that they are politically and socially neutral, and that they will flourish under any political regime — as long as they receive their proper share of the national revenue and public deference accorded the ruling elite. This, too, is a hypothesis which awaits validation by future events. It is also being argued that science and technology are shaping their own culture which will supersede all other historical cultures together with their political and social institutions, and, more important still, that scientific treatment will remove the one human foible most disruptive to the steady and rational improvement of human society, namely, the individual power urge. Thus dominant science and technology are credited with a power of self-abnegation which has been a stranger to all dominant cultures of history. This hypothesis falls under the rubric: the end of the *political*. For reasons stated below, it seems an implausible hypothesis. In any case, it can be validated only a good many years from now. Not all utopias need be impracticable. Yet all utopias are subject to the attrition of imperfect realization. The sustenance of this particular utopia — eternal scientific-technological potency — might be consumed by those uninvited guests who bear false gifts, gorge themselves and, for good measure, break the crockery.

Second, for good and sufficient reasons that organism called man conforms to the life cycle. Such life cycles as, for example, infancy, adulthood, and senescence; wakefulness and sleep; birth and death are constants. In turn, these constants, that is, constants of the individual organism's behavior, are governed by (are variables of) cosmic constants — such as day and night and the cycle of the seasons. In the language of contemporary American sociology, an organism seeks to maintain its pattern. Our daily routine can be defined as a means for maintaining our pattern: most of us go to bed sometime at night and arise in the morning; eat and drink several times during the day; and pursue various scheduled kinds of waking activities, including work. In brief, we are creatures of habit. Habit develops inertia. Most things we do we do because we are habituated to do them. Our social habits are derived from organic needs. Organic needs reinforce social habits. Without this inertia no social structure could be created. Yet, it is this inertia which slows or impairs the responsiveness of a society to sudden changes of the environment, the fact notwithstanding that these changes may have been wrought by that society itself. It is my hypothesis that our society has reached this critical point now. Yet, the response of our society to the critical challenge of the environment is to keep on doing the very things which engendered the critical challenge. Routine response to the challenge of deleterious developments, flowing from scientific-technological solutions, is a recourse to other scientific-technological solutions. In brief, we expect autonomous science and technology to provide the curative measures needed to cope with the idiosyncrasies of their own creation.

Much has been written about the helplessness of modern man faced by the complexity of our civilization. In many ways, modern man is less helpless than his ancestors. He rejoices in many assured creature comforts. He does not lack security — if by security is meant a high degree of probability of being fed, clothed, and cared for in old age, and in many, though not in all, places of being able to read, hear, and express all kinds of opinions without having to fear a charge of heresy. Modern man is free to make up his mind about many things heretofore reserved to the arbitrament of ruling castes, and to do a great many things his ancestor might have wished to do and could not do. But modern man, too, is a creature of habits. He learned to place his reliance upon science and technology. He keeps on relying on the scientist and technologist to control environmental change.

This common habit is reinforced by the ever-growing prestige of the scientist and the technologist. It is they who are the symbolic figures of our civilization. They merit deference; they cannot do wrong. Thus, our society turns to them in its search for health and happiness. It asks them to remedy its ills, including those which the careless uses of science and technology brought upon it. In brief, scientists and technologists are being asked, as scientists and technologists, to deal with social, political, economic, and aesthetical issues, with which they — as scientists and technologists — are not and should not be concerned. We need not examine here the question as to whether scientists and technologists should also be moralists. The fact is that, nowadays, institutional training and professional norms do not predispose them to be moralists. Thus far, they have given what they have had to give without asking society what it would or should do with it — except for demanding that their products be used for the enhancement of their productivity. The pursuit of knowledge for its own sake and the highest professional ethics do not translate themselves, as a matter of course, into personal integrity and social responsibility. The alleged revulsion of individual scientists against the end uses of their product, especially warlike uses, cannot be taken conclusively as a proof to the contrary. Individual idiosyncrasies may account for this deviation from the noncommittal norm. Furthermore, these scruples do not bespeak a foresight more impressive than that of the average, unscientific man. If such belated concerns prove anything, it is that the judgment of scientists and technologists about the social and human consequences of their labors is even worse than that of the average man. This fact notwithstanding, modern society looks to science and technology to deliver it from those predicaments which are rooted in the misuses of science and technology. Not so surprisingly, science and technology, complying with the demands of our society, provide the only kind of solutions they can provide, namely, scientific-technological solutions.

But, one might ask, cannot more germaine expertise be brought to bear on the *social-political* problems spawned by *scientific-technological change?* Can the social sciences not provide the answers? Alas, in their present state, the social sciences are unlikely to do so, for they do not possess intellectual tools as powerful as those forged over the last 150 years by the natural sciences, and they are discarding their normative tradition without having developed a rigorous empiricism of their own. In brief, they are ceasing to be *moral* sciences. As always in an interregnum, conditions are disorderly. A new and happy synthesis might be in the making. At present, it is not visible. Certainly, it is not yet visibly effective.

In their present embarrassed state the social sciences, in general, and political science, in particular, are humbly turning for help to those whom they should firmly guide, namely, the natural sciences and their related technologies. Thus far, the result has been a shrinkage rather than a widening of the fields in which the social sciences were once supposed to be competent. Now, they increasingly restrict themselves to "problem areas" which lend themselves to investigation by quantifying techniques and technological devices, and abandon those which resist such rigorous treatment. So dedicated to selective empiricism, the social scientist needs to pretend that he knows less and cares less about society, himself included, than he really does. In some "problem areas," especially those of pressing concern here and now, this pretense seems excessively cumbersome, if not wasteful and ludicrous. It is as if the data that cannot be measured were deemed not only incommensurate but also irrelevant data — as if the data that cannot be ground into the computer were data that do not matter. In brief, it is the tool of the investigator that sets the intellectual purpose of investigation. The findings are implicit in the mechanical device, its scope and limitations. To paraphrase Professor McLuhan: the technology *is* the message. To paraphrase de la Rochefoucauld: *La technique a des raisons que la raison ne connaît pas.* Put less arcanely: the voices of reason which cannot be put on the magnetic tape do not speak to a rising generation of social-political mechanics.

Third, the conception of the West's political ideas and the establishment of the West's political institutions preceded the Industrial Revolution. They antedate the scientific-technological revolution by, at least, three generations. The deviant philosophy of Marxism is grounded intellectually in eighteenth-century economic thought and, since it never prescribed political institutions of any kind, it is rooted spiritually in the utopianism of even more remote ages. The one and only political *innovation* of the last fifty years — the age of the scientific-technological revolution — has been totalitarianism. Indeed, it was scientific-technological progress which supplied the tools of totalitarian rule. Since only

183

total states can make total war, modern science and technology have fathered the peculiar style of modern international conflict. Conversely, this peculiar style has powerfully stimulated scientific-technological creativity. The old saying that "war is the father of all things," has never been the whole truth about material progress. In this century, it has been as close to truth as it has ever been. Although this sparse summary stints the immense complexity of the phenomenon, it circumscribes the contemporary problem of politics. Is the totalitarian state the one and only political answer to the exigencies of scientific-technological progress? Can only the power of the total state host the invited guests and eject the uninvited ones?

Not so surprisingly, the mushrooming state bureaucracies do not care to take issue with the "inevitable" expansion of state power, the one and only alternative for dealing with the "complexities of modern life." It is, however, surprising that the West's intellectual community which, for centuries, stood against the arbitrary power of the state, has reversed its position. Thus far, statistics are not available for determining accurately the attitudes of the Western intelligentsia towards state and man. The amorphousness of the intellectual-academic community precludes agreement on exactly who belongs to it and, hence, on representative attitudes. Yet, if the publications of leading scholars in most highly rated universities, the output of the most noted novelists and playwrights, and the drift of intellectual magazines can be said to express dominant attitudes, then the alienation of the Western intelligentsia from the ideals of representative government cannot be in doubt. The great majority of the most prestigious members of the intellectual-academic community either accept or advocate the expansion of central — "executive" — power and are either indifferent to or denigrate the role of parliamentary institutions as checks upon state power.

Admittedly, this summary indictment slights the lone protester as well as the uncommitted who goes quietly about his business — and awaits events. Yet, the lone protester and the inarticulate noncommitted do not set the style of the age. It is never easy to gauge in one's own age so volatile a substance as is the prevailing intellectual atmosphere. Stepping back by one hundred years, such an assessment becomes much easier. Indeed, there has been a fundamental change: the juxtaposition of liberal philosophy then and now suffices to make the point. Functionalism has carried the day: it is not meaningful, that is, scientific, to ask what man *is*, and to ask what is man's purpose upon the earth. Since first causes and ultimate consequences do not lend themselves to rigorous empirical treatment, it is meaningful, that is, scientific, to ask what man *does* and *how* he does it. Only insights thus derived can be verified empirically. Only from empirically verified statements can predictive theories be built. Armed with such predictive theories, it is possible to plan human activities in such a way that men will be able to do better whatever it is that they are doing. Here, theory becomes somewhat confused: Exactly what are the criteria for "better"? In general, these criteria are derived from such ethically neutral concepts of management science such as "effectiveness" and "efficiency."

To be sure, there is wide agreement that men ought to lead happier lives. But wherein lies happiness? This is another of those questions that, susceptible as they might be to rigorous formulation, do not lend themselves to empirical investigation. Within the limits of sociological empiricism, the ethical purpose of the social system shrinks to the axiomatic goodness of its smooth operation and maintenance — of its own survival. The political expression of survival ethics is the welfare-consensus state. In such a state, there is no need for political parties which, as brokers, stand between the people and their government. Since political parties can no longer play a functional role, there is no need for political ideologies. Since all the great ideologies of the nineteenth century were conceived in ignorance of modern science and technology, they have become obsolescent and, operationally, useless. Thus, politics now confines itself to the management of interest groups and of their shifting coalitions. Now, the range of political debate has narrowed to discreet technical, functional issues, such as, for example, the efficient management of transportation or educational systems; rates of communal services; and the provision of recreational facilities. The age of deep ideological cleavages has ended. Ideology is dead or dying.

The last flicker of the ideological conflagration cast upon this, the emerging society, a mellow afterglow: the society of luxury socialism — the society of plenty on equal shares, governed by the meritocracy of technical experts — is within sight, rid of the searing issues and fighting slogans of its predecessor. All it needs to do in order to survive forever is to tend and to perfect its more or less self-regulating controls.

Thus, the question before contemporary political science is how moral philosophy can be brought to bear upon political and social problems created by scientific-technological progress; how the facts of scientific-technological progress can be made relevant to moral philosophy; and how moral philosophy can design a strategy for the uses of scientific-technological productivity. This is an ambitious purpose; but, in the light of the above discussion, it is neither an impossible nor a trivial one.

Science and technology cannot jump over their own shadow. Now, they are being asked to do that. The result has been that our society is seeking to cure its ills by taking more of that same medicine which has not only proven ineffective, but has further aggravated the condition of the patient. The agents of destruction — the uninvited guests — will prevail as long as the *political* does not leap across the shadow of science and technology and assume that sovereign direction which, cowed by pretentious scientism, it has let slip out of its hands. Political science, if it can legitimately claim to be a science, must be a moral science. To be sure, there is the need for exploring empirical relationships and for employing the appropriate methodology in the pursuit of knowledge. But this pursuit, lest it go nowhere, needs to be guided and inspired by the idea of man as moral man. If we do not bestir ourselves now, our political institutions will dissolve into the political nothingness of totalitarianism.

HAROLD D. LASSWELL

Policy Problems of a Data-Rich Civilization

No doubt we can anticipate at least some of the policy problems of a civilization whose stocks of promptly retrievable data are vast and growing. If we were to carry on this exploration in a rigorously systematic fashion it would be necessary to canvass the world social process as a whole, and to give full consideration to trends, conditions, and projections for every territorial component and for the principal value-institution sectors of every society. In this way attention would be directed to the potential impact of the shaping and sharing of information on the shaping and sharing of every other valued outcome in human affairs.

We could use as a comprehensive model of the human social process the following: *Human beings* seeking to optimize *values* (preferred outcomes) through *institutions* utilizing *resources*. The giving and receiving of information is a preferred outcome (the *enlightenment* value); and if we examine the aggregate flow of information gathering, storing, retrieving, processing, and dissemination, we might draw up an annual balance sheet of the *gross enlightenment outcome* of the world (or any lesser unit). If we subtract the information losses (from destruction of information), it is possible to arrive at a *net* outcome figure. The *accumulation* (investment) total would be the amount of newly stored information in data-

From Harold D. Lasswell, "Policy Problems of a Data-Rich Civilization," *International Federation for Documentation, 31st Meeting and Congress, Proceedings of the 1965 Congress*, Washington, D.C., October 7–16, 1965. In cooperation with the American Documentation Institute (Washington, D.C.: Spartan Books, and London: Macmillan and Company, Ltd., 1965). Copyright © 1965 by The National Academy of Sciences.

Mr. Lasswell is Professor of Law and Political Science, Yale University.

banks, libraries, and other documentary collections, plus the increment of expert knowledge memorized by the scientific and scholarly community. The *enjoyment* would be the volume of information used by decision- and choice-makers during the year. (Note that, unlike some valued assets, an information re-use does not necessarily deplete the asset.)

As our civilization of science and technology moves toward universality, the rapid enlarging of its capital stock of available knowledge introduces repercussions in every value-institution sector. Problems arise whenever changes occur in the expectation map in reference to which past value demands have been partially stabilized by individual and group participants in the social process. By revising the map of expectation, the act of accumulating information introduces an accelerating tendency toward further innovation and possible instability. We might take the various value-institution sectors in sequence and attempt to foretell emerging problems. This would make it necessary to examine government, politics, and law; and also to explore the network of institutions specialized to enlightenment (mass media, research agencies, storage and retrieval facilities, for example). We would assess economic institutions (production, distribution, investment, consumption of wealth); institutions of well-being (concerned with safety, health, and comfort); institutions specialized to vocational, professional, and artistic skill; affection (family, friendship, loyalty); respect (social classes); rectitude (ethics, religion).

As a selective device we focus on three large policy areas that cut across the entire social context: world security, individuality, democracy.

Implications for World Security

As the world's stock of information increases, will the prospects of world security improve? The key point to be made in this connection is that big-scale information retrieval easily favors the making of rapid, highly centralized decisions. However, the decisions that most vitally affect world security are not made by a globally inclusive agency of public order. On the contrary; whatever the words in which international obligations are phrased, the effective decision-makers of Moscow, Peking, Washington, and other capitals do *not* expect to be able to rely on an efficient system that maintains at least minimum public order. Hence there is not prompt and open access to vital information. The nation-states will continue to seek to monopolize rather than share information which is supposed to bear immediately on national security. Great ingenuity will continue to be exercised in attempts to misinform the intelligence services of rival states.

Perhaps surprise will become more difficult as world social and political data are more inclusive, and cross checks are improved by means of better simulation models. On the positive side it will be possible in a data-rich world to spell out in far greater detail than hitherto the net gains of worldwide cooperation.

We must make full allowance for the strength of forces that favor monopolies that block the dissemination of information to the entire world community. In a world divided by the expectation of war and other forms of collective violence, the control of information falls seasily in the hands of governmental, party, or other private monopolies. In small countries of high economic, social, and cultural levels of activity, parochialism is diluted by rather high per capita frequencies of foreign travel, message exchange, and transnational publications. In world security terms, however, this is not the most significant trend. The modern communications revolution has been unable to universalize the outlook of mankind. The new instruments have been utilized by the managers of the information media to overcome localism. However, *the chief gainer from reduced localism has been, not a common world perspective, but intermediate attitudes of a more parochial character.* The great continental units — like the U.S.A., Russia, and mainland China — absorb the focus of attention of the overwhelming percentage of their population. National self-references rise more sharply than do more inclusive references. The flow of information is controlled to perpetuate the patterns of segregated access that correspond to the value-institution structure of a divided world arena.

It has been suggested that heroic policies must be adopted if the parochializing and divisive consequences of the present control of information are to be overcome. Drastic proposals include: give a World Communication Network legal access to all inhabitants of the globe (and if a regime in power is in opposition, engage in subversive circulation of tiny receivers); give a World Board of Education control of an hour a day of the attention of all school children; arrange for at least a year's education abroad before adolescence for all children, and another year between adolescence and young adulthood. It is perhaps unnecessary to point out that these proposals are at present unwelcome almost everywhere. More immediate policy suggestions favor the self-interest of scientists and scholars by proposing that facilities be greatly multiplied to allow foreign travel, study, and information services for at least ten percent of all professionally trained people each year.

Unfortunately it cannot be asserted with confidence that scientists and scholars will be more effective than the public at large in breaking through the divisive structure of world affairs. Top flight scientists and scholars have long distinguished themselves for their humane and enlightened approach to the problems of man. However, most of their less successful colleagues and competitors have shrewdly adapted themselves to the professional opportunities of a divided and nationalistic world arena. The inference would appear to be that *so long as those who specialize in the advancement of knowledge depend for support on sources that seem to benefit from a divided globe, the vested and sentimental interest in division will in fact continue.*

Implications for Individuality

We turn now to a brief examination of the implications of a data-rich civilization for individuality. It would be congenial to most scholars, at least, to be able to demonstrate that individuality varies directly with society's stock of information. Does not a fuller map of past trends and conditions, and of future probabilities, multiply the bases of inference for the creative imagination of mankind, and thereby provide more direct and indirect opportunities for human capabilities to find expression in socially acceptable diversity?

Unfortunately we cannot propose an affirmative answer without assessing the weight of counteracting factors. (1) New information may be employed to concentrate the management of motivation in the hands of a few, thereby reducing the flow of spontaneous creativity in the entire society. (2) Individuality (and creative expression) depends on more than simple exposure to information. An essential requisite is a motivation that welcomes and does not turn away from perceptions of possible change. (3) There is the question whether individuality can withstand the invasions of privacy that seem inextricably interwoven with a data-rich civilization. Let us consider each of these points in turn.

(1) It is to be assumed that the study of factors that condition human response will become progressively more refined, and therefore more available for manipulators of political, economic, and indeed all collective responses. We do not doubt, for example, that in popularly governed states rival parties and candidates will take full advantage of the current

stock of knowledge about the influence of culture, class, interest, personality, and crisis level factors on response. Pre-tests will provide information about audience predisposition toward contingent choices of issue and appeal. Rival political manipulators will continue to uncover new conditioning factors that will enable them to exert a relatively strong impact on the target (at least the first time around). While it must be conceded that the chief protection of public judgment from monopoly management is *competition,* a further safeguard is *open disclosure of knowledge about the predispositions of voters, legislators, administrators, or judges.* If popular government depends on an informed opinion, a category of particularly important information for everyone is knowledge of how he can be manipulated and thereby deprived of the degree of choice that one might have.

I note that *disclosing information about how they are manipulated to those who are manipulated* is a policy that can be applied far beyond the arena of politics. The policy may include permission to technicians and managers to use new knowledge of motivation for a short time prior to disclosing it to the target audience. The advantage of initial use is that it provides an inducement to research and to the cultivation of knowledge. Political parties can be required to turn over their data and simulation models after elections. Business enterprises, whether private or public, can be required to disclose their merchandising information regularly in order to put the consumer on guard. Charitable fund raising and missionary data can also be made public.

True, one does not necessarily alter one's opinion because he becomes aware of the factors that usually shape it. But if one's factor-determiners are continually brought to attention, the likelihood is improved that an individual will ask himself whether his response is, after all, satisfactory when reviewed in the light of all the information at his disposal. Consider Mr. A, who is reminded that his party, candidate, and issue responses can be attributed to his Republican or Democratic family tradition; to frequent association with neighbors and business associates of one partisan coloration; to selective viewing, listening, and reading of one-sided media; to local favors granted by the political machine (and the like). Mr. A may recognize his determiners and go on responding to them. Then again, he may begin to wonder, and thereby become more sensitive to other factors.

Although it is usually said that information about courts, commissions, legislatures, or electorates is important for purposes of prediction, this is not necessarily the chief objective. It may be argued that the principal social purpose served by information about motivating factors is insight; that is, making available to the chooser knowledge about his dispositions which, when recognized, may lead him to reflect critically on the appropriateness of his behavior as judge, official, or leader.

(2) We have said that information may be misperceived; and that acquired mechanisms of misperception can reflect a deep motivation to turn away from innovation and to abandon any attempt at creativeness. Both the advancement and the effective application of knowledge in a process of decision are conditioned by automatic modes of perception and selection. Clinical psychology, in particular, emphasizes the point that perceptions and choices are often made rigid by defense mechanisms that inhibit the individual from taking note of new events or of entertaining new options of thought. It is not to be overlooked that these defense mechanisms have positive as well as negative functions, since they protect the person from anxieties aroused when earlier conflicting drives are mobilized. The cost of new perceptions or of novel options is thereby made too high in sectors that are taboo.

Is it to be taken for granted that the children and youth of tomorrow will be socialized (educated) for the encouragement of novelty and creativity? Many of us would be skeptical of the educational programs of totalitarian societies. But the future of relatively open "mass societies" cannot be viewed with unqualified optimism. As the dangers of "mass society" become more obvious, is it not probable that influential elements in any state will seek to reduce erratic crowd responses by aiming education at more perfect indoctrination, especially in reference to the key symbols, doctrines, and rites of public policy?

Already we see the outline of techniques that, if stringently employed for indoctrination purposes, can circumscribe both the acquisition of selected categories of information and imaginative new uses of knowledge. Combinations of hypnosis with drug-induced states and the use of learning machines can evidently specialize the stores of information put at the command of individuals, and circumscribe their potentialities for retrieval. Sheer quantity of information does not guarantee wide-ranging use if either retrieval or processing is subject to crippling automatic mechanisms of regulation.

(3) Another factor whose impact on individuality (especially creativity) is worth considering is individual privacy. Although the issues are not in principle new, a data-rich world can have individual records of unheard-of detail promptly available. Shall we attempt to bar the gathering and storage of specified classes of information? Shall limits be set

192

on who shall have access to personal data, for what purposes, and by what procedures?

It is conceivable that human beings will undergo general revulsion against the invasions of privacy that become more common as man's auxiliary brains are put to more and more detailed use. A few years ago when modern psychiatry was first applied to the study of politicians, the London *Times* editorialized in a sardonic mood that in the future campaign biographers would feel constrained to demonstrate that even in the cradle the candidate had lived a blameless life. Will the implacable demand for data about the decades, years, months, weeks, days, hours, and minutes of career development require, in addition to gynecological and obstetrical data, a record of everybody's feeding schedule, toilet behavior, and test performances at frequent intervals? Are we going to take literally the maxim that whatever concerns man is necessarily of concern to mankind's storers of information?

I suspect that there is no limit to the data that may be regarded by some scientist as of research importance. There seems to be no clear way to prescribe a limit; hence the mighty man-machine tide of information will probably swell and swell. Only think of all the psychologists, sociologists, physicians, nurses, welfare workers, child specialists, educators, tax collectors, police officers, salesmen, creditor agents, personnel administrators (and so on and on) who will continue to collect and collect and collect.

Reflection suggests that the most likely areas of policy regulation are not information obtaining or storage, but access. Consider briefly a few past policies of restricted dissemination.

It is generally agreed that great damage can be done to children and young people if certain kinds of information are made public, even to restricted audiences. The stigma of illegitimacy is an example, or of interracial or intercast parentage where these matters are taken seriously. Protection is given to family medical records, especially when a traditionally low-respect blemish is involved (idiocy), or when a low-rectitude involvement is implied (syphilis). It is common to destroy or seal records of early delinquency or failure.

Adults also obtain the protection of non-disclosure, though the policy is less stringent than with children. In a society that affirms its commitment to human dignity, whatever causes anguish without significant social gain tends to be avoided. One historic policy is designed to obtain for the community the benefit of allowing people to make a new start, unencumbered by ever-present reminders of the past. In countries where great new resources lay idle until labor and capital were added, the tendency was to overlook a man's past in the informality of everyday life and also in official records. People were not asked to identify the eye color of their grandparents before they could get a job or a driver's license. In a world whose established systems were widely viewed as immoral, the refugee might have a seemingly crooked or contemptible past; but it was felt that in a land of opportunity he might very well make good. In all societies some form of reprive or statute of limitations seems to operate as a means of giving hope to the deprived classes. Thus prisons may be cleared at the birth of a royal heir, and political prisoners released on the coronation of a new monarch.

As the data-rich civilization closes in, these public policies are almost certain to become obsolete, as indeed they are nearly everywhere today. If we begin to open up new zones of settlement in outer space on natural or artificial satellites, these perspectives and policies may revive. But the trend is more likely to be in the opposite direction, emphasizing the area of careful selection of personnel on the basis of exhaustive information. Space explorers and colonists will presumably be carefully selected, owing to the cost of transfer.

It may be that the coming years will witness a drastically new approach to the problem of protecting self-esteem from the crippling effect of unnecessary deprivation, and of obtaining for society the advantages of a buoyant, self-confident, congenial contributor to human relations and to the cultivation of resources. Instead of adopting the strategy of privacy, even secrecy, which in any case seems most applicable to a rather isolated frontier community, a contrasting strategy of insight may win acceptance.

By the *strategy of insight* several things are meant. A data-rich society can provide information that reduces the false pride of any individual, family, or community. The distorting effect of facts such as illegitimacy, a history of mental disorder or of secret vice comes from the ego's sense of isolation and vulnerability. It seems quite possible to change such an outlook by enlarging the scope of accessible information about man and society. As we push our data back through the years (while also carrying it forward), the objective, scientific point of view toward psychology and culture will become more widely shared. Like old families, large community groups will discover the existence of closets full of skeletons — of criminals, mentally disordered, defective, and illegitimate — as well as men and women of eminence. *If the educational system takes care to train the individual to see his enormous potentialities, and to discover the many strategies by which a specific negative characteristic can be overcome or compensated, the resulting personality systems can be expected to do without much privacy.*

Implications for Democracy

Although our discussion of security and individuality has had many side-implications for democracy, the problem has not been given the direct treatment that is warranted by its importance.

We are told that a vast system of documentation that relies on automatic methods is almost certain to possess built-in biases that affect public policy in the direction of centralization, concentration, monopoly, regimentation, and monocracy. These biases are described as consequences of the seeming advantages gained by operating the technicalities of storage and retrieval in ways that obtain economies of scale.

The analysis suggests further that reliance on accumulated documentation establishes an attitude that, when over-emphasized — as is bound to happen in a data-rich civilization — is dangerous to genuine power sharing. The reference is to an *attitude of inquiry, exaggerated at the expense of commitment, conviction, and argumentation.* The attitude of inquiry includes the tendency to translate statements of preference or determination, when challenged, into a demand for further factual investigations. Hence the style of problem solving seems factual, objective, and emotionally calm. It becomes bad form to insist on arguing at length in support of a goal value, a policy objective, or a strategy. Hence the apparent philosophic composure of such a decision process. It operates with a built-in short circuit toward fact-form inquiry or manipulation.

However — the analysis proceeds — surface composure of this kind actually works in favor of the established system of public order. In totalitarian regimes this is obvious, since the devices of documentation are employed as instruments of planning to keep the top elites in place. In non-totalitarian regimes the consequences are less evident. But the most sophisticated programs are nevertheless likely to be initiated and run by and for the benefit of top elites in politics, business, and other positions. The analysis suggests that the procedure is consciously or unconsciously slanted for the perpetuation of the oligarchical or monocratic advantage of those on whom the technical personnel must depend for safety, income, and other value inputs.

Are there strategies at hand that may neutralize or even reverse tendencies of the kind? The inference is that there must be *explicit training in*

195

commitment. Willingness to come to a decision and act as a responsible leader must be rewarded in the educational process and not treated as an indication of an unsophisticated perspective. Similarly, *rewards must be forthcoming in the policy-forming and -executing processes* throughout society if temporizing and acquiescence are to be met by counter-effective forces. This implies genuine participation in power sharing, even in situations where unexamined tradition allows important decisions to be the prerogative of a few.

Another way to formulate what has been said here is to say that modern documentation technique strengthens the tendencies in every large scale society toward bureaucratism, and that *realistic awareness of the pervasiveness of the danger* is itself a prerequisite to the adoption of strategies to nullify the threat.

The case for the cultivation of decisiveness is totally insufficient as a strategy of democracy unless it is joined with command over comprehensive information. In a relatively open society it is conceivable that control of the basic stocks of information is effectively pluralized, and is not allowed to gravitate into oligarchic or monocratic hands. A *policy of pluralism implies that the same stocks of data are differently used and interpreted by influential voices in the decision process.* Military experts must be open to challenge, not only by military experts but by civilian officials; executive authority by legislative authority; government office holders must be open to equally informed criticism by party experts; party experts must be open to adequately grounded criticism put forward by the non-power sectors of society — economic, scientific, medical, ecclesiastical, educational, journalistic.

Issues of preference and volition, not of information, rise at many places in a problem-solving policy process. There are the questions that come up in the *clarification of goal:* shall we postulate moving toward a world of human dignity or a world of indignity, of caste supremacy? Some questions arise in connection with the *examination of historical trends:* how far back and how detailed shall our inquiries go, and how complete shall our attempts be to empathize with past generations? Questions occur in the scientific *quest to explain* the social and physical process: how willing shall we be to sacrifice life in experiments and in field expeditions? Questions also relate to the *projection* of future developments, and the *invention, evaluation, and selection of alternatives:* how much risk of loss shall we take in the hope of how much gain?

If an information-rich civilization is to share with its members a common image of past, present, and future, it must find effective ways of providing *comprehensive, selective, and realistic experiences of the whole map of knowledge and informed conjecture.* As a symbol of what is required I have sometimes spoken of a social planetarium adapted to the orientation needs of every region, nation, province, city, locality, and pluralistic component of the world community. Such a series of rooms, buildings, presentations would provide alternative interpretations of the past of civilization and of potential goals and strategies of future development.

We are suggesting that, *if the many pluralistic elements in modern industrial nations seize promptly on modern methods of documentation, it will be possible to sustain political initiatives in the decision process of sufficient intensity to support a public order in which power is genuinely shared.* Shared data means shared power; a monopoly of data means a monopoly of power.

Our exploration of some of the policy problems of a data-rich civilization suggests the wisdom of anticipating as early as possible the implication of these emergents for such problem areas as world security, individuality, and democracy. Once more we confirm and apply the maxim: knowledge is power.

ERICH FROMM

Humanizing a Technological Society

If we are now to consider the possibility of humanizing the industrial society as it has developed in the second Industrial Revolution, we must begin by considering those institutions and methods which for economic as well as psychological reasons cannot be done away with without the total disruption of our society. These elements are: (1) The large-scale centralized enterprise as it has developed in the last decades in government, business, universities, hospitals, etc. This process of centralization is still continuing, and soon almost all major purposeful activities will be carried on by large systems. (2) Large-scale planning within each system, which results from the centralization. (3) Cybernation, that is cybernetics and automation, as the major theoretical and practical principle of control, with the computer as the most important element in automation.

But not only these three elements are here to stay. There is another element which appears in all social systems: the system Man. . . . [This] does not mean that human nature is not malleable; it means that it allows only a limited number of potential structures, and confronts us with certain ascertainable alternatives. The most important alternative as far as the technological society is concerned is the following: if man is passive, bored, unfeeling, and one-sidedly cerebral, he develops patho-

Mr. Fromm is Adjunct Professor of Psychology at New York University.

198

logical symptoms like anxiety, depression, depersonalization, indifference to life, and violence . . .

It is important to stress this point, since most planners deal with the human factor as one which could adapt itself to any condition without causing any disturbances.

The possibilities which confront us are few and ascertainable. One possibility is that we continue in the direction we have taken. This would lead to such disturbances of the total system that either thermonuclear war or severe human pathology would be the outcome. The second possibility is the attempt to change that direction by force or violent revolution. This would lead to the breakdown of the whole system and [to] violence and brutal dictatorship as a result. The third possibility is the humanization of the system, in such a way that it serves the purpose of man's well-being and growth, or in other words, his life process. In this case, the central elements of the second Industrial Revolution will be kept intact . . .

My intention is to discuss the steps which, to me, are the most important ones: (1) Planning which includes the system Man and which is based on norms which follow from the examination of the optimal functioning of the human being. (2) Activation of the individual by methods of grass-roots activity and responsibility, by changing the present methods of alienated bureaucracy into one of humanistic management. (3) Changing of the consumption pattern in the direction of consumption that contributes to activation and discourages "passivation." (4) The emergence of new forms of psychospiritual orientation and devotion, which are equivalents of the religious systems of the past . . .

[All] planning is directed by value judgments and norms, whether the planners are aware of it or not. This holds true also of all computer planning; both the selection of facts which are fed into the computer as well as the programing imply value judgments. If I want to maximize economic output, my facts as well as my program differ from what they would be if I wanted to maximize human well-being, in terms of joy, interest in work, etc. In the latter case other facts are considered and the program is different.

Several serious questions arise here: How can one have any knowledge about human values except by accepting the traditional ones, which at least have the validation of consensus or are accepted as a matter of personal taste or bias? . . . I have referred to the fact that the state of well-being of man can be described as empirically and objectively as the state of ill-being; conditions conducive to well-being can be ascertained, as can those leading to ill-being, both physical and mental. A study of the system Man can lead to the acceptance of objectively valid values, on the grounds that they lead to the optimal functioning of the system or, at least, that if we realize the possible alternatives, the humanist norms would be accepted as preferable to their opposites by most sane people.

Whatever the merits of the source of the validity of humanist norms, the general aim of a humanized industrial society can be thus defined: the change of the social, economic, and cultural life of our society in such a way that it stimulates and furthers the growth and aliveness of man rather than cripples it; that it activates the individual rather than making him passive and receptive; that our technological capacities serve man's growth. If this is to be, we must regain control over the economic and social system; man's will, guided by his reason, and by his wish for optimal aliveness, must make the decisions.

Given these general aims, what is the procedure of humanistic planning? *Computers should become a functional part in a life-oriented social system and not a cancer which begins to play havoc and eventually kills the system.* Machines or computers must become means for ends which are determined by man's reason and will. The values which determine the selection of facts and which influence the programing of the computer must be gained on the basis of the knowledge of human nature, its various possible manifestations, its optimal forms of development, and the real needs conducive to this development. That is to say, man, not technique, must become the ultimate source of values; optimal human development and not maximal production the criterion for all planning.

Aside from this, planning in the field of economics must be extended to the whole system; furthermore, the system Man must be integrated into the whole social system. Man, as the planner, must be aware of the role of man as part of the whole system. Just as man is the only case of life being aware of itself, man as a system builder and analyzer must make himself the object of the system he analyzes. *This means that the knowledge of man, his nature, and the real possibilities of its manifestations must become one of the basic data for any social planning.*

What has been said thus far about planning was based on the theoretical assumption that the planners were essentially determined by their wish for the optimal welfare of society and the individuals which make it up. But, unfortunately, in practice such an assumption cannot be made.

200

(I am, of course, not speaking about the *ideas* planners have about their own motivations. They, like most men, believe their motives to be rational and moral. Most men need to have such rationalizations [ideologies] for their actions partly in order to support themselves by the feeling of moral righteousness, partly in order to deceive others about their real motivations.) On the level of government planning, the personal interests of the politicians often interfere with their integrity and hence with their capacity for humanist planning. This danger can be reduced only by a much more active participation of the citizen in the decision-making process, and by finding ways and methods by which government planning is controlled by those for whom the planning is done.

Should then government planning be further reduced and most planning, including that in the public sector, be left to the big corporations? The arguments for this idea are that the big corporations are not burdened with outmoded procedures and are not dependent on fluctuating political pressures; that they are more advanced in system analysis, immediate application of research to technique; and that they are guided by men who have more objectivity because they do not have to fight every few years in election campaigns for their right to continue their work. Most importantly, management and system analysis being now one of the most advanced types of activities, it stands to reason that it will attract many of the most advanced minds, not only in terms of intelligence but also in terms of a vision of human well-being. These and many other arguments are very persuasive but not convincing with regard to two crucial points: First, the corporation operates for profit, although very modified in comparison with the profit interest of the nineteenth-century entrepreneur, often interferes with the best interests of the community. Second, the private corporation is not subject to even that small control to which government is subject in a democratic system. (If one would object to this by saying that the corporation is controlled by the market, i.e., indirectly by the consumer, one would ignore the fact that the tastes and desires of the consumer are largely manipulated by the corporation.) To believe in the wisdom and good will of the management is not a sufficient guarantee that the majority might not plan in accordance with impersonal technical feasibility rather than for the sake of human development. Precisely because the more conventionally minded managers do not lack good will, but rather imagination and vision of a fully human life, they are even more dangerous, from the standpoint of humanistic planning. In fact, their personal decency makes them more immune to doubts about the methods of their planning. For these reasons, I do not share the optimism expressed by John Kenneth Galbraith and others. I propose that corporation planning also should be subject to controls, by the government and by independent bodies of those who are subjects of their planning.

. . . [One] basic requirement for his well-being is to be active, in the sense of the productive exercise of all [man's] faculties; that one of the most pathogenic features in our society is the trend 'to make man passive, by depriving him of the chance of active participation in the affairs of his society, in the enterprise in which he works, and, in fact, although more hidden, in his personal affairs. This "passivation" of man is partly due to the "alienated bureaucratic" method used in all centralized enterprises.

Here, as so often, people are confronted by a confusing false dichotomy. They believe that the choice is between an anarchic system without any organization and control and, on the other hand, the kind of bureaucracy which is typical both for contemporary industrialism and even more so for the Soviet system. But this alternative is by no means the only one, and we have other options. The option I have in mind is that between the "humanistic bureaucratic" or "humanistic management" method and the "alienated bureaucratic" method by which we conduct our affairs.

This alienated bureaucratic procedure can be characterized in several ways. First of all, it is a one-way system; orders, suggestions, planning emanate from the top and are directed to the bottom of the pyramid. There is no room for the individual's initiative. Persons are "cases," whether welfare cases or medical cases, or, whatever the frame of reference is, cases which can all be put down on a computer card without those individual features which designate the difference between a "person" and a "case."

Our bureaucratic method is irresponsible, in the sense that it does not "respond" to the needs, views, requirements of an individual. This irresponsibility is closely related to the case-character of the person who becomes an "object" of the bureaucracy. One cannot respond to a *case* but one can respond to a *person*. This irresponsibility of the bureaucrat has another aspect which has been a feature of bureaucracy for a long time. The bureaucrat, feeling himself part of the bureaucratic machine, most of all wishes not to take responsibility, that is to say, to make decisions for which he could be criticized. He tries to avoid making any decisions which are not clearly formulated by his case rules and, if in doubt, he sends the person to another bureaucrat who, in turn, does the same . . . Our bureaucratic method gives the individual the feeling that there is nothing which he can initiate and organize without the help of the bureaucratic machine. As a result, it paralyzes initiative and creates a deep sense of impotence. The basic principle of the humanistic management method is that, in spite of the bigness of the enterprises, centralized planning, and cybernation, the individual participant asserts himself toward the managers, circumstances, and machines, and ceases to be a powerless particle which has no active part in the process. Only by such affirmation of his will can the energies of the individual be liberated and his mental balance be restored.

The same principle of humanistic management can also be expressed in this way: While in alienated bureaucracy all power flows from above downward, in humanistic management there is a two-way street; the "subjects" of the decision made above respond according to their own will and concerns; their response not only reaches the top decision makers but forces them to respond in turn. The "subjects" of decision making have a right to challenge the decision makers. Such a challenge would first of all require a rule that if a sufficient number of "subjects" demanded that the corresponding bureaucracy (on whatever level) answer questions, explain its procedures, the decision makers would respond to the demand . . .

The first objection probably is that the type of active participation of the "subjects" would be incompatible with efficient centralized management and planning. This objection is plausible (a) provided one does not have any compelling reason to think that the present method of alienated bureaucracy is pathogenic; (b) if one thinks only of the tried and proven methods and shies away from imaginative new solutions; (c) if one insists that even if one could find new methods, the principle of maximal efficiency must never be given up even for a time. If, on the other hand, one . . . recognizes the grave danger for the total system of our society inherent in our bureaucratic methods, these objections are not as compelling as they are to those who are satisfied with the operation of our present system.

More specifically, if one recognizes the difficulties and does not start out with the conviction that they are unsurmountable, one will begin to examine the problems concretely and in detail. Here, too, one may arrive at the conclusion that the dichotomy between maximal centralization and complete decentralization presents an unnecessary polarization, that one can deal with the concept of *optimal* centralization and *optimal* grass-roots participation. Optimal centralization would be the degree of centralization which is necessary for effective large-scale organization and planning; optimal participation would be the participation which does not make centralized management impossible, yet permits the participants the optimum of responsible participation. This formulation is obviously rather general and not sufficient as a basis for taking immediate steps. If a problem of such magnitude emerges in the application of scientific knowledge to technique, the engineer is not discouraged; he recognizes the necessity of research which will result in the solution of the problem. But as soon as we deal with human problems, such difficulties tend to discourage most people or they flatly state that "it cannot be done."

We have, indeed, an unbounded imagination and initiative for solving technical problems, but a most restricted imagination when we deal with human problems. Why is this so? An obvious answer is that we do not have the knowledge in the field of the science of man that we have in the natural sciences and in technique. But this answer is not convincing; why don't we have the necessary knowledge? Or, and this is even more to the point, why don't we apply the knowledge we do have? Nothing can be *proved* without further study, but I am convinced that to find a practical solution for the integration of optimal centralization and optimal decentralization will be less difficult than to find technical solutions for space travel. The real answer why this kind of research is not done lies in the fact that, considering our present priorities, our interest in finding humanely more acceptable solutions to our social organization is only feeble. Nevertheless, while emphasizing the need for research, we must not forget that there has already been a good deal of experimentation and discussion about these problems going on in the last decades. Both in the field of industrial psychology and management science, one finds a number of valuable theoretical discussions and experiments.

Another objection, often combined with the previous one, says that as long as there is an effective control of decision making on the political level, there is no need for active participation in a corporation, since it will be properly supervised by the legislative and executive branches of the government. This objection does not take into account the fact that today government and the corporations are already so interwoven that it is difficult to say who controls whom — furthermore, that government decisions themselves are not under effective control by the citizens. But even if there existed a satisfactory active participation of the citizens in the political process, as it is suggested here, the corporation itself must become responsive to the will, not only of the participants, but of the public at large inasmuch as it is affected by the decisions of the corpora-tion. If such direct control over the corporation does not exist, it will be very difficult for the government to exercise power over the private sector of the system.

Another objection will point out that the double responsibility in decision making which is proposed here will be a source of endless friction between the top and the "subjects" and will be ineffective for this psychological reason. Talking about the problem in an abstract sense, we may easily find it formidable, but once such changes are ac-cepted, the resulting conflicts will be far less sharp and insoluble than they are if one looks at the picture in an abstract way. After all, the managers have an interest in performing, and so have the participants in an enterprise. As soon as the bureaucrat becomes "vulnerable," that is to say, begins to respond to desires and claims from those subject to him, both sides will become more interested in the problems than in preserving their positions either as authority or challenger . . .

If the bureaucratic mode were changed from an alienated to a human-istic one, it would necessarily lead to a change in the type of manager who is successful. The defensive type of personality who clings to his bureaucratic image and who is afraid of being vulnerable and of con-fronting persons directly and openly would be at a disadvantage. On the other hand, the imaginative, nonfrightened, responsive person would be successful if the method of management were changed. These considera-tions show how erroneous it is to speak of certain methods of manage-ment which cannot be changed because the managers "would not be will-ing or capable of changing them." What is left out here is the fact that new methods would constitute a selective principle for managers. This does not mean that most present managers would be replaced by the new type of manager. No doubt there are many who under the present sys-tem cannot utilize their responsive capacities and who will be able to do so once the system gives them a chance . . .

Even if most physical labor is taken over by the machines, man has still to take part in the process of the exchange between himself and nature; only if man were a disembodied being or an angel with no physical needs would work completely disappear. Man, being in need of assimilating nature, of organizing and directing the process of material production, of distribution, of social organization, of responses to natural catastrophes, can never sit back and let things take care of themselves . . . *If man is passive in the process of production and organization, he will also be passive during his leisure time* . . .

Even if machines could take care of all work, of all planning, of all organizational decisions, and even of all health problems, they cannot take care of the problems arising between man and man. In this sphere of interpersonal relations, human judgment, response, responsibility, and decision, the machine cannot replace human functioning. There are those, like Marcuse, who think that in a cybernated and "nonrepressive" society that is completely satisfied materially there would be no more human conflicts like those expressed in the Greek or Shakesperean drama or the great novels. I can understand that completely alienated people can see the future of human existence in this way, but I am afraid they express more about their own emotional limitations than about future possibilities. The assumption that the problems, conflicts, and tragedies between man and man will disappear if there are no materially unfulfilled needs is a childish daydream.

Active participation in the affairs of the country as a whole and of states and communities, as well as of large enterprises, would require the formation of face-to-face groups, within which the process of information exchange, debate, and decision making would be conducted . . .

W. H. FERRY

The Need for New Constitutional Controls

I shall argue here the proposition that the regulation of technology is the most important intellectual and political task on the American agenda.

I do not say that technology *will* be regulated, only that it *should* be.

My thesis is unpopular. It rests on the growing evidence that technology is substracting as much or more from the sum of human welfare as it is adding. We are substituting a technological environment for a natural environment. It is therefore desirable to ask whether we understand the conditions of the new as well as we do those of the old, and whether we are prepared to do what may be necessary to see that this new environment is made suitable to men.

Until now, industrial man has only marginally and with reluctance undertaken to direct his ingenuity to his own welfare. It is a possibility merely — not a probability — that he will become wise enough to commit himself fully to that goal. For today the infatuation with science and technology is bottomless.

Here is where all the trouble begins — in the American confidence that technology is ultimately the medicine for all ills. This infatuation may, indeed, be so profound as to undercut everything of an optimistic tone that follows. Technology is the American theology, promising salvation by material works.

From W. H. Ferry, "Must We Rewrite the Constitution to Control Technology?" *Saturday Review* 51 (March 2, 1968): 50–54. Copyright © 1968 Saturday Review, Inc.
Mr. Ferry was until 1969 a vice president of the Fund for the Republic, Inc., and a staff associate of its Center for the Study of Democratic Institutions.

207

A few cautionary words are in order.

I am aware of the distinctions between science and technology but intend to disregard them because the boundary between science and technology is as dim and confused as that between China and India. . . . At the same time, it must be granted that the scientists have been more conscientious than the technologists in appraising their contributions and often warning the community of the consequences of scientific discovery.

The first point to be made is that technology can no longer be taken for granted. It must be thought about, not merely produced, celebrated, and accepted in all its manifestations as an irrepressible and essentially benign human phenomenon.

Technology is not just another historical development, taking its place with political parties, religious establishments, mass communications, household economy, and other chapters of the human story. Unlike the growth of those institutions, its growth has been quick and recent, attaining in many cases exponential velocities. This is instant history. Technology has a career of its own, so far not much subject to the political guidance and restraints imposed on other enormously powerful institutions.

This is why technology must be classed as a mystery and why the lack of interest of the intellectuals must be condemned. A mystery is something not understood. Intellectuals are in charge of demystification. Public veneration is the lot of most mysteries, and technology is no exception. We can scarcely blame statesmen for bumbling and fumbling with this phenomenon, for no one has properly explained it to them. We can scarcely rebuke the public for its uncritical adoration, for it knows only what it is told, and most of the information comes now from the high priests and acolytes of technology's temples.

Quite a lot of imaginative writing has been done about the world to come, whether that world develops from the technological tendencies already evident or is reconstructed after a nuclear war.

The conditions imagined are everywhere the same. High technology rules. Efficiency is the universal watchword. Everything works. All decisions are made rationally, with the rationality of the machines. Humans, poor folk, are the objects of the exercise, never the subjects. They are watched and manipulated, directed, and fitted in. The stubborn few in whom ancient juices of feeling and justice flow are exiled to Mars or to the moon. Those who know how are the ones who run things; a dictator who knows all reigns over all; and this dictator is not infrequently a machine, or — more properly — a system of procedures.

I proceed to examples of the benign and malignant capacities of technology. I am aware that many will find unacceptable my treatment of technology as a semi-autonomous force.

I hope to demonstrate that technology has an ineluctable persistence of its own, beyond the reach of all familiar arguments based on the power structure.

My first example is privacy, today a goner, killed by technology. We are still in the early days of electronic eavesdropping, itself an offshoot of communications research, and at first celebrated as a shortcut to crime control. But now no office, schoolhouse, or bedroom is any longer safe from intrusions.

What are we to think of the proposal for a National Data Center, which will have the capacity and perhaps the responsibility to collect every last bit of information concerning every citizen? Not only tax records, but police records, school grades, property and bank accounts, medical history, credit ratings, even responses to the Kinsey sexual behavior questionnaire.

We have been reading a lot recently about the greatest intrusion on privacy yet dreamed up, in terms of numbers of people affected. I refer to the supersonic transport plane, a multibillion-dollar folly to which the nation is now apparently committed irrevocably. In a few years' time, the sonic boom of the SST will daily and nightly waken sleeper; worsen the condition of the sick, frighten tens of millions; induce neuroses; and cause property damage beyond estimate.

At least three European countries are considering putting the traveling thunderclap of the sonic boom on the forbidden list of passing legislation which would prevent SST's from flying over their territories. The position of these countries on this issue is people first, machines second.

The doctrine of the United States is that whatever can be done must be done; otherwise, the United States will fall behind in the technological race. That is the thesis. Therefore, if the SST can be built, it must be built. This technological imperative is bolstered by dozens of irrelevant arguments in support of SST. It is said that other nations will gather the glory and profit and jobs resulting from SST manufacture. American manufacture of SST will help the balance of payments. These arguments are as popular as they are off the mark. Against them are many equally valid.

It has not occurred to many that the argument should be about the superiority of SST, all things considered, as a means of getting from here to there. It should be about the benefits to the thousands and the dis-benefits to the millions. The pursuit of super-speed is being conducted by experts who might better be working to make present aviation super-safe. The socially necessary tasks to which these nimble minds might be turned are unaccountable if we should take seriously the proposition that people must come first, machines second.

When SST proponents are asked to justify the assault on the bodies and minds of human beings, the customary answer is, "They'll get used to it." Some technologists, however, are more direct. Speaking of the sonic boom, Engineer Charles T. Leonard gives this prescription: "A greatly more tolerant populace than is presently assumed to be the case . . . may well become mandatory if the SST is to realize its full potential."

It may turn out this way: We may be compelled to become tolerant of every and all techniques — but at what human expense we may not appreciate for generations.

That public servants can act with good sense and foresight when in-formed about the impact of technology is illustrated by the City Council of Santa Barbara. Responding to incessant boombarding of that quiet city, the council recently passed an anti-boom ordinance.

In only one case, that of atomic energy, has this country had enough imagination about results to put a stiff bridle on technology. The Atomic Energy Commission came into being partly because of the lethal poten-tialities of the new force and partly because of a few leaders — mainly scientists — who were able to convince Congress that this cosmic threat should never be a military monopoly.

What is needed is a firm grasp on the technology itself, and an equally clear conviction of the primacy of men, women, and children in all the calculations. This is a resounding prescription, and I regret to admit that I am more clear about ultimate steps than I am about how to do what needs to be done in the near future.

I am convinced only that political institutions and theory developed in other times for other conditions offer little hope.

I turn to my final example of technological invasion. American busi-ness executives a half dozen years ago wakened to the existence of a multi-billion-dollar market — education. It was hard to ignore. Today's real growth industry is education.

As always, the central claim is efficiency. Mass education, it is said, requires mass production methods. The result is already discernible, and may be called technication. The central image of technication is the student at the console of a computer.

Our educational purposes have never been very clear. Technication may compel removal of the ambiguities and establishment of straightforward aims. But who will undertake this task? How shall we assure that the result is the betterment of children and not the convenience of machines?

The perils are manifest. One of them lies in adopting the totally wrong notion that an educational system can be thought of in terms like those of a factory for producing steel plate or buttons. Another peril is to that indefinable relation between teacher and taught: Dare we think of it as a mere holdover from another world, as subject to the junkpile as the horse-drawn fire engine has been? A third peril is that the ends of education, already a near-forgotten topic, will be gobbled up by the means.

Technication means standardization. The history of factories shows the benefits and limits of standardization. Factories are fine for producing things, but their record with people is terrible. We cannot expect to hear the voices of democracy emerging from education factories; we can hear only the chorus. Technication, as Robert M. Hutchins observes, will "dehumanize a process the aim of which is humanization."

The effect on the taught is crucial. The rebellion at Berkeley centered on the indifference of the multiversity's mechanism to the personal needs of the students. When the protesters pinned IBM cards to their jackets — an act duplicated on campuses throughout the land — they were declaring against impersonality and standardization; and it cannot be said too often that impersonality and standardization are the very hallmarks of technology.

I have offered not-very-penetrating illustrations of the way technology is raising conspicuous questions about the social and personal welfare of Americans. Behind all these matters, as I remarked at the outset, are dangerous convictions that science and technology provide the panacea for all ailments. It is curious that this conviction should be so widespread, for life today for most people appears to be more puzzling and unsatisfactory and beset with unresolved difficulties than ever before. For most people — but not, I suppose, for the scientists and technologists, the priesthood of the modern theology that is more and more ruling the land, and from whose ingenious devices and fateful decisions we must find a way to make effective appeal.

Scientists and technologists are the indubitable agents of a new order. I wish to include the social scientists, for whose contributions to the technological puzzle I could find no space in this paper. Whether the political and social purpose of the nation ought to be set by these agents is the question. The answer to the question is no. We need to assign to their proper place the services of scientists and technologists. The sovereignty of the people must be reestablished. Rules must be written and regulations imposed. The writing must be done by statesmen and philosophers consciously intent on the general welfare, with the engineers and researchers summoned from their caves to help in the doing when they are needed.

The most comprehensive and thoughtful approach to the problem of regulation is that of U.S. Congressman Emilio Q. Daddario, chairman of the House Subcommittee on Science, Research, and Development. Representative Daddario starts with the necessity for "technological assessment," which he characterizes as urgent It will amount to a persisting study of cause-effect relationships, alternatives, remedies.

It is too early to guess whether Congressman Daddario's group will come out for certain statutory additions to the present political organization as the proper way to turn back or harness technology's invading forces. There is ample precedent.

We can regard the panoply of administrative agencies and the corpus of administrative law as early efforts in this direction. They have not been very effective in directing technical development to the common good, although I do not wish to minimize the accomplishments of these agencies in other ways. Perhaps they have so far prevented technology from getting wholly out of hand. America is not so much an affluent as a technical society; this is the essence of the dilemma. The basic way to get at it, in my judgment, would be through a revision of the Constitution of the United States. If technology is indeed the main conundrum of American life, as the achieving of a more perfect union was the principal conundrum 175 years ago, it follows that the role and control of technology would have to be the chief preoccupation of the new founding fathers.

Up to now the attitude has been to keep hands off technological development until its effects are plainly menacing. Public authority usually has stepped in only after damage almost beyond repair has been done: in the form of ruined lakes, gummed-up rivers, spoilt cities and countrysides, armless and legless babies, psychic and physical damage to human beings beyond estimate. The measures that seem to me urgently needed to deal with the swiftly expanding repertoire of toxic technology go much further than I believe would be regarded as constitutional.

What is required is not merely extensive police power to inhibit the technically disastrous, but legislative and administrative authority to direct technology in positive ways: the power to encourage as well as forbid, to slow down as well as speed up, to plan and initiate as well as to oversee developments that are now mainly determined by private forces for private advantage.

Technology is already tilting the fundamental relationships of government, and we are only in the early stages. A new and heavy factor has entered the old system of checks and balances. Thus, my perception of the situation is that the Constitution has become outdated by technical advance and deals awkwardly and insufficiently with technology's results.

Other critics tell me that we are sliding into anarchy, and that we must suffer through a historical period in which we will just "get over" our technological preoccupations. But I do not face the prospect of anarchy very readily.

So that my suggestion of fundamental constitutional revision is not dismissed as merely a wild gasp of exasperation. I draw attention to the institutions dominating today's American scene which were not even dimly foreseen by the founding fathers. I refer to immense corporations and trade unions; media of communication that span continent and globe; political parties; a central government of stupendous size and world-shattering capabilities; and a very un-Jeffersonian kind of man at the center of it all.

It seems to me, in face of these novelties, that it is not necessarily madness to have a close look at our basic instrument in order to determine its ability to cope with these utterly new conditions, and especially with the overbearing novelty of technique. Technology touches the person and the common life more intimately and often than does any government, federal or local; yet it is against the aggrandizement of government that we are constantly warned. Technology's scope and penetration places in the hands of its administrators gigantic capabilities for arbitrary power. It was this kind of power the founding fathers sought to diffuse and attenuate.

CORNELIUS E. GALLAGHER

Computing Power in Real Time

One of Norman Mailer's more fanciful conceits is that tuberculosis
was the disease which best characterizes the nineteenth century and that
cancer, in the same sense, is the disease of the twentieth century. Those
who quietly and elegantly languished, gradually diminishing into death,
seem to Mailer to sum up an age in which time moves slowly and medita-
tively. But the twentieth-century society is symbolized by a literal explosion of the life process; cells, reflecting hyperactive modern life, multiply so rapidly that they overwhelm their host.

Mailer's pungent metaphor is a useful and provocative comparison. In
terms of this audience, we should change the image to read the quill pen
expressing the ninteenth century and the computer characterizing the
twentieth. But we should not discard cancer, for Erich Fromm, in *The
Revolution of Hope: Toward a Humanized Technology,* says, "Computers should become a functional part in a life oriented social system
and not a cancer which begins to play havoc and eventually kills the system."

This is, admittedly, a rather oblique entrance into a speech called
"Computing in Real Time," but it does highlight a view of the computer
which is becoming increasingly prevalent. It is a view which must be

From Cornelius E. Gallagher, "Computing in Real Time," a speech given before the
Association for Computing Machinery Technical Symposium, June 19, 1969.

Mr. Gallagher is a Member of Congress from the Thirteenth District of New Jersey,
and Chairman of the Subcommittee on Invasion of Privacy of the House Government
Operations Committee.

recognized by computer professionals, for humanist doubts underlay the distrust of mechanistic decision-making.

From the vantage point of a century or so, it is possible to dismiss the Luddites in England as sadly disillusioned and rather pathetic figures. However, it is a fact that they were able to destroy machines and cripple factories. In the same sense, it is possible to dismiss computer critics today as merely naïve and uninformed anti-intellectuals who simply do not understand the rationale of computing. But computer professionals and managers must build in relevance to their computer applications. Many of your installations may suffer from a confrontation with those who act in a manner similar to the Luddites. One of the cries of the New Left is "open it up, or shut it down." In another hundred years it is to be devoutly hoped that these people will seem just as irrelevant as the Luddites do now. We can make sure that that happy projection becomes a reality if it is possible, now, to open up computerized information systems to the legitimate demands of the people whose dossiers create the input and the output of many systems.

It has not been the purpose of my investigations into computer privacy to encourage those who oppose all computer applications. The rewards and benefits of the computer are too essential to the health and survival of modern society. But it is extremely important that computer professionals realize that there is a body of opinion which questions the very foundations of your work.

You do not massage your data in a cloister; you are computing in real time.

But let us "disanthropomorphize" the discussion by considering some views of computer applications which restrict themselves to non-fiction. Many men, representing various viewpoints, have commented, rather unkindly, upon the current uses of the computer. I would like to give you four examples.

First is the New Left critic of American society Paul Goodman. Goodman is extremely distressed about the fact that giant corporations employ systems analysis to make computer generated decisions in areas where they have only developed the systems, not the expertise.

Goodman comments on the results of such insulated decisions regarding teaching methods: "Somewhere down the line, however, this cabal of decision-makers is going to coerce the life of real children and control the activity of classroom teachers. Those who are directly engaged in the human function of learning and teaching have no say in

215

what goes on . . . but the brute fact is that the children are quite incidental to the massive intervention of the giant combinations."

One does not have to agree with everything Goodman says to appreciate the perception of his insights. In addition, of course, he does represent the views of many disenchanted but deeply concerned people in our land.

Second, Robert Theobald is one of our most respected economists and social commentators. Theobald finds that a misapplication of computer technology may further aggravate situations they presume to cure. Although the computer is frequently beneficial in solving serious problems, Theobald says ". . . is also true that our attempts to reverse these trends will be frustrated if we continue to regard the ability of the computer to act with maximum efficiency in carrying out an immediate task as more important than all of our fundamental values put together. As long as we regard these values as of minor importance, to be upheld only when it is convenient to do so, we will be unable to recruit the computer to help us to attain our fundamental goals."

Almost all of Erich Fromm's book, *The Revolution of Hope,* is meaningful to the message of this speech. But I would like to repeat one thing he says about the computer's ability to store so much data that it assumes a virtually divine status. Core storage as God-head and print-outs as divine revelation can create decisions which are totally counter to a creative use of the intellect. Fromm describes men who rely totally on computer generated decision-making data in these terms: "However dreadful the consequences of their decisions may be, they need not have qualms about the rightness and legitimacy of the method by which they arrived at their decision . . . Like Dostoevski's Grand Inquisitor, some may even be tragic figures who can not act differently, because they see no other way of being certain that they do the best they can. The alleged rational character of our planners is basically not different from the religiously based decisions in a prescientific age."

All the questions which have been raised about the ultimate impact of the computer on society are stylishly summarized by one of the most knowledgeable men in America today: Dr. Emmanuel Mesthene, Director of the Harvard University Program on Technology and Society. In 1968, Dr. Mesthene asked: "What happens to traditional relationships between citizen and government, to such prerogatives of the individual as personal privacy, electoral consent, and access to the independent social criticism of the press, and to the ethics of and public control over a new elite of information keepers, when economic, military and social policies become increasingly technical, long-range, machine processed, information based, and expert dominated?"

These points assume major importance, for the computer is the world's fastest growing industry. In 1956, there were about 600 computers with a value of about 340 million dollars. Today there are more than 70,000 computers valued at more than 18 billion dollars.

Computer capacity has kept pace. IBM has stated that, in 15 years, computers increased in speed by 150 times, and the cost of each computation was reduced to 1/40 or less of the original level.

And it is predicted that by 1980 computers and computer applications will account for 20% of the Gross National Product.

If for no other than these financial facts, computing will increasingly be done in real time. And certain other problems have begun to surface.

When Judge Miles Lord of Minneapolis awarded 480 thousand dollars to a computerized accounting and inventory system user, he said, "His whole business was wrapped around a spool of magnetic tape which was not in his possession and was not even his property." The firm which sold the system attempted to claim that it was the user's own workers who were to blame, but the judge felt that under the circumstances, the user could not be faulted for failing to recognize that the system itself was unworkable.

In spite of the scientific, almost religious, mystique with which outsiders view computing, Judge Lord's decision once again signals the end of computing as pure science. Legal responsibility will probably ultimately rest on the creators of computerized data systems and you will continue to represent, in the main, a part of technology, not science.

In a May 1969 speech, Admiral Rickover described the distinction between science and technology better than I have ever seen it put before: "Science, being pure *thought,* harms no one; therefore, it need not be humanistic. But technology is *action* and often potentially dangerous action. Unless it is made to adapt itself to human interests, needs, values, and principles, more harm will be done than good."

And computing technology is certainly where the action is! And action takes place in real time. To carry the metaphor a little further, you must share time with human values. Unless society is to become a terminal patient, every computerized system must have a terminal to which mankind has access.

The Congress has taken tentative steps to address itself to the real time in which you are computing. When my Special Subcommittee on Invasion of Privacy initiated Congressional consideration of credit bureaus in March 1968, we had the benefit of the views of Alan Westin. I proposed the following question to Dr. Westin: "Is there a possibility of the formation of a data elite's manipulating American society by their manipulation of data on individual Americans?" I would like to indicate the range of his remarks by the following excerpts. "There is a dangerous arrogance that can be built up when a small group of people believe that they have the language, the system, and the most scientific way of making decisions. Failure to keep popular participation in public decision-making, and the developing mixture of private and public decision-making in our society creates a dangerous impersonality."

He describes a futuristic society in which ". . . there is a gap between those who have a high elite education and everybody else in the society. The people without high intellect feel they are the ones full of emotion, sentiment and love, and view the decision-making elite as cold and calculating. Such a separation is dangerous in a democratic political system because often what is required is not the wisdom of technical solutions or of scientific cost effectiveness, but a wisdom that has to do with leading and inspiring people and convincing them that they have a stake in the system."

"I think it will be a while before the line can be drawn between what can be achieved through new management science techniques and information systems and what still remains the art of the political process. I am afraid the line is going to get very blurred in the next half decade or decades because it is essentially the poor and the black who want access into and participation in the system. They have never had a voice of the kind the middle classes had in the political system."

Dr. Westin envisions society responding to people who want participation now in these terms: "We don't do things that way any longer; we have new technical ways of making decisions. Why don't you just ratify those? We can't let you participate because the planning is so complex that you don't even know the language and we will often have to make commitments that run 3 or 5 years ahead."

I am afraid that these opinions of Dr. Westin's are, in essence, correct. I find it very disturbing that computerized information systems for decision-making may be heightening rather than lessening our current agonies.

For it is a fact of the very real time in which we live that people are just not going to wait. Articulate and aggressive segments of our society are insisting upon the right to influence and alter decisions which vitally affect them. Blacks, hippies, students, ghetto parents, and members of the dissenting academy may seem like a wildly disparate group, but they are united on one thing. They all demand a greater piece of the decision-making action, or at the very least, a heightened sense of personal involvement in and control over their own destinies. It does not take an especially astute observor to discover that all around us there is real anger and a spreading disenchantment with the goals of government.

These uses of computerized information systems suggest two questions which I feel have yet to be explored in any formal or deeply meaningful way. The first question is: Can machine-based data systems assist in decentralizing decision-making? Is it possible for individuals who are not technologically sophisticated to interface with the data flow?

I have given you a segment of Dr. Westin's judgment on that issue and it is an opinion which, at this point in time, I share. However, I am also aware that there are those who claim that the computer's ability to digest so much data will permit a greater variety of views to enter the decision-making mix. Frankly, I do not think a definitive answer has yet emerged and I believe the Association for Computing Machinery could bring knowledgeable insights to the debate. I would urge you, both as individual members and as an Association, to address yourself to the question.

Second is a problem which, to the best of my knowledge, has never been studied in any coherent or disciplined manner. What are citizen attitudes and opinions regarding the disclosure of personal information to those who operate computerized data systems?

My staff and I have been forced to respond to the many people who have raised that question that probably the largest collection of citizen reaction to machine systems is contained in our own files. They bulge with thousands of letters from concerned people throughout our nation and with hundreds of editorials and articles which support our work in highlighting the issue of computer privacy.

This is, of course, a wholly unsatisfactory answer to you and I must admit, perhaps reluctantly, that it is also unsatisfactory to me.

Virtually every page of *Datamation* and *Computerworld* contains reports of new data systems being constructed and of new areas of personal information being reduced to machine-readable form. Yet, to the best of my knowledge, no dispassionate and scientific survey of the attitudes and opinions of the people whose dossiers are forming these systems exists. No answer has been forthcoming to the crucial question of whether these systems are the life-blood of society or are, in reality, a cancer.

When I began my studies of computer privacy, I had hoped to create a climate of concern. I believe that goal has been realized and that some effective and promising first steps have been taken by professionals in the computer field to translate that concern into practice.

I would hope that anyone who has reliable information about the citizen's attitude's toward the computer will communicate with me. Perhaps more important, I would hope that we might commence an in-depth study to discover just what we are doing to our society, and even more important, whether society will permit it.

For there is a disturbing body of evidence which suggests that the ordinary American — that most extraordinary of humans — is becoming supersaturated with the toxic in the tonic of technology. The myriad forms of pollution — air, water, noise — the bomb, highways which destroy neighborhoods, unresponsive federal and local agencies — the list of such outrages to which man is subject is depressingly long.

In March of this year, I had the privilege of addressing the Chicago Chapter of the Institute of Management Sciences. I touched upon these subjects and I described all the investigations I have made into privacy: the lie-detector, psychological testing, the National Data Bank, and business intelligence firms such as credit bureaus. I concluded that speech by developing a concept called "The Intellectual Imperative" which attempted to coalesce my investigations into a coherent theory. I would like to expand on that theme this morning.

Every individual must have certain areas over which his sovereignty is absolute, as long as he is pursuing legitimate aims. Lower animals have a body buffer zone and, as Robert Ardray has so compellingly pointed out, a territorial imperative. Perhaps this can best be represented by the bull ring where the bull himself outlines an area of his own called the *querencia*. This is a randomly chosen spot where the bull will always retreat when the pressure of his death struggle with the matador becomes too intense.

But where can modern man go to gather his strength when he is gored by society? Techniques to assert the individual's right to a space of psychological control have simply not kept pace with technology's ability to disclose almost everything to almost everybody.

In Chicago, I described the Intellectual Imperative and its necessity to the needs of modern man in these terms:

> Man may choose those in whom he wishes to confide. He may discuss any issue in any terms he may desire and be assured that an indiscretion of phrase or even an indecency of thought will remain private. A space of psychological control permits ideas to be discussed

freely within his territory and with the guarantee that strict public accountability will not follow. It is just this blurring of the public and the private which makes invasion of privacy so obnoxious to personal integrity and civilized society.

The control of the flow of information about yourself, about your actions, about your beliefs, is seen as a crucial aspect of a dynamic society. Urban mass culture has destroyed for most of us the opportunity to exercise freely the Territorial Imperative; the advance of computer and other technologies threatens the Intellectual Imperative. Physically, we are constantly in a crowd; intellectually, technology has provided devices to make our forgotten actions and our unacknowledged thoughts known to the crowd.

In short, I believe that the Intellectual Imperative is just as important to humans as the Territorial Imperative is for lower animals. It is extremely dangerous for a matador to violate the bull's querencia, and it may be equally fatal for society to presume that it can violate the space where the individual's basic nature resides.

It seems to be a basic contention of computer-oriented planning that the nature of man is infinitely malleable and that the individual can be made to adapt to any mold deemed suitable for him. If this were true, no one would ever quit a well-paying job and no society would ever undergo a revolution.

And if technology's might, acting on quantifiable data, could solve all problems, Vietnam would be just a pleasant memory.

So we must recognize that tools alone will not do the work of man. If we are to survive as a viable and free society, we must make sure that the light of humanity illuminates the direction in which we are moving and that we do not permit any of our technologies to extinguish the fires which warm a fully human life, and which create a spiritually satisfied mankind.

HAROLD SACKMAN

A Public Philosophy
for Real Time Information Systems

The diverse needs for a public philosophy on the use of computers for the regulation and control of social affairs stem from many cultural roots. Perhaps the most fundamental source is the accelerating tempo of contemporary change spurred by the advance of science and technology. Situations and events seem to be moving faster than we can recognize and cope with them. Social solutions which once had a useful half-life spanning decades now have useful total lives over much shorter periods and have to be constantly revised and updated along the way to keep pace with changing conditions.

The concept of the real time information system — a system that monitors events in a specified environment and controls the outcome of such events in a desired direction — is a leading technical concept that is being increasingly applied to cope with fast-moving changes in many walks of life. The power of computerized real time information systems to meet rapidly changing problems and situations has been garnered from over a decade of experience in computer-assisted command and control. The technique is well known: continual surveillance over the object environment to permit early warning of critical situations; identification of problems; corrective regulation and control in accordance with

Paper delivered at a Special Interest Session on "Real Time Information Systems and the Public Interest," Fall Joint Computer Conference, San Francisco, California, Dec. 9–11, 1968.

Mr. Sackman is Senior Research Leader, System Development Corporation, Santa Monica, California.

established standards of system performance; and evolutionary adaptation of system design and operations to meet changing conditions.

The real time information system is a new class of social institution, a more radically powerful and rapidly responsive social form to recognize, meet, and deal with specified problems at the time they occur and in time to modify their outcome. If we neglect to formulate desirable social consequences for these new systems, we neglect them at our own peril, and at public peril.

Information power is a new dilemma in modern society. Social control of information power is a focal problem for a public philosophy of real time information systems. Prior to the advent of real time computing systems, information was collected and stored in a manner that tended to separate knowledge from action, as in books and films. Radio and television allowed more timely collection and dissemination of information, but these mass media of communication were still not linked to direct social action. In real time computing systems, however, the collection, organization, and storage of information leads directly to action, to integrated surveillance and control over the object environment. This dynamic marriage of information and control in real time systems is a fusion of knowledge and action, and, through directed action in real time, information is expressed as power.

As more and more social knowledge becomes computer-accessible, so will more extensive, interlocking, and more powerful real time systems come into being. As surely as the night follows the day — or the day follows the night, depending on your outlook — so will computer-accessible information be followed by real time control. In a democracy, the public is the ultimate source of social power, and information power, accordingly, is ultimately a public trust. A public philosophy on information power needs to account for new democratic forms and procedures bearing on the organization and equitable distribution of social information.

Philosophical challenges are encountered not only in general areas such as meeting the tempo of contemporary change and coping with the institutionalization of information power, but also and perhaps most critically in the problems of social implementation. A workable philosophical position should provide guidelines for social method, for putting principles into practice. While many agree on broad principles, consensus often vanishes when details of implementation are hammered out.

There are many knotty questions facing the implementation of real time information systems in the public interest. Where does the domain of public information end and where does the domain of private information begin? Is the information utility a genuine public utility and, if it is, what kind of commodity is public information? Should information be distributed to the public on a metered basis, as we do with gas, water, and electricity, or should it be freely available as in radio and television? Should the cultural store of computer-accessible public information be available to all as a basic human right, supported by the government and the taxpayer, or should such public information services be supported by private enterprise, or do we need a judicious mix of public and private support? Who tests and evaluates real time information systems for social effectiveness and who evaluates the evaluators? What legal changes and what new social agencies are required to safeguard the public interest and to protect the private interest in the field of information services?

It should be apparent from the foregoing that the challenge of a public philosophy for real time information systems is, in many respects, unprecedented and extremely complex, at general levels, in details, and in implementation. At the same time, the need for such a philosophy is vital and long overdue. The next section is devoted to an inquiry into key elements of a public philosophy of real time information systems; this inquiry then leads to a synthesis of these elements into an initial philosophical framework.

Elements of a Public Philosophy

The desiderata of a public philosophy are developed in three stages, starting from definitions of the area of inquiry, proceeding to scientific and technical aspects, and culminating with social considerations. Each stage builds upon and incorporates the preceding stage. While the social stage represents the broadest set of elements and requirements, it does not attempt to describe a substantive public philosophy of real time information systems per se, which is the main business of the last part of this paper.

A philosophy of real time information systems presupposes some definition of the concept of "real time." Historical interpretations of time, and by extension, "real time," have assumed the varied forms of the conceptual containers into which notions of time, like a liquid, have been poured. These interpretations range from the ceaseless flux of Heraclitus to the flickering unreality of Platonic change, to Newton's geometrization of time, to Einstein's space-time, to probabilistic and indeterminate temporal constructions in quantum physics, to ecological statistical trends in evolutionary time. While probabilistic and contingent interpretations of real time seem to be gaining increasing ground in the physical, biological, and social sciences, controversy has been and still is the rule.

For present purposes, three aspects of real time are distinguished: real time events, real time information systems, and real time science. Each is defined and discussed in turn.

Real time essentially refers to events — their appearance and duration, their passage and succession, and the hypothesized interrelations of events as empirically tested and demonstrated in any referent system and its environment. Real time is thus the way events happen, our description of how they happen, and our best interpretations of why they happen as they do. The definition also implies that warranted interpretations are those empirically certified by experimental method in a systems context.

Real time information systems refer to systems that (1) continually sense and respond to selected changes in an object environment, (2) in a manner and in time to enable regulation and control over some ongoing events in the system and its environment while they occur, (3) within the bounds of minimal or acceptable levels of system performance as determined by continual test and evaluation of feedback from system events.

As mentioned earlier, the central feature of real time information systems is direction and control over selected system events while they take place; and in order to exert such cognizance it is necessary to maintain constant surveillance, identification (decision making), and control to modify the environment as required. Note that the definition does not mention computers. It essentially states that any system that is organized to sense and respond to an object environment according to some criterion of effectiveness is, in principle, a real time information system. The crux of this definition is that real time systems are not merely passive spectators of their own events, but are creators of desirable outcomes, that they are active agencies that mold a partially plastic environment in accordance with a preconceived image.

The next definition — real time science — moves into the second stage toward a public philosophy: the technical and scientific stage.

Real time science deals with temporally and situationally contingent events amenable to experimental method, and it results in an extension of human mastery over such events; it is broadly eclectic, borrowing freely from the methods and findings of the pure and applied sciences, and from any mix of interscience and new science as required and needed to understand and control real world events.

As we enter into the era of computer-catalyzed real time information systems, we need a scientific discipline to develop the theory and practice of real time systems, and the suggested discipline is real time science as defined above. This definition is different from conventional concepts of science in several leading respects. First, it explicitly fuses knowledge and action together as a single entity; no pretense is made for the pursuit of antecedent, abstract knowledge for its own sake. Second, the pursuit of knowledge is for human purposes, for improving human effectiveness. Third, the proper object of real time science is real world events — real time science belongs where the action is. Laboratory events and abstract constructions are not excluded, but they are preparatory rather than consummatory in the sense that they contribute toward the ultimate objective of understanding, shaping, and controlling real world events for human ends.

The eclecticism of real time science is a restless, fast-moving, aggressive eclecticism, itself changing in real time with new methods and findings. Real time science borrows freely from any established or new experimental discipline that contributes to improved real time system performance. Anyone who has worked in the design and development of real time information systems is acutely aware of the eclectic and pluralistic nature of such systems, of the requirement to optimize interdisciplinary teamwork, of the necessity to adopt new science and technology into system design and operations, of the open-ended, jazz-like need to improvise against residual uncertainty, of the need continually to test and modify system configuration throughout the entire life cycle of the system.

The relation of real time science to traditional forms of science is that real time science borrows experimental method and findings wherever and whenever they are useful for understanding and directing real world events. The common denominator is experimental method. With the advent of computer-serviced societies we may expect a flowering of new species of computer-catalyzed experimental method, particularly in real time information systems embedded in real world happenings.

A criticism that may be leveled against the foregoing definitions of real time events, real time information systems, and real time science is that they seem to be so broad and all-encompassing as to become meaningless; little is left out. The antidote to indiscriminate extension of real time concepts lies in the distinction from non-real time concepts. There are two basic senses in which non-real time may be construed — as an entity in its own right, and as failure in real time systems.

In the first sense, a non-real time information system is one that does not continually sense and respond to selected changes in the object environment in a manner permitting control over events at the time they occur. Analyses of past events and planning for future events fall into the non-real time category. In computer systems, batch processing is generally conducted in non-real time, and abstract simulations are typically non-real time operations.

The results of analyses of the past, of planning for possible futures, of batch information processing and of non-real time simulations may eventually be applied to a real time systems context, and as such, non-real time behavior may be interpreted as preparatory to real time behavior. Non-real time behavior may even have its own characteristic real time pace (as in accelerated real time simulation), but, insofar as immediate control is not exerted over ongoing events, such behavior is interpreted as non-real time for concurrent events. From a practical point of view, the heart of the distinction between non-real time and real time is the distinction between knowledge disembodied from immediate and con-current action versus knowledge expressed in action.

The second sense of non-real time is failure of a real time system to meet some specified standard of performance in controlling the system environment. Thus, in computerized real time systems, if SAGE does not destroy a hostile bomber before it reaches its target, if the Apollo space-craft is not being picked up by the ground tracking system, if SABRE air-line reservations are swamped with erroneous manual inputs, if the executive program of a time-sharing system has to handle too many users at one time, to that extent the real time information system deteriorates in performance and regresses to a non-responsive or non-real time mode of operations.

Turning now to the last stage, the social elements of a public philos-ophy of real time information systems are primarily concerned with social effectiveness. If the object of real time systems is to regulate selected ongoing events in the system environment, and if the object of real time science is to extend human mastery over real world events, then the aggregated effectiveness of such efforts is real time social effectiveness.

But just what does social effectiveness mean when applied to real time information systems? It was mentioned earlier that real time systems probably represent the most advanced technical means available for reg-ulation and control of social change, and that information power, in a democracy, ultimately resides in the public. Social change via real time information systems is thus self-change. The public, ideally, authorizes and warrants social change. Each individual is thus both experimenter and subject in the development of real time public systems; a new level of participant democracy is needed well beyond anything that has been attempted so far. A socially effective public philosophy correspondingly requires educational changes in the general population that can lead to enhanced participant democracy. The alternative is the eclipse of the public by a new technological meritocracy.

The way out of the dilemma of overconcentration of information power in some new elite is modification of existing democratic procedures with the aid of new technological capability. Pluralistic checks and balances between competing groups and interests, conducted in the open forum, is a time-honored method for preserving a dynamic democratic equilibrium. The design of pluralistic checks and balances for diverse real time information systems and public information services would be pouring new real time wine into old democratic bottles. The new real time information services can be applied to enable the public to exert closer scrutiny over elected officials by more frequent voting, and more frequent expression of public opinion by electronic polling on key issues as they arise. The electronic potential for public control is so great that we should also be concerned with overcontrol of public officials by a fickle and changeable public, overcontrol that could lead to a more virulent form of the tyranny of the majority (as Alexis de Tocqueville described it more than a century ago).[1] The knife cuts both ways — more power means more work and greater responsibility for the public and its representatives to maintain equitable equilibrium between shifting majorities and diverse minorities.

The foregoing should make it obvious that the determination of suitable checks and balances between competing groups, competing real time information systems, between the public and various elites, between majorities and minorities, will require a long and continuing course of social experimentation. Doctrinaire solutions are no match for systematic social experiment and verified empirical demonstration. An essential requirement of a public philosophy, then, is the institutionalization of social experiment in public affairs with a corresponding internalization of experimental values in thought and outlook.

Summing up, what are the key elements of a public philosophy for real time information systems? The philosophy requires an outlook that links knowledge with action; it needs the support of eclectic real time sciences concerned with the extension of human mastery over real world events; it is characterized by diverse democratic means to achieve plu-

1. Alexis de Tocqueville, *Democracy in America*, 1835.

ralistic social ends; and it requires an extension of experimental method and experimental ethos to social affairs. Do we have a philosophy that brings these elements together, or do we have to invent a new philosophy for the era of real time systems in computer-serviced societies?

The Promise of American Pragmatism

The thesis put forth in this final section is that we do have the fundamental elements for a public philosophy of real time information systems in the legacy of American pragmatism. The following discussion develops the grounds for this position in four steps: a brief description of the historical development of American pragmatism; pragmatism as a philosophical system founded upon and profoundly influenced by real time concepts and a real time outlook; pragmatism as a coherent experimental approach to the democratization of real time social control; and the extension of pragmatism into systems science and the era of computer-serviced societies.

The recurrent theme throughout the rest of this paper is that we already have the basic elements of a philosophy of real time in American pragmatism, constructed over almost a century of hotly contested philosophical labor, as represented by its principal originators, Charles Peirce, William James and John Dewey, and their successors.[2] These three founders portray the three faces of pragmatism — Peirce the mathematical and scientific side, James the psychological side, and Dewey the social side.

"Pragmatism" is derived from a Greek root signifying action. According to James (*Pragmatism*), pragmatism was first introduced into philosophy by Peirce in 1878. For Peirce, the meaning and value of a statement consisted of its conceivable consequences in practice, of its bearing on deliberate human control over future events. Peirce clearly envisaged the union of knowledge with action.

At the heart of Peirce's belief was his conviction of the superiority of experimental method over other methods for gaining and implementing useful human knowledge. The "truth" of statements is operationally determined by empirical verification of testable consequences achieved

2. Charles S. Peirce, *Collected Papers of Charles Sanders Peirce*, ed. Charles Hartshorne and Paul Weiss (Cambridge, Mass.: The Belknap Press of Harvard University Press, 1935); William James, *Pragmatism: A New Name for Some Old Ways of Thinking* (New York: Longmans, Green, 1907); William James, *A Pluralistic Universe* (New York: Longmans, Green, 1909); John Dewey, *Intelligence in the Modern World*, ed. J. Ratner (New York: Random House, 1939).

by iterative experimental inquiry, as it occurs in scientific progress. Peirce was the first to use the concept of inquiry in this context, a term later adopted and elaborated by Dewey. With Peirce, meaning, truth, and experimental inquiry were cast in a temporal frame, contingent upon and responsive to the cumulative consequences of ongoing human action. The long-range, evolutionary advance of science served as the idealized model for Peirce's vision of pragmatism which contained the seeds for a philosophy of real time science.

James was the popularizer of pragmatism and its most eloquent, almost poetic, spokesman. While agreeing with Peirce that the validity of statements is to be continually tested by their consequences, James broadened the domain of pragmatic meaning over the whole of human experience. His earlier preoccupation with the shifting stream of consciousness was expanded into an all-encompassing concept of experience (which he described as radical empiricism) that incorporated subject and object as an undifferentiated unity, a unity consonant with that described by Bertrand Russell as "neutral monism." [3] For James, the temporally conditioned stream of experience, flowing in a "pluriverse," displayed the same strung-along, partially connected, mosaic character as his stream of consciousness. This strung-along pluriverse was contrasted by James against the "block universe" espoused by idealists of all callings who believed in the Platonic tradition of a fixed, antecedent structure of the universe laid out in some grand, sweeping design. James' philosophical pluralism, more than that of other pragmatists, lays the groundwork for a virtually unlimited multiplicity of real time sciences and intersciences modeled after the kaleidoscopic configurations of real time systems.

Dewey was deeply concerned with the accelerating tempo of scientific and technological advance and the need for continual social reconstruction to keep pace with such changes. He seized upon the element of human control in experimental method, developed previously by Peirce, as the method of choice to implement and guide social reconstruction.

In a remarkable anticipation of systems science, Dewey attacked the efficacy of conventional notions of true and false and urged, in their place, the adoption of operational measures of effectiveness for human, organizational, and social performance. Social behavior is not true or false — it exists, for better or worse — and our concern, according to Dewey, is to find out how effective it is, and to do it in a manner that will permit us to improve upon it to meet new conditions.

3. Bertrand Russell, *A History of Western Philosophy* (New York: Simon & Schuster, 1945).

For Dewey, every existence is an event, and all events are potential experiments. Contrary to the prevailing laboratory view of science, Dewey saw the universal prospects of real world experimentation with real time events in his doctrine of experimentalism — the extension of experimental method to human affairs. Dewey effectively anticipated a philosophy of real time science by urging increased human control over social events through scientific method.

Dewey's concept of increasing experimental control over social affairs was consistently qualified as democratic control by an enlightened public. In *The Public and Its Problems,* Dewey put forth his prophetic vision of free social communication and democratized public control in a new machine age:

> We have but touched lightly and in passing upon the conditions that must be fulfilled if the Great Society is to become a Great Community; a society in which the ever-expanding and intricately ramifying consequences of associated activities shall be known in the full sense of that word, so that an organized, articulate Public comes into being. The highest and most difficult kind of inquiry and a subtle, delicate, vivid and responsive art of communication must take possession of the physical machinery of transmission and circulation and breathe life into it. When the machine age has thus perfected its machinery it will be a means of life and not its despotic master. Democracy will come into its own, for democracy is a name of free and enriching communion. It had its seer in Walt Whitman. It will have its consummation when free social inquiry is indissolubly wedded to the art of full and moving communication.[4]

The above sketch is only crudely indicative of the philosophies of Peirce, James, and Dewey. It is beyond the scope of this paper to set out the distinguishing characteristics and the current diversity of American pragmatism in any detail. But these brief remarks should suffice to point up the pronounced temporal thrust of American pragmatism, the continual reconstruction of present belief toward future behavior, with vigilant appraisal of fresh consequences leading to new guidelines for further action. Peirce stressed the self-corrective aspect of the inquiring process; James focused on the human implications of the pluralistic stream of experience; Dewey emphasized instrumental means and experimental control over growing social problems in a precarious world. The flux and pressure of real time events is written large in these philosophies, and social mastery over this flux is most apparent and most comprehensively expounded in Dewey's work.

4. John Dewey, *The Public and Its Problems* (New York: Henry Holt, 1927), p. 184.

Social control has become a terrifying notion when coupled with computers. It conjures up visions of Orwell's Big Brother and Wiener's Golem.[5] Dewey was always a great believer in democracy even though he was acutely aware of its many limitations as he saw them in his time. He also had an abiding faith in the public. He felt that if, in some manner, available social knowledge could be made freely accessible to the public, the effective intelligence of the public would be released, and the excellence of democracy would be enhanced. Is the imminent emergence of the public information utility the instrumentality through which Dewey's dream can be realized? If we design the computer utility to gather and distribute public information on an equitable basis to all, and if we integrate this utility with new, experimentally evolved democratic procedures that will enable the public to use this information wisely, then, to that extent, democracy stands to be the beneficiary of the new concentration of information power.

The development of such new democratic procedures would involve experimentation with prototype computer utilities to test alternative methods of man-computer communication in the management of social information. Results of such tests could be made widely available, openly discussed and debated, and incorporated into improved versions by public approval or through authorized agencies appointed and monitored by the public.

The concept of deliberate, institutionalized, continuing public experiment for public affairs is a new evolutionary force in democratic advance, a challenge that requires new attitudes and revised values. Each individual will have to learn to think of himself as both subject and experimenter, with lifelong responsibility for selecting and implementing new experiments, evaluating social effectiveness, and applying the results. The realization of this new experimental ethos will require far greater participation and public evaluation of social feedback than has ever occurred before in any democracy, including the personalized democracy of the city-states of ancient Greece. The information utility, linked to the public real time information base, could conceivably provide the leading instrumentality for the public to scan the social scene, identify problems, contribute to social control, and provide continuing corrective feedback on the interplay of pluralistic social experimentation.

The new experimental ethos will also require an infrastructure of continuing, lifelong education in real time, the acquisition of new knowl-

5. George Orwell, *1984* (New York: Harcourt, Brace and World, 1949); Norbert Wiener, *God and Golem Inc.* (Cambridge, Mass.: M.I.T. Press, 1964).

edge when it is needed, in time to meet problems as they arise. When education occurs in real time, it is responsively adaptive and education becomes indistinguishable from on-the-spot human problem-solving. Real time education will then articulate with the tumultuous flow of social experience, and education will become an integral part of such experience. The dusty dogma of the academic creed may become a relic of the past.

There are those who argue that experimental method is good, true, and beautiful, but only as long as it remains in the domain of natural science where it originated, and where, they claim, it belongs. As soon as experimental method is taken out of conventional scientific pursuits and is indiscriminately placed into such fields as democracy and education, into social affairs, then, these critics claim, you enter the never-never land of human values and transcendental metaphysics where statements become meaningless from a scientific point of view. Such is the position, for example, of the logical positivist and most behaviorists.

The pragmatist rejects this view since it would keep scientific method confined within the scientific priesthood and deny it to the public. Experimental method is the most precious legacy of scientific endeavor, and it is too important and too valuable to entrust it to any aristocracy, scientific or otherwise. The crux of the pragmatic position is that values may be formulated as hypotheses, operationally defined, quantitatively measured, and empirically tested with results subject to further test and evaluation as in any other scientific activity. If values are treated as hypotheses, then democracy and education, social attitudes and social change, when they are operationally defined under empirically verifiable conditions, are correspondingly amenable to social experiment.

The early pragmatists were in a difficult position in defending their stand on the possibility and validity of social experimentation because the means for the universalization of experimental method were not at hand and they could not point to concrete, real-world social experiments. They could defend their position in principle but not in practice — a vulnerable position for one who calls himself a pragmatist. But now conditions have changed dramatically, particularly with the advent of systems science and the proliferation of the high-speed electronic computer. Social experiment is now possible on a scale undreamed of by the early pragmatists.

It is commonplace to point out that computers make it possible to collect, organize, and process vast amounts of data quickly and reliably in real time experiments that were beyond the ken of the precomputer era. The computer is, in fact, revolutionizing experimental method in the physical, biological, and social sciences, and the end is nowhere in sight. Systematic experimental method is comparatively recent in human history, dating back only to the Western Renaissance.[6] It has changed rapidly since its inception and has received an electronic jolt with the emergence of the general-purpose digital computer since World War II. Social experiments are now possible in a bewildering variety of forms, for a growing number of variables, with real time collection, reduction, and analysis of social data. For many, perhaps most, the question is no longer whether to experiment on a social scale, but how to experiment in the best interests of the public.

The power of systems science in catalyzing and accelerating the extension of experimental method is probably not as well understood as the more obvious impact of computers. The concrete, tangible system, with its specified stages of definition, design, production, installation, and operation, with test and evaluation occurring at all stages, is the organizational vehicle for the break-through into real-world experimentation. If a coherent social activity is organized into a formal systems framework, then the system serves both as subject and object of its own evolutionary series of system experiments, for continuing system test and evaluation. The integrated system is the crucible in which the real-world experiment is forged.

The combination of computers and system science, in a concrete system context, makes possible the universalization of experimental method in an unprecedented manner. The computer complex can and has served as a built-in laboratory for test and evaluation of system performance. This has occurred most notably and dramatically in the earliest large-scale real time systems, in SAGE air defense and in Mercury-Gemini-Apollo manned spaceflight. In each case there was an attempt to make a great leap forward into new knowledge and new control over uncharted domains. The only way to achieve system goals within planned timetables was to experiment rapidly and boldly with new techniques and new findings.

The system configuration served as its own test bed in measuring and assessing system performance. Simulation, training, testing, and evaluation were indistinguishably intermixed in system development in a new experimental style — in computer-aided, interdisciplinary, mission-oriented, self-experimentation in real time, under common schedules and common system goals. With the advent of other and newer real time

6. George Sarton, *The Life of Science* (Bloomington: Indiana University Press, 1948).

information systems in industry, science, education, medicine, and now, on the threshold of computer utilities, the experimental dance is improvised oṅ new real time tempos.

To the extent that a systems approach is deliberately integrated into social organization, and to the extent that such systems are computerized, to that extent will potential experimental power grow for real-world social experiment. Saying that experimentation is good and noble is not enough, there must be the means and the explicit social configuration — the real time systems configuration — to make such experimentation feasible. The first step, then, in the evolution of real-world social experiment is the evolution from non-real time to real time systems. And the more advanced the computerization of such real time systems, the more potent are the possibilities for ongoing systems experimentation. Social experiment will spread as real time information systems spread and proliferate into interlocking networks, ultimately into ecological complexes of openly cooperative and competitive real time information systems.

The form that real time social control will take will depend on how real time information systems are implemented. If competitive social experiments are freely conducted in an open forum, if many alternatives are explored, if real, not rigged choices are open to the public, if grass-roots participation and feedback is built into the genes and chromosomes of object systems at the system design stage, if adequate checks and balances are devised between the public, the managers, the operators, and users of such systems, if these and related conditions are met, then real time social control may effectively turn out to be of the people, by the people, and for the people, rather than for the old plutocracy or a new technological elite.

When pragmatism was thrust with a "barbaric yawp" into the world of philosophy, mainly through the efforts of William James, a hue and cry arose from many quarters on the crassness and narrowness of this new outgrowth of American materialism. Pragmatism was maligned as opportunistic, self-indulgent, unscientific, anarchistic, and as an ideal comedian's philosophy. The semantic storm over the pragmatic as the narrowly practical was overwhelming; repeated onslaughts from the ideal, the good, true, and beautiful, from the pure and theoretical were launched against this newborn philosophy from all sides.

Peirce, disagreeing with James' exposition of pragmatism, insisted that his theory be called pragmaticism. James turned to the more technical concept of radical empiricism to ward off the semantic pitfalls of pragmatism. Dewey lingered longest over pragmatism, and somewhat reluctantly turned to instrumentalism and experimentalism to defuse the relentless onslaught from critics.

But the temper of the times has changed and the horrendous connotations of pragmatism have become more respectable in a world that desperately needs intelligent, practical solutions to mounting problems. While pragmaticism, radical empiricism, and instrumentalism remain as distinctive historical hallmarks of their creators, American pragmatism persists as the designation of their common origin, continued growth, and diversification in contemporary affairs. After being drummed out of court for challenging the established, absolutistic order, American pragmatism is experiencing a renaissance.

With the emergence of real time information systems, the pragmatic temper of American science and technology has received a fresh impetus and a powerful new thrust. Peirce's "knowledge of consequences" has become transmuted into the principle of real time feedback; James' "cash-value" has become mission payload and system payoff; Dewey's social inquiry and behavioral effectiveness has evolved into system and cost-benefit analyses; the early pragmatic focus on the regulation of future consequences has been transformed into human real time control. The philosophy of pragmatism has evolved into the philosophy of real time.

III. The Information Function in Organizational Decision-Making

Introduction

Defining the role and function of information within organizations and the effects of informational processes on decision-making is not a new concern. Long before computers and new communication systems were developed, the relation of information to policy-making had drawn the serious interest of sociologists, economists, political scientists, social psychologists, historians, and engineers.

In Part III, a group of selections has been assembled which discusses this issue primarily in terms of what might be called the conversion or "alchemy" problem. How does an organization, especially a government agency, turn the base metal of raw data into the organizational gold of knowledge, or policy-wisdom? If, as Pool, McIntosh, and Griffel argue, the social sciences are "data rich and theory poor"; if the definition of system and subsystem boundaries is elusive and our defining efforts often lead to agency self-deception or public delusion; and if the crucial problem in organizations is not a shortage of data, but insufficient time for executives to ponder and digest key samples of data, then the introduction of new data-mountains and electronically swift communication may well place more strain on organizations and produce less effective policy than ever before.

The selections in Part IV examine this problem from a wide variety of viewpoints. What they have in common is an effort by social scientists expert in organizational behavior and analytical processes to provide realistic statements of the information function in organizations. Drawing on social science findings and organization studies, they go behind the formal flow charts and organization manuals, and it is from this base of organizational realities that we will go on to debates over the specific components of technological information systems.

ITHIEL DE SOLA POOL,
STUART MCINTOSH, AND DAVID GRIFFEL

Information Systems and Social Knowledge

Most information systems may be considered to be exercises in applied social science. The data in them generally concern human beings and their institutions. There are exceptions. Meteorologists need large information systems. However, most large information systems, and certainly the examples we have generally used — urban information systems, health information systems, business records systems, survey data banks — are designed to facilitate the management of society and contain predominantly data about man and society.

We may single out four characteristics of the social sciences that profoundly affect the way in which they use computers.

First, the social sciences generally describe multivariate systems. Neither in the physical nor the social sciences are beautifully simple relations typical, such as those of the laws of gases in which the interaction of but two variables, temperature and pressure, give us highly precise prediction. Some aspects of economics, such as the quantitative theory of money and the microeconomics of price, are like that. So are some aspects of psychology, such as models of the memorization of nonsense syllables and some models of simple perception. Yet, generally speaking,

From Ithiel de Sola Pool, Stuart McIntosh, and David Griffel, "On the Design of Computer-Based Information Systems," a paper issued by the Massachusetts Institute of Technology, Cambridge, Massachusetts, 1968. Copyright © 1968 by Ithiel de Sola Pool, Stuart McIntosh, and David Griffel.

Mr. Pool is Professor of Political Science at the Massachusetts Institute of Technology. Mr. McIntosh and Mr. Griffel are members of the research staff of the Center for International Studies, Massachusetts Institute of Technology.

social science phenomena are extremely complex. What determines how a person votes? It is his class, his education, his age, sex, religion, region of origin, urban or rural residence. It is the personal influence of his family, friends, neighbors, and co-workers. A woman tends to vote as her husband. Also, ideology enters in. A principle of inertia keeps people voting for policies that were vital to them in their more formative youthful years, making them seem conservative relative to their times as they grow older. The great depression, Stalin, Hitler, the wars, all left their continuing mark on their generation of voters in ways that today's youth find hard to understand. Furthermore, a psychological craving for consistency affects how people vote. A person who thinks he is a Marxist, for example, wishes to support both the labor movement and internationalism, and finds himself in difficulty in those common situations when organized labor turns out to be chauvinistic and xenophobic. Furthermore, a person's vote is determined by structural facts that affect strategy. Is the candidate who has a plurality elected — so a well-organized and large minority has a chance — or does the law require him to get an absolute majority? If the latter, is a second-turn runoff provided or how are deadlocks broken? All of this affects whether to vote first for one's first choice or to settle for a second-best compromise candidate who has a good chance of winning. All of these demographics, social, ideological, and structural facts, affect how people vote.

The multivariate character of social situations could be illustrated by many other examples. What determines whether a city grows? Its geography and situation on lines of communication; the growth or non-growth of the neighboring urban centers; the state of the economy and all the myriad things that affect that; the net reproduction rate and all the biological and social facts that affect that; tax policies; building policies and technology; war and peace; refugee movements and migrations; the quality of government; and people's values and attitudes towards urban life.

Thus, there is a large class of unlikely outcomes, namely, ones where a clear-cut, widely recognized, reasonably confident social science analysis exists that demonstrates a more or less undesirable outcome of a course of action. The existence of that class of outcomes explains why so much of social science deals with multivariate systems. Where one or two variables dominate a situation, intelligent policy makers and activists are likely to foresee their consequences and see what to do about them. The dominant variables are then stalemated. The many other less obvious determinants then come into their own.

Clearly, society is not very good at running itself well. Social evils and catastrophes are rampant. But the ones that occur are most likely to be the outcome of interactions among a large number of complex variables so large and subtle that intelligent men walk into their fates unknowingly. Urban blight is a good example. Tax laws, immigration laws, business considerations, traffic choices, and technology all interact to turn neighborhoods from homesites into slums. These changes seem to work inexorably despite counteracting efforts of men of power and good will. If there were a single dominant variable, one could be quite sure that at least some mayors and city councils would have placed it under control long since. Indeed, they have done that with several potential dominant variables. They have created fire departments that prevent our cities from burning down. They have created traffic and utility systems that make it possible for millions of people to congregate in a small area. What remains unmanaged is the interaction of a series of less obvious variables, about which no one can be glibly confident as to the right course of action. It is their interaction that brings the downfall of large urban areas. Only careful multivariate analysis can help gain more control over those residual fluctuations of the system.

We have now established one key characteristic of the social sciences and the reason for it. The social sciences usually describe multivariate systems in which there are no one or two dominant variables to account for most of the variance, but rather a large number of weak variables in complex systems of interaction, and they do so because men control obvious dominant variables.

A second characteristic of the social sciences follows almost as a corollary. The social sciences are data-rich and theory-poor. The systems they analyze usually have to be described with large numbers of parameters measurements. On the other hand, theories are hard to come by that explain more than a few variables. Carl Hovland has pointed out that there are rather good theories that predict attitude change in a laboratory situation, but they seldom appear to have relevance to real-life attitude studies in the field. The reason is that, in the laboratory, subjects are paid to listen to a message to which they respond. In real-life uncontrolled situations, people choose what they will pay attention to, and they avoid paying attention to anything that will change their minds. Thus, our knowledge of real-life attitude change consists largely of poll statistics about what was believed by people at different times and places. We have little theory that could predict and thus eliminate the need for large-scale empirical compilation.

A third characteristic of the social sciences which also follows is that they are generally phenomenological, describing natural environments rather than working with well-controlled experimentation. There is some experimentation done in the social sciences, but, as we noted in the example just above, what it gains in rigor it loses in immediate relevance. The value of rigorous laboratory work is inestimably great. Nonetheless, quantitatively most of what students of society wish to know is specific to some contentual situation. It is a problem in some region, at some specific period of time, for some particular group of people. Thus, most of social science is phenomenological.

A fourth characteristic of the social sciences is that they are historical. Human beings, like animals but unlike most objects of the natural sciences, have memories. What they do is not only dependent upon the present condition, but also on everything they know from the past. A pendulum of a certain length pulled back a certain distance will swing the same way whether the experiment is done the first or the fiftieth time. A person given an identical task to do in identical circumstances may do a very different thing the second or nth time for his circumstances are really different each time, since he retains in memory the experience of the previous times. Thus, Markov chain models are often wrong for description of human behavior. They take no account of experience before the present state of the system. In most social science models, at least some variables must be time-dependent.

These four characteristics of the social sciences all make them particularly susceptible to help from computerization. Computers are instruments that efficiently store, search, organize, and reorganize large sets of data or other symbols. Up to now, however, the predominant use of computers by social scientists has not taken account of the distinctive characteristics of either the social sciences or of the computer itself. Up to now, computers have been used by social scientists mostly as large arithmetic calculators. Statistics is a discipline with a long and reputable history in the social sciences. The problems to which Galton, Pearson, Fisher, and others addressed themselves were generally social. Censuses and economic measures have kept most statisticians busy. The sophistication of social statistics is at least as great as that of statistics in any other field. To social scientists, with much statistical calculation to do, the arrival of the computer was indeed a blessing. It saved numerous hours of research assistant time.

That, however, is a use of the computer which illustrates the familiar phenomenon of the persistence of old habits in the use of a new technology. Early automobiles were built to look like horse carriages. Computers were originally designed by mathematicians and engineers who conceived of them as machines to compute. This is attested to by the misleading name "computer" which still clings to these devices for manipulating symbols.

The name has its effect. Even today most computation centers run with hardware-software configurations designed to optimize the ability to compute. Batch processing centers tend to evaluate their systems by how fast they perform the basic arithmetic operations. Most time-sharing systems provide the user at his console with what is, in effect, a desk calculator. Only a few sophisticated systems provide him with any facility for organizing and manipulating files.

For all these reasons the computer revolution in the social sciences may come a little more slowly than one might otherwise expect, given the natural affinity of the computer's capabilities and the needs of the social sciences. Whether slowly or fast, however, we can delineate some of the kinds of things that will increasingly be done with computers by social scientists and that will transform those disciplines. We can predict the increasing use of simulation models to represent multivariate systems too complex to allow of analytic solutions. We can predict the development of large data systems with automated retrieval and on-line analysis. The data files will come from many sources, much of them as byproducts of normal management record-keeping. At the same time, we predict, social indicators will be developed to measure such matters as discontent, health, and educational progress, to supplement such familiar economic indicators as GNP and unemployment rates.

Computer simulation models have been used in the social sciences in a number of applications. Social scientists have simulated the functioning of a business firm, an industry, and also the economy of a whole country. They have simulated bargaining between nations and the process of decision-making in a crisis. They have simulated the growth of population from generation to generation. They have simulated the spread of a fad and the spread of an innovation in a population. They have simulated the communication system of a country. They have simulated the electorate and how it makes up its mind. Simulations are useful when there are many and discontinuous variables in operation.

It is possible to represent in a computer model virtually any set of precisely expressed relations. Scientific theories are, after all, sets of symbols, whether in linguistic or graphical or mathematical form. Any of these can be expressed in computer interpretable code. If the original expression was unambiguous, then a computer interpretable translation is possible. For the social sciences, the computer interpretable formulation of the theory is particularly valuable because social theories are so complex and multivariate that the human mind is pushed beyond its limited capacity to keep things straight and to analyze them. The human mind is skillful at simplification. Intuition serves us well in homing in on key variables and relationships. However, the human analyst cannot begin to compare with the computer in accurate and detailed calculation of the interactions in a complex system.

If we are right in characterizing not only present but future social theories as predominantly multivariate simulations, lacking strongly dominant variables, then several important things follow. Predictions from such theories are highly dependent upon numerous empirical measurements. From the point of view of a person who controls any one variable, only a little can be predicted without entering large numbers of parametric measures on the other variables into his calculations. It is in the nature of things that the social sciences are data-rich and theory-poor. It is not just that we are at a primitive stage in them.

Measures of social phenomena are, therefore, central to the development of social science. The census and social statistics of all kinds are the basis of any social science. If we look at the history of economics, for example, we find that theory developed best on those topics on which statistics were readily available. The most precocious part of economics was the theory of foreign trade. It developed long before the theory of the domestic market, because at national frontiers the custom men collected data on everything that crossed. Similarly, the theory of banking grew early because banks generated records.

Today economics is the most advanced of the social sciences, very largely because business accounting makes it feasible to compile good economic indicators. We have available measures of cost of living, wholesale prices, GNP, bank transactions, stock averages, savings, investments, production levels, employment, unemployment, costs of production, and volume of trade.

Now the interest of the social sciences is increasingly turning to the measurement of satisfaction and of those behaviors in society that cannot be kept track of by money accounts. Today there is an increasing awareness of the need for social indicators that measure such matters as discontent, health, political attitudes, and educational progress. If society is to evaluate its performance in such fields as race relations, education, or citizen contentment, we need social indicators based upon measurement of noneconomic aspects of human behavior, and even on people's attitudes.

The identification of useful social indicators is a task calling for considerable theoretical sophistication. We usually measure society's progress in education by the increase in the average years of schooling. We have no idea, however, whether a man now completing the twelfth grade is better or worse educated than he would have been 30 years ago. In the United States, as a result of the revolution in race relations in the last few years, Negroes are filling better jobs than they used to, but their levels of aspiration are also properly rising. No one can say whether the degree of contentment or bitterness in the Negro ghettos is greater or less than it was two years ago. These are the kinds of phenomena for which standardized reliable measurements are necessary.

It will, of course, be objected that monetary measurements are easy, but that measurements of attitude, beliefs, knowledge, or contentment are somehow subjective and unfeasible. Clearly, they are difficult to make; that is why they have come more slowly. Yet, even today, we have available a few examples of well-accepted and reliable social indicators to provide an existence proof for their possibility. The I.Q. is an example of a widely accepted, reasonably reliable, and standardized measure of a subtle psychological fact. It is as stable and well accepted as many of the conventional economic measures. Another example is a social indicator that almost inadvertently has come to play a major role in American political life, namely, the Gallup Poll's repeated question, asking whether the citizens believe the President of the United States is doing a good job. This question is asked periodically of a national sample. The results are prominently reported in the press and awaited by the politicians. The movement of this indicator has become as politically important as many of the constitutionally authorized ballots, and certainly as important as many economic indicators. Major changes of national policy result from a loss of confidence in the President shown in this poll. His ability to influence Congress is seriously affected. One can no longer describe the American political system without reference to this political indicator.

All of this has nothing directly to do with computers. Computers are, of course, used to tabulate the results of a social survey, but what they contribute to that is a few days' greater speed in analysis. The computer as a tabulating machine does nothing that unit record equipment did not do before, or that even hand tabulation could not practicably do. The significance of the computer is not in our ability to compile any one social indicator, but in our ability to compile and manipulate very large masses of data, including large numbers of social indicators. For example, measurements of educational accomplishment need to be applied not only nationally, but school system by school system (school by school, and teacher by teacher). Measurements of public health need to be controlled by all the varieties of treatments, intentional and unintentional, which may affect the rates. The difficulties and the subtlety of analysis required to establish the conditions of diseases and health have been illustrated, in recent years, by the years it took to become aware of the medical consequences of smoking and the difficulty in establishing these conclusions firmly.

The benefits that can accrue from having computerized data systems that facilitate the application of social knowledge is clear. It is also clear that gaining power over our social destiny carries dangers. The dangers are minimized if knowledge is available for competitive use to all. The dangers are maximized if there is a monopoly of control over information. There is a widespread misapprehension that the computer centralizes information control. The assumption is that the planner sitting in the Capitol can see spread before him on his console all the details of the operation of the economy or society of his nation and can make decisions to control it. In the Communist world it is sometimes argued that he can thus make it function better. Clearly, this is an illusion, for it assumes the magnificent wisdom of the planner. But, the relevant point to make here is not only that such centralization of decision is unwise, but that it is an illusion and quite unnecessary in a computer-based information environment. The information facilities provided by the computer can equally serve as a decentralizing instrument. They can make available to all parts of an organization the kinds of immediate and complete information that is today available only at the center. The power of top leadership today is very largely the power of their information monopoly. Only they are served by the armies of clerks that compile the records of what is going on. A society with computerized information facilities can make its choice between centralization and decentralization, because it will have the mechanical capability of moving information either way. An information utility can make information available with unprecedented facility to people working at all levels.

If our picture of the future of social science and its applications is correct, then there are substantial implications for information systems.

The demand will continue to grow for large and comprehensive information systems, encompassing data to provide all sorts of parametric measurements of social phenomena.

The computer system needed is more than a retrieval system in that it must facilitate the entry of the retrieved data into simulation models and facilitate on-line manipulation of the models, followed by storage of the output as new data files. Like statistical packages, the simulation programs will be many, varied, and should be subject to choice and programming by the user. Convenient interfaces between data and simulation program must be provided, on-line. For example, traffic data needs to be easily usable in any of the many simulation models that have been developed to represent systems of moving vehicles.

Much of the data needed for social information systems will come online as a byproduct of managerial operations. Computer-controlled traffic lights that assess the flow of traffic by electric eye will incidentally provide data on traffic movement that will be much better than what is now collected by surveys. Computerization of hospital patient records and billing procedures will provide, as a byproduct, the basis for a health information system. Use of computer-aided instruction permits compilation of records of records of educational achievement. The frequency of use of special questionnaires may actually decline.

Some data will, however, have to be specially compiled if we are to have the social indicators we need for effective management of our complex society. Such social indicators will be the product, in part, of the data in social data archives, but, even more important, the indicators reported in regular time-series will be a major portion of the basic data in our social information systems.

The data that analysts want will never be all in one place. Communication networks among researchers via their respective information facilities will bring to each whatever data he wants and may legitimately have regardless of where it is normally housed or in what format.

ANTHONY G. OETTINGER

A Bull's Eye View of Information Systems

Research on management and engineering information systems has been neglected. To be sure, everybody who is anybody nowadays runs his payroll on a computer. There is a theory of sorting. There is a successful theory and practice of such isolated business functions as inventory control, and in areas where linear programming models are adequate, notably for example in the control of the production of petroleum products, a harmonious and fruitful wedding of operations research and computing technique has been consummated.

Yet all is far from well. Military or industrial management have again and again been promised timely, accurate, and relevant reports or, better yet, multi-colored wall-sized displays with instant access to vast stores of recorded information about any aspect of their enterprise on which a decision must be made. They have received huge bills for machines, huge bills for programs, masses of unreadable printouts, and, when enough honesty and courage could be mustered, some wry jokes about "GIGO," interpreted by trade wits as "Garbage In Garbage Out" or, worse, as "Garbage In Gospel Out."

The following observation goes near the heart of the matter:

Ironically, the basic problem which the computer poses is ineffi-

From Anthony G. Oettinger, "A Bull's Eye View of Management and Engineering Information Systems," *Proceedings of the Association for Computing Machinery, 19th National Conference,* Philadelphia, Pennsylvania, August 25–27, 1964. Copyright © 1964, Association for Computing Machinery, Inc.

Mr. Oettinger is Professor of Linguistics and Applied Mathematics at Harvard University and a Research Associate to its Program on Technology and Society.

ciency — because the computer *is* difficult to use. All communications between the user and the machine must first be formalized by large professional staffs of analysts and programmers before the user can achieve the necessary data processing capability at some future date. This is frequently unreasonable and sometimes impossible. The Air Force can't afford to spend precious man years in programming to find that it has only solved yesterday's problems. Nor can it afford to bow to Parkinson's Law and carry along hosts of programmers whose ranks will swell exponentially with the numbers of computers required.[1]

It is suggested that, to solve this "basic problem," the middle man be eliminated and the user be given direct access to his machine with means for building up processes and underlying data gradually and in his own way with what is described as "user controlled evolution and flexibility." [2]

The key notion here is not the dubious implication that formalization is necessary only because of the interposition of analysts and programmers while, on the contrary, a user directly coupled to the machine could somehow muddle through with great speed toward an undefined goal, if only he were given "complete freedom to work in the problem setting unconstrained by a fixed set of subroutines." [3]

Timing and vagueness are the key factors. Time lags in programming and time lags in querying through intermediaries are important, of course, but other delays of equal importance appear in a complete process: there is the time required to accumulate and to verify an initial data base; there is the time taken in gathering new information and updating existing files; there is the time taken in understanding information displayed. Mere access to information is of no value without confidence in the timeliness and accuracy of the information and, above all, raw information, however timely, accurate, and relevant, is not to be equated with knowledge or understanding. Formalization and structure — or vagueness, the lack of these — are also important factors, but they cannot be studied in the presence of change without due regard to timing.

It may well be asked how, if so much is wrong with computers and their users, anything gets accomplished at all. An answer should emerge from considering four categories of tasks, definable in terms of timing and structure, which govern the share of each task that is best allocated to men or to machines.

1. C. H. Terhune, Jr., "Address by Major General C. H. Terhune, Jr., to the American Federation of Information Processing Societies," Las Vegas, Nevada, November 12, 1963, Air Force Systems Command, Electronic Systems Division News Release, Office of Information, L. G. Hanscom Field, Bedford, Massachusetts.
2. Ibid.
3. Ibid.

In one of these categories the machine clearly predominates and has achieved unquestionable usefulness. In a second, unstable, category the value of machines is marginal at best, and the *necessary things get done simply because the official system is usually bypassed, machines and all.* It will be suggested that, in this interesting category, legitimizing surreptitious bypassing procedures and assisting *them* by machine should prove a fruitful avenue of exploration. In a third category, presently exemplified only in several frontier research areas, machines may prove useful in the future. The fourth category is, at present, entirely speculative.

	Cow	Bull
Steady State	Successful	Research Area
Transient	Troublesome (unstable)	Speculative

Fig. 1. Application of computers to four categories of tasks

The definition of the four categories is illustrated in Figure 1.

Time is characterized in terms of steady state and transient phenomena, concepts familiar in electrical engineering and in control theory. The other axis of the definition is described in terms of the familiar if slightly disreputable notion of "bull" and a complementary notion of "cow":

bull (pure): relevancies, however relevant, without data.

to bull (v. intrans.) or the act of bulling: to discourse upon the contexts, frames of reference, and points of observation which would determine the origin, nature, and meaning of data if one had any. (To present evidence of an understanding of form in the hope that the reader may be deceived into supposing a familiarity with content.)

cow (pure): data, however relevant, without relevancies.

to cow (v. intrans.) or the act of cowing: to list data (or perform operations) without awareness of, or comment upon, the contexts, frames of reference, or points of observation which determine the origin, nature, and meaning of the data (or procedures). To write on the assumption that "a fact is a fact." (To present evidence of hard work as a substitute for understanding, without any intent to deceive.)[4]

Although necessary to delineate the scope of bull as generally understood, the part of the definition in parentheses should be omitted for our purposes, good honest bulling being a basic and vital function of management. This sentiment is more conventionally expressed in the definition of management as the art of making decisions with insufficient information, namely as bulling with some contamination by cow. The parenthesized portion of the definition of cowing should likewise be deleted to remove moral overtones.

It is obvious from the definitions that cowing is what computers do best and that to bull is human. It should, therefore, come as no surprise that computers have been most effective and successful in coping with cow in the steady state. The steady state, to be more precise now, exists when neither the well-defined procedures nor the structure and scope of the data defining a task change significantly while the computer is operating on the data. Contemporary computers, of course, see their data as pure cow. It is the prior human act of specifying procedures and data structures which, if done with any care at all (and this brings up the vexing matters of problem definition, adequate documentation, and so forth) provides the human recipient of machine output with precisely those contexts, frames of reference, or points of observation which determine the origin, nature, and meaning of the machine output. The steady state hypothesis guarantees that machine output, when obtained, is germane to the task as seen by the user at that time, that is, it insures that the output is interpretable and *meaningful*. Under these conditions:

The masculine context has embraced the feminine particular, though itself "born of woman." Such a union is knowledge itself, and

4. W. J. Perry, Jr., *Examsmanship and the Liberal Arts—An Epistomological Inquiry*, Bureau of Study Counsel, Harvard University, March 1963.

it alone can generate new contexts and new data which can unite in their turn to form new knowledge.[5]

While the structure of data must be fixed in steady state cowing, data content may vary. However, output must be obtained while the input data on which it is based are still valid and, of course, in time to meet any deadline beyond which it becomes useless. If this is the case, normal usage says that the machine system is operating in *real time*. If this is not the case, the output loses not its meaning, but its value. The categories of Figure 1 are concerned with meaning and hence potential usefulness, while "real time" determines actual usefulness.

A few examples should help to lend concrete substance to the foregoing. Most conventional numerical analysis applications are prime examples of steady state cowing. This is certainly the case when the procedure is a well-established algorithm whose definition is known to be sound, when proper scaling has been performed to avoid overflow or underflow, and when input variables are restricted to a range for which the algorithm is known to work. The interpretation of output under such circumstances is predetermined and straightforward. An algorithm for weather prediction is meaningful not only abstractly but practically if it predicts today's weather correctly, but it is useless outside the realm of research if it makes this prediction only tomorrow, or when conditions have already changed, that is, not in real time. Payroll processing is, by now, an almost classical form of steady state cowing in real time. Determining the proper domain of steady state information processing in an integrated enterprise is still a major problem of contemporary data processing systems design.

Transients may arise in several ways. First, the amount of data may grow. Occasional spurts or benign long-term growth are usually easily handled by temporary or permanent additions to processing facilities. Periodic peak loads and long-term growth of the volume of checks in the banking system are good contemporary examples. However, malignant data growths also occur, typically in military and space data-reduction activities, although the "historical records" of ordinary business are not immune, the urge to "gather statistics" being so much stronger than the capacity for digesting them. Any thought of using these data in real time is rapidly abandoned. Surgery — selling the records for scrap — and time — just forgetting their existence — are the great healers; nothing is lost but time, effort, and money.

More serious are the transients induced by changes in the procedures,

5. Ibid.

data structures, and data scope defining a task. Unless such changes can not only be reflected in machine operations, but also perceived and assimilated by the recipients of machine output, the resulting cow, nearly of laboratory purity, is mismatched with all available bull, and sterility inevitably ensues. Such transients are of least trouble when they occur in periodic systems and can be handled within a period. The additions of new regular employees to a payroll, and similar changes in scope, are usually handled with great ease in well-designed systems, which then return to the steady state. One-time procedural or structural changes, for instance a change in income tax withholding rates, or a changeover from piece work to time rate throughout a factory, can be handled in periodic systems when there is enough lead time to plan, execute, and test the necessary modifications and to explain them to all concerned before cut-over to a new mode at an appropriate time in some future cycle. As anyone who has ever participated in a conversion of this type can testify, it is often no easy matter and always requires the most minute and care-ful planning. It can, however, be done and has been done successfully without amplification and propagation of the transient, and without loss of confidence in the automated system. A good deal of careful and pro-tracted backstage bulling thus stabilizes the transient into an instantane-ous switch from one mode of steady state cow into another.

When aperiodic demands are made of a periodic system, when task components change more rapidly than the processing period, or when there are no well-defined or definable periods, critical instabilities ap-pear. Malignant data growth "merely" obliterates real time; periodic transients can be stabilized; in either case meaning remains stable. In the aperiodic case, cow and bull stampede and union becomes impossible.

Aperiodic demands on periodic systems are frequent and they are han-dled by bypassing the system in a characteristic way. For example, the pay of an employee who leaves his job between payroll dates is, more often than not, either estimated or calculated by hand on the basis of information available from printouts made at the last period and brought up to date by information obtained by telephone or other ad hoc means from his supervisors. The system itself remains ignorant of the event un-til the next periodic updating when appropriate information is intro-duced, typically via a change file. It is not atypical for adjustments to be made to the estimated pay when more precise calculations can be made at the normal point in the period.

Rapid changes in task components or absence of any periodicity are less frequent and, although computer people tend to take it for granted, the need for aperiodic instantaneous operation should be very strongly questioned:

> Most companies find a month too short a period of time for an accurate budget on financial reports. Would management want hourly or daily profit information? Ridiculous! This information requires periodic accumulation and analysis. In fact, the shorter the period covered, the less reliable it is. What, then, could be the value of having this type of information available in a computer's memory for management to interrogate at will? [6]

Lack of periodicity and rapid change of task components are most marked in the large defense and space research and development projects. The attempts to use PERT [Program Evaluation and Review Technique] techniques in these realms provide us with an outstanding case history of unstable transient cow.

The outlines of the PERT ideal are too well known to warrant re-iterating them here. The reader in need of refreshing is referred to two excellent summaries, one from the business point of view and one from the computing point of view, each accompanied by an extensive bibliography.[7] Although the bulk of the literature is either stolidly neutral and narrowly technical or else fervently proselytizing on the matter of the value of PERT, some skeptical voices are being raised:

> Though there is no statistical accumulation of data concerning the success and failure of PERT on particular programs, it seems safe to say that as many PERT-ing attempts have failed as have succeeded. And of those which have been deemed as successful, many have been so in name only. That is, there may have been impressive graphics and expensive computer runs, but managers were actually basing decisions upon more conventional techniques.[8]

Typical benefits cited for PERT are the following six:[9]

1. *"The development of an intelligent, intelligible and efficient plan."* This point is unassailable. Doubtlessly, a positive requirement for explicit planning, coupled with the Hawthorne effect, will be beneficial to any activity. The PERT network is, in many instances, a very apt mode of representation for plans.

6. J. Dearden, "Can Management Information Be Automated?" *Harvard Business Review*, March–April 1964, pp. 128–135.

7. A. B. Kahn, "Skeletal Structure of PERT and CPA Computer Programs," *Communications of the ACM* 6 (August 1963): 473–479; A. R. Dooley, "Interpretations of PERT," *Harvard Business Review*, March–April 1964, pp. 161–172.

8. R. T. Boverie, "The Practicalities of PERT," *IEEE Transactions on Engineering Management*, March 1963, pp. 3–5.

9. Ibid.

2. *"The accurate measurement of progress against the plan."*

3. *"The prognostication of task accomplishments and goal achievement."*

4. *"The signalling of potential problem areas before they actually occur."*

Were steady state cowing attainable, benefits 2, 3, and 4 could conceivably be obtained. Unfortunately, for projects with well over 100,000 activities reported at the lowest level of detail, data are weeks old when they come to be processed by the PERT programs of a sub-contractor. The output of these programs is next interpreted by "professional" PERT analysts whose principal function, aside from panning for nuggets of meaning in unreadable printouts prepared by "professional" programmers, is to make sure they and their company will stay out of trouble. Appropriately interpreted data are then fed with due delay into a contractor-level network. Some more iterations of this process eventually yield condensed data for the attention of top management. It is now months since the data so presented has been collected at the sub-contractor level.

Were it only for this lapse of real time, the resultant data might have at least historical meaning. They are, however, cow without bull: needless to say, in the meantime the real network has changed many times over; hence, no part of the computer system actually reflects the network as it is now, nor are subnetworks in phase with one another. What does the manager do under these circumstances? He telephones his subordinates to get their current estimate of progress, accomplishments, and problems.

Such short circuits are occasionally excused on the grounds that

> The older, conventional techniques will be readily utilized by much of management because they are part of management's heritage. Regardless of the relatively poor past performance of conventional techniques in depicting problem areas, predicting status, and forcing planning, the weak known is preferred over the strong unknown.[10]

The problem is surely more fundamental than that: where management needs fresh bull, PERT supplies stale cow. In many cases the implementation of PERT systems has fallen into the hands of (1) professional PERT analysts with an old-fashioned accountant's outlook, who treat PERT networks as if they were audit trails rather than planning tools, (2) hosts of programmers dedicated to polishing to an exquisite shine multitudes of infinitesimal variations on the basic PERT theme,

10. Ibid.

257

and (3) an occasional precise theorist who suggests from the sidelines that it would be well "to introduce a fourth time estimate into the calculations for fitting β distributions to activity completion times. The fourth time estimate would make it possible to remove the constraint that $\beta = ((b - a)/6).$" [11]

To keep the balance it is only fair to add that such means as milestone or bar chart reports hardly fare better. They too are bypassed by the phone call to Joe.

5. *"The capability to simulate and optimize plan changes and to determine impact upon program goals."*

6. *"The capability to maximize the effective use of resources."*

These last two benefits are hardly ever bestowed by any actual PERT system. Where the attempt is made to simulate or maximize, it is the basic network concept and network manipulation which is useful, since the data massaged tend to be hypothetical data or some kind of estimates without direct relation to the flow of cow from below.

The problem of maintaining the structure of PERT networks up to date is itself reminiscent of another major and currently fashionable object of unstable transient cowing. This is the process now being popularized as *Configuration Management*. The essential problem is to keep effective track of the hierarchy of components and assemblies fitting into one another or combining together, ultimately to form some single unit of interest. This problem is serious enough in any industrial situation, but particularly so during development and early production when design changes and other modifications are the rule rather than the exception.

A manual which makes recommendations for a refined system of Configuration Management has this to say with respect to an important input to the reporting and control system, the so-called ECP or Engineering Change Proposal:

> If the initial message is other than a written communication, it shall be confirmed by written message or ECP form within 24 hours. When written messages are used, a formal ECP on an ECP form shall be prepared and submitted within 30 days after the initial communication. The same change identification number shall be assigned to the formal ECP as was assigned to the written message, except that the "E" code shall be dropped. This formal ECP shall

11. J. E. Murray, "Consideration of PERT Assumptions," *IEEE Transactions on Engineering Management*, September 1963, pp. 94–99.

258

reference the original communication, the individuals contacted and the status of contractual authorization.[12]

Elsewhere we find:

The exact cycling of the updating report to and from the agencies responsible for its preparation and updating shall be established by the applicable Configuration Management Office (CMO).[13]

It is a safe bet that here too phone calls will be necessary to find out what is really going on.

It might be argued that Configuration Management, unlike the problems to which PERT addresses itself, is justifiably a matter of cow and not of bull. It is a vital matter, for example, to know precisely what parts should be in what equipment at what time. Granting this to be the case, the argument remains that a system which provides for time lags up to 30 days in the formalization of one vital part of the reporting cycle and leaves the timing of others at local discretion, cannot achieve its objectives. The contexts and frames of reference simply shift too fast.

About such matters the computer profession has shown a remarkably unprofessional head-in-the-sand attitude bordering on solipsism. It is not true of management and engineering information systems in general and only partially true of PERT that "theory and systems are well expounded," although truly "the harsh practicalities of PERT have remained in the background." [14] The same comments apply to our partners in crime, the systems and procedures people, the management specialists, and management itself. In the rush for sales, for writing "sophisticated" "advanced" programs (giant economy size), for the prestige of a bigger and faster machine than that of the competitor next door, fundamental questions remain unasked and unanswered.

Who has objectively investigated the dynamics of the PERT reporting process? Or the need for it? How long does it take to get data from their source to the point of use? How long need it take? Why should the data be gathered at all? And supposing one assumes that "operational control data would be the only information that it makes any sense to collect and update continuously," what would be the conclusion?

All the computer could supply, when interrogated, would be such things as inventory levels (by any part desired) or production records!

12. Anonymous, "Configuration Management During the Definition and Acquisition Phases," AFSCM 375-1, Symposium Workshop Draft, January 1, 1964, Headquarters, Air Force Systems Command, USAF, Exhibit VIII, paragraph 6.4.8.4, p. 19.
13. Ibid., Exhibit XVII, paragraph 6.1i, p. 3.
14. Boverie, "The Practicalities of PERT."

And what is management to do with this information when it is flashed on the board room screen? There is only one thing that it can do — harass operational personnel. Notice also that you do not need an elaborate computer installation to communicate when something is seriously wrong in the operating area, which is the only time when top management should be concerned. The usual procedure is to accumulate the information that is collected for the operational managers and to submit it to top management. (Remember, if top management needs the data, the person directly responsible must need it, and, therefore, it has to be collected for his use in any event.)[15]

One conclusion is inescapable: when management needs good bull it goes to the best sources, namely introspection or consultation of subordinates. This is invariably the case when attempting to operate machines in the transient cow mode. There is also good reason to believe that it would remain the case even if "all" information could be made available instantly, since, as has already been noted, information and knowledge are not synonymous, and a good subordinate is a better aid to understanding than raw data. What is needed, therefore, is not instant cow but, if anything, instant bull. If it is true that "many managers today are making decisions using less than one-tenth of the information that would be made available to them *without a computer*,"[16] then surely good bull is the rarer commodity.

Vannevar Bush has made much the same observation, although what he said has been grievously distorted. He said, to repeat, "The investigator is staggered by . . . *findings and conclusions . . . many of which he cannot find time to grasp, much less to remember*,"[17] and he did not say *staggered by the papers and the reports . . . most of which he cannot find*. So much time and effort have been spent chasing the will-o'-the-wisp of automatic document and data retrieval that far too little attention has been paid to those positive phenomena which have kept the show going in spite of the alleged "information explosion." References have indeed been made to "invisible colleges" whose members supply one another with scientific and technical information either orally or through the exchange of informal, otherwise unpublished literature. However, the whole procedure is viewed as irregular, slightly perverted, and possibly subversive. But a similar phenomenon makes the industrial and military world go round.

That part of scientific and technical information that can be freely

15. Dearden, "Can Management Information Be Automated?"
16. Ibid.
17. Vannevar Bush, "As We May Think," *Atlantic Monthly,* July 1945, pp. 101–108.

handled is in articles, reports, abstracts, chapters of books, and the like — collections of words in a form that can be reproduced or stored. *The unhandleable part — in people's minds, rough notes, and conversations — which is often of greater importance, still escapes all tools of information pursuit except human memory.*[18]

A poor manager may think that if he does not know, nobody knows. A good one knows that when he needs information about *A* he calls on Joe and when he needs information about *B* he calls on George. Joe and George, in turn, either know or know who should know, and so on down the line. Across the line also, for in spite of in-groups, interdepartmental jealousies, competition, and other isolating influences, the horizontal component of the velocity of information is often much higher than the vertical, and the colleague in the same job at the other place almost always can and does find out everything but explicitly confidential information appropriate to his level long before any supervisor on either side does. Thus, information that might take two months to travel up and then down the official channels from division *A* to division *B* veritably leaps across if only Joe knows who George is.

It would be a healthy first step if these pervasive and vital underground practices could be discussed in management and computer circles at least as frankly as sex. Computer people might then be tempted to explore new realms of application for steady state cowing techniques. For instance, it might turn out that keeping track of organizations, formal and informal, might be both easier and more rewarding than keeping track of equipment or documents.

In a stable, old-time company everybody who matters knows who knows what, and it is a sad day when old Ginny, who always had last year's sales reports at her fingertips, or old George, whose thirty years of design experience were available to anyone for recall, interpretation, and discussion, retire. This, of course, is of no use to the newcomer to the organization who must spend a long time finding out who's who, a process accepted as a traditional form of corporate hazing. The information needs of the rank and file deserve at least as much if not more attention as those of management.

In the rapidly growing industries, and almost everywhere programmers are employed, reorganization, expansion, and turnover are so common that hardly anybody knows who knows what. Finding Joe is a serious problem at *all* levels. To compound the difficulty, most organizations

18. J. W. Tukey, "The Citation Index and the Information Problem," Annual Report for 1962 under Grant NSF-G-22108, Statistical Techniques Research Group, Princeton University.

guard their internal organization charts, job assignments, and telephone books, if indeed they have any up-to-date ones, from their employees, other divisions, or competitors with all the jealous concern of a brooding hen.

While there are legitimate reasons to guard privacy, at least part of this concern arises from a mistaken confusion of information gathering with the exercise of authority. Clearly, the opening of information lines up, down, and across would legitimize a leaping over organizational boundaries that, while essential for real accomplishment, is done nowadays only at official risk and peril. Organization lines reflect lines of authority, but while knowledge is power, the gathering of information is not the exercise of authority. It seems, therefore, perfectly proper for a manager to leap several levels down in search of answers, for a subordinate to leap across organization lines and occasionally over his boss's head, so long as decisions and orders travel by normal channels and care is taken to protect legitimate confidences such as, for example, actual salary figures. As pointed out elsewhere:

> President Kennedy . . . has insisted not only on the right, but the necessity, to talk to those who are informed and not only to those who, by some quirk of accident, occupy positions of authority.[19]

Hence, the use of machines to maintain detailed, accurate, and up-to-date organization charts ought to be seriously investigated, aiming toward a quasi-automatic Joe-finder which strikes an acceptable balance between accessibility and privacy. Key-Work-in-Context techniques, associative network methods, and the like might prove useful in preparing an index of the organization by functional areas and in aiding the tracing of paths through the organization. A few such attempts have been made, but none have received sufficient encouragement to proceed to detailed formulation or significant testing. It should also be noted in passing that the updating of an organization chart can be controlled through a mechanism neither president nor detail draftsman will care to bypass, namely the payroll file.

In summary, the range of tasks described as transient cow are ripe subjects for fresh studies free from preconceptions. Too many of these tasks have been mistaken for steady state cow, and machines intended for them stand bypassed and useless as expensive monuments to the accountant's love of pure cow, to the programmers' unprofessional pursuit of their needlessly esoteric art for art's sake, and to widespread management neglect of its own information problems and those of its sub-

19. J. H. Hollomon, Letter to the Editor, *Science,* January 31, 1964, p. 429.

ordinates. The accountants must learn to distinguish history from plans. The programmers must think of themselves less as mathematicians manqué or as aristocrats of accounting and more as engineers, for programming is, if anything, a major new incarnation of the vanishing older engineering professions. Programmers are not scientists, and their role is too important and too professional to permit treating them as technicians or clerks. The practice of *program engineering* with the ethical and intellectual standards and obligations of an engineering profession should be encouraged. Management must learn to apply to information problems, to program engineering, and to programming or software the same expectations, the same standards, the same controls, and the same status it applies to other engineering aspects of its enterprise.

The two remaining categories of tasks may now be disposed of rather briefly, since relatively little is known about them. Steady state bull may be characterized as a task in which one or more of the procedures, the data structures, and data scopes which define it are allowed to vary in a controlled way. Concern here is not primarily with the rapid processing of vast amounts of data but rather with the shaping and understanding of contexts, frames of reference, and points of observation.

This is the realm of developing and testing new methods of numerical analysis; the realm of simulation, of "the capability to simulate and optimize plan changes and to determine impact upon program goals" and of "the capability to maximize the effective use of resources." [20] It is also the realm of interesting experiments in computer-aided design and planning and of renewed speculation about the "Memex," which Bush visualized as an aid to thought and not as a vast automatic garbage can full of undigested documents.

Were some of the time, effort, and money heedlessly spent on premature, ill-conceived, and vast cowing schemes applied to studying the dynamics of information flow in organizations and to encouraging research and development — but not premature application — of methods and devices suitable for steady state bulling, there would be a much greater likelihood of genuine progress toward meeting management's need for good honest bull spiced but not drowned by a dash of relevant cow.

The absence of any control over procedures, structures, scope, or content characterizes transient bull. This highly speculative area encompasses a fair amount of serious research on what would be popularly described as "thinking machines." In this paper, however, further exploration of this realm at this point could lead only to bad pure bull.

20. Boverie, "The Practicalities of PERT."

RUSSELL ACKOFF

Management Misinformation Systems

The growing preoccupation of operations researchers and management scientists with Management Information Systems (MIS's) is apparent. In fact, for some the design of such systems has almost become synonymous with operations research or management science. Enthusiasm for such systems is understandable: it involves the researcher in a romantic relationship with the most glamorous instrument of our time, the computer. Such enthusiasm is understandable but, nevertheless, some of the excesses to which it has led are not excusable.

Contrary to the impression produced by the growing literature, few computerized management information systems have been put into operation. Most have not matched expectations and some have been outright failures. I believe that these near- and far-misses could have been avoided if certain false (and usually implicit) assumptions on which many such systems have been erected had not been made.

There seem to be five common and erroneous assumptions underlying the design of most MIS's, each of which I will consider. After doing so I will outline an MIS design procedure which avoids these assumptions.

Most MIS's are designed on the assumption that the critical deficiency under which most managers operate is the *lack of relevant information*. I do not deny that most managers lack a good deal of information that

From Russell Ackoff, "Management Misinformation Systems," *Management Science* 14 (December 1967): B-147–B-156. Copyright © 1967 by The Institute of Management Sciences.

Mr. Ackoff is Chairman of the Graduate Faculty in Operations Research, The University of Pennsylvania.

they should have, but I do deny that this is the most important informational deficiency from which they suffer. It seems to me that they suffer more from an *overabundance of irrelevant information.*

This is not a play on words. The consequences of changing the emphasis of an MIS from supplying relevant information to eliminating irrelevant information is considerable. If one is preoccupied with supplying relevant information, attention is almost exclusively given to the generation, storage, and retrieval of information: hence emphasis is placed on constructing data banks, coding, indexing, updating files, access languages, and so on. The ideal which has emerged from this orientation is an infinite pool of data into which a manager can reach to pull out any information he wants. If, on the other hand, one sees the manager's information problem primarily, but not exclusively, as one that arises out of an overabundance of irrelevant information, most of which was not asked for, then the two most important functions of an information system become *filtration* (or evaluation) and *condensation*. The literature on MIS's seldom refers to these functions let alone considers how to carry them out.

My experience indicates that most managers receive much more data (if not information) than they can possibly absorb even if they spend all of their time trying to do so. Hence they already suffer from an information overload. They must spend a great deal of time separating the relevant from the irrelevant and searching for the kernels in the relevant documents.

Unless the information overload to which managers are subjected is reduced, any additional information made available by an MIS cannot be expected to be used effectively. Even relevant documents have too much redundancy. Most documents can be considerably condensed without loss of content.

It seems clear that condensation as well as filtration, performed mechanically or otherwise, should be an essential part of an MIS, and that such a system should be capable of handling much, if not all, of the unsolicited as well as solicited information that a manager receives.

Most MIS designers "determine" what information is needed by asking managers what information they would like to have. This is based on the assumption that managers know what information they need and want it.

For a manager to know what information he needs he must be aware of each type of decision he should make (as well as does) and he must have an adequate model of each. These conditions are seldom satisfied. Most managers have some conception of at least some of the types of decisions they must make. Their conceptions, however, are likely to be deficient in a very critical way, a way that follows from an important principle of scientific economy: the less we understand a phenomenon, the more variables we require to explain it. Hence, the manager who does not understand the phenomenon he controls plays it "safe" and, with respect to information, wants "everything." The MIS designer, who has even less understanding of the relevant phenomenon than the manager, tries to provide even more than everything. He thereby increases what is already an overload of irrelevant information.

One cannot specify what information is required for decision making until an explanatory model of the decision process and the system involved has been constructed and tested. Information systems are subsystems of control systems. They cannot be designed adequately without taking control in account. Furthermore, whatever else regression analyses can yield, they cannot yield understanding and explanation of phenomena. They describe and, at best, predict.

It is frequently assumed that if a manager is provided with the information he needs, he will then have no problem in using it effectively. The history of OR stands to the contrary. For example, give most managers an initial tableau of a typical "real" mathematical programming, sequencing, or network problem and see how close they come to an optimal solution. If their experience and judgment have any value they may not do badly, but they will seldom do very well. In most management problems there are too many possibilities to expect experience, judgement, or intuition to provide good guesses, even with perfect information.

It is necessary to determine how well managers can use needed information. When, because of the complexity of the decision process, they can't use it well, they should be provided with either decision rules or performance feed-back so that they can identify and learn from their mistakes.

One characteristic of most MIS's which I have seen is that they provide managers with better current information about what other managers and their departments and divisions are doing. Underlying this provision is the belief that better interdepartmental communication enables managers to coordinate their decisions more effectively and hence improves the organization's overall performance. Not only is this not necessarily so, but it seldom is so. One would hardly expect two competing companies to become more cooperative because the information each acquires about the other is improved.

When organizational units have inappropriate measures of performance which put them in conflict with each other, as is often the case, communication between them may hurt organizational performance, not help it. Organizational structure and performance measurement must be taken into account before opening the flood gates and permitting the free flow of information between parts of the organization.

Most MIS designers seek to make their systems as innocuous and unobtrusive as possible to managers lest they become frightened. The designers try to provide managers with very easy access to the system and assure them that they need to know nothing more about it. The designers usually succeed in keeping managers ignorant in this regard. This leaves managers unable to evaluate the MIS as a whole. It often makes them afraid to even try to do so lest they display their ignorance publicly. In failing to evaluate their MIS, managers delegate much of the control of the organization to the system's designers and operators who may have many virtues, but managerial competence is seldom among them.

Let me cite a case in point. A Chairman of a Board of a medium-size company asked for help on the following problem. One of his larger (decentralized) divisions had installed a computerized production-inventory control and manufacturing-manager information system about a year earlier. It had acquired about $2,000,000 worth of equipment to do so. The Board Chairman had just received a request from the Division for permission to replace the original equipment with newly announced equipment which would cost several times the original amount. An extensive "justification" for so doing was provided with the request. The Chairman wanted to know whether the request was really justified. He admitted to complete incompetence in this connection.

A meeting was arranged at the Division at which I was subjected to an extended and detailed briefing. The system was large but relatively simple. At the heart of it was a reorder point for each item and a maximum allowable stock level. Reorder quantities took lead-time as well as the allowable maximum into account. The computer kept track of stock, ordered items when required, and generated numerous reports on both the state of the system it controlled and its own "actions."

When the briefing was over I was asked if I had any questions. I did. First I asked if, when the system had been installed, there had been many parts whose stock level exceeded the maximum amount possible under the new system. I was told there were many. I asked for a list of about thirty and for some graph paper. Both were provided. With the help of the system designer and volumes of old daily reports I began to plot the

267

stock level of the first listed item over time. When this item reached the maximum "allowable" stock level it had been reordered. The system designer was surprised and said that by sheer "luck" I had found one of the few errors made by the system. Continued plotting showed that because of repeated premature reordering the item had never gone much below the maximum stock level. Clearly the program was confusing the maximum allowable stock level and the reorder point. This turned out to be the case in more than half of the items on the list.

Before the day was out it was possible to show by some quick and dirty calculations that the new computerized system was costing the company almost $150,000 per month more than the hand system which it had replaced, most of this in excess inventories.

The recommendation was that the system be redesigned as quickly as possible and that the new equipment not be authorized for the time being.

The questions asked of the system had been obvious and simple ones. Managers should have been able to ask them but — and this is the point — they felt themselves incompetent to do so. They would not have allowed a handoperated system to get so far out of their control.

No MIS should ever be installed unless the managers for whom it is intended are trained to evaluate and hence control it rather than be controlled by it.

The erroneous assumptions I have tried to reveal in the preceding discussion can, I believe, be avoided by an appropriate design procedure. One is briefly outlined here.

1. Analysis of the Decision System

Each (or at least each important) type of managerial decision required by the organization under study should be identified and the relationships between them should be determined and flow-charted. Note that this is *not* necessarily the same thing as determining what decisions *are* made.

Decision-flow analyses are usually self-justifying. They often reveal important decisions that are being made by default and they disclose interdependent decisions that are being made independently. Decision-flow charts frequently suggest changes in managerial responsibility, organizational structure, and measure of performance which can correct the types of deficiencies cited.

Decision analyses can be conducted with varying degrees of detail, that is, they may be anywhere from coarse to fine grained. How much detail one should become involved with depends on the amount of time and resources that are available for the analysis. Although practical considerations frequently restrict initial analyses to a particular organizational function, it is preferable to perform a coarse analysis of all of an organization's managerial functions rather than a fine analysis of one or a subset of functions. It is easier to introduce finer information into an integrated information system than it is to combine fine subsystems into one integrated system.

2. An Analysis of Information Requirements

Managerial decisions can be classified into three types:

(a) Decisions for which adequate models are available or can be constructed and from which optimal (or near optimal) solutions can be derived. In such cases the decision process itself should be incorporated into the information system thereby converting it (at least partially) to a control system. A decision model identifies what information is required and hence what information is relevant.

(b) Decisions for which adequate models can be constructed but from which optimal solutions cannot be extracted. Here some kind of heuristic or search procedure should be provided even if it consists of no more than computerized trial and error. A simulation of the model will, as a minimum, permit comparison of proposed alternative solutions. Here too the model specifies what information is required.

(c) Decisions for which adequate models cannot be constructed. Research is required here to determine what information is relevant. If decision making cannot be delayed for the completion of such research or the decision's effect is not large enough to justify the cost of research, then judgment must be used to "guess" what information is relevant. It may be possible to make explicit the implicit model used by the decision maker and treat it as a model of type (b).

In each of these three types of situation it is necessary to provide feedback by comparing actual decision outcomes with those predicted by the model or decision maker. Each decision that is made, along with its predicted outcome, should be an essential input to a management control system.

3. Aggregation of Decisions

Decisions with the same or largely overlapping informational requirements should be grouped together as a single manager's task. This will

269

reduce the information a manager requires to do his job and is likely to increase his understanding of it. This may require a reorganization of the system. Even if such a reorganization cannot be implemented completely what can be done is likely to improve performance significantly and reduce the information loaded on managers.

4. Design of Information Processing

Now the procedure for collecting, storing, retrieving, and treating information can be designed. Since there is a voluminous literature on this subject I shall leave it at this except for one point. Such a system must not only be able to answer questions addressed to it; it should also be able to answer questions that have not been asked by reporting any deviations from expectations. An extensive exception-reporting system is required.

5. Design of Control of the Control System

It must be assumed that the system that is being designed will be deficient in many and significant ways. Therefore it is necessary to identify the ways in which it may be deficient, to design procedures for detecting its deficiencies, and for correcting the system so as to remove or reduce them. Hence the system should be designed to be flexible and adaptive. This is little more than a platitude, but it has a not-so-obvious implication. No completely computerized system can be as flexible and adaptive as can a man-machine system. This is illustrated by an example of a system that is being developed and is partially in operation.

The company involved has its market divided into approximately two hundred marketing areas. A model for each has been constructed as is "in" the computer. On the basis of competitive intelligence supplied to the service marketing manager by marketing researchers and information specialists, he and his staff make policy decisions for each area each month. Their tentative decisions are fed into the computer which yields a forecast of expected performance. Changes are made until the expectations match what is desired. In this way they arrive at "final" decisions. At the end of the month the computer compares the actual performance of each area with what was predicted. If a deviation exceeds what could be expected by chance, the company's OR Group then seeks the reason for the deviation, performing as much research as is required to find it. If the cause is found to be permanent the computerized model is adjusted appropriately. The result is an adaptive man-machine system whose precision and generality is continuously increasing with use.

Finally it should be noted that in carrying out the design steps enumerated above, three groups should collaborate: information systems specialists, operations researchers, *and managers.* The participation of managers in the design of a system that is to serve them assures their ability to evaluate its performance by comparing its output with what was predicted. Managers who are not willing to invest some of their time in this process are not likely to use a management control system well, and their system, in turn, is likely to abuse them.

271

EDGAR DUNN

Distinguishing Statistical
and Intelligence Systems

Intelligence systems generate data about individuals *as* individuals. They have as their purpose "finding out" about the individual. They are widespread and common and essential in our private and public business.

A *statistical* information system produces information that does not relate to the individual. It only identifies characteristics that relate to groups of individuals or so-called "populations."

The important point to emphasize is that a statistical system is concerned with generating aggregates, averages, percentages, etc., that describe relationships characteristic of groups or populations of individuals. No information about the individual is generated as output and no information about the individual needs to be available to anyone outside the system under any circumstances for the statistical information system to perform its function.

This distinction divides the issue of personal privacy into two parts. The first part of the issue is reflected in this question: Can a statistical information system be developed and administered in a way that assures that it cannot be used as an intelligence system? The author is sure that the answer is yes.

We have seen that the coordinating requirements in the statistical system often will require reformulation of programs in the production of data. Thus, over a period of some years, a modification of the system

From Edgar Dunn, "The Idea of a National Data Center and the Issue of Privacy," *The American Statistician* 21 (February 1967): 21–27. Copyright © 1967 by American Statistical Association.

Mr. Dunn is with Resources for the Future, Inc.

will have to proceed with only those limited subsets of all conceivable existing files that are relevant to the most urgent policy requirements. Consequently they will deal mostly with traditional statistical records that have contained information dealing largely with the public face of the individual (such things as the demographic characteristics like age, race, sex, etc.) in contrast to the private face of the individual (such things as criminal records, medical records, psychological tests, etc.). In the future, as the system evolved in scope and effectiveness, it would be possible to extend the legal and procedural protections against the misuse of a statistical system for intelligence purposes. Computer technology cuts two ways. It provides us with new and powerful techniques for controlling and protecting the misuse of the record.

The skepticism of the Congressional hearings on the federal data center in 1966–67 grows out of (1) the fact that a statistical system must contain information about individual respondents, thereby rendering it potentially useful for intelligence purposes; (2) the fact that no system designed exists for providing *foolproof* protection against file misuse in this way; and (3) the argument that the pace of technology is proceeding so fast that there will be no technical limitations on accumulating "all of the data about everyone."

A statistical information system of greater utility for policy cannot be developed without making substantial changes in production practices.

Subsets of traditional files will need to be modified and integrated for matching purposes on an incremental basis with priorities established by important requirements.

No one is going to plan a complete integration of all statistical records over any short-run period of time. It would cost a great deal, and regardless of cost it would take a considerable period of time to put into effect.

An *intelligence* system, if it is going to be efficient, has to be as nearly complete as possible. Ideally it should constitute a census so that every possible individual search request could be fulfilled. There has been an implicit assumption in committee hearings that this is also true of a statistical system, but it emphatically is not. We have found increasingly that the efficient statistical system (since it generates related information about groups of people and never about individuals) doesn't want "all the data on everyone." It only wants some of the data on some of the people — enough to be relevant for the important problems of analysis by private business, government, and researchers and enough to support reliable inferences. To build a complete file is inordinately expensive, and for most statistical purposes less reliable. Indeed, the national "census," since it is conducted primarily for statistical purposes rather than intelligence purposes, is a complete census for only a very few attributes of the population. The bulk of information is collected on a sample basis only.

The existing statistical systems have had considerable experience and an admirable record in protecting personal privacy through legal regulations supplemented by operational procedures. Initial moves to improve the matching characteristics of federal statistical records for *statistical purposes* could be carried out under an extension of well-established protection procedures.

Often data that is irrelevant for intelligence purposes (concerning deceased respondents, no longer existing enterprises, etc.) is a prized content of a statistical file because of its utility in permitting the analysis of statistical trends and other indicators of social change.

In short, the changes in the Federal Statistical System currently needed would not generate files sufficiently comprehensive in either scope (that is, the numbers of individuals) or content (data would be primarily restricted to the public face of the individual) to turn it into a comprehensive intelligence system. It is, furthermore, already protected by well-established procedures that can be extended and improved. A statistical file would have so many gaps in the kind of information important for intelligence use and contain so much information irrelevant to intelligence use that it would be a grossly inefficient instrument as a source of personal intelligence. The incentives to pervert such a statistical system for intelligence purposes are missing because less costly and less risky intelligence sources are already available and are more complete.

Can a "foolproof" system be developed to prevent the misuse of a statistical system for intelligence purposes? The answer is no. But this is not the relevant form of the question. Mankind has never been able to develop a foolproof method of safeguarding any human value. It is unreasonable to expect anything different here. If one asks whether the cost of improper use can be made prohibitive, the answer is an unqualified yes, and we already know a lot about the techniques for accomplishing this and have a good record to build on as far as statistical systems are concerned. Suffice it to say that statistical systems are still far enough away to allow ample progress in technology and law to protect personal privacy adequately as statistical systems develop in flexibility.

We have heard impassioned demands that we halt any improvement in the statistical system until complete protection of personal privacy can be designed. Such an argument condemns us to failure before the start.

Systems like this are not designed in the abstract. They emerge out of practice and experience in meeting requirements. One reason we are in such a strong position to proceed with adequate protections against the invasion of personal privacy is the fact that, through practice, we already have developed useful techniques and experience that can be extended in new system design.

What has been happening in the recent public controversy seems to be understandable and probably necessary. Every major social and technological innovation in the advance of human society serves as a powerful stimulus both to man's legitimate dreams and to his legitimate fears.

It is not surprising that, in the face of untempered dreams, we should encounter untempered fears. The specter of the negative utopia of Orwell seems an obvious instrument to counterbalance the scale. The public conscience seems to become obsessed, in turn, with the benefits and then the costs. The public education about complex issues often seems to require such a dialectic exchange. Our task for the future is to guide the dialogue to a joint evaluation of the cost-benefit ratio. We need to develop the capacity of dream and fear at the same time and reconcile the two in the day-to-day task of getting the job done.

The necessity of the latter is an inescapable aspect of the human condition. Every personal and public advance is won at some cost, because each individual and each society have competing interests. They have to be reconciled in the day-to-day process of personal development and social evolution.

The competing interest between personal privacy and public information is one of this ubiquitous class of conflicts. It has many facets of much wider significance than has been recognized in the current record of investigation and public controversy. Just to identify a few important subsidiary problems, there is the issue of personal privacy versus effective government; personal privacy versus behavioral research; personal privacy versus law enforcement; and personal privacy versus free dissemination of the news.

But expressing the conflicts of interest in this way has the effect of making the conflict appear to be a contest between governments and individuals. How often our thinking becomes trapped in this oversimplification. The conflict, in the end, is between conflicting aspects of our own individual personal interests. Law enforcement, behavioral research, freedom of the press, and effective government enlarge some of our personal freedoms through the instrument of at least partially restricting others. The problem, of course, is that we have never devised a way, in a free society, to allow every individual an unrestricted choice in his market basket of freedoms and still maintain the viability of the society upon which all freedoms depend.

It is not proposed that the problem of establishing a socially acceptable balance in this area of information and personal privacy is necessarily of the same order of importance as all other conflicts of interest. The instinct of the Congressional committees and of the public is correct. The question of how to develop information and how to use it is without a doubt one of the most vital of all public issues. Information is power. But both information and power are morally neutral — each has the ability to enslave and to release.

Here on the most general and philosophic plane we have the issue restated. In the final analysis what are the benefits to be derived from improved information systems? The stake is our success as a nation in our complex world. The future of mankind is bound up in the accumulation and effective use of pertinent information. In our case, if there is any critical deficit, it is in the realm of information that will serve society's need to establish policy and manage its public affairs.

But if the stake is large, so is the risk. The risk is the dehumanization of man: or perhaps, put more accurately, that we shall fail in our long-term effort to become fully humanized.

This brings us to a critical point. In the end, the important thing is not that we must strike an operative balance in solving these problems, as we will and must. The important thing is what standards serve as our guide as we attempt to strike the balances and restrike them every day and year. What is it that motivates our purpose? Which will be the dominant ethic — if you will?

In short, the issue of personal privacy is really only part of the larger and more fundamental issue: How can information, which is really the codification of all human knowledge, be made to serve the goal of national development and human enrichment? In this context the long-range evolution of statistical systems is seen to be essential to the achievement of these goals.

HAROLD L. WILENSKY

The Road from Information to Knowledge

A managerial revolution has taken place but its form is less dramatic than that envisaged by Max Weber and Thorstein Veblen and popularized by James Burnham. Instead of scientists, engineers, and other technical staff coming to power by virtue of their indispensability, there is a shift in power to administrative leaders — in the economy, to coalitions of top managers and experts, each acquiring some of the skills of the other; in government, to the executive branch, gaining at the expense of the legislature. Information is now, as before, a source of power, but it is increasingly a source of confusion. The proliferation of both technical and political-ideological information and a chronic condition of information overload have exacerbated the classic problem of intelligence. An increasing share of organizational resources goes to the intelligence function; structural sources of intelligence failures become more prominent; doctrines of intelligence — ideas about how knowledge should be tapped and staff services organized — become more fateful.

At the same time that problems become more complicated and technical, available information technology and expert staff present more possibilities for solutions. Whatever the national variations in ideologies justifying economic activity, whatever the degree of pluralism in political life, there is a universal increase in information-consciousness at the top; elites in every rich country are moved to break through mere slogans and

Reprinted from pp. 173–191 of *Organizational Intelligence* by Harold L. Wilensky, © 1967 by Harold L. Wilensky, Basic Books, Inc., Publishers, New York.
Mr. Wilensky is Professor of Sociology at the University of California, Berkeley.

grasp reality. Their success in understanding internal operations and external environment is affected by the shape of the organizations they command and by their defenses against information pathologies.

In this [paper] I will discuss two implications [of my analysis] for administrative practice. . . . (1) Some gains in the quality of intelligence are possible from a reorganization of the intelligence function; but (2) much of an organization's defense against information pathologies lies in (a) the top executive's attitude toward knowledge — a product of his own education and orientation, his exposure to independent sources, his capacity to break through the wall of conventional wisdom, and (b) the intelligence specialist's capacity to affect the general tone of policy discourse.

An approach based on reorganization of formal structure has a deceptive simplicity. If the hierarchy is too tall, flatten it; give more experts more autonomy by having them report to fewer bosses. If departmental rivalry blocks communication, set interdepartmental task forces in motion. If experts and executives are parochial, move them about from job to job, agency to agency; send them back to school to stretch their minds; seek new sources of manpower. If secrecy and security regulations prevent the recruitment of skillful interpreters of data — men with scholarly imagination — then change the regulations, use secrecy only where it is functionally necessary, apply loyalty criteria only in posts of extraordinary sensitivity in time of clear and present danger.

Such redesign of structure, however, meets its limits where it entails large losses of efficiency, coordination, and control, and where structural resistances to change are strong . . . [Intelligence] failures are built into complex organizations. On the one hand, the most readily accomplished revamping of structure turns out to be mere organizational tinkering. Establishing an interdepartmental committee makes formal what was unofficial before — the selective sharing of inside information, the public restatement of fixed departmental positions. On the other hand, even when the reorganization of formal structure is pushed to its limit, the basic sources of distortion remain in some degree: insofar as the proper mastery of the task calls for specialization and the need to motivate and control personnel necessitates hierarchy; insofar as coordination demands centralization; insofar as the exigencies of decision seem to require direct answers, if not short-run predictions of the future; insofar as internal security and outside competition necessitate secrecy — to the extent that these other organizational interests must be protected — a singleminded attention to administrative reforms that facilitate the flow of accurate information is inappropriate. And, finally, many sources of intelligence failures are natural to the state of the organization's development and are therefore substantially beyond its control; if swiftly growing organizations in contact with a fluid environment and facing urgent problems are less vulnerable to structural and doctrinal distortions of information, that is no help to a more established, slower-growing organization coping with more routine crises.

Thus, the alert executive is everywhere forced to bypass the regular machinery and seek firsthand exposure to intelligence sources in and out of the organization. In matters delicate and urgent, more imaginative administrative leaders typically move to points along the organization's boundaries: looking toward the bottom, they rely on internal communications specialists such as education directors and auditors; looking outward, they rely on contact men such as press officers, technical salesmen, foreign service officers, lobbyists, mediators. They talk to reporters and researchers investigating their organizations; they establish study commissions or review boards composed entirely of outsiders, like the members of British Royal Commissions; they institutionalize complaints procedures and thereby subject themselves to systematic, independent criticism from below, as in the case of the Ombudsman; they assemble ad hoc committees, kitchen cabinets, general advisors, personal representatives. These unofficial intelligence agents, some of them defined as peripheral, may constitute the most important and reliable source of organizational intelligence. They are sufficiently sensitive to the culture of the executive to communicate, independent enough to provide detached judgment; they bring to bear the multiple perspectives of marginal men.

[A] difficult but crucial area for research is the effect of the new information technology and of related managerial techniques on the problem of intelligence. Glib talk about the computer taking over executive functions runs rampant. It is said that systems researchers, bemused by their mathematical models, are taking all the creativity out of decision, and presumably the joy out of living. If we combine the rapid handling of information by computers, the application of mathematics and statistics to administrative problems (linear programming, simulation, operations research, and systems analysis), and the recruitment of better-educated managers who are smart enough to use the staff to put these methods to work, then we have a formula for revolution in administrative leadership. The speculation is that it will mean greater centralization of authority, clearer accountability of subordinates, a sharper distinction between top management and staff, and the rest of the organization, and eventually a transformation of the planning and innovating functions. It is not at all clear, however, that these changes, if they do spread widely, will weaken the roots of intelligence failure. No one argues that in these highly programmed systems there will be less specialization, less accent on hierarchy and command, although there is considerable question about the degree and forms of centralization. It is likely, too, that the new flood of information will not make the doctrines of "all the facts" and "short-run estimates" less attractive.

. . . [From] the growing demand for experts who can supply a blend of technical and political intelligence, however, we can infer one fact of the matter: whatever the uses of electronic data processing (EDP) in routinizing decisions involving large-scale repetitive operations (as in accounting, inventory control, production scheduling and control) and whatever the expansion of applied research on narrow technical problems, there remains a great shortage of generalized policy advice. The systems analyst, symbol of the new "Whiz Kids," reflects one of many efforts to meet that shortage. No doubt, lower-level technical experts are susceptible to technicism; they sometimes exaggerate the importance of their methods, substituting means for ends. But this phenomenon is not new; dedicated specialists have always pushed their specialties. More important, the graphic horror of directionless machinery taking over denies the main functions of both top staff experts and executives. Experts who move into policy circles typically provide analytical advice defining major alternatives in a situation of great uncertainty. Top executives typically incorporate analytical judgments, value judgments, practical experience, and intuition into policy decisions. Neither the expert nor his boss can long remain preoccupied with means and methods; both strain toward a synoptic view. With the diffusion of more efficient information technology, the good sense of the questions asked, the relevance of the categories used for analysis, and the reliability of the data become even more important . . .

I do not wish to minimize the dangers of technicism. The question of the conditions under which the tyranny of technique prevails deserves serious attention, but to talk about the age of "technological idiots" and "cheerful robots" clouds the issues. Consider the problems of the United States Defense Department, symbol of the new managerial revolution . . . Nowhere is the price of irrational decision or poor judgment greater, and nowhere has the apparatus of modern management been more aggressively and skillfully applied. To evaluate the claims for these techniques is premature because they have prevailed in Defense only a few years and have spread to such agencies as the Office of Economic Opportunity only recently . . . Moreover, data on the impact of information technology and of such related ideas as "cost-benefit analysis" or "systems analysis" are either nonexistent or not publicly available. Using the Defense Department as a model, however, we can glimpse the broadest implications of the new managerial revolution for government and industry. The most likely outcomes are the following.

1. At every level there will be increased pressure to explicate assumptions and goals more clearly and to subject them to quantitative analysis. There is no doubt that the techniques of systems analysis have made choices among weapons more conscious and rational, sometimes resulting in the liquidation of glamorous hardware preferred by bellicose congressmen. The controversy about Secretary McNamara's decision to move from bombers to missiles provides several examples. At one point Air Force enthusiasts in Congress demanded the continued development and procurement of the Skybolt air-to-surface ballistic missile (which would have cost about $3 billion, not counting the cost of additional warheads) and the purchase of a fifteenth wing of B-52 bombers. McNamara's cost-effectiveness studies gave him strength to resist such demands. Strangelovian philosophers in the Air Force and elsewhere found the Secretary a formidable opponent.

2. Insofar as top managers know what questions to ask, and can elicit good data (i.e., overcome the structural and doctrinal roots of intelligence failure), their decisions will be more efficient. More data bearing on more alternatives will be explored, longer chains of causation analyzed, the consequences of a policy decision for a whole organizational system more often grasped. Whatever one thinks of American foreign policy, it would be difficult to argue that the shift from "massive retaliation" to "graduated response" and "flexible, balanced defense," carried out during the administration of Secretary McNamara, decreased the range of options.

3. Insofar as top managers ask the wrong questions and muster poor intelligence, wrong decisions will be more efficiently arrived at, and poor judgment, now buttressed by awesome statistics, will be made more effective. Wherever the new tools and perspectives are institutionalized, more weight will attach to data and systems analyses, whatever their quality. The chance is increased that information errors will ricochet at high speed throughout the system.

4. The number and influence of information technologists will increase and the power of executives in charge of such staffs will be enhanced, at

least in the short run. The most significant fact about the Defense Department story is that with far less formal reorganization than that attempted by his predecessors, Secretary McNamara succeeded in shifting the locus of authority to central civilian management; he revolutionized the processes of decision-making. PPBS gave him the ability to cut across organizational lines and particularly to integrate both complementary and competitive functions of rival services — an effective substitute for unification, a goal that had eluded everyone else.

5. As executives who are well equipped with information technologists expand their influence, competing executives, not so well equipped, find that they have lost room for maneuver and bargaining. For instance, when an organization adopts PPBS and gives a planning and analysis group review powers, the budget proposals that are skillfully cast in formal cost-benefit terms receive preferential treatment; others lose out. In a university budget scramble, a library unit that shows how an $80,000 expenditure for additional staff will permit a better schedule of hours, which in turn will increase the circulation of books and the use of reference services by X amount and decrease student waiting time by Y amount, and, further, that this small cost will yield greater gains than equivalent investment in any other library services — that library unit will outpace competitors who use traditional methods of budget justification. In such situations, executives who lose are moved to resist. Either they fight fire with fire, assemble and train the staff and master the techniques (which results in a general, competitive upgrading of manpower), or they resist implementation of policies based on the new techniques (which increases dysfunctional conflict between departments and ranks), or, having resisted unsuccessfully, they are forced to leave.

6. The gulf between top executives and the information technologists, on the one hand, and men whose work is more programmed, on the other, will widen. One troublesome expression of this gulf is the issue of how much information about goals and conflicts of goals and about priorities in the allocation of scarce resources can or should be shared, once goals and means have become more explicit and quantitative at central headquarters. The problem is partly technical. It is difficult to compare different preferences within similar categories of activity (library service measured by book circulation rates versus classroom service measured by teacher-pupil ratio, the circulation of Mickey Spillane versus that of Plato), let alone preferences in contrasting categories (library services versus research on air pollution). The problem is also partly political and moral . . . If the university using systems analysis gives priority to ap-

plied research product over teaching and to the professional schools over the liberal arts, should those interested in scholarship and general education be informed? . . . If all value conflicts, all clashes of interest, are made explicit every year, so that administrators can compare every item in a budget with every other and eliminate those that contribute little to an explicit value scheme, two consequences follow: (1) latent conflicts become manifest and positions become more polarized; (2) the administrator is tempted to keep a larger fraction of what he knows to himself; he avoids explaining the relative insignificance of powerful programs (public information policies become more manipulative, credibility gaps widen). In short, information technology may aggravate the "honesty problem." It is like the familiar dilemma of central planners everywhere: the target plan is announced, the real plan is kept quiet, but word creeps around . . .

The most difficult claim to assess is that information technologists, oriented to the measurement of gains and costs, inevitably drive out the "soft" in favor of the "hard" variables, that instead of wisdom and good sense the tyranny of technique prevails. Information technologists argue that there is nothing intrinsic to their methods that prevents proper respect for qualitative variables and judgments. To quantify what it makes sense to quantify and to avoid quantifying what cannot be quantified is not to give the easily measured variables undue weight. Moreover, even the most "technical" of experts are valued primarily for their interpretive skills and creative judgment . . .

In the absence of studies of the influence of information technologies in diverse settings, we cannot assess these claims. In order to bring the issues into focus, however, consider . . . the case of the Defense Department's role in the continuation of the Vietnam war . . . In the mid-1960's the Defense Department displayed a remarkable taste for ghoulish statistics — body counts and kill ratios in Vietnam villages. One can argue that this was not the result of systems analysis or any other modern method of management. Nor was the Vietnam intervention a case of evaluation techniques molding the objective — that is, technicism. Rather, the statistics resulted from a desperate effort to find a substitute for the old-fashioned battle line that told the warring nation whether it was ahead or behind. And the policy resulted from political leaders being seized by specious analogies — Vietnam is seen as Munich, as Greece, as Czechoslovakia; Southeast Asia, with per capita incomes in the range of $100, becomes Europe with incomes twenty to thirty times as large; the 1930's and 1940's are the 1960's; civil wars accompanied by multiple outside interventions are simple wars of aggression; unpopular military dictatorships are the same as popular legitimate governments; wholesale destruction of property and life and corruption on a grand scale are called "saving our allies from Communism" and "maintaining world order."

But it is equally plausible — and it follows more directly from our analysis of the obstacles to gathering reliable data on such matters — to argue that the statistics are full of error, and that even if they were accurate, analysis of the easy-to-measure variables (casualties suffered by the Viet Cong and the South Vietnamese) was driving out consideration of the hard-to-measure variables and long-run costs (the nature of popular support for a South Vietnam government, the effect of the war on the Western Alliance and on domestic civility, the effect of bombing on the will to resist). It is even possible that cost-benefit approaches tend to rivet the attention on relative outcomes (if the enemy continues to lose more than we lose, relative to resources, he will give up) while the absolute level of current investment (are the high costs in money and blood and in hard-to-measure losses worth the effort?) fades into the background. In any case, if in assessing our policy in Vietnam in the 1960's top decision-makers were taking their data seriously — perhaps because kill ratios and the like represent a touch of spurious certainty in a highly uncertain world — the availability of the data and of the analysis techniques must be counted a determinant of foreign policy.

Assuming the availability of accurate data and a continued decline in data processing costs, the crucial limitation is not that information technologists are necessarily restricted in their intellectual perspectives by the techniques of their job. Rather, it is that on average their training does not overcome their limited political and social sensitivities. The integration of values, theory, and practice nowhere depends more on the supply of talent. The danger of technicism is in direct proportion to the shortage of educated men. Too often the new technologists are methodical and exact in their specialized fields, but impressionable, naïve, and opinionated on broader issues of policy. Like the executives they advise, they lack a sense of relevance and analogy — the critical common sense and trained judgment that mark an educated man.

That breadth of view combined with technical skill is a requisite for effective policy advice is especially true when social science is to be incorporated into decision-making. Insofar as the users of social research mainly demand short-run predictions — forecasts of the demand for soap, estimates of whether internal dissension in Peking will make the Chinese more or less likely to greet a bombing escalation with a troop commitment — they deprive themselves of the main contributions of social science. Although there have been many successes in prediction, notably in demography, in economics, and in polls of voting intentions (where the question is simple and the forecast is very short), the specific data of social sciences are typically outdated in the short run. They are far more useful for constructing comprehensive pictures of social reality and for understanding extended social trends. They are a primary source of political and ideological intelligence.

Given the institutional roots of intelligence failures, scattered about like land mines, given the urgency of so many big decisions, what counts is the top executive's preconceptions — what he has in mind when he enters the room and must act. The role of experts and intellectuals in shaping these preconceptions, in and out of the organization, is little understood . . . If education in social science does not yield direct answers to immediate questions, perhaps it does break through executives' cruder stereotypes, enhance their understanding of themselves and their organizations, alert them to the range of relevant variables, and make them more skillful in the use of experts.

Similarly, the symbols that surround the executive in his daily life shape his orientation. Experts and intellectuals who can write, speak, and present ideas quickly and easily have a major influence on speeches and resolutions, by-laws and contracts, press releases and house organs, legal, economic, or scientific briefs and testimony. In private conference and committee meeting they set the tone of policy discourse. No one who examines the history of such doctrines as "strategic bombing" and "massive retaliation," or the sad tale of foreign intervention in such places as Cuba and Vietnam, can be impressed with "the end of ideology," if by that we mean the end of illusions that systematically conceal social reality. And in all these cases, intellectuals have played their part in creating and sustaining the symbolic atmosphere within which men calculate. Many a brittle slogan has perpetuated a policy long outmoded.

To read the history of modern intelligence failures is to get the nagging feeling that men at the top are often out of touch, that good intelligence is difficult to come by and enormously difficult to listen to; that big decisions are very delicate but not necessarily deliberative; that sustained good judgment is rare. Bemoaning the decline of meaningful action, T. S. Eliot once spoke of a world that ends "not with a bang but a whimper." What we have to fear is that the bang will come, preceded by the contemporary equivalent of the whimper — a faint rustle of paper as

285

some self-convinced chief of state, reviewing a secret memo full of comfortable rationalizations just repeated at the final conference, fails to muster the necessary intelligence and wit and miscalculates the power and the intent of his adversaries.

IV. Emerging Information Systems: The Policy Debates

Introduction

For Part IV, I have chosen selections about the social impact of computerized databanks and management science techniques that rest on factually informed judgments about the advantages and disadvantages of these new techniques. Neither straight ideological statements nor popularized discussions which skip blissfully over the hard issues have been included here.

Most of the essays represent what might be called "middle-range" commentaries. The authors tend to be persons who are or have been involved in government, or have worked with the new technologies and techniques, or have had direct contact with such experiments as social science observers. There are obviously some not-so-gentle essays included, such as Ida Hoos' discussion of systems promoters as "foxes in the henhouse," Robert Boguslaw's attack on the "coercive utopia" of systems designers, and Thomas Conrad's critical assessment of "systems analysis at the service of the Liberal Establishment."

But I suspect that the assumptions shared by the authors represented in this part about the problems involved in organizing a complex society under a democratic political system are more significant than their disagreements over the current uses and effects of information technology. Thus a Conrad, fresh from his critique of Simon Ramo's primer urging greater use of systems analysis to avert social chaos, ends his piece by warning left critics that they will be "historically irrelevant Luddites" if they assault technology per se. "There is nothing inherent in systems analysis which makes it useful only for elitists and totalitarians." On the contrary, Conrad says, "There are basic intellectual and ethical strains in systems analysis which are of vital usefulness to radical social critics."

Not every author, even those reprinted here, would necessarily agree with that judgment. But these commentaries are the debates within the key political and intellectual communities which are factually informed and personally experienced on the early experiments with information technology. Until empirical case studies are published to provide detailed accounts of how information technology entered and progressed through American governmental agencies during the 1960's and early 1970's, the commentaries presented here offer the best projection of the social, political, organizational, and technical issues involved in this area.

DONALD N. MICHAEL

Democratic Participation
and Technological Planning

It is commonplace today to recognize the necessity for moving in this
direction [long-range planning] in order to deal more adequately with
the operating requirements of day-to-day government. Crime control, tax
records, urban data banks, program planning and budgeting systems, and
so forth all depend or are expected to depend on the computer's data-
storing and data-processing capabilities. But using the computer for long-
range planning in a context of social perturbations will demand a collaboration among planners, policy-makers, and politicians that will
threaten the practice of democracy. This threat can, perhaps, be mitigated
by using the computer in ways we shall examine later. First, however, we
should be clearer about the nature of the threat.

Its source is twofold: the increasing dependence of those with political
power on esoteric knowledge and the decreasing ability of the concerned
citizen to get the knowledge he needs to participate in matters of importance to him.

All decision-making related to a city government or made by agencies
of a government has a substantial political component, even those decisions based heavily on the kinds of information the computer and its
human adjuncts provide. Any political decision is made with the intent

From Donald N. Michael, "On Coping with Complexity: Planning and Politics,"
Daedalus, Journal of the American Academy of Arts and Sciences, Boston, Massachusetts,
volume 97, number 4 (Fall 1968), pp. 1179–1193. Copyright © 1968 by the American
Academy of Arts and Sciences.
Mr. Michael is Professor of Psychology and a Program Director of the Center for
Research on Utilization of Scientific Knowledge, Institute for Social Research, Uni-
versity of Michigan.

of preserving or expanding the base of power, command, control, and influence of the organization or persons involved. Mayors, authorities, chiefs or commissioners of this and that do not choose to weaken their personal power, nor do their organizations deliberately act so as to lose control over their traditional mandates.

In the urban world of 1976 that control, that power, will increasingly be based on access to and control of information and the means for generating new knowledge out of it. Information will provide an increasingly potent basis for "adjusting" the outside world so that it is compatible with the survival and growth aims of the agency and for internally adjusting the agency so that it can respond to what it perceives as pertinent to it in the evolving complex environment. This is not a new situation; organizations have always acted to monopolize the knowledge they need for influence and for control of decisions and their implementation even when the knowledge served essentially a ritualistic or rationalizing purpose rather than as a realistic efficient basis for choosing options.

But the situation takes on significant new aspects when the computer provides an improved basis for choosing among options. Then the politician (and I include the agency chief and the advocate planner), working in tandem with his technological advisers and program designers, is in a position to put forth interpretations of "urban reality," programs to deal with it, and evaluations of those programs as implemented based on knowledge either unavailable to those who might challenge him or unavailable at the time that a challenge might be most effective.

This situation characterizes the way military affairs and military policies are planned and operated (for example, the Vietnam war), but it is also true, and will be increasingly so, in more and more domestic areas. The partisan use of incomplete or selectively emphasized technological knowledge is already the case with regard to the justification offered for the supersonic transport or a man on the moon by 1970. It is beginning to be so with regard to methods advocated for pollution control, mass transport, educational technology, and social welfare. As these areas of planning and operations become more rationalized, the agencies and persons responsible for such plans and programs will try to protect their decisions and actions from effective criticism or impedance. We can expect this conventional organizational reflex to continue to operate, certainly over the next decade or more when bureaucracies will still be dominated by those who were trained in and rewarded by the traditionally successful operating styles. And given the nature and the basis for decision-making and operations — increased social complexity dealt with through increased conceptual complexity — it will be easier to obscure the organizations' situation than it was in a simpler day unless we specifically design means for keeping these reflexes from operating too well.

No computer-based, technology-based set of options will be exhaustive. Our knowledge about the nature of the urban present, although greatly improved, will be incomplete and our theories for interpreting that knowledge will be flawed. And since more and more of the urban tasks will be long-range ones, policy-planners and decision-makers will have to commit themselves on the basis of estimates of an essentially unpredictable future. (And citizens, choosing among the options offered, will be even more ignorant because a realistic estimate of the long-range consequences associated with an option requires an evaluation of the knowledge on which the option is based.) The politician, when choosing among any set of options, will face two facts of life he has customarily shared with the voter as little as possible. The first is the fallibility of the programs and plans to which he commits himself and his organization, the inherent uncertainty about the nature and distribution of costs and benefits. The second is that, given this state of uncertainty about the future, present political considerations pertaining to the preservation and extension of his power through time deeply influence his decisions. In the conventional situation, the politician and professional could cover up these two facts of life quite well most of the time. In the future, it will be even easier to cover them up because computer-based options will, by virtue of their source, carry great weight with many policy people and voters. The overwhelming complexity incorporated into the derivation of the options will make it excessively difficult to know in what ways the politician is covering up conceptual and data limitations in the computer program providing those options.

By 1976 not all agencies will be using computer aids to the extent they might. In many situations the changeover to such rationalized methods will be too threatening to those in power, too upsetting to their definitions of self, purpose, and status for them to move easily and quickly into the new arrangements, styles, and rewards appropriate when computer aids are used for planning. Given the mixed bag of autonomous, interlinking, semiduplicative, and competitive agencies and activities that characterize the urban condition of governance and control, foot-dragging will be difficult to overcome. These "foot-draggers" will, however, feel that they must give their clients the impression that they indeed know where they are going and that, in the mode of the times, their knowledge somehow derives from the approved, sophisticated "systems" thinking.

Thereby, they will have an additional reason for hiding their interpretative and programmatic fallibility, a fallibility appearing and in fact sometimes being greater for their dependence on "old-fashioned" non-computerized approaches.

These anticipated characteristics of urban governance suggest that we should be preoccupied with developing not only the means for making the political system manipulable by the poor, but also the new means that will enable affluent, concerned citizens to get at the political system in years to come. Unless we do so, the citizen of 1976 may find himself unable to judge whether he knows enough about a particular proposed policy or a proposed or ongoing program to discern where his and the community's interests lie. He probably will not be able to identify the set of options or the conceptual model used to transform the data. He will not even know what data were fed into the program or how adequate they were. Nor will he be able to judge which costs and benefits of the secondary and tertiary impacts reverberating out through the urban environment have been taken into consideration and by whom. (Given the autonomy of various agencies in the urban government, he will probably be safe in assuming that some of the "interface" issues have not been dealt with or even recognized by agencies indifferent to or ignorant of them — or by those avoiding them for political reasons.) Thus, even when he is offered a choice of programs, his ignorance about the assumptions made by the planners regarding the supposed future context in which the programs will operate and eventually "pay-off" will prevent him from choosing wisely, from committing himself to a long-range risk with an understanding of what the costs and benefits are thought to be.

If the concerned citizen felt ignorant or impotent in the past, he could take solace in the knowledge that the capacity of organizations to change things was usually small and potentially subject to some revision at the next election. That solace will disappear, however, when the requirement for long-range programs means that many programs will have to carry on through many elections if they are to have any chance of success.

This source of comfort will be gone, too, when the citizen comes to realize that computer-aided planning and operations allow programs to have a much greater impact on the urban environment, and that the intense and wide-ranging interaction within this environment encourages secondary and tertiary consequences of perhaps even greater impact than the primary ones. Obversely, the citizen will find no comfort in those cases where he wants some great impact on the environment, but where considerations — mostly unknown to him — result in choices that have little impact. The concerned citizen's discomfort will be increased in a new way: He will know he is unskilled in manipulating and evaluating the information from which the computer-based options are derived. Not only will he realize that he lacks some of the facts; he will know that he is unable to work with them, even when he has them.

These sources of discomfort suggest the direction in which we shall have to look for new arrangements allowing the citizen a meaningful role in influencing his urban destiny. The citizen must have as much access to the procedures of social planning and evaluating data as do those in the system who propose programs and evaluate their implementation. The citizen will need this access both during the period when the agencies and the politicians are developing the program and continuously once the program is in operation. The citizen would then be able to criticize more effectively a program's quality and relevancy, and he could be aided enormously in this process by the computer.

To do so, the citizen ought to be able to ask questions such as: What were the sampling procedures used to obtain the "raw data"? How accurate and how valid are they? How are they aggregated? What sensitivity to change or stasis is lost or gained by clustering the data demographically, temporally, economically, and so forth? Then he should know which conceptual models were used to relate various data so that interpretations could be made. These models may be mathematical or logical, based on economic theory or on social-psychological theories, perhaps supplemented in part by the decision-makers' hunches and wisdom. To the extent that the models provide a basis for sharing ideas and clarifying choices, they can be made explicit in words or mathematical statements. The citizen should also know how logic and data are related in the computing program. What are to be the measures of costs and benefits? What range of economic or social variation is to be considered and how are these variations related to one another? How does the computing program emphasize or alter the meanings of the data and the conceptual model for the sake of computing convenience? (For example, one way of averaging out variations in demand for a service may indicate no special need for an increase in that service; another way of averaging those variations may indicate very real needs in certain groups under certain variations in circumstances, but whose need-indicating behavior was "washed out" in the former averaging method.) What value assumptions are operating? What goals for the plan are revealed by the methods for ranking the options generated by the computer-manipulated data? Some of the options may be generated directly by computer analysis; others may use computer outputs supplemented by considerations outside the computer's option-generating program and introduced by politicians. One way or another, the variables attended to in creating the options will reveal underlying value preferences. Are economic savings to override other social gains? To what extent is the computerized option-generating model to operate within the constraints of the private enterprise value system? Is an assumption made that inequities for 4 per cent of the target population are acceptable, but unacceptable for 5 per cent? Will monitoring the plan in action require data about people presently considered private? Why is this "invasion of privacy" presumed to be worthwhile?

In principle, the citizen ought to be able to look over the shoulder of the planner and decision-maker as they prepare their plans and decisions. He ought to be able to ask all the questions of the computer that could be asked by the professionals working for the urban agencies — such questions as: "What happens to the ratio of costs to benefits when I use the same data the planners have used, but another definition of costs or benefits?" "If in *my* conceptual model the rate at which average personal income grows has consequences for the larger community that differ depending on the ethnic background of those whose income is changing, at what rate will the average personal income in district Y grow compared to district Z if the proposed industry is in location A rather than B?" Citizens with different perspectives and interests than the planners and politicians almost certainly will ask questions that the professionals forgot, thereby discovering significant implications the professionals overlooked. In this way, the professionals will have thrust on them a larger set of considerations to reconcile. Few professionals will embrace this additional decision-making burden or the challenge to their professional omniscience, but the advantages of this burden and challenge are too obvious to bear elucidation here. On the other hand, it is also obvious that the professionals could be immobilized by the effort involved in responding to the citizens; clearly, means for establishing a mutually useful balance have to be invented.

Again, in principle, the means for such citizen involvement exist today, operating in the form of multiple-access computer systems in which many people use the same computer and share one another's programs, data, thinking, and solutions. Each user has his own terminal equipment for instructing the computer and for receiving information from the computer. The terminal may be an especially adapted typewriter or a glass surface, like a television, that displays information and can receive instructions from the user via a pen that writes signals on it with a narrow beam of light to which the computer responds by a visual display on the screen or by printed symbols on paper. Thus whatever numerical data, charts, graphs, or designs are used, and whatever computer programs are used, the information can be stored in the computer and displayed through these terminals and the computer can be queried from them.

Imagine, then, similar terminals spotted around the urban area in the center cities, the suburbs, and the contiguous rural centers. Each of these could be linked to the same data banks and computers that the urban planning and governing agencies tie into. The laws could be so written that it would be illegal to deny these "citizen terminals" access to any of the data that the agencies use. Since agencies cannot use data legally defined as private or privileged without special permission, misuse of such data may be discovered if the computational results the citizens obtain differ from those of the agencies, even though both are supposedly using the same data and computer programs. The law could further require that the computer programs for manipulating data and the conceptual schemes that the programs presumably reflect also be public information. And all ancillary information that the planners may not store in the computer, such as maps, must be displayable for the citizens' use. Thus, all the information and methods for manipulating information available to the planners and decision-makers would also be available to the citizen. If information was privileged or proprietary, this would have to be indicated when a citizen requested that information. Means would have to be established allowing the citizen to determine the significance of that information for the proposed plan or related project. Since such information is sometimes critical for choosing among options, confrontation procedures would have to be developed.

The hunches, biases, and political sense that usually influence the planner's preferences and the politician's choices probably could not be detected or evaluated by such means. The citizen *would* know, however, what there was to know about the data-based and theoretical relationships of the issue to the options. He could then apply his own hunches, preferences, and biases and push for one option or goal rather than another. Thus, this approach would not eliminate or reduce the political or emotional factors in the pursuit of urban goals.

This approach seems to carry with it more than just a new means for maintaining an uneasy balance between the citizen and the urban government. Because we must cope with urban complexity by long-range planning, citizen participation responsive to the same methods and types of data the planners use can help produce citizen attitudes oriented to the

297

future and preferring the long-range planning approach to the ad hoc and spasmodic styles that have typified the American way of dealing with urban problems. Because long-range planning must be flexible and responsive to changes in the human and material environment as the plan works its way out over the years, the government must be alert to and responsive to feedback about the general environment as well as the specific environment the plan is intended to effect. With access to all the data the government agencies will have about what is happening to their areas of responsibility, it can be expected that the citizens' various interests will result in one or another group scanning each pertinent situation, alert for new data revealing unexpected gains or losses that can be attributed to the working out of one or another plan. These continuing monitoring efforts could force the agencies not only to appropriate programmatic responses to what the citizens discover, but also to collect new types of data needed for improved evaluation of the programs.

Most important of all, the extraordinary degree of openness required to operate this way could mean that, over time, the political system, including the citizen, could come to recognize error and failure as natural products of trying to cope with a complex urban environment. No longer would the government have the need to cover up: The degree of ignorance about the feasibility and implications of any program would be evident to the recipients of the program at the time it was initiated as well as all along thereafter. Knowing that some error and failure are inevitable, both government and citizen would be able to accept social experiments more easily for what they are, making changes candidly and quickly when needed, without pretending or expecting that the initial plans were more certain to succeed than realistic estimates would suggest. And no one doubts that we will have to experiment socially if we are deliberately to invent a better urban world.

Even after one discounts the large majority of citizens who will be uninterested in such sophisticated participation in the conduct of the community, most of those who do want to take part will be unable to do so directly, being untrained in the statistical, social, and technological concepts involved in querying and interpreting the computer outputs. Specialists will be needed to do this, people who see the issue writ large, who can play with data, who see what is and is not in a computer program, who can invent alternative programs, who can sense the ethical and social problems and opportunities implicit in the planning options. Although the individual citizen can usefully contribute to the elucidation of some of these issues on the basis of his own circumstances, much of what he will need to transform his concerns into decisive queries to the information system will have to be provided by specialists. Analogous roles are filled today by lawyers, crusaders like Nader and Carson, some theologians, advocate planners, and even an occasional systems analyst, technologist, or scientist caught up in an urban issue that impinges directly on him. But the present roles are not refined enough to provide a readily accessible resource for linking citizens with computers.

A more specific delineation of specialties will be needed to implement the proposed system. These would provide the functional equivalent of the "shadow" planning, policy-making, and program-evaluation agencies of urban government. These specialists, retained by citizen groups, could be individuals or consulting firms that do not take government contracts and thus avoid conflicts of interest. The affluent ought to be able to pay for some services. As mobility and affluence increase, their interests in overlapping issues in nonoverlapping geographic locales should also increase.

The poor or the less affluent will need subsidization in this area much as we are beginning to provide them with legal services and other professional aid services. Perhaps foundations will help. Perhaps specialists could contribute their services part time as some do now in other activities. Universities might find some answers to their presently fumbling search for relevancy by providing such services on a nonpartisan basis. Their faculty members could raise the questions, pose alternative conceptual models and computer programs, and interpret findings in the light of their expertise. Just as universities encourage faculty members to consult in conventional ways, they may also encourage this sort of service, compensating their faculty members accordingly. Political parties might find ways of matching the interests of citizens and party by supporting particular efforts, publicizing the results, and using political leverage to get the alternatives attended to.

For those who want to participate in the political process, the opportunity to challenge the system or to support it on the basis of knowledge *as* the government develops its own position and then to monitor and criticize *continuously* the implementation of whatever policy prevails should be a heady incentive for extensive use of such computer facilities. But the approach proposed here involves no casual laying-on of minor modifications in the conduct of urban government. Opening up the information base of political decision-making would be one of the most painful wrenches conceivable for conventional styles of governing. Those now involved who have devised over their political lifetimes elaborate strategies for maintaining operational power and a complimentary personal self-image would find themselves naked, having to armor themselves anew and in new ways. Many simply could not do this, and many will fight such an approach with the cunning and commitment elicited by threats to survival. As a result, the scheme proposed here would hardly be in fully effective use in any urban area by 1976. Political and dollar costs and the technical complexity of installing citizen terminals might be too great for more than a few experimental terminals to be operating. Moreover, the numbers and types of experts available to aid citizens might be too small to man more than a few terminals. Perhaps the most that can be done is to ensure that citizens have access to the computer in the offices of the planners so that they can query the computer there during periods when the planners are legally obligated to free it for citizen use.

Indeed, it is not at all clear that this scheme would, in fact, realize its goal: more vigorous and knowledgeable participation by even a small percentage of the population. Citizens doing the same sorts of professional-political thinking and feeling as those legally empowered to run the government full time may turn out to be as destructive of a workable democracy as citizens not participating meaningfully. We shall have to experiment over many years to discover if we can have *both* long-range planning and democracy — that is, if we can have a viable, complex, huge, and dignifying urban condition. Thus, an approach such as this to inventing mutual urban and democratic viability must be attempted, and we had better have made a good start in this direction by 1976. We really have no choice in the matter if we wish to maintain the reality of democracy. If one expects that the conventional political system will fight computer-based long-range planning or exploit it in order to preserve conventional political power, then one must expect that those who plan and decide for urban government will try to do so ever more protected behind impenetrable barriers of complexity. In that case, the citizen would be less and less able to assess the implications of what the government proposes in his best interest. Being unable to assess his interest, he would be forced either to abdicate political participation based on a knowledgeable assessment of the situation or to accept out of ignorance what the planners and politicians offer him. And in the urban world of 1976 these alternatives would, I hope, be unacceptable.

ALAN F. WESTIN

Civil Liberties Issues in Public Databanks

From the earliest days of the American Republic, our legal and political system has been devoted to placing limits on the powers of surveillance that authorities can conduct over the lives of individuals and private groups. This tradition of limiting surveillance goes back to a stream of development in Western history that begins at least as early as the democratic Greek city-state and represented one of the keystones of the American Constitution.

When the Framers wrote, physical surveillance over individuals and groups was possible only in terms of actual entry onto property, eavesdropping on conversations by ear, and overlooking individuals. To place limits on these forms of surveillance, the American Constitution required that searches and seizures by government be "reasonable," describing specifically the places to be searched and the persons or things to be seized. Reasonableness was determined by a judicial inquiry in which law enforcement officers had to establish probable cause and were examined by a judge about the scope and conduct of the enquiry.

When the Framers wrote, psychological surveillance over individuals was possible only by torture to extract information or beliefs, or proceedings to compel individuals to testify against themselves. To meet these threats to psychological security, the American Constitution forbade torture and self-incrimination.

From Alan F. Westin, "Legal Safeguards to Insure Privacy in a Computer Society," *Communications of the ACM,* vol. 10, no. 9 (September 1967), pp. 533–537. Copyright © 1967, Association for Computing Machinery, Inc.

The other remaining form of surveillance known to eighteenth-century life was the record and dossier system maintained by European monarchies to control the movement of population and the activities of "disloyal" groups. In the United States, the openness and mobility of our frontier system and the deliberate refusal to employ a passport and dossier system of police control guaranteed that the American citizen would be free from these means of surveillance over his life.

Until the late nineteenth century, this legal framework was thoroughly adequate. The reasonable search and seizure principle allowed the balance to be struck by the courts and legislatures between the individual and group claims to privacy on the one hand and the needs of law enforcement and government information systems on the other. Then, late in the nineteenth century and accelerating rapidly during the first half of the twentieth century, technological developments began to erode the legal system for guaranteeing a libertarian balance of privacy. The invention of the telephone in the late 1880's meant that conversations were now projected outside the home and a network of wires, conduits, and central offices contained the speech that originated in one private place and was meant for reception in another. Telephone tapping by police and private adventurers began virtually simultaneously with the installation of telephone systems in the United States, just as telegraph tapping had begun in the 1850's when the telegraph first became an important means of communication. At about the same time, in the 1890's, the microphone was developed and quickly applied to the problem of monitoring speech through surreptitious devices. The law enforcement agencies and the Pinkerton Detective Agency made "dictaphone detection" a by-word of the late 1890's and the pre-World War I era. With these developments, the erosion of physical boundaries on which the reasonable search and seizure concept of the Constitution had been based began to create stress in the application of Constitutional protections to privacy from physical surveillance. During the same period, advances in techniques of psychological surveillance also grew. The polygraph, developed in the 1920's, provided means of measuring the physical states and emotional responses of individuals under stress, and this was picked up both by law enforcement agencies for questioning suspects and by private employers for investigating business employees and business crimes. Paralleling the polygraph development was the spread of deeply probing psychological tests of personality. Using a variety of approaches, from sentence completion and multiple choice tests to projective tests of situation and picture interpretation, psychologists applied measures of emotional adjustment and personality traits to the selection of individuals for a variety of purposes in governmental and corporate life. On the whole, American law drew a simple line in these areas — it forbade the use of polygraph or personality test results as legal evidence in courts but did not interfere in any way in the use of such tests for personnel selection and other non-judicial decision-making by authorities.

In the area of data surveillance, American society began the expansion of records and information-keeping in the period between World War I and World War II, events which represented the natural outcome of an industrial society with a growing regulatory and welfare function by government and an increasingly large bureaucratic structure in private organizational life. For the most part, American law dealt with this problem by setting general standards of confidentiality for information given to government agencies under compulsion of law (such as census data, social security information, and income tax records). However, the prime protection in this area remained the inability of government agencies and private authorities to use the mountains of information they had secured in anything like a centralized and efficient fashion.

Now, the contemporary era of electronics and computers has provided the final coup de grace to the technological premises on which the classic American law of privacy has been based. Micro-miniaturization, advanced circuitry, radar, the laser, television optics, and related developments have shifted the balance of power from those who seek to protect their conversations and actions against surveillance to those who have access to the new devices. What was once Orwell's science fiction is now current engineering. In the field of psychological surveillance, the enormous expansion of polygraphing and personality testing into personnel selection in the 1950's has been matched by new technological developments such as covert polygraph measures, new truth drug research, and the possibilities of reading emotional states currently opened by computer readings of brain-wave responses. Fears of manipulation and of penetration into the intimate spheres of autonomy through such techniques have made worried protests against "Big Brother" a growing response to such psychological surveillance.

The area which has undergone the greatest leap forward in technological capacity, however, is not physical or psychological surveillance, but data surveillance. The impact of data processing by computer is altering, in a way so profound that we are only barely aware of it as yet, the relation between individual spontaneity and social control in our society. As computers have made possible the collection, storage, manipulation, and use of billions of bits of information, at quite cheap prices and through operations done at incredible speeds, ours has become the greatest data-collecting society in human history. Government agencies, corporations, universities, churches, labor unions, and a host of other organizations now handle more volumes of personal data than they ever did before. More organizations exchange information from their files than ever took place before. More centralized records are growing up to collect information according to certain functional aspects of individual life — education records, employment records, military service records, medical records, security clearance records, and many others. At the same time, the pressure to move from our present cash and check economy, with its relatively small-scale credit card sector, to a money-less transaction system, based on a computerized flow of credits and debits to central bank accounts for each individual (and fingerprint, voiceprint measures for unique identification) represents the most far-reaching utilization of computer capability, yet many experts in banking, government, and corporate life state confidently that such an automated transaction system is on the way. Finally, as government has had to deal with its increased responsibilities in social welfare, law enforcement, civil rights compliance, economic regulation and forecasting, and national security, the pressures have mounted for centralized information systems that would apply large-scale data analysis on both a statistical and personal dossier basis.

Of course, the collection and storage in computers of vast amounts of personal data about individuals and private data about groups does not mean that we currently possess the technology to make all the comparisons, syntheses, and retrievals that proponents of computer information systems sometimes claim or their critics sometimes envisage. A great deal of work is currently underway to make either the general data bank for statistical purposes or the "intelligence system" for specific enforcement yield up its capacity data in usable form. The more complicated the mix and match operations called for, the more difficulty this poses for the computer in its present form.

This brief sketch of the interaction between technology, law, and social values in American society during nearly two centuries suggests in the briefest possible way the revolutionary character of the situation we are facing today. An enormous leap forward has been made in the power of public and private authorities to place individuals and private groups under close surveillance. In reaction, American society has stirred in alarm over the "Big Brother" prospects presented by these developments and has mounted an energetic campaign to either outlaw or control the techniques that have outstepped classic legal and social restraints. This is the situation we find ourselves in in 1967. Among thoughtful segments of the American public and the law-making community, the search now is for a whole new framework for defining privacy in a technological age. A host of interventions, from statutes and judicial decisions to administrative rules and professional standards, must somehow be devised to replace the current restraints which originated in and serviced an earlier period in our nation's history, but are outmoded today.

I am concerned here with only one area of this problem — what I call data surveillance, and the remainder of my remarks will be directed to this aspect of the problem. However, it is because this problem arises in the context of the technological advances in physical and psychological surveillance and public alarm over these threats to privacy that the computer issue must be seen in a larger context.

In many ways American law is in the worst possible shape to deal with information processing and privacy, much worse than the task of modernizing its concepts in the fields of physical and psychological surveillance. In the physical and psychological areas, American law has clear-cut concepts to build from — ideas such as trespass, intrusion, physical rights of property, etc. — but consider the difficulties of applying constitutional standards to the information process. First, American law has no clear cut definition of personal information as a precious commodity. It has well-developed notions of proprietary information, corporate records, and similar business information, derived from medieval law on the secrets of trades and professions and codified in the American patent system. But when information is not needed to make a profit, when it involves the flow of disclosure about the individual among those he comes in contact with and those who exercise authority over him, American law has had no general theory of value, no set of rights and duties to apply as a general norm. Second, American law has had no general system for dealing with the flow of information which government agencies and other levels of government control, apart from a few examples such as census data (which has been closed to any additional circulation) and income tax (which has been given a set of additional areas of circulation controlled by statute or executive order). On the one hand, we have traditions of free circulation of information that arise in our credit investigation and public opinion collection processes. On the other hand, we have traditions of confidentiality and classified-secrecy which mark the other boundary. How information can circulate between these two poles and what to do with information systems that are likely to contain all of these types of information are problems that American law has not considered. Third, American law has not developed institutional procedures to protect against improper collection of information, storage of inadequate or false data, and intra-organizational use of such information for reaching decisions about individuals outside or inside the organization. Again, we have been most creative where tangible property rights have been involved. The Federal Administrative Procedure Act of 1946 assured businessmen facing federal regulatory agencies that they would know what information about them was going into the records in certain key types of government hearings, that they would have opportunities to present other information to challenge or modify this data, and that the record produced by such a procedure would be subject to review through higher administrative and judicial processes. The development of such a theory of information and government action was set back badly during the late 1940's and 1950's, when the loyalty-security problem produced large-scale information collection about individuals without open hearings which provided full due process. Without the opportunity to know what was in the record, to cross-examine those who had given the information, and to challenge the evaluation put on the information by government security officials, individuals were left without effective protection in their personal reputations and job rights. It is important to note that American law never came to a final resolution of this dilemma. Supreme Court decisions limited the scope of the loyalty-security process in government to truly sensitive agencies and trimmed back its application in various marginal areas such as the granting of passports. But it has never been held by the courts that an individual has a right to full due process in loyalty-security matters and thus one model for information challenge that still exists is a model which rejects the obligation of government to give individuals whose loyalty has been questioned the kinds of remedies that are available to businessmen when property rights are involved.

Finally, American law is seriously challenged by some of the technological aspects of computer information systems which tend to work against the kinds of reasonableness standards that the law tries to apply where balancing is necessary among privacy, disclosure, and surveillance. If, for example, there were ways to assure that statistical data banks, such as the proposed Federal Data Center, could be set up so that they could not be transformed by those who run the system into a means of obtaining various sets of information about known individuals, American law could well set carefully differentiated standards for data banks and intelligence systems. But the clear message of the technological specialists involved is that identifying names or numbers must be left attached to statistical data if information from various sources is to be put together for statistical purposes and if longitudinal studies are to be made of specific individuals through time. When this is the case, American law must confront the possibility that data banks might become intelligence systems and it is this hard dilemma that is now deeply troubling the congressional committees and legal writers concerned with the first wave of data-pool systems for federal and state governments.

This short summary of the ways in which American law is not well prepared for developing new doctrines to control mis-use of information collection does not mean that the future is gloomy. What it does mean is that the same kind of imaginative thinking and systematic programming and planning must be applied to this problem as went into the development of the technology for the information systems themselves. This is a job in which the most fruitful discussions can take place among the computer scientists, lawyers, social scientists, and public officials. The sharing of expertise, the recognition of needs and values, and the setting of new balances are the key developments. To suggest the kind of approach that I think American society should take to information systems, let me sketch the response that I think sets these balances most sensitively. At the outset, I would have the courts and legislatures adopt as their guiding principle the concept that an individual's right to limit the circulation of personal information about himself is a vital ingredient of his right to privacy and this should not be infringed without the showing of strong social need and the satisfaction of requirements for protective safeguards. The First Amendment to the American Constitution which guarantees our rights to freedom of speech, press, and association must have as its necessary corollary the fact that we have a right not to communicate. It must also mean that we have the right to choose those to whom we communicate and the terms on which we do so. Any action by government that "turns us on" without that consent violates the right to silence that the Framers intended to give in the First Amendment just as much as the right to communicate. I would predict that this principle will come to be the guiding constitutional approach of the United States Supreme Court in dealing with the areas of physical, psychological, and data surveillance. Following this approach, when government takes information from an individual for one purpose (such as income taxation, social security, government licensing and employment) and uses it to influence, regulate, or prosecute the individual on unrelated matters, this

307

raises a question about violation of the confidence under which the information was originally given. The more that centralized information pools on individuals are assembled, the more serious the unrestricted flow of information becomes. This suggests that we need in our legal system some procedure for classifying information into various categories and distinguishing the rights to use of such information according to such classifications. For example, personal information could be divided into matters of public record that are expected to be open to virtually everyone; confidential information that is given in trust to certain individuals or agencies with the expectation of limited use; and security information which is either given under the expectation of complete non-circulation or which contains derogatory information about individuals that has been obtained by physical and psychological surveillance. Different standards must be set for the receipt, storage, and circulation of such different classes of information. This could be done by federal and state legislation, by administrative rules, and by the way in which information systems are technologically related to one another.

With these general proposals established, our policy-making would turn to the technological safeguards that could limit the capacities for mis-use of information systems. It is important to realize that storing data in computers rather than on pieces of paper in metal files allows us to create far more technological protection for sensitive information than in the era of written records and physical manipulation. For example, information "bits" in the memory banks could be locked so that only one or several persons who have special passwords could get to it. Computers could be programmed to reject requests for statistical data about "groups" which are really attempts to get information on specific individuals or organizations. A data system could be set up so that a permanent record was made of all inquiries and the "audit trail" could be subject to annual review by the management of the information center, independent "watch-dog" commissions of public officials and private citizens, and legislative committees.

Although many other ways to set system controls on information systems could be discussed, the fact remains that the system could still be "beaten" by those in charge of it, from the programmers who run it and the mechanics who repair breakdowns to those who are in charge of the enterprise and know all the passwords. This means that a network of legal controls is absolutely essential. For example, a federal statute could specify that the data put into a statistical center is to be used solely for statistical purposes. It could forbid all other uses of the data to influence, regulate, or prosecute anyone, making such use a crime, and excluding all such data from use as evidence in judicial or governmental proceedings. It could forbid all persons other than data center employees to have access to the files, and the data could be specifically exempted from subpoena. An Inspector General or Ombudsman-type official could be set up to hear complaints about alleged misuse, and judicial review for such complaints could be provided for.

A far more extensive set of safeguards are required when intelligence systems are involved. These must deal with which individuals go into the system at all, which public officials have access to the information, what classes of information are completely excluded and what safeguards are provided for challenging both the information collected and the use made of it. Regulations for mis-use of the information by the intelligence system personnel and by agencies which use the information would have to be provided and, again, some form of outside review of the system would be required, preferably by both an indedependent executive agency and legislative committees.

At the moment, American society is barely entering the beginning stage of this debate over data surveillance. We can see that three quite different approaches are already appearing. One position, reflected by the initial views of many newspaper editors, civil liberties groups, and congressional spokesmen is to oppose creation of data centers and intelligence systems completely. The need for better statistics for policy analysis or of richer information systems for criminal justice purposes is seen as inadequate when weighed against the increase in government power and fears of invasion of privacy that such systems might bring.

A second view, reflected in the initial thinking of many executive agency officials and computer scientists, assumes that traditional administrative and legal safeguards, plus the expected self-restraint of those who would manage such systems, are enough to protect the citizen's privacy. The more reflective spokesmen in this group would add that a large-scale decrease in the kind of personal privacy we have through inefficiency of information collection may well be on its way out, but that this would be something individuals could adjust to and would not seriously threaten the operations of a democratic society.

The third position, which I have tried to describe in my earlier discussion, assumes that neither the "total ban" nor the "traditional restraints" positions represent desirable alternatives. What is called for is a new legal approach to the processing of personal information by authorities in a free society and a new set of legal, administrative, and system protections to accomplish this objective. The fact is that American society wants both better information analysis *and* privacy. Ever since the Constitution was written, our efforts to have both order and liberty have succeeded because we found ways to grant authority to government but to tie it down with the clear standards, operating procedures, and review mechanisms that protected individual rights. A free society should not have to choose between more rational use of authority and personal privacy if our talents for democratic government are brought to bear on the task. The most precious commodity we have now is the few years of lead-time before this problem grows beyond our capacity for control. If we act now, and act wisely, we can balance the conflicting demands in the area of data surveillance in this same tradition of democratic, rational solutions.

ANTHONY DOWNS

The Political Payoffs
in Urban Information Systems

The glamorous capabilities of computerized "urban information systems" appear so dazzling that no major city planning proposal is considered respectable unless it contains at least one section on EDP, ADP, or an urban data bank. Nevertheless, automated data systems are still regarded with uncertainty and uneasiness by many key urban decision-makers. How can anyone — even a trained data technician — judge whether these systems are really worth the huge costs involved? Even more significant, how will these systems affect the relative power and influence of various individual decision-makers?

Ultimately, the answers to these questions depend upon assessing the final payoffs from urban data systems. *Final payoffs* are actual *improvements in government or private action,* as distinguished from *improvements in the information* on which such action is based.

Up to now, most of the concern with urban data systems has not been focused upon final payoffs for three reasons. First, the technical design of these systems has seemed more exciting, more novel — and more amenable to analysis. Second, most detailed analyses of the decision process have been performed by members of computer hardware firms. Naturally, they have concentrated upon describing the impressive improvements in information they can undoubtedly deliver. Third, it appears obvious that better data in urban decision-making would have huge final

From Anthony Downs, "A Realistic Look at the Final Payoffs from Urban Data Systems," *Public Administration Review* 27 (September 1967): 204–209. Copyright © 1967 by American Society for Public Administration.

Mr. Downs is Vice President of the Real Estate Research Corporation of Chicago.

payoffs, because it has hardly been doubted that better information would reduce both the frequency and the magnitude of planning mistakes.

This intuitively plausible but actually misleading assumption has caused us to deemphasize final payoffs. Therefore, this article will concentrate upon analyzing them.

All final payoffs from urban data systems consist of improvements in the effectiveness of decision-making. *Technical payoffs* are at least potentially beneficial to all participants in the decision-making process. They result from technical improvements in data inputs, processing, and outputs. Examples are greater speed of processing, greater consistency among outputs, and wider distribution of information. *Power payoffs* are gains in one person's decision-making effectiveness made at the expense of another person's. They are *redistributions* of the benefits of decision-making.

In reality, every change in urban data-reporting or data-processing systems has both technical and power repercussions. Hence anyone analyzing the impact of automated data systems upon urban decision-making, or forecasting the attitudes of government officials towards such systems, must take both types of impacts into account. Yet in almost all studies of urban data systems, power payoffs are considered too political and too controversial to discuss. As a result, we get one-dimensional dialogues about problems which in reality have two or more dimensions.

It is time we faced this reality by taking a hard look at power payoffs. But first it is necessary to examine technical payoffs in more detail.

A careful analysis shows that the technical payoffs from urban data systems are smaller than intuition would lead us to suppose. Also, they have certain characteristics which will strongly influence the forms of future urban data systems.

Computerized data systems could improve the data underlying current urban decisions by providing the following:

1. Lower operating costs of data processing.
2. Faster availability of information.
3. Wider distribution of information.
4. Generation of new information never before observed, recorded, or reported.
5. Greater consistency in reporting data.
6. Reduced distortion of data reported to top levels.
7. Eventual development of a giant data inventory. This could ultimately be used to formulate, test, and modify theories about causal relationship in the urban environment which we can now only guess at.

8. Greater freedom from routine record-keeping.

On the other hand, the following technical costs are required to gain the above improvements:

1. Increased capital costs including both hardware and software.
2. Demands for much more highly skilled personnel.
3. A tendency towards greater reliance upon quantifiable and measurable variables.
4. Increased narrowness of comprehension, particularly concerning incipient changes in the environment. Machine systems can respond only to stimuli they have been programmed to perceive, and in ways they have been programmed to react. Hence they are not sensitive to new types of data or of nuances in information that may signal changes in the entire situation.
5. Reduced sensitivity to the opinions and self-interest of intermediate-level officials in operating organizations. Information sent "straight through" from events to top-level administrators by automatic systems does not contain the interpretations of middle-level officials which often help place it in context, even though such interpretations always embody some biases.

These costs are often vastly outweighed by the improvements described above. Nevertheless, a balanced and impartial view of urban data systems must consider both.

The increased capabilities described above can greatly improve the data available to urban decision-makers. However, three factors make it hard to prove that these better data will lead to more effective decisions.

First, it is extremely difficult to measure the effectiveness of many decisions vital to urban affairs. The errors of such measurement are often likely to exceed by a wide margin even the most generous estimates of possible increases in effectiveness caused by better data.

Second, even when the effects of decisions can be readily measured, variances in those effects may be due to factors other than data inputs. Whenever the same kind of decision is made over and over, it may be possible to test one set of decisions based upon "old fashioned" data vs. another set based upon all the same inputs except data from an automated system. However, it is difficult to do this before installing the automated system when such knowledge is critical to deciding whether the system is worth its cost. Moreover, it is impossible to set up adequate controls concerning unique or irreversible decisions to measure the degree of improvement in their effectiveness created by better data.

Third, many persons with different goals are affected by every decision. Whether given payoffs should be considered positive or negative — and to what extent — depends upon whose values are used in making the calculation.

All these major obstacles to measuring the technical payoffs of urban data systems become more severe the broader the decisions involved. For truly "sweeping" choices, (1) the relative effectiveness of alternative decisions is harder to estimate, (2) the number of factors considered other than quantitative information is much larger, (3) the decision is more likely to be unique and irrevocable, and (4) there is a higher probability that more groups with conflicting values will be affected. Consequently, *it is much easier to prove that urban data systems will provide positive technical payoffs concerning narrow operational decisions than concerning broad policy or operating choices.*

Much of the academic and intellectual support for urban data systems has resulted from the seemingly enormous technical payoffs to be gained from truly comprehensive systems. Such systems (1) service all government departments from a central data processing complex, (2) link these departments in a single information and report-printing network, (3) provide a single massive memory based upon a uniform coding system, and (4) allow instantaneous random access to this "joint memory" from remote stations in each department. In theory, such a comprehensive system should be able to bring together and analyze masses of data from all the various departments affected by even the broadest municipal government decisions.

But in reality, even if such huge systems existed, it would be tremendously difficult to *prove conclusively* that they provided significant technical payoffs concerning broad decisions. This is true for the reasons set forth previously. Yet comprehensive systems are immensely expensive. Much narrower data systems often provide the greatest *demonstrable technical payoffs* in decision-making — at least in relation to their costs, which are much lower. This implies that, in the near future, many urban politicians will buy narrowly designed data systems (such as those serving individual city departments) rather than comprehensive, "all-department" systems.

In the long run, the biggest technical payoffs from improved urban data will probably arise from better knowledge of underlying causal relationships in the urban environment now shrouded by ignorance. But developing theories about these casual relationships, and then testing those theories, requires an enormous stockpile of data about how each factor varies under a wide diversity of conditions. Hence this important technical payoff may not become available for something like a decade after massive urban data systems are installed and working. This situation will further discourage many urban governments from initially purchasing comprehensive urban data systems.

The large extra costs of a comprehensive system must be borne immediately, or soon; whereas the extra payoffs it generates will not accrue for years. Even then, their appearance is by no means certain. Moreover, human judgment can never be eliminated from the application of results derived from even the most sophisticated computer analysis. But when urban decision-makers realize that no data system, however comprehensive, will ever "give them all the answers," many will be reluctant to pay huge additional costs for what will probably seem like only marginal gains in final payoffs. After all, the bigger the role of judgment in the final decision, the greater the probability that a wise man will make the right choice without the help of a comprehensive computerized system.

For all these reasons connected with purely *technical* payoffs, it seems likely that many — though not all — cities will avoid early commitment to costly comprehensive data systems. As we shall see, consideration of *power* payoffs further strengthens this conclusion.

Most of the technical payoffs promised by promoters of urban data systems require continuous data acquisition after the systems are installed. Such updating creates a major cost in any data system — in the long run, often the single largest cost, even exceeding the cost of hardware.[1] This huge on-going burden is tolerable only if the system itself is associated with an operating department which continuously procures the necessary data anyway as part of its normal behavior. This is another reason why many urban data systems are likely to start out as narrow departmental tools rather than as broad comprehensive ones.

Because of the uncertainties connected with the technical payoffs from urban data systems, power payoffs loom large in the minds of those who must decide whether such systems will actually be built and installed.

Power payoffs arise because every change in organization, techniques, or decision processes shifts the relative power of at least some of the individuals involved. Invariably, these individuals place heavy weight upon such shifts in judging the desirability of proposed changes. True, in public they rarely if ever speak of these power shifts. Instead they usually refer only to the technical impacts of the changes being considered. But this does not fool anyone who really knows what is happening.

The power payoffs from urban data systems spring from four technical

1. Melvin M. Weber, "The Roles of Intelligence Systems in Urban-Systems Planning," *Journal of the American Institute of Planners* (November 1965), p. 294.

impacts of such systems. First, automated systems tend to transmit many data directly from events themselves to top-level officials, or at least to reduce the number of intermediate steps separating these two extremes. As a result, lower- and intermediate-level officials often have little or no opportunity of "filtering" important data before they reach top-level officials. "Filtering" can mean either distorting information by altering or leaving out parts of it, or adding personal interpretations to it, or both.[2]

Second, urban data systems inevitably shift some emphasis in decision-making towards more easily quantifiable factors and away from immeasurable ones. Third, such systems free lower-level officials from many routine reporting and recording chores. Fourth, they provide those officials capable of understanding and using them with much better information about certain aspects of urban affairs than those persons who do not use them.

The technical impacts of urban data systems described above tend to produce seven specific power shifts among the various "actors" in the urban decision-making process. The net power gainers from such shifts regard the data system causing them as having positive power payoffs; whereas the net power losers regard its power payoffs as negative. Any given person may gain from one power shift and lose from another. In fact, a single system might provide him with far more power regarding certain decisions or actions, and far less regarding others. Nevertheless, most well-informed people affected by a given data system will have definite opinions about whether it improves or worsens their overall power.

Automated data systems cause the following seven power shifts in urban decision-making — or in decision-making at state and federal levels when introduced there.

1. *Lower- and intermediate-level officials tend to lose power to higher-level officials and politicians.* The reduction in "filtering" of data at lower and intermediate levels of city hierarchies deprives officials there of some of their former influence, since machine systems often bypass them entirely.

2. *High-level staff officials gain power.* Since lower-level officials no longer condense data as it moves upward, an enormous amount of information flows directly to the "top of the heap." The politicians and line executives located there simply cannot cope with all this information

2. George P. Shultz and Thomas J. Whisler, eds. *Management Organization and the Computer* (Glencoe: Free Press, 1960), p. 13.

unaided. So they rely on expanded staffs, or ever-more-overworked staffs, to provide the interpretation and filtering formerly done by lower-level officials.

Since the politicians and top-level executives concerned receive "filtered" information both before and after urban data systems are installed, it might seem that they are not net power gainers. However, this conclusion is false for three reasons. First, automated data systems often provide certain types of highly useful information never available before, or now available much faster. Second, staff advisors are likely to be more directly loyal to their top-level bosses than lower-level line operators, who have strong loyalties to their departments. Third, expanding one's staff creates additional channels of information which can be used to check up on the activities of operating departments. As every public and private executive knows, development of such seemingly redundant channels of information is crucial to keeping oneself well informed about "what is really going on down there."

3. *City and state legislators tend to lose power to administrators and operating officials.* The latter are generally more sophisticated, have more technical training, are equipped with larger staffs, devote more time to their city jobs, can focus more intensively upon narrow specialties, are in a better position to control the design and operation of urban data systems, and are more likely to receive continuous reports from those systems by virtue of their positions.

4. *The government bureaucracy as a whole gains power at the expense of the general electorate and nongovernmental groups.* Government officials have continuous "inside access" to the data generated by automated systems, and they also control which data are built into those systems. No matter how idealistic they are, they will vigorously resist universal accessibility to these data. This occurs because accurate and detailed reporting of the behavior of any large organization — private or public — will inevitably reveal operating deficiencies that would be embarrassing if widely known. Moreover, the general electorate and most nongovernmental groups are not technically sophisticated when it comes to understanding and interpreting complex data.

5. *Well-organized and sophisticated groups of all kinds, including some government bureaus, gain power at the expense of less well-organized and less sophisticated groups.* The former are much better equipped than the latter to collect, analyze, understand, and react to the data outputs of automated systems. However, organization alone is not enough to counter-

act potential power shifts caused by urban data systems. Even well-organized groups may lose some power if their members are not technically sophisticated.

6. *Within city governments, those who actually control automated data systems gain in power at the expense of those who do not.* Most city officials are acutely aware of this potential power shift. Each operating department naturally wants to retain as much power as possible over its own behavior and its traditional sphere of activity. Its members are especially anxious to prevent "outsiders" from having detailed knowledge about every aspect of the department's operations. Hence nearly every department with operations susceptible to computerized management will at least initially fight for its own computer and data system controlled by its own members.

At the other extreme, city planners and budgetary officials will both eventually espouse centralized data systems. They will view such systems at least in part as means of gaining control over the information channels vital to all operating departments — and thereby capturing some of the latter's power. Therefore, *much of the controversy which is sure to arise concerning the proper design and operation of urban data systems will reflect a power struggle for control of those systems.*

7. *Technically educated officials within city governments gain power at the expense of old-style political advisors.* The latter are the "wise old (or young) men" found clustered around the head of every local, state, and national government. Their function has always been to provide good judgment in the face of uncertainty. But urban data systems tend to substitute new types of uncertainty (such as that concerning statistical reliability) for old (such as that concerning the accuracy of individual insights). Well-educated data technicians will seem much more capable of coping with these new uncertainties than will the traditional "wise men."

However, politicians will soon discover that data technicians cannot really deliver on their promises to make accurate predictions of crucial variables. Our ignorance is still too profound for such accuracy. Hence a new advisory role will appear for men who possess *both* technical sophistication and wisdom. Although many men can learn sophisticated techniques, true wisdom is extremely scarce; so such advisors will acquire increasing power.

The power shifts described above will markedly affect the attitudes of specific groups and individuals towards the use of automated data systems. However, not all power losers will oppose the system, and not all power gainers will support it. In the first place, most people who will be affected by a new system will be uncertain about whether they will gain or lose when it is introduced. Hence their attitudes will be ambivalent, unless they oppose it out of sheer inertia. Second, some power losers may accept the system because of its large technical payoffs, and some gainers may oppose it because its costs outweigh the technical payoffs they perceive. Third, some people who realize in advance how a new data system will affect their power will not attempt to influence the decision about whether to use it. Either they feel they cannot affect that decision, or they believe its impact will be slight. Therefore, only a minority of the persons whose power will in fact be affected by a new urban data system are likely to support or oppose it in advance because of their beliefs about its power impacts upon them.

Nevertheless, this minority will exert very significant influence for two reasons. First, a minority with strong opinions about highly technical matters almost always has great influence in our democratic society concerning those matters. The majority of persons are too ignorant or apathetic to express any technical views at all. Second, the only people likely to be in this particular minority are those who hold powerful positions in the urban decision-making structure — especially within the city government.

The officials in this minority will consist of two groups. On the one hand, city planners, administrative assistants to mayors and city managers, and other high-ranking staff members, plus some top politicians, will press for early introduction and widespread use of fairly comprehensive data systems. On the other hand, many officials in specific operating departments will drag their feet about introducing automated systems, restrict the use of such systems sharply, and insist upon allowing each department to set up and operate its own system.

In the long run, the former group will prevail. The higher technical payoffs of comprehensive systems will eventually become clear to everyone. But in the short run — which may last for a decade or even longer — the latter group will be more powerful in many cities in spite of its lower rank. In most city governments, the people who run the everyday affairs of each operating department invariably exert much greater influence over how those affairs are carried out than central staff members or even top-level elected officials. Introducing any automated data system into an ongoing department requires great changes in day-to-day procedures. Therefore it necessitates overcoming the department's inherent inertia.

319

Few mayors or city managers, however powerful, are strong enough to fight such inertia in all departments simultaneously. Yet that is precisely what they would have to do in order to install a single comprehensive system covering all city operations, unless individual department heads become convinced that such a system would greatly aid their own shops. Furthermore, resistance to automated data systems within each department will be greatly reduced if its top-level officials have a strong incentive to use them. They would if those systems were designed specifically for their benefit and operated by them. Therefore, *perception of power payoffs by departmental officials is likely to cause many cities to adopt a highly piecemeal approach to the adoption and use of automated urban data systems.* Thus both piecemeal and comprehensive approaches will be followed by different cities in the next few years.

It is quite likely that the total costs of eventually arriving at a single integrated data system in any city will be much greater via the piecemeal route than they would via initial adoption of a comprehensive system. The former approach will require gradually developing links between disparate individual systems not initially designed to function as a unit. The cost of such development will probably exceed that of providing such links right from the start in one integrated system. Moreover, some of the data necessary for development of basic theories about causal relationships in the urban scene can emerge only from an integrated system. But it will take much longer to create an integrated system through piecemeal construction. Hence technical payoffs based on knowledge of these causal relationships may be delayed for years. Similarly, under the piecemeal approach, those parts of government which receive automated systems last will not enjoy the technical payoffs thereof until much later.

In spite of these drawbacks, it is at least arguable that the piecemeal approach has sizable advantages for technical reasons as well as power payoff reasons. If cities refrained from installing any automated data systems until adequate research for fully comprehensive systems were completed, they would have to pass up sizable technical payoffs which can be achieved immediately in certain departments. Moreover, any attempt to install a comprehensive system in a large city might wind up as a piecemeal approach anyway. By the time the last "integrated" units were installed, technical changes might have made the first units obsolete.

It can hardly be doubted that automated data systems will soon have profound effects upon government and private decision-making in urban areas — and at state and federal levels too. Nor is it debatable that these revolutionary impacts will spring from the immense technical improvements in data which such systems make possible. Nevertheless, the future form and use of automated data systems will not depend solely upon improvements in data. Rather they will depend upon the ways in which data improvements increase the effectiveness of actions and change the power positions of the actors involved. These two outcomes constitute the *final payoffs* from using automated data systems.

Therefore, in order to forecast how automated data systems are likely to be designed and used in government, we must shift our attention from the dazzling technical capabilities of computer systems to the ways in which men apply those systems in the real world.

Three major conclusions emerge. First, significant technical payoffs from automated data systems are much more ambiguous and difficult to demonstrate than technical improvements in data. Second, the ways in which public (and private) officials use automated data systems will be determined just as much by their perceptions of the resulting shifts in personal power as by their desire to reap technical benefits for the public interest.

Third, the nature of both technical and power payoffs implies that many city governments — as well as state and national governments — will develop automated data systems in a piecemeal, department-by-department fashion. Hence the glamorous comprehensive urban systems we hear about from "computerphiles" are likely to be a long time in coming in many areas.

One final observation is warranted. Experts who set up urban and other automated data systems should pay more attention to power payoffs in designing those systems. Every data system serves real flesh-and-blood men. These men sorely need the help obtainable from automated data systems. But they will not accept or effectively use such help unless it is offered to them in a way that takes their own interests into account.

OLIVER E. DIAL

Why There Are No Urban
Information Systems Yet

This monograph [a bibliographic essay on urban information systems, prepared in 1968] was constructed from a screening of some ten years of literature on the subject of urban information systems. Upon completing a reading of it, one is left with the distinct impression that there are no great problems remaining; that urban information systems are performing reasonably well in many cities; and that remaining developments will be of a technological nature, reflecting improvements in hardware, software, and displays.

To test this impression, the author visited a number of the cities which had the longest experience in developing urban information systems. *In none of them did he find a computerized-based urban information system in being.* Furthermore, after conferring by telephone with officials in selected other cities, and after attending a conference on the present "state of the art," it could only be concluded that *there are no such systems in existence today.*

One city which had participated in a federally funded program with four other cities over a period of more than four years to develop an urban information system had succeeded only in creating a single basic file which had never been up-dated and *which had never been used.* Officials of that city stated that they would not consider re-involvement

From O. E. Dial, "Urban Information Systems: A Bibliographic Essay," published by the Urban Systems Laboratory, Massachusetts Institute of Technology, 1968. Copyright © 1968 by Oliver E. Dial.

Mr. Dial is Visiting Professor of Public Administration at Long Island University and Director of the Municipal Information Systems Research Project.

in such a scheme for some years. So far as they were concerned, the study never took place. They agreed that they had learned from it, but they learned how *not* to build an urban information system, not how to build one.

Another city in the same group developed a basic file, but was unable to update it. The file was used twice in six years, each time for a nongovernmental client and for a trivial fee. Each time, also, the software demanded some ten levels of processing, e.g., the output of the first run became the input of the second, and so on through ten passes in the computer. Time required was in excess of 24 hours' computer time. That particular city is clinging to the notion that it can be done and persists in its efforts.

In a city which had a much touted computer-based police dispatching system, it was learned that those lights on the numerous map displays did not really move, nor did they indicate the location of a police car. They merely indicated the identity of police cars unassigned at the moment and located somewhere within one of eight extremely large geographic areas of the city. Communication moved from the originator through two human interfaces, one of whom completed a hand-written dispatch card before the police car received his assignment. The weight of the dispatch card placed in an appropriate slot served to open a micro-switch, thus putting out the light relating to that vehicle on the map board. Ingenious? The literature of urban information systems would suggest not, and yet that city is well ahead of all others in its police dispatching system.

Another large city had developed some two hundred computer-based files, and was unable to link any two of them at this writing. Thus, they required continued duplication in information handling.

One city complained that the program documentation provided by a software consulting firm was so sketchy that they had to assign a programmer to "live with the program." After applying himself full-time for about a year, he was able to document the portion which he was able to decipher, and devise substitute sub-systems for the portions which he could not unravel. Repeated calls and letters to the consultant brought no additional documentation. City officials concluded that the consultant was concerned that detailed documentation might make the program too freely exportable to other communities.

It is obvious that most large cities in the United States have moved from electronic accounting machinery to electronic data processing, and that in the transition some people genuinely believe that they have achieved an urban information system. There clearly is some confusion in terms. Nor does the literature do much to relieve this confusion. Rather, the literature tends to exploit it.

A total urban information system can be analyzed into five sub-systems. First, and most well developed, is an administrative sub-system. This is the system which was first to exploit the efficiencies of electronic accounting machines (EAM), and then to change to electronic data processing (EDP). The system is conventionally used for personnel accounting, property inventory and control, finance management, billing and receipting, and so on. It seems doubtful that this sub-system in itself can constitute an urban information system.

A second, and somewhat less well-developed, sub-system is in support of operations. The system is a resource for police, fire, and other emergency vehicle dispatching, for controlling an array of traffic lights, and for other control, alert, and dispatching functions in a city.

A third sub-system may be created in support of planning. This system provides a computerized base for problem solving in the field of engineering, but it may include a geocoding system and an analytic and modelling capability for purposes of transportation simulation, PERT, and CPM. Ideally, this system would also support health and social planners, with a computer capacity and software choices which make it possible to massage large volumes of data about people and places.

The fourth sub-system is perhaps furthest from being achieved. This is a management sub-system. It automates the PPB System, thus making it possible for policy-makers to know the consequences of policy alternatives which they are considering for decision. It yields a degree of rationalization to the programming and budgetary process which cannot be achieved by any other known method. Equally important, this sub-system provides a situational display to the city manager and/or urban policy makers. The sub-system utilizes exception reporting and priority reporting techniques, thus permitting a manager to have prompt knowledge of significant variance from the routine in all aspects of the urban system. The system would utilize electronic and non-electronic displays, both computer based, as well as conventional graphic displays. The system would support periodic briefings in all phases of the activities of an urban system.

The final sub-system is a research facility. This system differs from all others in its demand for historic data in specified times and periods. Computer based, it would have a geocoding system together with a variety of software permitting a wide range of analytic solutions to problems.

There are examples, to some limited degree, of each of these sub-systems today. While it is easy to separate them analytically, in real life they are merged to some extent. For example, an administrative system may also support planners, and both may support management.

The question remains, however, at what point do we properly describe a city as having an urban information system? If the question seems difficult to answer, we cannot with any consistency be critical of cities which have fragments of one or more of these sub-systems and yet acclaim theirs as an urban information system. There are no established criteria for this judgment. Nor, for that matter, should the classification into five sub-systems described above be regarded as having found authoritative concurrence. A review of the literature will quickly reveal a confusion between authors in this respect where one regards an urban information system to be a management information system, and another a planning information system, and so on.

But as we seek to settle the waves of disagreement as to the name of what we are talking about, it seems essential to resort to some such classification as that discussed above. This need stems from one of the most difficult problems facing urban information system designers today, namely, how does one begin? What should be the point of departure? It is obvious that the point of departure will be different according to which sub-system you are going to design.

For example, the point of departure in one city was to take note of every item being recorded, either on forms, in journals, or on maps. A chart of frequencies, formats, codes, volumes, and flows was then prepared. This quickly developed into a deluge of flow charts that defied recapitulation. The effort was given up.

Another city, under the guidance of its consultant, used the "event" as the point of departure. Each "event" in the city, a fire, for example, generated a flow of information to various departments of the city administration. To the police, if arson were suspected; to the assessor, if significant property damage resulted; and to other departments insofar as the event generated information of interest to them.

Whatever the approach, it seems clear that none will be successful until the information system has been rationalized. Providing a computerized base to a system does not assure any degree of rationalization whatsoever. Instances of duplication continue to obtain; information required to be reported at one point in the history of a city may no longer be needed in another, more modern period; information conventionally reported at the source by human interfaces will in all probability continue to be reported this way in a computerized system; and distribution lists for varieties of reports become quickly outdated with additions and rare deletions.

It is obvious that some degree of systems analysis and the revisions to the system that this analysis yields must precede automation of the system. While systems analysis is in progress it is clear that it must be constrained by the capabilities and limitations of computer hardware, software, and displays. It seems clear, too, that systems analysis should impose a disciplined files-and-forms management technology upon the urban community as a first point of order. Whether or not this would be digestible remains to be seen.

The "total system" concept has become anathema in the literature of urban information systems. But it has not been replaced by any organized scheme of sub-systems. Rather, the term "incremental" development of the system will be heard and echoed from author to author. Whether this is justified on the basis of insufficient funds, personnel, knowledge, or hardware and software in being is a choice which each author selects from his own experience. Incremental seems to mean "feel your way," "develop the system step-by-step from modest origins." Given the state of the art, it is difficult to disagree with this position, yet it seems clear that continued effort ought to be made to conceptualize the entire system in theory at the very least. Incremental development of existing systems ought to accord with that theory. Where it fails to do so, both should be closely examined for defect.

That is exactly the point which this caveat seeks to make. Theory, as represented in the literature of urban information systems, is seriously at odds with what actually exists today. The literature would seem to be inflated as one software developer and hardware manufacturer after another boasts the virtues of his own ware. This is not difficult to understand since there are no agreed-upon standards or specifications by which one item might be compared to another. Then, too, there is no existing urban information system by which the claims, with exceptions, might be tested. Testing of software and hardware is more often than not necessarily confined to the optimum conditions of the laboratory.

Government bureaucracy at all levels, but particularly the federal, consulting firms and individual consultants, not excluding exponents of academe, have a vested interest to be served which too often causes them to be excessively optimistic while minimizing difficulty, maximizing theoretical success, and claiming achievement when the product has fallen well below the mark.

Finally, there is evidence that systems designers tend to see all the problems in the light of their own expertise. This tends inevitably to a narrowness of thought which denies any potential for contribution by persons in other fields. One example should make this clear, although many will be in evidence while reading the literature. At a recent conference on the present state of the art of urban information systems, there was a reluctance to consider the potential for power re-diffusion and re-organization as aspects of urban information systems. The reason for this became clear when it was learned that the conference was sponsored by the department of education of that university, and that there was absolutely no consultation or intercourse with the political science, sociology, or business departments. What, indeed, did they have to offer? The chairman saw the entire problem from the perspective of a city planner dealing with merchants of hardware and software.

The subject, urban information systems, is more complex than the literature suggests. In all probability it will involve far more disciplines than are presently involved as efforts towards its realization become progressively more successful.

KENNETH L. KRAEMER

A Model for Urban
Information Systems

As a concept for approaching data handling, the databank has roots in
the U.S. census beginning with 1790. However, the signal stimulus for
local government experimentation with the concept was provided by
Hearle and Mason's RAND Corporation study [Edward F. R. Hearle and
Raymond J. Mason, *A Data Processing System for State and Local Governments*] of data processing in state and local governments, published
in 1963. The study severely criticized the housekeeping approach and
advocated the databank concept as a better alternative, thereby initiating
a series of efforts during the 1960's to develop urban databanks.

The databank advocates asserted that urban governments needed data
about both the environment they served and about internal operations.
They argued that much data collected as a result of day-to-day administration could be utilized for planning and management as well as for
operations. Data needs should, therefore, be conceived on a government-
wide basis. A data pool or bank would be established. It would be subject
to manipulation by a generalized programming language to allow for
frequently repeated routine processing, analysis, and reporting requirements. A wide range of data relating to persons and property would be
included and, except for confidential data, be available for a wide variety
of governmental decision making. The data base would be maintained

From Kenneth L. Kraemer, "The Evolution of Information Systems for Urban Administration," *Public Administration Review* 29 (July–August 1969): 389–402. Copyright
© 1969 by American Society for Public Administration.
Mr. Kraemer teaches at the University of California at Irvine.

by the operating agencies which generate and keep data current in the course of their daily operations. Thus, the urban information system envisaged was a massive data retrieval file, updated by operating agencies, continuously on call to its users, supplying them on a routine basis with the information they required.

Some databanks, such as the land-planning oriented, Tulsa-based Metropolitan Data Center Project, the Campbell and Le Blanc study for the Department of Housing and Urban Development, and the Pittsburgh Community Renewal Program (CRP), were developed or proposed for a single governmental function; others, for general governmental use: the Alexandria, Va., databank, the Metropolitan San Diego Data System, and the Los Angeles Automated Planning and Operational File (APOF); still others, for use by both public and private agencies: the Portland Metropolitan Databank, the Cincinnati Urban Data Center, and the Pennsylvania-New Jersey-Delaware (PENJERDEL) Area Data System.

Experience with urban databanks has been disappointing. An implicit assumption of the concept was that a core data base existed which was common to the needs of various levels and functions of urban government. This assumption is probably correct. However, neither the theoretic studies nor the application efforts faced the task of defining that data base. Data were included in the system because they were available, because they were presently used, because people said they needed them, or all of these. Such considerations may be necessary criteria for including or excluding data, but they are not sufficient. The key criteria — organizational decision and operations requirements and their information needs — simply were not included. The failure to define a core data base adequately resulted in creation of a data wasteland somewhere between operational and management needs. Thus, databanks were not used.

While top managers were not served by the databanks, their direct investment was low. That of the operating agencies was high, because these units bore the burden of creating the data base and keeping it current. The databank design did not integrate these tasks into ongoing operations such that current data would be developed as a by-product of operations. It established data base creation and updating as additional burdens. Thus, the cost-benefit ratio of participation was high and few operating agencies chose to cooperate. Since the development of a databank, whether for one function or an entire governmental unit, requires the involvement of other agencies as data sources, most databanks have not been kept current.

The first two weaknesses led to a third. Because a core data base was not defined and updating could not be achieved, or, because the life of certain data elements was too short to be accommodated by the updating procedure, the data in the banks represented a static, i.e., one point in time, portrayal of the community. Because of rapid change in the community, the utility of this static data base was short-lived.

A Redefinition of the Urban Information System

In view of the information field's evolution to date, it is important to develop a generic definition of an urban information system.

An urban information system consists of people, computer equipment and related programs, a dynamic data base, and institutional procedures interacting in a prescribed systems pattern. It is designed to collect, store, update, and facilitate the automated use of data on a continuing basis. Such data and its processing and analysis are related to both the internal affairs of government and the external environment. The manifold purposes of such an information system are to meet operational requirements; to facilitate various summarizing or analytical techniques relevant to the definition of community problems; to assist the search for program goals; to generate cybernetic flows for evaluation and control; and to permit the exchange of information among governmental units and with the public.

Several key ideas underlying or contained in this definition should be noted:

1. An information system is an integrated series of subsystems, the development of which can be characterized by definable phases — though the phases interact and proceed in reiterative fashion.
2. Housekeeping applications, databanks, models, and process-control systems are included in the system as identifiable stages in system development and ultimately as elements of an integrated system.
3. The system involves a series of interfaces relative to internal governmental affairs, to the external environment served, and to other levels of government.
4. Feedback control is a basic feature.
5. Information systems are most meaningful when they serve to integrate the processes of administration and enable urban governments actually to improve government or private action.

A Suggested Approach to Urban Information Systems

While developmental work remains to be done on each of the several elements of an urban information system, it is becoming increasingly critical that work be initiated to build the linkages creating an information system capability such as that suggested by the foregoing definition. Now is the time to bring together the various approaches in the development of urban information systems and to search for a creative synthesis going beyond past experimentation. Such an approach is developing, and probably will continue well into the 1970's. A convenient phrase to designate this development is the systems approach.

As used here, the systems approach is an attempt to view broadly and within a unified framework the processes of government and the use of information for decision making within those processes. The aim is to embrace all consequential ramifications, interactions, and exterior connections, taking full cognizance of the particular place, time, and context.

The utility of information technology rests in its potential contribution to improving the information and decision processes in urban governments. To achieve that potential, information must be viewed first as a part of governmental decision-making processes and secondarily as data to be handled. However, improvement of information and decision processes requires simultaneous improvement in several related dimensions of the governmental system. Chief among these are organization structure, people, knowledge about information systems, and the social milieu of government. The key reason for these concomitant requirements is that, given the nature of systems, improvements must reach a critical mass in order to influence the aggregative working of the system. Improvements which do not reach the relevant impact thresholds will be neutralized by countervailing adjustments of other components, or may actually reduce the quality of the system. Thus, a systems approach to urban information system development requires simultaneous improvements aimed at: (1) integrating information technology and decision processes, (2) realigning organization structure, (3) developing personnel, (4) expanding the stock of knowledge about information systems, and (5) altering the social milieu in which information systems are built.

Integration of Information Technology and Decision Processes

Urban government can be viewed as an information system in which data are collected, organized, stored, managed, analyzed, and retrieved — all ultimately for decision-making purposes. The system of information is not simply an inventory of data but a time-related dynamic flow in which the information is displayed in a variety of patterns over time as the organization acts and reacts to its significance. The information flow reveals interfaces which are inter- and intra- and extra-governmental in character. At any single point in time, the governmental system and any of its components may be described not only by their information content and flow but also by their history, which is both the aggregation and distillation of information about previous patterns in space and time.

In the process of producing and distributing services, each component generates and receives information. Some is of interest only to that component; much is important to other components and to the governmental system. This information is generated primarily from daily operations, but also from secondary data sources and from ad hoc data collection efforts. The processes which generate the information are in some sense "organized," at least by the inner logic of the particular component served. Urban information system development requires the rationalization and formalization of these existing informational activities in terms of the decision requirements of each component and the governmental system. The information system then can be designed as an organized part of both the daily operating, monitoring activities of government and the longer-term policy-testing activities. In this way the development of a wide range of physical, social, political, and economic data about the environment can become built-in features of governmental administration along with highly specific and detailed information about governmental effectiveness in changing the environment.

To achieve such multifaceted data bases, the stocks and flows entering the system must be selected to reflect both the clearly defined operating information needs and the analytic needs of government. Here lies a major controversy in the urban information systems field. Some people hold that information systems must be based in the operating activities of urban government and that these activities provide, or can be made to provide, the many information needs. Others criticize this position because the quality of data obtained from operations is poor and because data are collected for one purpose in operations and used for different purposes in the system. The first problem can be managed in systems design by attention to standardization of data definitions, identification, and classification, and by improved collection procedures. The second problem is more difficult. The critical issue here, and one which has not received positive theoretical or practical attention, is to define that data base which is common to the components of a particular government and which permits multiple utilization. A related issue is the design of the information system so that it is sufficiently open-ended to permit the addition and deletion of data elements and the addition of new components as experience and changing conditions indicate the need. Using the same data for several purposes, then, involves further aggregation or disaggregation, rearrangement in time or space, or some other form of reorganization.

But, in a very general way, everything in the system relates to everything else and a boundary problem results. The problem is to determine where, in this ever-expanding universe of data and information impacts and uses, it is reasonable to rationalize the information flow in some fashion and to include or exclude particular streams from the design of the integrated system. It is here that the analytical forms of theory, models, socioeconomic indicators, and other symbolic representations to aid thinking become important and constitute a basis for data selectivity in addition to that of the existence and use of data in the operating activities of government. That is, these analytical constructions provide an additional basis for deciding what information is relevant and what is not. This they do because they are explicit propositions about the key variables that underlie various urban phenomena and about the impact of particular governmental actions in effecting changes in those variables. Conversely, the data produced by the government operations in the community provide the empirical data base against which these symbolic propositions can be tested and affirmed as significantly reflective of reality.

Realignment of Organization Structure

Related to improvement of information and decision processes are organizational structures. Examination of the information flows in a number of governments indicates that information processes and organization structure are interrelated. Either information or structure may be viewed as the independent variable. In many cases, the most desirable way to organize may be determined only after information needs and points of decision have been determined. This is a critical consideration because in the social milieu behavior can be modified almost only by the transfer of information. The points of information generation, aggregation, and dissemination become key decision centers and the focus of organizational capacity to influence action. Thus, the reworking of old structures becomes an integral part of information systems design. So does the creation of new structures. Among these are units and arrangements for the development of policy regarding information system development (e.g., data sharing and exchange among components and other units of government, confidentiality, data manipulation, and dissemination), for the management of information handling processes, and for the continuous evolution of the information system itself.

Development of Personnel

Improvement of the human decision makers in the governmental system is also required. Nearly everyone in the system is a decision maker and potentially contributes to or utilizes information. Therefore, development of information-related knowledge and skills is required at all levels of a governmental organization. A variety of educational and training programs exist for technical and professional personnel, but most fail to be concerned with matters beyond the mechanics of information technology. Educational programs for managers and politicians are almost nonexistent.

Indoctrination, technical training, use of new procedures, the human and organizational impacts of information systems, and change strategies are basic requisites of personal development. So is sophistication in the use of information. Recent experiments have indicated that decision makers, when free to call for information from a ready-access source, are extremely wasteful of these resources. In addition, given the complex problems facing urban governments, policy makers are tempted to grasp at measurable dimensions in order to represent an underlying reality. In the process of political discourse and debate the statistical abstraction is often confused with a particular reality. Statistical, mathematical, and logical abstractions are important. But generalized descriptions and explanations are needed also. Such explanations should make possible a constant reminder that statistics which show, say, a decrease in the number of poor families can exist side by side with increased militancy of certain poor elements in the population.

Expansion of the Stock of Knowledge

Improvement is also needed in the basic stock of knowledge about information systems—their design, construction, operation, use, and impacts. As pointed out by Crecine and others, few systems or their components are documented sufficiently to transmit the considerations involved in a particular design. Failures, whether technical or behavioral, are never reported in the literature. Research, frank experimentation, and documentation is needed if the knowledge and experience with information systems is to be transmitted and if there is to be a basis for theory building and improvement of practice. Since information system development is an activity largely carried on in operational settings, those responsible for development cannot leave this function solely to academicians. Development efforts can be designed as experiments conducted in a scientific manner and reported on for replication and testing in other contexts.

Alteration of the Social Milieu

A final area of needed improvement is the culture of government. Information systems are change agents. They cannot be accomplished without change in attitudes and existing ways of doing things. More fundamentally, they cannot be accomplished without change in the way information systems are viewed. As long as these systems are viewed as something apart from, rather than integral to, the normal processes of government, their full potential will remain unrealized.

As yet, there is no thoroughgoing urban government experience with this approach that can be evaluated, although several partial efforts are proposed or under way. If past experience is any indicator, however, even recent and proposed efforts will not constitute the ultimate in urban information systems development. They will provide simply one more group of experiences to push the state-of-the-art a little farther and open up new possibilities and insights. They will result in a somewhat greater capability to take future considerations into account, manage the urban environment, and adapt to rapid change.

MYRON E. WEINER

Trends and Directions
for Urban Information Systems

The field of urban information systems has reached a stage where those involved in its development are searching for a strategy that can serve as a practical guide for the next ten years. There are several basic questions closely related to devising such a strategy: Are "piecemeal" and "integrated" systems development incompatible? What should be the focus and objectives of the systems to be developed? How can they be developed to make maximum use of new developments in hardware and software? . . . to relate to other systems being developed by other local governments, and by other government agencies on other levels of government? To what extent should a municipality attempt to develop its own system or cooperate in multijurisdictional efforts? What level of education in the technology is required for municipal professionals to engage in urban systems development? What is the primary potential that information technology holds for urban management and what approach should be taken to tap this and secondary potentialities for the complex task of coping with the problems of an urbanized, pre-twenty-first-century American society?

This paper will attempt to answer these and similar questions, to indicate the major trends and directions for urban information systems, at least for the next decade, and I hope, to help those groping today for a systems development strategy. In doing this, we shall first evaluate how

A paper delivered at the American Institute of Planners Conference, Pittsburgh, Pennsylvania, October 14, 1968.

Mr. Weiner is Director of the Municipal Information Technology Program of the Institute for Public Service, University of Connecticut.

far the field has progressed in its first decade, and from this evaluation indicate the goals it has set for itself and how it can best achieve these objectives.

Evaluation: How Far Have We Come?

Any evaluation of the impact of information technology on urban government must be made from a perspective that takes into account the following observations.

1. Municipal automation is hardly out of its infancy. Every technology takes decades before its use becomes developed on any kind of a sophisticated basis. Indeed, after fifty to sixty years of literally billions of dollars of research and development, transportation systems utilizing the automobile and aerospace technologies are still very much in a state of flux and apparently will continue in such a condition for several more decades. Part of the evolutionary nature of technology is technical, related to the fact that research and development is resource bound and tends to be slow, since knowledge compounds in much the same manner as interest grows on capital invested. More important, however, is the process of continual search for the role that technology will play in society. The berthing of the Queen Mary and the Queen Elizabeth is not unrelated to a changing concept of leisure time "delivery systems" that is being formed in America (i.e., air travel to Europe may be more expensive but the "payoff" in maximum vacation days spent "on site" rather than "in transit" is more important to a once-in-a-lifetime sightseeing tour of Europe). The same technology/system search process is evident also in Dr. Philip Leighton's observation that *one* automobile in Los Angeles needs more oxygen than that required by *all* of the people presently residing in L. A. County.[1] Automobile-bound transportation may fail unless the technology can cope with total system boundaries that, today, must include critical air pollution problems.

Thus, we must constantly keep in mind that the urban information system/technology is still in its infancy and most probably will take at least a quarter of a century to develop some level of sophistication.

2. The crystallization of any technology (technically and conceptually) is intimately related to the ecology of the American society. The turbulence of the 1950's and 1960's is universally recognized. We have not yet concluded our first half-century as an urban nation; small wonder that

1. Philip Leighton, "Education for Ecstasy," *Look Magazine*, September 17, 1968, p. 40.

in the current process of rapid urbanization our nation shows signs of extreme tensions that are a result of a "cultural lag" in our ability to cope with high-density living. Urbanization alone does not account for today's turbulence; it is related to the rapid technological changes around us, and, equally important, to our return to the uncompleted work of social reform in the United States. "It would be a mistake to describe America's return to social reform as merely a reaction to racial group protest. . . . 'Affluent America' has a troubled conscience. It has found the 'Other America.' As a consequence, the moral basis of American civilization is undergoing its most severe test since the Civil War." [2] In a decade when the television technology reaches into practically every American home to show, instantaneously, moon-bound spaceships, from a technology barely ten years old, small wonder that American politics of the late '60's is fraught with extremism and violence.

The turbulent '60's have also had significant impact on urban management. Dedicated men, political and professional, are attempting to operate from outmoded forms of government and to deal with extremely complex problems: How should a municipality cope with environmental problems created by a high-density society? How can effective services be delivered to maximize the human resources of a community? How can community resources be focused and allocated to structure the type of society we set out to achieve almost two centuries ago?

Although not popularly understood as yet, the role and process of government in our society is being reconstructed. I have previously indicated that "increasingly, the traditional municipal role of 'public servant' is being replaced with a function that can best be described as 'controller of community development.' " [3] Bill Mitchel expands this concept by pointing out that urban governments must move from being "reactive" to "active" instruments of change. "Municipalities have shown themselves to be quite structured and rigid. . . . Even though many municipalities perform traditional functions efficiently, most have not adjusted themselves to meet new and emerging urban needs affirmatively and effectively." [4] More and more governments are being recognized as systems, in

2. Edward A. Lehan, "The Municipality's Response to Changing Concepts of Public Welfare," in *The Revolution in Public Welfare: The Connecticut Experience* (Storrs, Conn.: Institute of Public Service, University of Connecticut, 1966), p. 45.

3. Myron E. Weiner, *Information, Technology and Municipal Government* (Storrs, Conn.: Municipal Information Technology Program, University of Connecticut, 1967), p. 2.

4. William H. Mitchel, *The Municipal Information and Decision System: Phase One Final Report* (Los Angeles: School of Public Administration, University of Southern California, 1968), p. 30.

total, and as components of a complex, highly interrelated intergovernmental system sometimes referred to as "dynamic federalism." (Ken Kraemer's description of urban government as a system excellently portrays this concept.)[5] Often confused in these days of restructuring of American government is the fact that *urban* governments are, potentially speaking at least, the only true effective instrumentality for achievement of our society's "domestic" goals.

This "reformation" of government has also had its impact on all urban professionals who suddenly find themselves searching for a new identity and role in the management of urban America. This is true as much for professional urban planners as for other professionals; Ken Kraemer[6] and others have already indicated this. Professions also seem to evolve conceptually, along with technology. Witness the education or the recreation professions, both of which are in a period of serious "goal/process search." Their growth as professions followed a pattern. Both seem to have passed through a phase of stressing "opportunities"; this can be illustrated by the tremendous concern on the part of the park professionals for pleasant, green surroundings in which people could enjoy leisure, at their own pace. Success here was measured in acres of green or number and types of trees. The next phase seemed to be a compulsive concern for "programs" and "activities"; success was measured in the number of different programs and number of people involved in these programs. Now, these professions seem to be moving into another phase, perhaps because of our growing interest in "systems analysis," where the focus seems to be the individual and how to build an environment responsive to his needs; i.e., we are suddenly "human resource development" focused. Thus today the key concern of education and recreation professionals, along with professional planners, is how can we create a total environment in which the human can flourish according to his interests and capabilities, to meet his individual needs as he copes with the tensions of high-density life. The next ten years will note continued struggles by all professionals participating in the forging of an urban society with the translation of this focus into reality.

On top of all of this has been the sudden realization that fifty years of scientific management with its almost fanatical concern for specialization, functionalism, hierarchy, etc., has created straitjackets for our efforts

5. Kenneth L. Kraemer, "An Automated Planning Subsystem," in *The Municipal Information and Decision System: Technical Report No. 4* (Los Angeles: School of Public Administration, University of Southern California, 1967), pp. 11–15, 56–57, fig. 1.
6. Ibid., p. 54.

to deal effectively with the late-twentieth-century problems of an urban society. "Taylorism" is slowly being replaced with "McLuhanism" as we gird ourselves for the twenty-first century; urban management professionals of all fields are now part of a highly interrelated team, in concert with politicians, struggling to find organizational mechanisms and processes just to cope, let alone lead.

How Far Have We Come? Not Very Far!

Having developed a perspective which can serve as a basic framework from which we can evaluate our progress to date in the field of urban information systems development, let us turn to such evaluation. Briefly, such an evaluation can be stated as follows:

- How far have we come? Not very far.
- What have we accomplished? Laid the basic foundation.
- Where are we today? Finally understanding where we should be going.

But let us view this in a more detailed fashion.

How Far Have We Come?

In attempting to make this evaluation, there are two methods of measurement: (1) statistically counting the municipalities and/or planning units utilizing the technology, or (2) judging the systems developed empirically or through research during the past ten years.

Statistically, according to James Enright of the Public Automated Systems Service, "a 1967 study made for the Municipal Yearbook shows that there is a data processing capability in 253 cities with populations above 10,000. Even if we exclude the 1,200 cities in the ten to twenty-five thousand population class, it still is clear that only about three cities in ten are presently making use of data processing in any form." [7] When viewed more carefully from a functional point of view, the use of automation in the urban setting is heavily skewed toward financial activities, mainly because of the control exercised by the municipal finance officer over this technology thus far. The functional/professional use of computers in municipalities is spotty from profession to profession: "high" on the list of users are such urban professions as police, planners, town clerks (land recording), educators, public utility and health administrators; "low users" would be town engineers (which is ironic), fire pro-

---

7. James E. Enright, "Municipal Automation: State of the Art — 1968," in *Municipal Automation: State of the Art* (Storrs, Conn.: Institute of Public Service, University of Connecticut).

fessionals, recreation, redevelopment, and building inspectors. But "high" or "low," functional use of computers in municipalities is fairly low; Clark Rogers and Claude Peters, in the 1967 AIP Survey of Automated Information Systems for Urban Planning, found only 14 municipal planning units with systems actually under development or in use.[8]

Viewed singularly, these statistics are discouraging. However, when taken into account along with the research and development in the field, the picture is somewhat brighter. Ken Kraemer excellently summarized these efforts in his work on the *Evolution of Information Systems for Urban Administration*.[9] I will not attempt to repeat his effort, except to emphasize the important role played by planning professionals beginning with the pioneering effort by the Metropolitan Data Center project.[10]

While not reviewing the history of R & D in urban information systems during the past decade, I would like to evaluate the work accomplished in order to draw conclusions that can be of great significance to all of us who will continue these efforts in the next decade.

1. For a technology still in its infancy, a great deal of research and development has been devoted to highly specialized areas in the overall system, rather than concentrating on establishing basic foundations. A great deal of effort and many resources have been expended in municipal automation systems development on data banks, geo-coding systems, and attempting to construct fairly sophisticated models. Without meaning to deflate the importance of such efforts, in terms of priorities it could be compared to efforts for constructing a hi-fi system by putting the major effort in the development of an extra-fine speaker without having first developed the tuner/amplifier; or, in the automobile industry, devoting most of the research resources in developing safety tires before having solved the systems problems concerning the mass production of the engine. In other words, our research focus has been out of focus in respect to priorities. We should have been concentrating our efforts on building the "guts" of a local government information system, i.e., a wide series of interrelated, operational components for the full range of municipal computer subsystems. As it is, in most of the identifiable local government information subsystems, very little work has been done; these would in-

8. Clark D. Rogers and Claude D. Peters, "Directory of the Status of State and Local Systems," in *AIP Survey of Automated Information Systems for Urban Planning: Part I* (Pittsburgh: American Institute of Planners, 1967).

9. Kenneth L. Kraemer, *The Evolution of Information Systems for Urban Administration: Need for a Unified Approach* (Irvine, Calif.: University of California–Irvine, 1968).

10. Tulsa Metropolitan Area Planning Commission, *Metropolitan Data Center Project* (Tulsa, Okla.: Metropolitan Data Center, 1966).

clude the public works, building inspection, code enforcement, fire administration, redevelopment, personnel, and recreation subsystems.

2. With a few notable exceptions, attempts to develop urban information systems for municipalities have not used an integrated approach; instead, most have attempted to impose upon the local government's operationally-grounded information system an "extra-organizational" information system. No municipal or urban information system will be maintained on a dynamic basis unless it is an integral part of a system that has at its base the satisfaction of operational requirements of local government agencies and then, as a critically important by-product, maintain the data base for that system.

3. Typifying the general approach to urban problems that has been the unfortunate pattern of the 1950's and 1960's, the major efforts expended in computer systems development for urban organizations have been functional in focus in such fields as police, health, libraries, transportation, and education. To their credit, these efforts have been multijurisdictional on several levels of government. But they have failed to take into account, during their design and development stage, the need in the near future to relate and interrelate with other urban information systems both functional (vertical) or jurisdictional (horizontal) (see J. Richard Vincent[11] and Joel Kibbee[12] for their concern over this matter). It has reached such ridiculous proportions, states William Mitchel,[13] that a city manager in southern California must first request permission from his chief of police before he can retrieve information from the statewide California stolen-car automated system (AUTOSTATIS).

4. The functional approach to the design of urban information systems most probably reflects the form of federal grants now available for research in information systems — all granted on a functional basis. However, we should not lose sight of the fact that collectively it is doubtful if all of the R & D efforts into urban information systems during the past ten years would total $100,000,000. NASA's R & D budget for information systems alone would exceed that figure, not even to mention the Depart-

11. J. Richard Vincent, "Crisis in Government Information Technology: Need to Coordinate EDP Systems," in *Connecticut Government* (Storrs, Conn.: Institute of Public Service, University of Connecticut, 1968), p. 4.
12. Joel M. Kibbee, "The Scope of Large-Scale Computer-Based Systems in Government Functions," in *Governing Urban Society: New Scientific Approaches* (Philadelphia, Pennsylvania: The American Academy of Political and Social Science, 1967), pp. 195–196.
13. William H. Mitchel, "Municipal Automation: State of the Art — 1978," *Municipal Automation: State of the Art* (Storrs, Conn.: Institute of Public Service, University of Connecticut).

ment of Defense's investment in information systems development. Our main failure, albeit that we are not guilty, has been the fact that we have only begun to scratch the surface of urban systems R & D requirements.

What Has Been Accomplished?

Our efforts to date, however, have not been in vain; on the contrary, practitioners and researchers alike have gained tremendously during this past decade and have laid the basic groundwork upon which the urban information systems of the '70's and '80's will be built.

Figure 1 makes an attempt to trace the evolution of the basic concepts

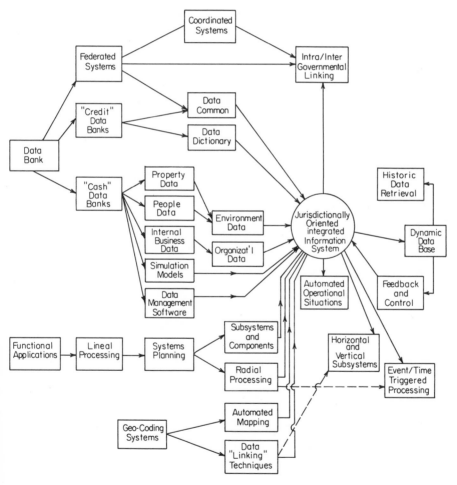

Fig. 1. Evolution of basic concepts for municipal information system design, 1958–1968

343

that today serve as the foundation of the principles required for the design and development of municipal or urban information systems. It should be noted that it is hard to pinpoint exactly when a particular concept was first conceived and by whom. With the lack of any central coordination or even common channels of communication, it is interesting to note how the same concept was arrived at by two parties or groups of people widely separated by geography. In addition, as concepts continue to evolve, they become continually refined; thus a concept in its original form may be quite altered in name and appearance by the time it is generally accepted in the field. Rather than attempting to pinpoint exactly who contributed what concept, a general reference is made to all parties who collectively participated in these efforts. One would also be quick to add that such a list is not all-inclusive, since many contributors will remain anonymous; they probably are not even aware of their own contribution to the field.[14]

The basic concepts, as we now recognize them, will be discussed briefly later in this paper under the description of the approach required for the development of urban information systems for the next two decades. It is sufficient here to note the manner in which concepts evolved in a nuclear fashion from two basic approaches: *applications* (which originated completely from an empirical base) and *data banks* (which were conceived from a theoretical, planned research base). Herein, perhaps, lie the seeds of what appears to be a conflict of approaches in the design and development of urban information systems: piecemeal versus integrated systems. It is also interesting to note from Figure 1 that as we mature in our conceptual understanding of this field, the approaches themselves begin to merge. Perhaps there really is no conflict in approaches?

One further point of interest that Figure 1 points up is the three orientations delineated by Ken Kraemer: processing, analysis, and management control.[15] Applications were the major thrust of the processing orientation, being primarily concerned with cost reduction/economy/efficiency. Data banks were the major focal point for the analysis orienta-

14. The list of contributors to this evolution would include among others Hearle and Mason's Rand Corporation study; the Metropolitan Data Center Project; John Parker's work with Informatics at Alexandria, Virginia; Myron Weiner's research into an Integrated Data System for Connecticut municipalities; Lockheed's State-wide Federated Information System study for the State of California; and Mitchel and staff's research effort at the School of Public Administration, University of Southern California, into a Municipal Information and Decision System.

15. Kraemer, *Evolution of Information Systems,* pp. 11–12.

tion, being concerned for the most part in improved decision alternatives for maximum community development. Beginning with radial processing and now concentrating on event/time triggered processing, the management control orientation has been concerned first and foremost with effectiveness, improved decisions, and above all improved services to the taxpayer. A jurisdictional integrated information system indeed merges these three orientations to satisfy all requirements for municipal automation.

Where Are We?

We stand on the threshold of ten to twenty years of steady, increasing, solid growth of municipal automation, evolutionary in nature — not explosive. The trial and error of the infancy period will not go to waste. Already there is a recognition of the necessity to plan carefully for municipal information systems similar to the way in which we have so carefully invested in the preparation of master physical, economic, and social development plans for a community. A municipality must develop a long-range plan for automation, one which is based on evolutionary growth tied in with improvements in technology as developed and with a better understanding of the potential of the computer technology for urban management. The City of Los Angeles is an excellent example of such an approach to municipal automation and of such a long-range plan.[16]

There is also a growing realization of the need for basic, large investment in R & D in this field; the decision of IBM to make such an investment in their New Haven research effort and that of a consortium of federal agencies, as discussed at the recent URISA conference in St. Louis, are examples of such realization.[17] Only larger problems of resource allocations for government programs during the '70's will affect the trend toward substantial investment of resources in R & D for municipal automation.

The next ten to twenty years will see a sifting and refining of concepts developed thus far with rapid extensions in the knowledge thus accumulated. Perhaps most important of all, we seemed to be poised just now, ready to break out of the clouds which seem to have obscured the concepts that underline the primary role and potential of the computer technology for urban governments.

16. *City of Los Angeles Municipal Information System, LAMIS* (Los Angeles, California: Data Services Bureau, City of Los Angeles, 1967).

17. "Urban and Regional Information Systems" (URISA) annual conference St. Louis, Missouri, September 5–7, 1968, panel on "The Federal Government's Role in Urban Information Systems Development."

Where Are We Going and How Do We Get There?

Before turning our attention to these questions let us first be reminded that the basic issue at hand in the next two decades will be an attempt to understand the role of governmental management for a high-density, urbanized society. Patience and endurance will be our by-words, for, as Dr. James Wilson has pointed out, having solved the easier problems in our society, we in America are now down to the really tough problems of structuring life in the high-density type of living we have chosen for our society.[18] Information technology will play a critical, supportive role in the solution of the "tough ones," provided several prerequisites can be met.

Recognition of the Primary Potential
of Computer Technology for Urban Management

To understand this primary potential, one must neither underestimate nor overestimate the role of information technology in municipal management. Information systems are an essential part of complex urban systems for controlling the quality of life for men interacting with their environment. There are several subsystems and components that make up the urban management system, most of which we do not yet know how to structure and interrelate. There are the communication/intelligence/information systems which include not only the technical problems of equipment and "software" for the use of the equipment, but all of the dynamics for man-machine interfaces. Early warning of rat infestation is quite possible from intelligence systems manned by garbage collectors who come in direct contact with all structures in a city at least once a week; but would such information be acceptable to well-educated and experienced sanitation professionals who man the housing-code enforcement units of our urban governments?

While urban management systems should be "service delivery" oriented, our current functional organizations seem to prohibit municipal "service delivery" particularly to the disadvantaged. With a few notable exceptions (i.e., the experimentation in New York City), are judicial administration systems designed to serve the public arrested late Saturday night or are they designed for the convenience of working hours of judges, lawyers, legal clerks, etc.? There is sufficient documentation today which

18. James Q. Wilson, Keller Memorial Lecture, University of Hartford, Hartford Connecticut, 1968.

illustrates the fact that today's urban government organizations are not problem-, program-, or people-focused; on the contrary, people must focus on the urban government bureaucracy. We are surrounded by examples of such dysfunctional focusing. How many municipal agencies or departments deal with an unemployed man, whose wife has an active case of tuberculosis, with a family of six children in the public school system (one of which has a record with the juvenile delinquency unit of the police department), living on welfare in an urban renewal area in a structure due for demolition within six months? Care to count the number of separate information systems in such a case concerning health only: health department (mother and child clinics; TB unit); school system health office; municipal hospital; not to mention a minimum of four other separate health information systems on other levels of government and in private health agencies — and we have only been talking about health information systems. Yet in all of this, is our urban management system focusing for delivery of services to this citizen or do we expect him to enter the "Automat" of municipal services and pick his way through the various delivery doors that can be opened by those initiated in the present system? Perhaps the time has come to change from the cafeteria form of urban management systems and go to the form of system where one waitress stands poised ready to fill the citizen's needs. Can you picture the fundamental difference in information systems design between two such widely different urban management systems?

As if this is not complicated enough, we are also faced with another major change in management systems that involved the governed; popularly coined "participatory management systems," right or wrong, they seem to surround us, from teacher unions' participation in educational management to the involvement of the disadvantaged in community action programs. Bothersome as they may seem to some, they must be taken into account even if only to fulfill the needs of scientific management. The City of Charlotte, North Carolina, is quite aware of such a need. Currently engaged in a joint effort to experiment with the application of systems analysis to urban management, the City is cautious.[19] In a previous study, recreational centers for the disadvantaged were located according to the recommendations of a linear programming exercise; once constructed, some of the centers subsequently were closed due to non-use by the disadvantaged. The interests, habits, preferences, and group dy-

19. Research Project for "The Application of Systems Analysis to Urban Government" jointly sponsored by the International City Managers Association, American Society for Planning Officials, National Bureau of Standards, and the Fels Institute of Local and State Government, University of Pennsylvania.

namics of the Negroes living in the neighborhoods affected were not taken into consideration. The data collection system used for the computerized linear program that pinpointed the "ideal" locations for the recreation centers was formulated by scientists using white norms; it is now being redone with the active participation of representatives of the areas to be served.

The forging of urban management systems 'required for the twenty-first century will be an extremely complex task. Development of information systems will be a vital, integral part of this task, but the objective of this effort must not be lost; creating an urban management system will emphasize the necessity of interrelating the variety of subsystems that must be developed.

With the above points in mind, what then is the primary potential of information technology for urban management? It now seems clear that this answer should be to improve the quality of life for human beings living in a democratic, technological, affluent, high-density, urbanized society. In short, the primary user of urban information systems must be the public citizen himself and only secondarily the urban bureaucrat and professional.

Let it be understood clearly that contrary to popular thought, computer technology within a properly designed urban management system is the only hope that *all* citizens have of being treated as human beings in an increasingly dehumanizing society and under an increasingly dehumanizing urban government apparatus. Why must human beings face the indignity, in their hurried lives, of long waits in registration lines only to face a bureaucrat who, despite all good will, never heard of the registrant before? Yet even with our current-day computer systems, this is a daily occurrence in government offices ranging from registration to motor vehicles and unemployment check-processing to registering for classes in our institutions of higher learning. The airlines and the hotels have pointed the way, albeit at fantastic investments, with a "register-at-home" system. Let us follow their path.

Beset with enormous tensions that result from high-density life (even those which occur in the "solitude" of man's domicile as the noise pollutors roar by at abnormal decibel levels), why should *not* an urban management system assist the head of a household in selecting from a variety of recreational program alternatives recorded on his telephone-computer connection and then, once his family's choice is made, make all the reservations and even plot out an itinerary. True, a travel agent could do all of this but: (a) Who could afford their services if used every weekend? (b) If we did use their services, there would have to be a million-fold increase in the number of travel agents or more properly named "leisure time consultants." (c) Would such consultants be equipped to advise us on recreational programs that only end up with sending the taxpayer across town to a municipal facility?

All of this seems farfetched? Think through the automatic machine-based systems that serve us today that were once based on human power. Would there even be enough human beings around to operate machine-less systems for our society today? Quality of life — this must be our focus. In Northampton, Massachusetts (population 30,000 approx.), there is a manned telephone system where the taxpayer can reserve a picnic table in lovely Look Park and arrive relaxed, free of the tension of waiting or looking for a picnic site. Could the City of Los Angeles (population 2,695,000 approx.) ever provide such a service for equally as lovely Griffith Park based on the same type of system as Northampton? It is doubtful. Well, why then should the quality of life in Northampton be different than in Los Angeles? Our choices are clear; either reconstruct our urban centers to create (probably with force not unlike the Soviet Union) a low-density society *or* cope with high-density life by means of technologies at hand.

In every urban profession, the primary focus should be *direct* services to the human beings in our society; *direct,* not indirect by means of "improving our professionals' capabilities of better management decisions to improve the citizen's quality of life." The latter must be a *by-product,* important and vital, but none the less a by-product of our main thrust — systems to serve the public directly.

Anthony Downs was concerned with the approaches (piecemeal or integrated/total) that can be taken to the development of urban information systems; he evaluated these in terms of two types of "payoffs" — "technical" and "power." [20] "Technical payoffs . . . include greater speed of processing, greater consistency among outputs, and wider distribution of information. Power payoffs are gains in one person's decision-making effectiveness, made at the expense of another person's." [21] ". . . the future form and use of automated data systems will not depend solely upon improvements in data. Rather they will depend upon the ways in which data improvements increase the effectiveness of actions and change the power positions of the actors involved. These two outcomes constitute the

20. Anthony Downs, "A Realistic Look at the Final Payoffs from Urban Data Systems," *Public Administration Review* 27 (September 1967).
21. Ibid., p. 204.

final *payoffs* from using automated data systems . . . city governments will develop automated data systems in a piecemeal, department by department fashion. Hence the glamorous comprehensive urban systems we hear about . . . are likely to be a long time in coming in many areas." [22]

Some of Downs' conclusions are sound: "technical payoffs" are dubious; "power payoffs" do impede the development of integrated urban information systems since they threaten the power relationships of professionals and bureaucrats; comprehensive urban systems will take a long time in coming. But Mr. Downs' focus and frame of reference is incorrect. The same "payoff" measurement problem exists for all technologies. Who could have measured the "technical payoffs" of the automobile or television during the infancy of their respective technologies? True, local government is primarily an arena of "power conflicts and payoffs"; but how long can governments suffer intense problems of high-density urban life before "power payoffs" between narrow groups broaden to include the "public welfare?" Witness the intense struggle of rapid transit systems versus the automobile, with its attendant side effects. Eventually society will reach the point where there will be no choice — power struggles or otherwise. And besides, the concept of "power payoffs" sells short the will of many professionals and politicians alike who show willingness to *reduce* their power status for the "public good." Indeed it may be technology's role to broaden the band of communications between the electorate and the elected to replace our current narrow band of pressure groups and thus widen the arena of power conflicts.

But most important of all, Downs starts from the premise that "all final payoffs from urban data systems consist of improvements in the effectiveness of decision-making." [23] It is my contention that this is only a *secondary*, by-product payoff of such systems; the most important payoff, one in which the ultimate payoff can be measured, will be in "Service Payoffs." To what degree will the taxpayer be serviced directly by urban information systems so that their quality of life can be improved? In every other technology that has had an impact on human beings, this was the only "final payoff" in society's terms. Philosophers can argue that life was more rewarding in the days when grandfather was only able to travel 10 miles in one day by horse and buggy and then *hike* to the top of a mountain. But grandfather never dreamed of seeing the Grand

22. Ibid., p. 210.
23. Ibid., p. 204.

Canyon or fishing in Nova Scotia within his economic bracket of life. In our society we start from the point of view that technology can and will be rewarding to the quality of life of human beings. Perhaps we are not willing to pay the price for such a point of view. But if we hold this view, then it is incumbent upon us to apply the concept. Thus, in the field of information technology as it can be utilized for urban life, there can only be one final payoff.

A Basic Approach to the Development
of Urban Information Systems

Is there a dichotomy between the "piecemeal" and "integrated, comprehensive" approaches to the development of urban information systems? The more one becomes familiar with the field, the more he is convinced that no such dichotomy exists. It would be nice to tell everyone in the field to do nothing for ten years while R & D of a "total" system could be undertaken; but no technology evolves in this fashion. Even with a complete set of specifications for urban information systems, the approach would be that which most of us are coming now to recognize — piecemeal evolvement of a *plan* for integrated municipal information systems. At the present time the plan to be used can only be based on systems' guidelines, not detailed specifications. But this is the only logical option today; it also calls forth the second most important specification for the plan today — maintenance of a flexible position in the incremental, evolutionary development so as to utilize all the benefits of new concepts and hardware and software improvements as they occur. All technologies develop in this manner. You will recall that the first specification was: focus on systems objectives for 1985, namely, servicing human beings in their struggle to improve their quality of life.

Before turning our attention to the specific guidelines that should be used for the development of urban information systems during the next decade, I think it is important to stress the need during this period for a cooperative stance on the part of all, practitioners and researchers. The next ten years will require large investments of critical resources for software development in this field. The limited nature of these resources within our GNP forces all of us to cooperate and share in systems and software development. This is not to say that during the '80's we will not go our own ways, with our own hardware (this is quite likely). It is only to stress the necessity that all levels of governments currently involved or soon to be involved in urban information systems development approach this development cooperatively. The key issue at hand is the vital necessity for linkage.[24] Sharing, transferability, exchanging, linking generalized systems must all be bywords for urban systems development during the coming decade.

What then are the basic guidelines to be followed for the design and development of information systems for municipalities and urban areas? The following is a list, not set in priority, of such guidelines with a very brief definition of each. For a more detailed explanation of each guideline, the reader can turn to several original sources, among which are the publications of the Municipal Information Technology Program of the Institute of Public Service, University of Connecticut; those of the Municipal Decision and Information Systems Research at the University of Southern California, School of Public Administration; and the preliminary technical manuals of the IBM-New Haven Joint Information System Study.

1. *Satisfy urban government operational requirements first.* The primary thrust in urban information systems development must be the meeting of the operational needs of the local government agency. Improving the flow of information for better decisions and actions must be a by-product of this effort. A large portion of municipal operational activities can be rationalized and thus automated; however, be sure to recognize the need to refocus current urban delivery systems to meet the needs of human beings as our society prepares for the twenty-first century.

2. *The basic "building block" of urban information systems is the MUNICIPALITY.* This pertains to any type of urban information system whether jurisdictionally (area) oriented or functionally oriented (for several jurisdictions on various levels of government). The basic data for all urban information systems originates with a municipality; thus it must be the foundation.

The major impact or effect of the above two guidelines is to create an urban information system that is built into the main stream of information flow concerning our urban life. With this approach data are maintained on a current basis because it is primed to satisfy basic operational needs of the municipality. No extra-organizational information reporting systems are placed upon the municipal government agency. Data are fed into urban information systems at their source as an *intrinsic* part of operations.

24. Myron E. Weiner, *Cooperation as a Model for Municipal Use of Computers* (Storrs, Conn.: Municipal Information Technology Program, Series No. 3, 1968).

3. *Maintain a "dynamic data base."* The first two guidelines are also directed toward the maintenance of a "dynamic data base." The difference between a "dynamic data base" and a data bank, in William Mitchel's terms,[25] is the difference between a freeway and a photograph of the freeway. In the former example, the vehicles are continually moving dynamically; in the latter, the vehicles are "captured" in a static fixed position.

A "dynamic data base" has several requirements for its maintenance including:

a. *Linkage.* Identifiers in all data files which permit the linking of related subsystems and components. It is in this area that quite a bit of work in "geo-coding" systems is currently underway in various parts of the United States.[26]

b. *Specification of common data.* The various subsystems in municipal information systems have a great deal of data that are common to more than one subsystem. These must be identified and included in the data base design.

c. *Data dictionary.* Each data file, record, and data element in subsystems developed must be described in detail and cross-indices created. "Standard" data elements should be so noted along with data elements that can be interchanged.

d. *"Event/time triggering."* The design and development of urban information systems must be so rationalized that the automatic updating of all related data files are "triggered" either as a result of an "event" (a fatal accident occurs at Second and Chestnut streets) or of the arrival of a time period (end of month reports).

e. *Internal/External data focus.* For maximum utilization of all concerned with urban information systems, the data base must be focused to include data that describe both the urban area and the agencies interacting with that area. This description must be all-inclusive according to the needs of all system users.

f. *Aggregate capabilities.* For analytical purposes, primarily, the data base must be so designed as to facilitate the aggregation of data for both current identified needs and any possible future requirements.

4. *Open-ended systems' design.* Urban management systems' requirements can always be considered dynamic in nature. Consequently the design of urban information systems must be open-ended, with the flexi-

---

25. Mitchel, *Municipal Information and Decision System*, p. 123.

26. There are several universities, federal agencies, and private agencies who have expended a great deal of effort in the field of geo-coding for urban information systems, the foremost of which are the University of Washington, Harvard University, and the New Haven Census Use Study of the Bureau of the Census.

bility to eliminate and acquire subsystem components, data files, and elements as the need arises. This is particularly true during periods of rapid change that can be anticipated for the next two decades.

5. *Multijurisdictional linking capability.* Based on the guidelines described above, the capability for the linking of all information systems dealing with urban matters must be an important design feature for all concerned with this field. The number of interrelated urban information systems will be almost limitless. Thus the capability for linking is essential. It is also essential where comparable data are important and where data can be exchanged electronically.

6. *Design for utilizing the full potential of the technology.* Kenneth Kraemer delineates three potentialities of the computer for urban information systems: operations, monitoring, and analytical.[27] The writer agrees with the first two, but subdivides the latter potential into calculating and researching.[28] Regardless of the breakdown, the systems developed must make *full use* of *all* potentialities of the computer technology for municipalities.

7. *Design for "visual" based urban management systems.* Marshal McLuhan has pointed out that our society for several centuries has been based on the technology of typesetting, but that this is gradually shifting to a society based on electricity, on visual technologies. Such massive efforts as preparation of model cities' proposals that measure six inches in depth of typewritten pages will eventually be replaced with electronic communication of data among government agencies. While hardware and software developments are required before such systems can be economically implemented, eventually they can be anticipated. The design of urban information systems must take this probability into account.

8. *Utilize the "systems' approach."* The construction of information systems for municipalities must take an extremely broad "systems' approach" in the development of its various subsystems and components. All of the various systems and data interrelationships must be taken into account along with the interactions of men and machines. The analysis and development must be independent of any municipal departmental organization, oriented more toward "situations" (the term popularly used by Donald Luria).[29] Systems, therefore, should not be developed on a

27. Kraemer, *Evolution of Information Systems*, pp. 11–12.
28. Myron E. Weiner, *An Integrated Data System for Small-Medium Sized Local Governments* (Storrs, Connecticut: Municipal Information Technology Program, January 1966).
29. Donald Luria is Director of the IBM–New Haven Joint Systems Study currently underway.

department-by-department basis; while subsystems can be implemented on a "piecemeal" basis, their planning and development must be on an integrated basis.

9. *Prepare a long range systems development plan.* A prerequisite to all of the above guidelines is a long-range systems development plan that must be prepared very carefully before the detailed design and implementation of the subsystems of an urban information system can be initiated. This is basic to the "implement 'piecemeal' within an 'integrated' development plan approach."

Conclusion

This paper has indicated the progress made to date in the field of urban information systems and made a strong case for the refocusing of systems' goals so as to meet our primary goals of directly servicing the public in order to assist human beings in their struggle to improve the quality of their lives in the high-density, urbanized society we have created in pretwenty-first-century America. The purported dichotomy between "piecemeal" and "integrated" systems development will not exist if guidelines developed over the past ten years are used during the coming decade. It remains only to delineate two additional requirements for success for those venturing into the field of urban systems development in the '70's.

1. Our most crucial need in the field actually is education at all levels, both for budding professionals and especially for those already in the field. It is both ironic and somewhat alarming that more attention is not now being given to this critical area. Estimates of the manpower requirements for urban information systems on a municipal level alone range from 500% to 1,200% *growth* over current personnel levels to meet the needs of 1980.[30] Unless general and technical educational efforts on a comparatively massive basis are undertaken, the users will not keep up with developments in the systems fields and the large investment, minuscule as it may be compared to Defense Department R & D investments, will be underutilized and to a large extent wasted. Equal attention and investment must be made to education in this field along with our increased efforts in the systems design, development, and implementation phases of this field. It is here that professional associations can play their most vital roles.

30. James E. Enright and Myron E. Weiner, "Manpower Requirements for Municipal Automation: 1978," *Municipal Automation: State of the Art: 1968* (Storrs, Conn.: Municipal Information Technology Program, University of Connecticut).

2. The most crucial ingredient for success is probably patience. Our generation will probably never really understand the full potential of this technology for urban America. But we must patiently expend our maximum effort so that the next generation can take benefit of these potentialities.

BERTRAM M. GROSS

The New Systems Budgeting

Within less than a year after his 1964 election to the American presidency, Lyndon B. Johnson announced "a very new and very revolutionary system of planning and programming and budgeting throughout the vast Federal Government." [1]

Subsequently, he boasted that "this system — which proved its worth many times over in the Defense Department — now brings to each department and agency the most advanced techniques of modern business management." [2] Toward this end, "systems analysis" experts (mainly microeconomists) were moved from Secretary Robert McNamara's Department of Defense to various civilian agencies of government, including the Bureau of the Budget and the White House itself. With new experts hired and some old-time civil servants co-opted, a prodigious effort was made to adapt Defense Department methods to less tangible "soft" civilian programs — both traditional ones and the new and potentially expensive Great Society "seedlings."

Since 1965, the new system has spread rapidly. It is now being introduced, used, or misused by:

From Bertram M. Gross, "The New Systems Budgeting," *Public Administration Review* 29 (March–April 1969): 113–133. Copyright © 1969 by American Society for Public Administration.

Mr. Gross is Distinguished Professor of Urban Affairs and Planning, City University of New York, Hunter College.

1. Statement by President Lyndon B. Johnson, News Conference of August 25, 1965.
2. President Johnson's Message to Congress on the Quality of American Government, March 17, 1967.

— hundreds of bureaus and divisions throughout the federal government

— the Comptroller General as a tool in trying to modernize the General Accounting Office

— Congressional committees in appraising executive program proposals and writing legislative prescriptions for future program review

— many governors, mayors, and state and local agencies (a tendency accelerated by a growing belief that applications for federal aid may be more successful if justified in PPB terminology).

Interest in the new system is rapidly growing in foreign countries, both industrialized (or "developed") and industrializing (or "developing"), both more socialist and less socialist. In industrializing countries, officials still struggling to assimilate the performance budgeting reforms of the Hoover Commissions (1947–49 and 1953–55), are now seeking technical assistance to explain the new reform.

The spread of the new budgeting system in the United States has been accompanied by mounting confusion. As with any significant innovation, it has been met by both inertia and hard-fought resistance — particularly among old-time budget personnel. This has led to ritualization, over-formalization, and overdocumentation. Indeed, the flood of PPB paperwork, clogging the channels of government communication, has in some cases threatened the very capability for rational action that it was supposed to enhance.

PPB was initiated, as with many other managerial techniques, "in a burst of grandiose claims of 'breakthroughs' and exaggerated application to irrelevant situations." [3] It has been pioneered by many technical specialists who — with little understanding, less interest, and no experience in general management — tend to propagate the "fallacy of management (or administration) as technical gadgetry." [4] As with most innovations in public management, the roots in, and implications for, politics and policy have been ignored, concealed, or distorted. As in innovation associated with Robert McNamara's service as Secretary of Defense (1961–68) and Lyndon Johnson's as President (1963–68), it cannot be easily disassociated from the deep controversies engendered by their policies and programs. Those willing to give McNamara credit for a "managerial revolution" in the strengthening of military capability must ponder his role — and

3. Bertram M. Gross, "Systems Guidance in the 1970's," in *Organizations and Their Managing* (New York: Free Press, 1968), p. ix.

4. United Nations Department of Economic and Social Affairs, Public Administration Branch, *The Administration of Economic Development Planning: Principles and Fallacies,* United Nations, New York, 1966 (ST/TAO/M/32), p. 12.

that of cost-effectiveness analysis — in an Asiatic military operation of high costs, low effectiveness, and questionable wisdom. Those who, in reaction to his Vietnam policies, are unwilling to give Lyndon Johnson credit for anything, may find it difficult to appreciate the historic implications of the new system.

All these confusions have been magnified by fantastic terminological tangles. Into the older jargons of budgeting, accounting, and efficiency engineering have been mixed new terms from microeconomics, systems engineering, and business management. Bumbling attempts at popularization have been successful in little except slowing down the essential processes of improved conceptualization. "System," "output," "planning," and "programming" have become "fad words," used with a false sophistication that often masks narrow-minded naïveté. In fact there seems to be an unspoken "gentleman's agreement" that basic terms need never be defined.

As a result of all this, the greatest of all confusions centers around the question "just what is the new system?" The extent of popular misconceptions on the matter was revealed in testimony before a Senate committee by Alain Enthoven, Assistant Secretary of Defense for Systems Analysis: "Hardly a week goes by that I don't read some fantastic descriptions of systems analysis in the Pentagon. If I believed that even a small fraction of such descriptions were accurate, I would recommend to Secretary McNamara and Deputy Secretary Nitze that they fire me." [5] More significant, deep confusion has developed within the very "control tower" of the new system: the Bureau of the Budget. By the summer of 1967, Budget Bureau officials reluctantly but officially found that "the longer term objectives of PPBS [which was supposed to clarify the objectives of other agencies and identify national goals with precision] are now unclear to many." [6] By identifying many alternative future relations between PPBS and "*the* budgetary system," they highlighted the fact that the new system was merely an increment on top of the old and that integration between the two in the near future is unlikely.[7] Indeed, they even came to the conclusion that within the Bureau itself, "*The definition of PPBS is a source of disagreement and confusion.*" [8]

The most responsible proponents and defenders of PPB have tended

5. Testimony of Alain C. Enthoven before the Subcommittee on National Security and International Operations, Part II, 90th Congress, 2nd Session, 1968, p. 72.
6. U.S. Bureau of the Budget, *The Work of the Steering Group on Evaluation of the Budget: A Staff Summary*, July 1967, p. 2–11.
7. Ibid., pp. 2–6 to 2–10.
8. Ibid., p. 2–5.

to be very clear about what PPB is *not*. They have repeatedly stressed that it:

— is *not* dependent upon tight mathematical models or computerized calculations
— is *not* a system for replacing human judgment
— does *not* deal directly with such sector-proportion questions as the relative emphasis placed upon health versus education, transportation versus communications, or military versus civilian expenditures.

Nonetheless, many otherwise well-informed people still think that PPB is one or all of the above. This may be explained, in part, by the fact that PPB'ers face greater difficulty — if not disagreement and confusion — in explaining what PPB *is*. There are many good reasons for this difficulty.

One is that the PPB spirit is more important than the letter. Some offices practice PPB without knowing it; others go through all the formal motions without coming anywhere near it. Moreover, *there is really no one system*. Rather, there are a large variety of PPB-type services; and organizations will differ greatly in the specific mix ("output mix" in the terminology below) provided during any one period. Above all, PPB is in an early state of growth — and more changes are probably taking place in it than anyone could possibly track down.

The spirit of PPB is a marriage between program planning and budgeting. Without such union, planners can easily lose touch with the constraints imposed by scarce resources, while budgeteers can easily be divorced from the content of plans and programs. This spirit pervades the otherwise spiritless (and often confusing) verbiage of the many Budget Bureau bulletins on the subject. It is embodied in the provisions of these bulletins dealing with: (1) an "analytic capability," (2) a specialized information cycle, and (3) the concepts on which such information is supposed to be based.

The analytical capability, according to the Budget Bureau, is supposed to consist of "a specialized analytic staff reporting directly to the agency head or his deputy." [9] In actuality, this has meant a program and review staff to supersede or dominate the specialized old-time budget staffs already reporting to the top officials. In the early stages the designers of PPB tried to recruit to such staffs people who had worked for the RAND Corporation or in McNamara's office or had background in econometrics or welfare economics. This "old school tie," together with some specialized

9. Bureau of the Budget, Bulletin No. 68-2, July 18, 1967, p. 12.

terminology, facilitated communication and cooperation in fighting the good fight against old-time budgeteers. It also helped maintain a "true believer syndrome" on the part of those early PPB'ers who, regarding themselves as the standard bearers of advanced rationality, had little regard for traditional budget staffs. After three years of PPB, there were probably about 1,000 people in special PPB positions throughout the government, with about half of these representing a net increase in positions. Since many of these lacked the old school tie and familiarity with the new terminology, steps were taken to send them back to school through special training programs. In addition, a growing volume of analytical services has been purchased through contracts with private research organizations and consulting firms, including the RAND Corporation.

The specialized information cycle is supposed to present "data in meaningful categories essential to the making of major decisions by agency heads and by the President." [10] The traditional budget cycle remains more or less the same — with each agency formally submitting its annual budget requests in September of each year, the President transmitting his NOA (new obligational authority) budget requests every January, and Congress presumably passing appropriation statutes by the end of the fiscal year in June. The new information cycle seems almost designed to fill in the "valley" in old-time budget activity after the "peak" of the President's Budget Message. From January to June particularly, each agency works on three kinds of documents: (1) a program memorandum (PM) outlining the objectives, broad strategy, major choices, and tentative recommendations with respect to each of its programs; (2) a multiyear program and financial plan (PFP) to show "the present and future budgetary and output consequences of the current year's decisions"; and (3) special studies (SS) that are to provide "the analytic basis for decisions on program issues in the PM." [11] It is only in the SS's, much fewer in number than the PM's and PFP's, that occasional efforts are made in the direction of formal analytical models along the lines used in some kinds of defense system analysis. At their best, these documents bring into the open many considerations that were previously tacit and hidden from view. To the extent that this is done, they promote a structured form of debate within the Executive Branch, with analysis being met by "counter-analyses." Formally, all such documents — whether controversial or harmless — are hidden from Congress and its committees.

10. Bureau of the Budget, Bulletin No. 66-3, October 12, 1965, p. 2.
11. Bulletin No. 68-2, p. 9.

Nevertheless, they unquestionably serve to prepare the rationale for agency appearances before Congress. Each PFP is supposed to include a reconciliation (called a "cross-walk") between the newer program categories and the appropriation and fund categories of appropriation statutes. All the documents may be drawn upon (if not leaked to the press) in preparing formal justifications, testimony, and the arguments used in other forms of legislative persuasion and pressure.

The concepts underlying the informational cycle and the work of the analytical staffs are PPB's greatest source of strength. Yet at present they are incompletely developed and ambiguously presented in the formal documents. Essentially, to use a formulation based more on advanced practice (as I interpret it) than official prescription, they relate to: (1) inputs and their costs, (2) outputs (end products or services), (3) effects (benefits or disbenefits), and (4) alternatives. These concepts provide the basis for both quantitative measurements and for looser qualitative information. They provide the substantive content — both short-range and long-range — behind other terms (objectives, plans, programs, etc.) referring to goal-oriented behavior. As parameters of system performance, they provide the basis for information on past and present performance as well as probable or desired future performance.

From time immemorial budget mobilizers have been justifying their requests by arguing that if they get what they ask for, the effects on many others will be very beneficial. Their justifications have ranged from claims concerning benefits for specific groups to sweeping generalizations on presumed contributions to such broad objectives as national defense, full or fair employment, economic growth, physical or mental well-being, social justice, or any other broadly stated "national purposes." The rhetoric of the claimants has usually been more impressive than the cause-effect argumentation. It has traditionally been met by deep skepticism and shallow analysis on the part of resource rationers.

During the 1930's and the 1940's giant battles developed between competing claimants in the area of water resource development — particularly between the Army Corps of Engineers and the Bureau of Reclamation. In the 1950's similar battles developed between different military services on alternative missiles, airplanes, and other "defense systems." In both cases the conflicting programs involved readily identifiable, albeit highly complex, end products. In both cases the conflicts involved not only embattled federal bureaucracies, but also the vital interests of thousands of workers, farmers, contractors, suppliers, local governments, and their representatives in Congress. In both, new techniques of conflict management were needed to help identify the problems, choose among alternatives, and legitimate the choices made.

The result was a long sequence of new analytical techniques — some developed by mobilizers (particularly in the Bureau of Reclamation) and some by rationers (as in the Office of the Secretary of Defense under McNamara). The essence of these techniques, as I see it, was to provide more explicit and logically organized information on the effects, or outcomes, of specific programs or projects — usually referred to as "benefits" or "disbenefits." In providing such information on effects, there has been a constructive sequence from narrower to broader approaches. Thus early "cost benefit analysis" emphasized benefits that could be expressed in monetary terms. This allowed both mobilizers and rationers to develop ratios of monetary costs to monetary benefits. Competing projects could thus be ranked on a ratio scale. This process raised sharp objections on the ground that many of the monetary measures were arbitrary, if not completely fictitious, and that other important measurements were neglected. The more advanced "cost-effectiveness analysis" consisted of little more than broadening the sphere of information allowed into cost-benefit calculations. The first phase of broadening has been to include side effects or indirect effects measurable in monetary terms (as in the early cost-benefit analysis of water resource projects). This has been followed by the inclusion of such information in nonmonetary terms, as when estimates are given on lives saved by a health or safety program without necessarily trying to place a monetary value on human life.

A major difficulty, however, is that even those microeconomists who have repeatedly used term "effectiveness" have been chary about admitting, let alone explicitly stating, that they have been engaging in attempts at cause-effect analysis. Once this is brought into the open, it becomes clear that estimates of presumed results must take into account many possible causative factors other than the program under analysis, and that many of such factors, being social, psychological, and political in nature, are not readily understandable in terms of economics or any other single discipline. Moreover, in real life, benefits and disbenefits (no matter how calculated) are never disembodied. They are enjoyed or suffered by real people, groups, or institutions — and some power wielders will always fail to welcome, or even be amused by, frank answers to the question of just whose ox has been gored or fed.

Nonetheless, the microeconomists' more explicit approach to effects (no matter how narrow or broad) has invariably been associated with more sophisticated approaches to inputs and outputs. On the input side, major stress has been laid on estimating capital costs over the lifetime of a capital investment project. This involves an enterprise-style approach to capital accounting — with the annual burden of capital costs estimated over a time period for possible comparison with benefits over the same period. This, in turn, has led to intricate disputes as to the appropriate interest rate to be calculated on government-provided capital (with somewhat less attention to the no less difficult problem of the time period chosen). On the activity-output side, encouragement has been given to operations research, PERT, critical path methods, and other techniques for improvements in complex work flows. Major work was done — particularly in the Department of Defense — in setting up appropriation accounts and accounting controls based on broad, interagency (or interservice) programs. Where detailed long-range planning had previously existed, this type of programming led to closer relations between planning and budgeting.

With this set of technical advances, a second channel has been established for the entry of professional economists into positions of influence. In this case, the reformers have been the microeconomists. Their theoretical background has been much weaker than that of the macroeconomists, since price theory and marginal utility theory has much less relevance to program and project analysis than Keynesian theory to fiscal policy. Many of them have tried to squeeze relevant concepts out of welfare economics, one of the more arid branches of economics. A few, more successfully, have obtained some theoretical and conceptual underpinnings from managerial economics. Yet this weakness has been in some ways a source of strength. It has shielded the new analysts — whether their approach is cost-benefit or cost-effectiveness analysis — from the vigorous and widely advertised public controversies that have characterized macroeconomics. This has contributed to the rather widespread idea — vigorously denied by many, subtly promoted by some — that the new techniques lead toward objective scientific solutions of what had previously been political problems.

The exploration of effects through the micoreconomic method of cost-benefit and cost-effectiveness analysis has led unmistakably to the consideration of broader alternatives: programs of different magnitudes, entirely different kinds of programs, indirect effects, and nonmonetary or even nonquantitative information on each.

This broader approach to alternatives is often referred to as "systems analysis." This usage is well illustrated by Charles J. Hitch's definition: "Systems analysis . . . involves a continuous cycle of defining military objectives, designing alternative systems to achieve these objectives, evaluating these alternatives in terms of their effectiveness and cost, questioning the objectives and other assumptions underlying the analysis, opening new alternatives and establishing new military objectives, and so on indefinitely." [12]

The careful reader will detect in the above two closely related, but nonetheless different, meanings of the term "system." On the one hand, Hitch uses the word to refer to "defense systems" or, more particularly, "weapons systems." On the other hand, Hitch also uses the word "system" to refer to a systematic method of analyzing hardware methods and procedures used in operating a concrete system. The two meanings come closest when systems analysts develop conceptual models to represent concrete systems. In the case of smaller components, this may be done with tight mathematical models; in the case of larger hardgoods systems, much looser models are needed. In either case, the tendency is to deal with much broader problems than are handled by operations research.

Whenever systems analysts go beyond hardware systems, the two meanings usually diverge rather widely. Problems develop, in fact, whenever military analysts — or even systems engineers — begin gingerly to bring people into their models in order to simulate an aircraft crew or a missile team. These problems become increasingly acute with respect to more complex social systems involved in military affairs — such as Defense Department, the aero-space complex, the South Vietnamese Army, NATO, or the guidance component of any of these. This is one of the reasons, apart from merely playing it safe, that the Defense Department systems analysts have confined themselves mainly to procurement and supply, considering strategic alternatives in relation more to the design and delivery of hard goods than to their deployment or use as instruments, and shapers, of U.S. policy.

In most areas of governmental decision making where machine systems are not under consideration, the present PPB-style of systems analysis may, in most cases, be described as *a systematic way of thinking about nonsystems.* Very rarely, if at all, have the PPB'ers developed models of a "social system" — in terms of either the organization or the complex of organizations involved in planning and implementing a given program or project. When input and output concepts are used, little if any explicit indication is given as to the structure of (or internal

12. Charles J. Hitch, *Decision-Making for Defense* (Berkeley and Los Angeles: University of California Press, 1965). Quoted in Samuel A. Tucker, ed., *A Modern Design for Defense Decision: A McNamara-Hitch-Enthoven Anthology* (Washington, D.C.: Industrial College of the Armed Forces, 1966), pp. 126–127.

changes in) the system or subsystem which obtains the inputs and transforms them into outputs. In the case of federal aid programs, the tendency is to ignore the elaborate societal network composed of competing donors, multiple intermediaries, and the final recipients who use the resources in ways that are rarely subject to close control. Thus a set of special studies prepared in the Department of Health, Education, and Welfare (sometimes used as showcase demonstrations of top-grade PPB) confine themselves to federal aid at one end and presumed results at another, with practically no recognition of all the intervening factors. Their major value has been to get more sophisticated processes of program planning under way through a series of reports, which (although each is an unsophisticated starting point) *in toto* provide something of a symbolic legitimation for HEW's new "analytic capability." They also help call attention to some relations among various programs.

Nonetheless, the emphasis on the formulation of alternatives has been very healthy. This is particularly true when PPB'ers have crystallized alternative magnitudes of operation for presently designed programs.

When alternative program levels are formulated (no matter what the quality of the comparisons between incremental costs and benefits), this may put more order into the complex process of program expansion or contraction. Some officials connected with field operations maintain that this gives field officers a constructive role in planning advances and retrenchments instead of leaving them entirely at the whim of central office "pie dividers." More ambitious systems analysts take a more creative approach to the reformulation, not only of existing and presently proposed programs, but also of the more general objectives they are supposed to serve. As Edward S. Quade has pointed out, "Objectives are not in fact agreed upon. The choice, while ostensibly between alternatives, is really between objectives or ends. . . ." [13] Formally, the most ambitious form of systems analysis is directed at comprehensive, zero-based (rather than incremental) budgeting. Yet this takes major investments of time and money by analytical staffs. More important, it requires considerable political clout. It is easier to do comprehensive, "root and branch" analysis on small programs, particularly the new weaker and relatively defenseless ones. It is quite another thing to take on such sacred cows as the supersonic civil air transport (SST), the new antiballistic missile systems, the Apollo program and other programs that soak up billions of dollars that could be devoted to urban problems. Here political courage

13. Edward S. Quade, ed., *Analysis for Military Decisions* (Chicago: Rand McNally, 1964), p. 176.

and political backing are not enough. It is also necessary to formulate very specific alternatives within the selfsame fields. A typical example would be a specific program of non-manned space exploration by automatic spacecraft of the Ranger, Mariner, Orbiter, and Surveyor classes. In addition to unfreezing billions for urban uses, this would also contribute to improved knowledge of outer space and safer and cheaper manned exploration at a later stage. But such a program cannot be meaningfully developed without considerable expenditures — indeed, by at least doubling NASA's current expenditures of about $75 million for unmanned interplanetary flight. Although many of the best PPB'ers would welcome such an adventure, any serious actions along such lines would entail a long and difficult conflict with elements in the aerospace complex who would rise to the defense of the far more expensive Apollo program of manned exploration.

As with previous budgetary advances, the new systems budgeting has involved improved approaches all along the line:

Input costs. An important emphasis on "total system costs" helps bring into the sphere of attention both total outlay costs (including those that are indirect or hidden from initial sight by appearing on another budget) and opportunity costs. Indeed, the basis is being laid for accounting and control systems that, like the Defense Department's PRIME, aim at more effective use of accounting in program planning and implementation.

Input related to output. The emphasis on output concepts has facilitated the analysis of input-output relations. Unfortunately, much of the earlier work was done by microeconomists who tended to use the term "output" to refer to results of an organization's end products, which in business management and systems engineering are themselves regarded as the outputs. As this difficulty is being overcome, PPB'ers are bringing into the new systems budgeting more advanced output or activity concepts: (a) the "output mix" of any system or subsystem, where changes in relative proportions are often the most important short-term alternatives; (b) distinctions between intermediate and end-product output, thereby facilitating the analysis of "output flows" within a system; (c) outputs that represent investments in the producing system itself and that, in diverting resources from end-product services, may contribute to a greater service capability in the future; (d) multiple-agency programs (and jointly produced outputs) financed by "multi-pocket budgets"; and (e) the many and often conflicting dimensions of output quality (as initially discussed in Werner Hirsch's important but long-neglected "Quality of Government Services").

Effects of total spending. In the earlier stages of the Keynesian revolution in fiscal policy, enthusiastic macroeconomists often took the position that what public money was spent on did not matter; it was the aggregate level that had the important effects on economic activity. With more refined analysis of the effects of specific programs and of program alternatives, fiscal policy analysts now have more information at their disposal and can more readily discern major fiscal effects stemming from the substance of programs as well.

Effects of specific programs. As already indicated, the systems analysts tend to handle any relevant information on the effects of specific programs or projects, rather than confining themselves to monetary or other quantifiable data. This makes it easier for PPB'ers to: (a) identify specific parties at interest, including clientele networks, suppliers, controllers, associates, etc.; (b) begin to think of complex money-and-influence flows, as with federal aid programs; (c) come to grips with the problem of cause-effect presumptions under conditions of multiple causation; and (d) help develop improved "social indicators" and other kinds of result area data that go beyond program accounting and deal more directly with the people and institutions presumed to be affected by government programs.

Whirling computers, "whiz kids," and the stern, ultralogical countenance of Robert McNamara tend to dominate the public image of the new "systems analysis." The PPB'ers themselves try to establish an image of "interdisciplinary generalist," a valiant effort which indicates a genuine effort to broaden their interests and skills. Unfortunately, many of those most active in developing this image are essentially microeconomists who prefer an "old school tie" milieu and are something less than receptive to truly interdisciplinary concepts. Many of them have not yet tooled themselves up on the accrued inventory of past budgetary terms, concepts, and practices. Many cannot even square their terminology with that of the macroeconomists (for whom input-output analysis, for example, means something quite different). Few are even barely familiar with some of the most relevant concepts of production engineering or systems engineering, let alone business or public management. When criticized sharply by old-timers for using difficult jargon, they may respond defensively by retreats into colloquialism and old-fashioned "governmentese" instead of efforts to reach higher levels of "concept attainment" and communicability.

Nonetheless, the genuine prestige of the best PPB'ers — particularly those who are more systems analysts than microeconomists — stems from their performance itself. "The good systems analyst," in the pungent words of Aaron Wildavsky, "is a 'chochem,' a Yiddish word meaning 'wise man' with overtones of 'wise guy.' His forte is creativity. Although he sometimes relates means to ends and fits ends to match means, he ordinarily eschews such pat processes, preferring instead to relate elements imaginatively into new systems that create their own means and ends. . . . He looks down upon those who say they take their objectives as given, knowing full well that the apparent solidity of the objective will dissipate during analysis and that, in any case, most people do not know what they want because they do not know what they can get." [14]

The users of budgetary analysis want more than information to guide decision making; they want the "hokum" needed to legitimate decisions in their own eyes and those of others. The forte of the creative, system analysis "chochem" is that he can provide both at the same time — a phenomenon supported indirectly by my own etymological research, which suggests that the Yiddish "chochem" (based on the Hebrew "chochma") is probably the source of the word "hokum." If the less able PPB'ers have overtly routinized minds and behave in compulsively rigid fashions, the most brilliant innovators among them — largely because of their scarcely concealed contempt for lesser breeds — are not always the most likeable human beings. As innovators, they have little time to sit down and state explicitly what they are doing; so the difference between their actual and self-described performance may be quite large. To paraphrase Harry Truman's remark about political heat, "If you can't stand the hokum, get out of the kitchen." That is the way new ideas are cooked up. That is also the way sacred cows are attacked. Since such attacks generate considerable heat, there is a discernible tendency for the bolder and more conscientious systems analysts to create situations in which they themselves are sooner or later invited (or thrown) out of the kitchen.

"The art of systems analysis is in about the same stage now as medicine during the last half of the nineteenth century," Alain C. Enthoven has suggested. ". . . It has reached the point at which it can do more good than harm on the average." [15]

To appreciate the wisdom of this observation [one] need merely assume that during the 1970's the accelerating processes of rapid diffusion, briefly referred to above, will bring the new systems budgeting and planning into the citadels of power in federal, state, and local government agencies. One must also assume that the "state of the art" will advance both rapidly and unevenly, with a larger variety of PPB-type services leading

14. Aaron Wildavsky, "The Political Economy of Efficiency: Cost-Benefit Analysis, Systems Analysis and Program Budgeting," *Public Administration Review,* December 1966, p. 298.

15. Alain C. Enthoven, "Choosing Strategies and Selecting Weapons Systems," in Samuel A. Tucker, ed., *A Modern Design,* p. 138.

less toward a single style of PPB system than toward new claims of reforms and breakthroughs. Such diffusion will probably mean more, not less, confusion.

One of the great strengths of the new systems budgeting is that it cannot be associated with any political party. This probably means that under most circumstances the innovational potentialities of systems budgeting will exist and may even grow. At the same time it is more likely that its equally great potentialities for curbing innovations will tend to be more fully exploited. This question is associated, of course, with changes in the volume of government expenditures. As Paul Hammond has sagely pointed out, McNamara's "management techniques — including the economizing ones — were instigated in an expansive environment." [16] This illustrates a fundamental operating principle of bureaucratic growthmanship — namely, the resource mobilizers who prove their capacity in enlarging the pie will have greater success in propagating their ideas on how to cut the larger slices. Many PPB'ers have felt that the inverse of this principle was demonstrated by the difficulties they faced when, with military expenditures rising in the 1966–69 federal budgets, civilian programs and hopes faced sharp retrenchment.

In a broader sense, the new systems analysis has already had an important effect on political structure and political style. PPB-type arguments and justifications are becoming an increasing part of political debate. Even old-style politicians and interest group leaders are eager to establish their own "stables" of systems analysts or purchase reliable services from research institutions, consulting firms, and other private companies. The new "technipols" — far from marking an end to pressure group politics — are becoming important elements in the complex networks of our power elites. On the whole, all this may tend to accelerate the growth of executive power, with a corresponding decline in the roles of federal, state, and local legislatures. Nonetheless, many legislative committees and enterprising legislators — particularly those backed up by technical work done for them in government agencies, private organizations, and special legislative staffs — have already used PPB-style methods. This will probably continue as a minor countervailing tendency. Many executive officials who see budgetary reform as a way of keeping legislators out of the petty details of input listing will not be so happy when it involves legislators in making unpleasant policy decisions on major programs.

16. Paul Y. Hammond, "A Functional Analysis of Defense Department Decision-Making in the McNamara Administration," *American Political Science Review* 62 (March 1968): 64.

Some political scientists and sociologists see in PPB-style methods an inevitable, single-dimensional trend toward the professionalization, large-scale institutionalization, and "depolitization" of politics through monopoly by technocratic politics of what Wildavsky calls "total efficiency" rationality.[17] The more one concentrates on executive agencies, legislatures, and political parties, the more appealing is this general viewpoint. The picture looks somewhat different, however, when one takes the broader view that "the more 'advanced' industrial societies — particularly in the United States and Western Europe — are in the throes of an uneven and unsettling transformation to post-industrialism." [18] From this vantage point it may be seen that the growth of post-industrial service societies may involve more social dislocation, greater societal breakdown, and deeper tensions, confusions, and frustrations than the industrial revolution had in the West during the nineteenth century or are having today among the so-called "developing nations." In this perspective, present-day systems analysis may thus be seen as one of the technological factors that tend to promote disorder and discontinuity rather than social systematization. On the basis of recent political development in Western and Eastern Europe as well as the United States, Ghita Ionescu has taken issue with the idea that governmental oppositions have succumbed to the "three-pronged pressure of consensus, institutional fatigue and the technical expansion of the powers and responsibilities of governments." [19] He has surveyed the recent outbreaks of "antipolitics-politics" in the form of racial disturbances, student rebellions, and other less conspicuous forms of rebellion by the post-industrial intelligentsia. He finds that such activities tend to be supremely political in an anti-institutional, extra-party, and extraparliamentary fashion. It is doubtful that we have seen the end of such phenomena. The diffusion of systems analysis of the more narrow variety could provoke continued enlargement of anti-institutional politics — particularly if systems analysis [is] used by political leaders as window dressing for a "welfare-warfare State."

Thousands of top executives in government agencies throughout America and the world are facing — or will soon face — decisions on the installation of "systems analysis" capabilities. Pressures in this direction will come from not only central budgeting agencies but also from other

17. Wildavsky, "The Political Economy of Efficiency."
18. Bertram M. Gross, "The Coming General Systems Models of Social Systems," *Human Relations* (November 1967), pp. 357–374.
19. Ghita Ionescu, "Politics in a New Key," paper presented to the Salzburg Round-Table on *Modernization of Politics*, International Political Science Association, September 16, 1968.

sources of financial support, from external controllers and advisers, and from their own more ambitious technicians.

A creative response to these pressures must be based upon something more substantial than blind acquiescence or mere conformity to regulation or fashion. Executives will have to learn that there is no one PPB or "systems analysis" system and that, in fact, they have options to establish a rather wide variety of analytical services. They will have to learn how to appraise alternative budget improvement programs in terms of their outlay and opportunity costs and of their various effects, both more desirable and less desirable ones. In other words, whether this is done formally or by intuition alone, they will have to use cost-effectiveness or systems analysis concepts in choosing among alternative plans for installing or improving programs for cost effectiveness or systems analysis.

In appraising the possible costs and effects of various systems' analytical services, it is essential that executives not make the error propagated by many technicians in the field — namely, assuming that information on costs, outputs, and effects is useful only if expressed in statistics. They would do well to heed the warnings issued by Arthur M. Ross upon leaving his post as U.S. Commissioner of Labor Statistics. In an article entitled "Overblown Affinity for Numbers," Ross points out that "Government officials are prone to take statistics too literally, to ignore their limitations and to confuse partial truths with the whole truth about complex realities." He then asks the question: "Is it a coincidence that the most elaborately measured war in American history is also the least successful?" His answer: "I do not think so. On the contrary, the egregious use of statistics contributed directly and substantially to the outcome."[20] This interpretation of the Vietnam war should be kept in mind whenever executives are asked to follow the example of McNamara at the Department of Defense. At the same time, it would be a mistake to assume that all military programs are "hard" and civilian programs "soft." In the former, there are many intangible activities (such as the threats involved in presumed deterrence) and many tangible activities (such as military operations themselves) whose most important effects on morale and political stability can be measured only in nonquantitative terms. In the latter, there are many forms of hard goods, particularly public works, that require highly quantitative measurement.

Finally, in making judgments about the installation and development

---

20. Arthur M. Ross, "Overblown Affinity for Numbers," *Washington Post,* June 30, 1968, reprinted in Hearings of the Senate Subcommittee on National Security and International Operations, Planning-Programming-Budgeting, Part 4, pp. 240–242.

of the new informational services, executives should keep in mind the still-unfinished business of all the budgetary reforms, including the latest. This is good reason not merely to avoid arousing prematurely high expectations, but also to invest some resources in experimental work that cannot yield big payoffs in the near future. The fine art of nurturing creative technicians lies in providing them with challenging problems, opportunities to be heard, the necessity of interacting with other experts, and sustained criticism. It does not consist of building them into a "statistocracy" that is given some behind-the-scenes power in exchange for the legitimating services of advanced number magic.

Further use of PPB-style methods will unquestionably lead to important technical advances (some of which have been touched upon in the previous sections) with respect to the concepts of input, output, effects, and alternatives. Above all, their logical development will lead the developers into the use of fundamental systems concepts that they have thus far largely ignored: the social and physical environment of a system (and system-environment relations), the structure of systems and subsystems (and the role of planned or unplanned structural change), and aspects of system performance (or functioning) other than the bare transformation of inputs into outputs. Above all, *this means putting people and institutions — with their motivations, divided interests, and unpredictabilities — into the models,* a task far more difficult than putting a man, or even a colony, on the moon.

But this does not mean jumping from the one extreme of machine models to the other extreme of human relations models abstracted from such hard realities as land, buildings, equipment, machinery, and money. It means the development of multidimensional models of people-resource (or to use the Tavistock phrase, "sociotechnical") systems. With such models to provide a general framework or perspective, systems analysts will be in a better position to develop their creative skills in designing the sequences of special, unique, or partial models needed in the unending sequential processes of decision making.

Second, the sustained application of systems concepts — even the present immature ones — to government programs may involve larger numbers and kinds of professionals, natural scientists, and social scientists (other than economists) in competing with economists as experts in public policy. In so doing, many will follow the example of those economists who have operated on the basis of either false neutrality or the exaggerated relevance of more neutral techniques in real-life issues. Others will follow the example of the greater economists — in the tradition of Adam Smith, Karl Marx, and John Maynard Keynes — who knew that to be honestly relevant, they must be frankly controversial. The sociologists have gone rather far in this direction. There are even signs of political scientists going beyond the nonpolitical science of process analysis and girding themselves for full entry into the public policy politics of the 1970's. All this will require building upon, rather than rejecting, the advances made in the past two decades of positivism, behavioralism, and burgeoning empiricism. But it will also mean that present-day conventional wisdom concerning resource allocation, rationality, and decision making can no longer be used as a starting point. It will require imaginative new concepts that refashion our premises on:

— resource distribution, with *resource mobilization and utilization* activities seen as the context in which "resource allocators" try to influence events
— rationality, with consideration of *desirability* seen as no less important than consistency or feasibility, and *rational action* in phenomenological terms seen as often more important than explicit calculational processes
— decision making, *with competition, conflict, and the exercise of power* seen as an integral part of decision-making processes and legitimation (for rationalization) as an essential element in the viability of the outcomes.

Hopefully, developments along these lines might provide more integration among the ideas, terms, and practices that originated in past phases of budgetary reform. But it would be unrealistic to expect very much very soon — or without new infusions of creativity, drive, and wisdom far beyond those of the 1961–68 budgetary developments.

THE EDITORS OF THE *YALE LAW JOURNAL*

PPB for Police Forces

In Hartford, Connecticut, the residents of a large area in the center of the Negro ghetto are victims of over one-third of the daylight residential burglaries in the city. Yet during the daytime only one of Hartford's eighteen patrol cars and none of its eleven foot-patrolmen is assigned to this area. Sections in the white part of town about the same size as the central ghetto area receive slightly more intensive daytime patrol even though the citizens in the ghetto area summon the police about six times as often because of criminal acts.

One would think that Hartford's decision to protect whites more than Negroes would come under public scrutiny at least once a year, when the City Council considers the police budget. But the traditional police budgeting process is poorly designed to reveal *any* policy decisions. As a result, not only racial discrimination in police protection, but the relative effort expended against various types of crimes is likely to be hidden from public officials examining the budget and even from the police themselves. The traditional line-item budget does not even give Council members the chance to channel funds to specific police activities, such as foot patrol or residential burglary investigations. Rather they must choose among such amalgams as wages, office supplies and capital investment.

Reprinted by permission of The Yale Law Journal Company and Fred B. Rothman & Company from *The Yale Law Journal*, Vol. 76, pp. 822–838. Originally published under the title "Program Budgeting for Police Departments." Copyright © 1967 by Yale Law Journal Company.

Hartford's budget process displays the shortcomings of traditional budgetary review. The annual cycle begins in November, when the Director of the Budget holds closed hearings in which he, the Chief of Police, and the captains in charge of the various divisions of the police (patrol, traffic, detectives, vice, records) discuss the department's needs for the coming year. In hearings [1966] each division captain gave a brief speech describing the pressures on his division and stating that even barely adequate service in the coming year would require more men. The budget officer has special knowledge of police operations, which enabled him to ask intelligent questions about police policy and efficiency. But the police officials parried questions about policy with assertions that their present practices were clearly "the most efficient." The police rarely offered factual support for these claims, but on most questions the budget official had no facts with which to refute them.

In one illustrative exchange during the November, 1966, hearings at Hartford a budget official managed to put together information from two lists and a map on the wall and formulated the question: "Why are your beats of equal size when there are fourteen times as many complaints about crime coming from one as from the other?" He was told that the present force distribution was the most effective one possible, and the issue was dropped.

From the police officer's point of view, the function of these hearings is to convey not information but an impression — an impression of a dedicated and overworked department, beset by adversity, and desperately in need of men and money. The budget official has no way to evaluate this impression or to measure the various requests against one another, much less against the requests of other city departments. He must rely for the most part upon his opinion of the chief's and the captain's abilities.

In early December the City Manager holds public budget hearings. Each city department is allotted about two hours to make its requests for the coming year.

During the next two months the Hartford City Manager prepares the entire city budget. He submits it to the City Council in January, in time for two private Council hearings and one public hearing before approval in late February.

Approximately twenty-five hours are spent each year in public and private hearings on the police budget. At no time are the police called upon to show, with any rigor, how they determine public "needs" for police service and decide which demands for their services are to receive priority.

The form of the traditional budget document is one important reason why time spent scrutinizing the police budget does not contribute to review and control of police policy. The traditional accounting-style budget is designed to keep track, in minute detail, of the expenditure of public funds. It is organized into such categories as "personnel" (wages and salaries, overtime), "non-personal expense" (gasoline, office supplies), and "outlay" (communications equipment, furniture). It is an excellent device for assuring that public funds are not lost or stolen, but tells almost nothing about what is done with them. It does not show how police resources are being allocated, either by neighborhood or by function. A citizen or councilman who wants to know what types of activities the police are emphasizing needs a great deal of unpublished data, such as maps of the car patrol districts and the foot beats, lists of calls for service by neighborhood, and records of case investigations. Even then, he must laboriously piece together the information and attempt to coax inferences from fragmentary data. An efficiency-minded councilman might wish to invest in crime prevention only up to the point at which the city pays no more for additional crime prevention than it saves in losses prevented, but no such calculation is possible unless the many functions of the police are separated, and a cost attributed to each of them. With the present budgetary system, city officials and the public must wait for fairness and efficiency to emerge spontaneously from within the police department.

Since the City Council has no way of identifying wasteful or undesirable police practices, its members economize in the only way the budget permits: by not appropriating enough funds to put radios in patrol cars, for example, or by refusing each year to replace the police department's ancient typewriters.

But it is difficult to control law enforcement policy with empty storerooms and triplicate requisitions. The device of a program budget allows the public to observe and modify police practices. A program budget shows how much an organization is spending on each of its various jobs. It does not attempt to show in detail what an organization buys — the exact sums spent for manpower, gasoline, or office supplies. Rather it attempts to show what an organization does — in the case of the police, how much money is to be spent for investigation, patrol, and arrest.

A budget following this kind of format would show the emphasis which the police give to each major task, such as crime suppression and crime investigation. If the police were also required to furnish such information for particular regions of a city, imbalance in their services would be visible.

The use of program documents is well within the ability of most police departments, especially those in large cities. First of all, police work in different cities is similar enough to allow use of a model program budget. Each city government can make such minor modifications as it wishes in the model budget, but it will not have to create its own budget format.

Second, data gathering and processing should not prove unduly burdensome. Detailed information on how officers spend their time can be gathered with little difficulty in brief sample periods during the year. Although computers may be required for some stages of the data processing, time-sharing schemes and the introduction of microcircuity should radically decrease computer costs in the near future.

A program budget will require police officials to make explicit their objectives and priorities. City Councils would then have to take public responsibility for approving or restricting specific police policies. At present, the police often disguise their policy choices for tactical reasons, hiding their exercises of discretion behind the myth of "full enforcement" of the criminal law. They may fear that by acknowledging their policy decisions they will leave themselves open to public criticism, or that courts will reverse convictions on the ground of discriminatory enforcement.

But not all the ambiguity in police objectives is calculated. Traditional management procedures can leave even the police unsure as to why a certain pattern of enforcement has developed. One good example is the common police practice of arresting persons for gambling only when they are in a group whose members don't know one another. It is assumed that this is a sure sign that the gambling is "organized." This policy treats social gambling by the poor more harshly than social gambling by members of the middle class, because in low-income neighborhoods purely social gambling for small stakes, usually with dice, is quite common among unacquainted people. But the practice is not ordinarily a product of conscious discrimination; rather it has simply calcified because no one has thought to question the assumption.

Of course a program budget will not instantly expose all police activities to public view. It will not reveal whether police officers are habitually rude, but it could reveal, for example, whether the department makes it a practice to establish roadblocks on holidays to check for drinking. If, for example, a 200-man department uses 10 men around the clock on six days a year to establish such roadblocks, this would require about one-half of one percent of the total available man-hours for that year. This figure is large enough to be made a sub-category of a program budget. Some patterns of discriminatory service would also be spotlighted. If the police customarily send only a patrolman to do a cursory investigation of burglaries in the ghetto, but send a squad of detectives to investigate burglaries of wealthy homes, this policy would be revealed by the program budget, because the cost per investigation in the ghetto would be far below the cost per investigation elsewhere.

Some police policies, such as the decision to use "aggressive patrol" in a particular area, may be controlled through the budgetary process even though the program budget will not itself reveal such policies. Public hearings on a program budget, focusing on such topics as "15 more man-years of patrol for the North Side" rather than "$100,000 more for the police department," will be an effective forum for complaints about the police.

So far we have been discussing the contribution which program budgeting can make toward discovering and guiding police policy. Once policy decisions have been made, however, program budgeting can help police officials use their limited resources efficiently so that objectives are met at the least possible expense.

"Cost-effectiveness planning" or "systems analysis" [can be] developed to guide efficient resource allocation.

For some government jobs, such as providing irrigation, it is possible to find a common denominator, such as dollars, for both the cost of a method and the benefits it will produce. For other jobs, such as crime control, it is difficult to find any commonly accepted quantitative measure of benefits. This does not mean that the technique is useless for improving efficiency in these tasks. It merely means that the analysis must compare the cost of each method with the effectiveness of that method in accomplishing a specific goal, such as preventing a certain number of crimes against the person. Program budgeting is the first requirement for efficient allocation by such methods.

Police administrators must decide whether to patrol an area with one-man cars, two-man cars, motorcycles, or foot patrolmen. Most patrolling work is done by the officers in the patrol division, but some is done by detectives, juvenile squad members and traffic officers. All of these officers, however, perform many other functions as well. A budget which indicates only how much patrolmen and detectives cost the city gives no useful information about the overall cost of the job of patrolling, much less the cost of each method of patrol. A police administrator must know how much effort, in man-hours and dollars, is being expended for each method of patrol before he will even find it useful to ask questions about the relative effectiveness of each method.

Police officials are generally skeptical of attempts to analyze police effectiveness. This is doubtless due in part to the same sort of insularity which reigned before McNamara came to the Pentagon. But in part the police have had good cause to be skeptical. Many purported tests of police effectiveness have been exercises in public relations. The best-known experiment in police methods was New York City's "Operation 25" in 1954. Twice the usual force of policemen was installed in New York's Twenty-Fifth Precinct for a four-month period. All police activities were increased dramatically: patrol forces (foot and auto), detectives, traffic details, juvenile squads, and administrative staff were all bolstered. By comparing 1954 statistics with those for the same period in 1953, the police found a sharp reduction of reported felonies.

The experiment had two serious shortcomings. No one analyzed crime rates in adjacent precincts, nor did anyone examine the possibility that a change of *any* kind in police practices might alter the apparent crime rate. Also the study made no attempt to pinpoint the effect of any one activity. The Police Commissioner of New York City stated that one of the experiment's main purposes was to make a case for a dramatic increase in police manpower.

Recently, work has been begun on more sophisticated experiments which seek to pinpoint the effect of specific police practices. Currently the Computer Center of the St. Louis Police Department is attempting to test the effectiveness of uninterrupted police patrol. Patrol cars in the test zone answer no calls for service; these are handled instead by centrally based cars. Cars in the control zone answer calls in the usual manner. Careful records are kept in the test zone, the control zone, and the area surrounding the test zone to determine whether criminal activity is being suppressed or simply displaced. In addition, crimes are recorded as "suppressible" or "non-suppressible" depending upon their type and location.

Experiments less rigorous than that in St. Louis may yield ambiguous results. If a city merely tries to change some police practice to measure the effect on the crime rate, it will usually find that the effect of the police action is washed out by political and economic changes. This problem is another reason for police skepticism about measurement of efficiency. But well-designed experiments, such as that in St. Louis, can correct for all effects except one specific change in police practice, and can thus yield persuasive results. A police administrator would then be able to compare the cost of each patrol method with the effectiveness of that method.

Cost-effectiveness studies, however careful, can give only rough results. [It has been suggested] that unless studies show that one method is at least two or three times as efficient as another, the differences are probably small enough that the decision can be made on other grounds without worrying about efficiency.

In addition, these studies cannot resolve hard questions about values — such as the issue of lives versus property. But they can make it possible to tell a decision-maker something like this: "Patrol of type A can probably prevent about $1 million of property loss next year, reduce the number of serious assaults by thirty or forty, and prevent five to ten forcible rapes. Patrol of type B is likely to be only about half as effective as A in preventing property loss, but will probably be about three times as effective in preventing both rapes and assaults." Thus, it is at least clear what is at stake in choosing one type of patrol rather than another.

Thus although results may be rough and value judgments will still need to be made, studies such as that in St. Louis can be extremely useful. A police department can use program budgeting to see how much it now costs to perform each police function. Then cost-effectiveness studies can determine whether the individual functions are being performed in the most efficient manner.

Program budgeting and systems analysis permit city officials not only to compare the costs of various police operations, but also to determine whether some other city agency could perform a traditional police function at equivalent or lower cost. The scarcity of qualified policemen and the tension which police patrol can produce in some parts of a city should encourage the search for alternate forms of protection.

The police function which might be dealt with most readily by other city departments is crime suppression. "Pure patrol" — mere walking or driving — accounts for 50 percent of patrol force time and over 30 per cent of most police budgets. The patrolman seeks to suppress crime by creating an "impression of omnipresence." But it might be possible to make potential offenders fear discovery in other ways, such as by improving street lighting. It would be helpful to compare the costs and the effectiveness of lighting to those of pure police patrol time. Although the idea of making such comparisons is not new, program budgeting assures that they will be made systematically, promotes their use, and increases the precision of the data.

Similarly, although police commonly check the doors of commercial establishments at night, Oakland, California, has recently experimented with a compulsory burglar alarm ordinance, a measure which may prove to be both more effective and less costly than door checks by patrolmen.

It is too early to say whether program budgeting for the police will turn out to be more significant because it lays a groundwork for improved efficiency or because it shatters the police's monopoly on policy-making. Either offers a persuasive case for its adoption.

THOMAS SCHELLING

PPB and the Complexities of Foreign Affairs

One must speak with diffidence on the Planning-Programming-Budgeting System (PPBS) in relation to foreign affairs. Foreign affairs is a complicated and disorderly business, full of surprises, demanding hard choices that must often be based on judgment rather than analysis, involving relations with more than a hundred countries diverse in their traditions and political institutions — all taking place in a world that changes so rapidly that memory and experience are quickly out of date. Coordination, integration, and rational management are surely desirable; but whether it is humanly possible to meet anything more than the barest minimum standards is a question to which an optimistic answer can be based only on faith.

Furthermore, PPBS is a method or procedure whose worth depends on the skill and wisdom of the people who use it. Identifying coherent objectives, relating activities to objectives, identifying costs with activities, comparing alternatives, and weighing achievements against costs are bound to be unimpeachable activities if properly done. But human ingenuity is so great that hidden assumptions can be introduced into any analysis, benefit of the doubt can be prejudicially awarded, quantitative data can be subtly made prominent to the detriment of important qualitative considerations, and even the objectives themselves can be gathered into the wrong packages. The success of PPBS in the Depart-

From Thomas C. Schelling, "PPBS and Foreign Affairs," *The Public Interest,* no. 11 (Spring 1968): pp. 26–36. Copyright © 1968 by National Affairs Inc.

Mr. Schelling is Professor of Economics and a faculty member of the Center for International Affairs, Harvard University.

ment of Defense over the past half-dozen years — and I think there can be no doubt that the system has been a great success — may be due as much to the quality of the people engaged, and their confidence in one another, as to the logic of the system.

I should like to emphasize another point. PPBS, backed up by a competent analytical staff, can hardly fail to be helpful to a decision-maker who insists on making his own decisions and on understanding how he makes them; it can be a seductive comfort, and in the end an embarrassment, to a lazy executive who wants his decisions to come out of a process in which his own intellect does not participate. PPBS can be a splendid tool to help top management make decisions; but there has to be a top management that wants to make decisions.

Let me use an analogy, if I may. A courtroom adversary proceeding has been evolved as a comparatively good way to provide the judge in the dispute with the arguments and evidence on which to base a decision; but the crucial element in the proceedings is the judge himself. Systems analysis and other modern techniques of evaluation require a consumer, some responsible person or body that wants an orderly technique for bringing judgment to bear on a decision. PPBS works best for an aggressive master; and where there is no master, or where the master wants the machinery to produce his decisions without his own participation, the value of PPBS is likely to be modest and, depending on the people, may even be negative.

A third point I would emphasize is that PPBS works best, and historically has been mainly applied, in decisions that are largely budgetary. Budgetary choices are typically choices among *good* things, some of which are better than others, when there are limits on what things or how much of them one can have. The question is not, "What is good?" but, "Which is better?," not whether more is better than less, but whether it is enough better to be acquired at the expense of something else. A budgetary proposal never arises in the first place unless someone thinks it has merit. A bad budgetary judgment is usually — not always, but usually — bad in proportion to the money that is misused; outside the budget big mistakes are cheaper. Having more bombs than necessary is bad only because they cost money; using bombs, or failing to use them, can be bad irrespective of what the bombs cost. In foreign affairs, more of the hard decisions are of this nonbudgetary sort; bad decisions are not merely wasteful of money, and good decisions do not merely promote efficiency.

Even in defense there are plenty of decisions that are not mainly budgetary; the defense budget, though, is so big that the scope for good budgetary practice is ample, and no one can deny the significance of PPBS if it "merely" helps to spend 50 or 75 billion dollars per year more sensibly. In foreign affairs, quite broadly defined, annual expenditure is about a tenth of that. The Director of the Budget has cited a figure of $5.6 billion, exclusive of expenditures on military forces and intelligence. No one will claim, I am sure, that decisions made in the field of foreign affairs are only one-tenth as important as those made in the field of military affairs; and indeed a good many of the nonprocurement decisions in the field of military affairs can be construed as a specialized part of foreign affairs.

I shall not question the worth of being more efficient in the use of $5 billion, even though the amount seems small compared with the defense budget. Furthermore, those of us who think that foreign affairs sometimes receives stingy treatment in congressional appropriations, compared with defense procurement, must be especially concerned that scarce resources not be wasted. Nevertheless, few among us, when we think about the management of foreign affairs, have an overriding concern with how the $5.6 billion gets spent. Money is not the primary consideration in nuclear proliferation, recognition of the Greek military regime, or new commitments to Thailand. Indeed, PPBS, if too much focused on costs and other "tangibles," may even divert attention from those elements of a decision, sometimes dominant elements, that cannot be translated straightforwardly into budgetary terms.

There is consequently genuine concern that PPBS and other techniques of management that are essentially budgetary or quantitative may be not only of less positive value when applied to foreign affairs but even, through their tendency to distort criteria and to elevate particular kinds of analytical competence, of positive harm. A rather striking manifestation of this concern is the extreme reluctance with which governmental officials approach the question of whether the Central Intelligence Agency is part of "foreign affairs" and ought to be subject, not only to similar program planning, but to the same process of planning, programming, and budgeting.

I nevertheless believe the spirit of PPBS, even some of its most familiar techniques, is as much needed in handling nonquantitative and nonbudgetary "costs" as in the more traditional budgeting; the "costs" of, say, meeting certain objectives in Jordan or India may be the sacrifice of certain objectives in Egypt, Algeria, Israel, or Pakistan, and the disciplined judgment that PPBS demands may prove an advantage. The estimates will have a higher component of judgment in them, a lesser component of organized data; at the same time, the temptation to hope, or to pretend, that the "system" gives answers, instead of merely providing the framework for disciplined judgment and confrontation, will be correspondingly smaller.

My fourth general observation is that any discussion of PPBS is unrealistic unless it is acknowledged that budgetary processes are a means of control, as well as a means of evaluation. Secretary McNamara surely did not use PPBS and other techniques of financial management merely to cut waste and to improve efficiency or to save money. He took advantage of his central role in the defense-budgeting process to exercise what he believed to be his authority over military policy. Some people have more instinct than others, or better training than others, for using the purse strings as a technique of management and a source of authority; but almost anyone concerned with administration sooner or later discovers that control of budgetary requests and disbursements is a powerful source of more general control. (This is true of universities as well as government agencies.) Anything that makes budgeting more effective will add to the authority of those involved in the budgeting. Budgetary procedures provide invaluable opportunities for holding hearings, demanding justifications, spot-checking the quality of planning, identifying objectives, and even enhancing competition among lethargic subgroups. Furthermore, the budgetary process being geared to an annual cycle, it provides a regular and systematic way of repeatedly examining these subjects.

My own experience on this score has been quite vivid. In 1951 Congress passed the Mutual Security Act. All aid funds were appropriated to the President, who could delegate authority to the Director for Mutual Security. Appropriations for all aid programs were first authorized and then appropriated in a single act, the titles of which were differentiated by region, not by agency or program. Both in going up to the Hill, through the Budget Bureau and the President, and in getting apportionments of appropriated funds, the several operating agencies were subject to coordination by the Director for Mutual Security. An extraordinary degree of centralized coordination occurred. It was accomplished by a small staff working closely with the Bureau of the Budget. The extent of coordination was undoubtedly more satisfying to the coordinators than to the coordinated; but there can be no question that coordination occurred, and that it occurred precisely because the Director for Mutual Security was put directly at the center of the budgetary process.

This is important. It means that in talking about enhancing the budgetary effectiveness of the Secretary of State or his office, we are talking about enhancing much more than that. A real test of whether an aid program, an information service, an agricultural program, an intelligence activity, or a peace corps is subordinated to the executive authority of the Secretary of State is whether, and how aggressively, he exercises authority over their budgets. (His authority over their personnel ceilings would be a second such test.) I have no doubt that the coordinating role of the State Department in respect of foreign aid would have been greatly enhanced, perhaps permanently so, had the Mutual Security Act of 1951 given budgetary authority to the Secretary rather than to a Director for Mutual Security. (And I have little doubt that the Congress knew exactly what it was doing.)

My fifth and final observation about PPBS and foreign affairs — and the one most directly related to whether the experience in Defense could be translated into the State Department — is that the budget does not yet exist to which PPBS might be applied in the field of foreign affairs. When Secretary McNamara assumed office, he was at least fifteen years ahead of where the Secretary of State is now in having a recognized budget. There is a "defense budget"; there is not a "foreign affairs budget." Both legally and traditionally the defense budget is fairly clearly defined; around the edges there are the Atomic Energy Commission, some space activities, perhaps the Maritime Commission, that one may sometimes wish to lump into a comprehensive "defense total," and over which the Secretary of Defense does not exercise direct budgetary authority. But he has always had his $50 billion or more that were unmistakably his responsibility; and money spent by the uniformed military services evidently came under his authority. The Secretary of Defense makes an annual comprehensive presentation of his budget, typically in the context of a broad evaluation of the military threat to the United States; it is a "State of the Union" insofar as national security is concerned. The committees in Congress that deal with the defense budget have no doubt that they are dealing with national defense and no doubt about what budget it is that they are considering.

Not so the Secretary of State, whose own budget of about a third of a billion dollars a year corresponds, to take a very crude analogy, to the budget that the Secretary of Defense might present for the operation of the Pentagon building and the people who work in it. The $5.6 billion cited by the Director of the Budget is neither a "State Department Budget" nor a "Foreign Affairs Budget." It is a composite figure that makes a lot of sense to the Director of the Budget but has no official status and corresponds to no appropriations procedure. I have no doubt that his composite is a reasonable one; but if I were to come up with my own figure I'm sure that it would be different, because there is no official definition that keeps me from adding, on the basis of judgment, a few things that his figure leaves out or deleting, on the basis of judgment, a few things that he and his staff think it expedient to include. Even he acknowledges that his figure leaves out intelligence as well as all expenditures on United States military forces; and while I may agree that it makes practical sense at the present time to put intelligence in a wholly separate category, it is not for "official" reasons. We know that the CIA is outside the defense budget because we know what the defense budget is; we do not know whether the CIA would be outside a "foreign affairs budget," because we do not even know whether there will be one.

Let us imagine that Mr. Charles Hitch had been, instead of Assistant Secretary of Defense (Comptroller), Assistant Secretary of Foreign Affairs (Comptroller). If he were to perform a task in the field of foreign affairs comparable to what he and Secretary Enthoven and others did for Secretary McNamara, he would have had to invent a budget, not merely to rationalize one. There would not have been a history of "Foreign Affairs Reorganization Acts" defining his budgetary jurisdiction. Nor could he have simply folded into one comprehensive foreign-affairs budget the budgets of several subordinate agencies; not all the agencies would have been subordinate, and some programs over which he might have wanted some coordinating authority would have been lodged in agencies, such as the Department of Agriculture, whose primary responsibilities were not in the field of foreign affairs. By a heroic exercise of both intellect and authority, and with the full cooperation of the Budget Bureau, he might have achieved a welcome consolidation of budgetary plans on their way through the White House to Capital Hill, but there the whole package would have had to be disintegrated to correspond to the Congressional appropriations structure. This would have been a different task, and in many ways a harder one, than the budgetary task that he actually took on — and that one itself was a task that an ordinary mortal would have shrunk from.

I called my fifth generalization "final," but I'd like to make one organizational comment about the Department of State. It has been widely remarked, especially in the early years of the McNamara regime, that there were frictions between civilians and the military in the Pentagon, that "civilian control" was occasionally resented, that there was not always mutual trust and respect as between civilians and the military, and that the civilians lacked direct experience in military command and the conduct of ground, air, or naval operations. Just suppose the reverse had been true, and the Chief of Staff of the Army were *ex officio* Secretary of Defense, all his Assistant Secretaries chosen from the Army, all of their "whiz kids" being bright, promising young Army officers. I think the situation would have been impossible. The entire OSD, being strictly Army, would have had no experience in naval command or the conduct of modern strategic air operations; professional bias and service loyalty would have made it beyond the credulity of the Air Force and Navy that they were receiving fair, sympathetic, and impartial treatment. Secretary McNamara had the disadvantage that he and his staff were a class apart — civilians — but he had the great advantage that he was unambiguously a civilian, not identified with a particular service, with no special bonds of personal sympathy or loyalty to any one service, and not obliged to devote part of his time to running one service while being the rest of his time the President's executive manager of them all.

The Secretary of State presides over, or can aspire to preside over, a number of civilian services and operations. But he is also traditionally identified with one particular service, the Foreign Service. The Department of Defense is essentially OSD, "the Office of the Secretary of Defense"; the Department of State is both OSS — "the Office of the Secretary of State" — and the Foreign Service. (It is also quite ambiguously related to ambassadors abroad, who are nominally the President's representatives, but who are more and more expected to be professional graduates of the Foreign Service.) The Congress has never quite recognized the OSS function of the Department of State; putting the Marshall Plan under an independent agency, the Economic Cooperation Administration, was a Congressional vote of "no confidence" in the executive talents of the State Department. Resentment and distrust of "State" by people in foreign aid programming, through a long sequence of agency reorganizations, has been not wholly dissimilar to the distrust that the military allegedly have for civilians in OSD.

Furthermore, by putting some of the specialized professional responsibilities in quasi-independent agencies such as AID, USIA, and Peace Corps, the Executive Branch and the Congress have precluded the State Department's acquiring the professional talents, the internal organization, and the executive experience to lord it over these other agencies. No uniform distinguishes the AID official from a country director, or Deputy Assistant Secretary of State; but he may feel a little the way an Air Force officer would feel if the Congress had created the Defense Department by elevating one service into executive status while preserving the operating role of that service.

I have to discuss this because, as I mentioned earlier, techniques and procedures that are intended to enhance the budgetary role of a particular office tend, when successful, to enhance the executive authority of that office. The matter is not simply one of providing better analytical staff work to a senior official of the government; more than that, the issue is how to generate more coherent planning and better coordinated operation in the field of foreign affairs. The first thing to decide is whether we want more coherence, more coordination, and an identified responsibility for executive direction. If we do not then PPBS probably becomes an analytical specialty that is not really worth the attention of foreign affairs specialists. If we do, then I believe we have to recognize that the Department of State presently combines both what might be called the "Office of the Secretary of State," and the Foreign Service, and that this constitutes an encumbrance that the Department of Defense did not have to suffer.

Now let me turn — "finally," if I may use that word again — to the first rudimentary step in the establishment of PPBS. It has nothing at all to do with computers, little to do with systems analysis, and in the first instance little to do with analysis of any kind. It harks back to the first elementary thing that Secretary Hitch did in the Department of Defense, something that is nowadays too little recalled when analytical techniques are being judged.

The most crucial thing that Secretary Hitch ever did was to identify his basic "program packages" — what are sometimes called the "outputs" of the defense budget. It is important, in thinking about a "foreign-affairs budget," not to pass on too readily to the examination of "program elements," and to all the techniques of analysis that can thereafter be applied. Eventually most of PPBS is likely to be concerned with the evaluation of "program elements" and comparisons among them, with cost estimates and so forth. But this is already way beyond what first needs to be done in foreign affairs; that all comes after the basic program packages have been identified.

What is it that corresponds, in the field of foreign-affairs planning, to the original program packages that were developed under Charles Hitch? I believe the Director of the Bureau of the Budget gave his answer when he recently said, "First," — and I am glad he put it first — "*individual countries constitute useful categories* under which to analyze an agency's foreign affairs activities as a means of achieving U.S. objectives." Let me say it differently: Individual countries are the basic "program packages" for foreign affairs budgeting. (I do not at this point want to argue with people who think that regions rather than countries are the basic packages; I think they are wrong, but they are not the ones I want to argue with.) The basic package is not the program — Peace Corps, intelligence, AID, agricultural surpluses, technical assistance, Ex-Im bank credits — but the country. Secretary Hitch identified originally, I believe, about seven basic packages. I wish in foreign affairs we could get along with as few; as Charles Schultze has indicated, the number of countries we now recognize in the world has grown to 119. I'm afraid this is an irreducible minimum number of packages, except as we can exercise selectivity in treating some as far more important than others.

Mr. Schultze understated it; individual countries are more than "useful categories," they are *the basic packages* for not only budgetary decisions but most other policy decisions. Countries cannot, of course, be treated in isolation — India separately from Pakistan, Jordan separately from Syria and Israel, Thailand separately from Vietnam and Cambodia. But neither can the Defense Department's strategic defenses be considered wholly in isolation from strategic offenses, or "general purpose forces" from sea-lift and air-lift. The point is that the basic program package is not Peace Corps, financial aid, military aid, agricultural surpluses, propaganda, or diplomatic representation; the basic package is the country.

Maybe somebody can think of a better package. But what we are presently struggling for in our budgetary procedures is an identification of the objectives or "outputs" toward which our programs are supposed to be oriented. Just getting recognition that the country, rather than the agency or program, is the basic unit of analysis would be a heroic step. After that the people with specialized analytic talents, with schemes for the orderly collection of data, and with professional training in PPBS can go to work. The first step toward PPBS is officially identifying program packages; and that step has not yet been taken.

To say that the basic program package in foreign affairs is the individual country can provoke either of two objections — that it is wrong, or that to say so is trivial. Those who object that it is wrong do not worry me; I share their discontent with the country as the basic package, but do not believe they can identify a better package, and in the end we shall, equally discontent, settle on the individual country as the least unsatisfactory basic package for most foreign-affairs budgeting.

Anyone who says that the individual country is so obviously the basic package that in saying so I have said nothing is plain wrong. What I have said is trivial as far as analytical budgeting is concerned; but bureaucratically it is revolutionary. Charles Schultze is a sensible and responsible man; that does not mean he is not revolutionary, only that he makes his revolution slowly, carefully, and responsibly. The revolution is *in considering all programs for a country together, rather than all countries for a program together.* It is examining what the United States does with respect to Greece, Thailand, Brazil, India, or Nigeria, rather than what the United States does with aid, Peace Corps, agricultural surpluses, military assistance, and propaganda.

This is revolutionary, not just because somebody would be looking at the totality of United States programs with respect to a particular country, relating them to the same set of objectives, comparing them with respect to their effectiveness, demanding that the same set of objectives be acknowledged in the consideration of each program, eliminating inconsistency, and reducing duplication. Nor is it that, once the basic country packages are identified, countries would be compared with each other as claimants for United States resources and United States attention.

No, what would be revolutionary is that somebody or some agency has to do this, and it has to be decided who or which agency would do it. (It also has to be decided whether the Congress wants this done; and that may depend on who does it.)

Who should do it? An easy answer is that the Budget Bureau should do it; the Budget Bureau is the centralized agency that brings consistency and compatibility to the claims of diverse governmental programs, foreign and domestic. But what I said earlier about the relation of budgeting to control commits me to the belief that we are talking about the question, "Who coordinates foreign policy?" I do not believe the answer should be the Bureau of the Budget.

Maybe the answer is "nobody." Maybe, as a practical matter, the answer is that the coordination will be fragmented, and the Budget Bureau will exercise a good part of the coordination. But if both the President and the Congress want this responsibility fixed unambiguously, in the absence of a drastic reorganization of the Executive Branch it would be hard to identify any formal locus of responsibility except the Office of the Secretary of State.

But to put this responsibility on the Secretary of State is to give him both a means and an obligation to assume the kind of executive authority that has never, in spite of executive orders and the logic of ideal government, either been wholly acceptable to the Department of State or freely offered to it. This is to put the purse strings directly into the hands of the Secretary of State with encouragement to use them in the executive management of foreign policy.

I think it makes sense, but I am not sure that this is what the Congress wants nor sure that this is what Secretaries of State and their senior staffs want. But this is where we are led by the philosophy of PPBS; and we are led there not by fancy analytical techniques but by the simple logic of "program packages" and the need to develop policies, as well as budgets, in a coherent process that recognizes the country as the primary unit of budgeting and policy-making.

I am not trying to lead the reader, through any line of reasoning or casuistry, to a particular conclusion. If we were concerned exclusively with bureaucratic architecture, we would end up with a good case for demanding of the Secretary of State that his office do this kind of budgeting and do it with the impartiality that would estrange the Foreign Service from the Office of the Secretary of State. But these issues cannot be settled by reference to the aesthetics of organization charts. These are pragmatic questions. Do we want coordination at the price of centralization? Can we split the Department of State into an executive foreign-affairs office and a foreign service? Does coordinated, centralized programming undermine the decentralized initiative and responsibility of such programs as the Peace Corps, AID, or cultural exchanges? Does the Congress itself lose bargaining power when the Executive Branch gets better organized for foreign affairs, and is the Congress willing to encourage this?

I should like to see the Office of the Secretary of State accept the philosophy according to which it becomes the executive arm of the President for foreign affairs, and is emancipated from the Foreign Service. I should like to see it use the budget process to clinch its authority and to rationalize its decision processes. I should like to see all overseas programs and activities brought under the purview of an "Office of the Secretary of State," streamlined to provide executive direction. And I should like to see the Department of State enjoy the benefits of modern analytical techniques of the kind that Secretary Enthoven has brought to the Department of Defense, as well as other kinds. But I cannot — I wish I could, but I cannot — declare with any confidence that this can be done. I come back to the remarks with which I began. Foreign affairs is complicated and disorderly; its conduct depends mainly on the quality and mutual confidence of the people who have responsibility; decisions have to be based on judgments, often too suddenly to permit orderly analytical processes to determine those decisions. The best — the very best — performance that is humanly possible is likely to look pretty unsatisfactory to the Congress, to Washington correspondents, to the electorate, even to the President who presides over the arrangement. The system can be improved, but not to anybody's complete satisfaction. In this improvement, PPBS will eventually have a significant role.

JAMES SCHLESINGER

Two-and-a-Half Cheers for Systems Analysis

The purpose of this paper is to evaluate how systems analysis, the set of analytical procedures featuring cost-benefit calculations being introduced throughout the government, will function in a highly politicized environment.

Viewed abstractly, systems analysis implies rigorous thinking, hopefully quantitative, regarding the gains and the resource-expenditures involved in a particular course of action — to insure that scarce resources are employed productively rather than wastefully. It is almost tautological therefore to state that systems analysis, effectively employed, will be beneficial. The real questions arise when we descend from a high level of abstraction and begin to grapple with the practical issues. Attention must be given to such issues as (1) the quality of the information base, (2) methodology, (3) bias, and (4) the impact of politicized environments on analytical efforts and analytical results.

These issues cannot be treated wholly in isolation. The quality of information, for example, is very much influenced (and biased) by the structure of and alliances within the bureaucracy. The methodology chosen for analytical efforts will in itself introduce a specific form of bias. These in turn, reinforced by the specific interests and functions of separate sections of the bureaucracy, will increase tensions within the gov-

From James Schlesinger, "Systems Analysis and the Political Process," © *Journal of Law and Economics*, vol. 11, no. 2 (October 1968), pp. 281–298.

Mr. Schlesinger, an economist, is Assistant Director, U.S. Bureau of the Budget, Washington, D.C.

ernment and make more costly the introduction of changes which might objectively be regarded as desirable.

Where gross wastage and irrationality have flourished it is relatively easy (in principle) to indicate very improved patterns of resource allocation even in the face of rather skimpy data. In all other cases the quality of the underlying data will determine the quality of analysis. The fact must be recognized that the data presently available to the government for analytical work are not good. In part, this problem will yield to steady effort especially as more trained personnel become available. However, it would be utopian to expect agencies automatically to provide data useful for analytical purposes. Knowledge is a form of power, and most institutions exhibit an understandable reluctance to dissipate this power in the absence of compensating advantages. While newer or favored agencies, which anticipate expanded budgets, are likely to prove cooperative, the old-line agencies, especially those that have established a degree of independence, are likely to prove obdurate. In many cases data of appropriate quality can only be obtained through the wholehearted cooperation of the relevant agencies. Since the indicated tactic for many agencies will be to hide some information and to release much of the balance in warped form, many decisions will continue to be based on deficient information with only limited confidence being placed in the results.

The existence of an established methodology creates problems which ought not be ignored, even though a sense of proportion does suggest that the potential payoffs from analysis substantially exceed the risks involved. In the first place, the availability of analytical tools may obscure the unpleasant reality that many public policy problems are highly intractable. The real problem is not method but understanding; the linking of costs and benefits is only as good as man's knowledge. Yet, there exists an image of systems analysis in which expert practitioners apply their methods and grind out solutions to policy problems — in the absence of a deep knowledge of the relevant social institutions or real-world mechanics. That image is false. But it easily may lead to pseudo-solutions based on nonsense relationships incorporated into a model.

Reinforcing this tendency, the background of systems analysis in lower-order operations research problems has resulted in a lingering preference for formal models, preferably mathematical. In numerous cases this leads to the neglect of important variables which are not readily subject to manipulation by the existing methods. The normal association of model-building and simplification cannot be avoided in analytical work in the social sciences, but there is cause for concern if such analytical work becomes the sole basis for decision-making. The stress on quantifiable elements is particularly risky in cost-benefit work where objectives are hard to define or subject to change. In most cases the cost elements can be reduced to money terms. By contrast, objectives may be numerous, mutually incommensurable, and reducible to money terms only on the basis of rather arbitrary and subjective judgments by the analyst. When and if systems-analytical work becomes routinized, the risks implicit in methodological bias will rise.

As distinct from methodological bias, the more general forms of bias reflect the pressures of a large and variegated organizational structure. Among the causes of bias are: asymmetry in the sources of information, disproportionate attention by the analyst to preferred information sources, prior intellectual commitment on the part of the analyst, selectivity in organizational recruitment, and other bureaucratic pressures. From these sources a great deal of bias, reinforced by slipshod and mechanical work, inevitably slips in, even on those occasions that it is not deliberately introduced. It scarcely needs saying that in so complex an organization as the United States government, viewed from its highest levels, the deliberate introduction of misinformation and distortion is no insignificant problem in itself.

[A] very large proportion of total bias springs from honest conviction rather than the attempt to deceive, and it is particularly difficult to compensate for bias in this form. Contrary to a widespread hope, the solution does not lie in the training and upgrading of personnel — in getting more honest (or more intelligent and capable) personnel. The most damaging forms of bias spring from an honest, if misguided, conviction of the correctness of one's own views. Where biases clash they may be viewed with less apprehension under the classification of the "competition of ideas." But all too frequently biases are mutually reinforcing. And, in any event, the introduction of bias (inevitable in all save the lowest-order decisions) contaminates the detached and quantitative analysis which a widespread myth holds to be attainable.

The final question bearing on the effectiveness of systems analysis for governmental decision-making is the impact of politicized environments on analytical efforts and analytical results. The deliberate introduction of distortion and fuzziness to improve the competitive position of one's own agency or division is an unavoidable and dominant feature of the bureaucratic landscape. At lower levels the tendency to pick and choose those data which support one's position results in analyses which may be uncritically accepted at higher levels, if the conclusions are palatable. Only if the conclusions are unpalatable, will searching questions be raised regarding the underlying data. Not infrequently, the very agencies whose premises are most questionable, are the very ones which are most adept in handling the new quantitative tools, and in developing a superficially convincing presentation that may beguile those charged with responsibility for review.

The techniques of deception are legion, the effectiveness of intelligence operations and the available sanctions frequently low. In the variegated structure of the government (with innumerable agencies and sub-agencies), deliberate distortion is reinforced by honest conviction, bias, recruitment, limited information, and the structure of power. It becomes impossible to separate one such element from another. How much systems analysis can do to counteract the pernicious results of such tendencies remains an open question. Certainly it can accomplish something — hopefully a great deal. Nonetheless, the resistances to the application of systematic and rigorous analysis in a highly politicized environment are sufficient to make even the stoutest heart grow faint. Our purpose is to examine how analytical techniques will fare in this political environment.

With perhaps a tinge of self-satisfaction on the part of its practitioners, systems analysis has been advertised as the application of logical thinking to broad policy issues. The implication is that logic comes in only one guise. Yet, whatever the doubts of those who seek to rationalize politics, the political process is dominated by a species of logic of its own, one that diverges from the brand germane to systems analysis. The domain of politics is a far broader system than that to which systems analysis is typically applied.

The criterion is some substantive (and presumably measurable) utility which is more or less directly relevant to the enhancing of national security or citizen well-being. The pride of systems analysis is its ability to take a long-run view and to disregard prior commitments, if they are too costly or nonproductive.

By contrast, in politics one is concerned with more than the substantive costs and benefits involved in a specific decision area. One is engaged in mobilizing support by words and by actions over a wide range of ill-defined issues. The ultimate criterion will remain the psychological and voting responses of the general electorate and of important pressure groups. Positive responses in this realm are only irregularly correlated with those actions preferred on the basis of cost-benefit criteria. The focus of political action tends to be short run. The wariness with which the approaching election is watched is tempered only by the precept that the half life of the public's memory is approximately three months.

Put quite briefly, political decision operates under the normal constraint to avoid serious risk of the loss of power. The tool of politics (which frequently becomes its objective) is to extract resources from the general taxpayer with minimum offense and to distribute the proceeds among innumerable claimants in such a way as to maximize support at the polls. Politics, so far as mobilizing support is concerned, represents the art of calculated cheating — or more precisely how to cheat without being *really* caught. Slogans and catch phrases, even when unbacked by the commitment of resources, remain effective instruments of political gain. One needs a steady flow of attention-grabbing cues, and it is of lesser moment whether the indicated castles in Spain ever materialize. The contrast to the systems-analytic approach with its emphasis on careful calculation of resources required to implement real alternatives could not be greater. In political decisions, the *appearance* of effort, howerev, inadequate, may be overwhelmingly more remunerative than the costly (and thereby unpleasant) implementation of complete programs.

Consider two of the guiding principles of systems analysis: (1) the avoidance of foot-in-the-door techniques leading to an unintended commitment to large expenditures, and (2) the orientation of analysis and allocation decisions toward output rather than input categories. These go to the heart of systems analysis with respect to the quest for the proper relating of resources provided and goals adopted. Output-orientation is designed to measure the extent to which adopted goals are actually achieved. Avoidance of foot-in-the-door is designed to prevent the preliminary wastage of resources on purposes for which one is unwilling to pay full costs. These are laudable principles, but they conform poorly to the realities of political decision.

Politics, it was hinted above, requires the systematic exploitation of foot-in-the-door techniques. One wishes to attract current support from various voting groups by indications or symbolic representations that the government will satisfy their aspirations. One wishes to attract the support of many groups, but there are limits to the size of the budget. Consequently, resources are applied thinly over a wide array of programs. The symbolism of concern is enough, and the last thing that is desired is the toting up of the full costs of a program with the implication that one should not go ahead unless willing to incur the costs involved.

Similarly, in the real world of political decision, it is immensely diffi-

cult to concentrate on outputs rather than inputs. A very large proportion of political pressure is concerned with the sale or preservation of
specific types of socio-economic inputs. The preservation or expansion
of vested interests implies that political decision will be much concerned
by and may be overwhelmed by inputs rather than outputs.

The systems analyst may search for new and more efficient means for
achieving objectives, but these new means are by definition likely to
have little political support [and powerful opposition] both within and
without government, depending on affected groups.

Consequently political leaders who are interested in maintaining a consensus (as all political leaders must be) must continue to pay close attention to input-oriented interest groups.

Endorsement of systems-analytic techniques at the highest political
level implies, in principle, the partial renunciation of the most effective
tools of the politician. [Introduction of] systems-analytic techniques
throughout the federal bureaucracy in [the Johnson Administration was]
both understandable and ironical. It [was] an administration with high
aspirations and expanding programs [and also highly] alert to the direct
political implications of domestic programs.

The keynote of the Great Society has been the launching of new programs associated with substantial increases in government expenditures.
Goals were announced (like the elimination of poverty) before the means
of achieving them had been developed. Neither alternative policies nor
the costs were studied until *after* a decision had been reached. My point
here is to suggest the inherent difficulties of reconciling such procedures
with the precepts of systems analysis.

These problems are not new ones. For generations men have sought
methods for introducing more "rationality" into the government allocations. Systems analysis is a powerful technique, but, like all techniques,
it will be germane only when there is a willingness to employ it systematically in dealing with issues of public policy.

In many, perhaps most, lines of activity, we already know — even without systems analysis — how to improve efficiency and shave costs by eliminating obsolescent activities. In principle, we could easily do far better.
The problem is not absence of knowledge; it is rather that appropriate
actions are constrained by political factors reflecting the anticipated
reactions of various interest groups. In such lines of activity, if analysis
is to be useful, it will not be by contributing to knowledge, but rather by
serving as a political instrument through which the relevant political
constraints can be relaxed. This is both a more modest and a more am-

bitious objective for systems analysis than is generally stated, but it is suggestive of the role that analysis can play once we recognize the serious limitations imposed upon it by the political process.

The application of cost-effectiveness techniques in the Department of Defense since 1961 is regarded as a model for reform. While unspoken, there exists an underlying premise that "what's good for the Department of Defense is good for the rest of the government bureaucracy." This may be true with regard to the *role* of analytical probing, but it is not necessarily the case with regard to the *implementation* of analytical results. It is necessary, therefore, to explore certain differences between the Department of Defense and other elements of the bureaucracy.

The Department of Defense, relative to other components of the bureaucracy, has provided an abnormally easy place to apply program budgeting and systems analysis. With the support of the President, the Department of Defense can follow *internally generated* guidelines, rational or otherwise, with only ineffectual resistance from below or outside. Moreover, the bulk of Defense's allocative decisions are internal to the Department. The linkages to allocative decisions by other Departments or Agencies are relatively weak, by contrast to the major civilian programs.

For those civilian programs in which improved-performance-through-analysis is hoped for, the situation is far less favorable. A number of the newer Departments represent a gathering-in of pre-existing entities with the tradition of independence and outside sources of support serving to sustain that independence. The Secretary is in a weak position to impose decisions; he is rather like a weak feudal overlord attempting to control some ill-governed baronies. The equivalent of the Defense Reorganization Act of 1958 does not exist to establish the authority of the Secretary. This condition applies, moreover, to some of the older Departments in which nominally subordinate units are in reality independent baronies.

The services provided by the various bureaus and agencies regularly create clienteles within the electorate, whose interests it is politically risky for the President to override in preparing his Budget. These interests are strongly represented in Congress, and even a bold President could not afford to take on too many of them within a brief span of time.

The weakness of the Departments, relative to the Department of Defense, implies that allocative decisions cannot be based upon *internally generated* guidelines. Consequently guidelines must be imposed from above, which is both difficult and politically risky for the President and his principal aides. More important, the appropriate analytical and decisionmaking domain is much broader than the individual bureaus and agencies in question. There are important linkages and spillovers in costs, in technologies, and particularly in payoffs across agency lines. The improvements to be obtained by intraorganizational changes are small relative to those obtainable by interorganizational adjustment. This is particularly dramatic, for example, in the natural resources area. Here the Bureau of Reclamation, the Corps of Engineers, the National Park Services, the Forestry Services, the Bureau of Land Management, and the Bureau of Mines are only the more prominent among the *federal* agencies involved (whose activities must be reconciled with such state entities as the Texas Railway Commission). Each has a position to maintain and a "suboptimizing" mission to perform. The concept of that mission is frequently based upon obsolescent views and obsolescent professional functions. Each, moreover, is involved in a symbiotic relationship with a clientele, which it partially supports and from which it gains significant political backing. The "systems" to which "analysis" should be applied are far broader than the ones which are the concern of the existing entities. Yet, the existing organizational structure makes it virtually impossible to implement the recommendations which would come from good analyses. Thus, the underlying question remains: how strong is the will and ability to achieve a modernization of the structure of the federal government?

To this must be added one final point. Both intensive and extensive research had been done on the problems of defense before 1961. For most of the civilian programs, very little policy-oriented research bearing on allocative decisions has been done. In some areas the problems have not even been formulated. Consequently, there is no capital of preexisting research to be milked. It may be years before adequate analyses have been performed. While in no way does this suggest that analytical effort should not be pushed, it does suggest that our expectations should not be pitched too high with respect to immediate benefits.

Let us turn briefly to consider the actual workings of evaluative procedures as opposed to an idealized model. We must bear in mind that analytical work is performed and decisions are reached, not by disinterested machines, but by individuals with specific views, commitments, and ambitions. The normal bureaucratic tendencies may be weakened, but will not disappear. We might anticipate the following:

> Where centralized evaluative procedures are applied, certain proposals, towards which the reviewers are predisposed, will be subject to less rigorous scrutiny than with other proposals.
> An administrator will have powerful incentives to preserve his own

options by vigorously suppressing foot-in-the-door attempts by *his* subordinates. He may have a strong desire to commit his superiors or his successors to those policies that he personally favors. Moreover, there may be a weak impulse to preserve options favored by subordinates, but which he opposes.

Finally, while the impulse to justify the commitments or disguise the errors in judgment of subordinates may be weak, the impulse to justify policies and programs to which one's own name has become attached may be correspondingly strong. Consequently, the hope that prior commitments can be disregarded appears utopian. Over time, current decisionmaking may increasingly be influenced by prior decisions.

Enough has been said to suggest that there is some discrepancy between the theory and practice of systems analysis. While the theory is unexceptionable, the practice is subject to the temptations and distractions that characterize the real world. Actual experience in the Department of Defense ought not be treated as synonymous with the idealized theoretical statement of the procedures. Perfection and elegance exist but rarely in the real world. When the natural impediments to implementation, which were encountered in the experience of the Department of Defense, are extended to the more raucous and politicized environment of the civilian programs, we should not be too surprised if this experience proves to be a rather inexact model for what will actually take place.

In predicting how systems analysis will fare as it encounters the passive resistance of the bureaucracy, one might start with E. L. Katzenbach's observation in his classic study of the Horse Cavalry that "history . . . is studded with institutions which have managed to dodge the challenge of the obvious."

For the military, Katzenbach indicates that the difficulty of serious inter-war testing of the effectiveness of forces partially accounts for the longevity of obsolescent institutions. But Katzenbach wrote prior to the impact of systems analysis, and it is arguable that the new techniques have eased the problem of testing and have made it more difficult for obsolescent institutions to withstand the challenge of the obvious. In civilian activities, however, the problem is less one of devising suitable instruments for testing than of overcoming inertia and the political strength of supporting constituencies. It is rare that the obsolescence of civilian functions becomes *obvious*. The dramatic evidence of an opponent's military capability is absent. The civilian agencies make contributions to the well-being of portions of the electorate, and it is difficult to make a persuasive case that the functions or technologies in question have been superseded. Perhaps only dramatic, interest-arousing events are sufficient to persuade the public that the productive period of an institution's life is near its end.

Collectively the programs of the government resemble an iceberg with only a small portion appearing above the surface. The older agencies will resist either the imparting of information or the development of analyses which would cut into their treasure troves. Unhappily, the new agencies, from which better things might be hoped, are put under unremitting pressure to produce glamorous new programs — before the necessary analysis has been performed.

These are "obvious" obstacles, but there are others more subtle and less obvious.

First, there is the ease with which all parties may fall into describing as "end use" or as outputs what are essentially inputs. The temptation is strong to continue to describe as an output what it has always been the agency's purpose to produce. The organization of the government for providing "outputs" has normally been on an "input" basis. The Forestry Service nurtures forests; the Bureau of Reclamation builds dams; the Corps of Engineers creates canals and flood control projects; the Atomic Energy Commission is charged with the responsibility aggressively to push the development of *nuclear* power. What is needed is a broader view of power developments or water resources developments or land use — with the evaluation of the relative benefits that component programs could provide on an integrated basis. But the existing organizations are in no position, either by structure or by disposition, to provide such an evaluation. Even where an agency is organizationally charged with a broader responsibility, confusion may remain regarding just what the "output" is. The Forestry Service is charged not only to manage the forests efficiently for production purposes, but to provide recreation for the public. However, the Forestry Service is dominated or strongly influenced by professional foresters, sometimes known as "timber beasts." Foresters certainly love trees and productive forests as such, and may view the town-dwellers who invade their forests as a nuisance to be tolerated. Consequently, the suggestion is hardly surprising that the Forest Service has overinvested in timber production and underinvested in recreation. Moreover, the Forest Service is interested in *timber* rather than in *lumber*. Yet, from the national standpoint, it is arguable that small sums invested in research and development on sawmill operations would have a much higher payoff than much larger sums invested in expanded tree production.

This leads into the second difficulty, which may be the most baffling and intractable of all. This is the orientation of research personnel in the agencies to prevailing notions of professional standards and scientific integrity. This orientation tends to overshadow a concern for the broader policy objectives of the agency. Reduced payoffs in this case reflect the highest rather than the lowest motives, but the impact on government efficiency may be the same. Researchers who respond mainly to the interests of their professional peers in universities and elsewhere may keep the research shop so pure that it is of little use to the agency in developing improved techniques or policies. This is the opposite extreme from use of research as an unimaginative and low-level tool for management, but it can occur within the same organization.

Effective policy research — at an intermediate level high science and prosaic managerial research — must be carried out somewhere in the government, if the new analytical techniques are to be exploited. The reorientation and broadening of professional attitudes is an essential ingredient for the more effective performance of many governmental functions. Yet, it is a problem that is easier to indicate than to solve. At best, many years will be required before the professional bodies are appropriately reoriented.

Third, there exist certain fundamental issues of choice, which even complete modernization of the governmental structure cannot resolve. Analysis cannot bridge the gap between irreconcilable objectives. At its best, analysis can shed some light on the costs of accepting one objective at the expense of others. But there is a danger that analysis may help to disguise fundamental choice problems as efficiency problems. Analytical techniques have been most successful in obtaining efficient mixes through the compromising of several objectives. But some objectives are not susceptible to compromise, and such objectives could easily be ignored in the simple-minded quest for efficient solutions.

One must face the fundamental choice issue *before* one seeks efficiency, or the issue of choice will be prejudged. The difficulty in the extended discussions of improved managerial or analytical tools is that it distracts attention from these more fundamental questions which deserve study in depth. By establishing efficiency as a goal one is deflected from examining those positions in which the question is: how much "efficiency" should we sacrifice in order to preserve a particular style of life or physical environment?

These are examples of the less obvious obstacles in the path of improved-government-service-at-lowered-unit-cost through analysis. We should be deterred from pushing ahead with the development and the exploitation of analytical techniques. These problems will yield to persevering effort. In the long run, they may prove to be less of a barrier than the more obvious one embodied in the formidable powers of resistance represented by the existing organizational structure and division of labor within the government. To accept the spirit of systems analysis is exceedingly hard, but to learn the language is rather easy. There is a danger that the same old programs will be presented in new costumes.

A number of the agencies which were early users of cost-benefit techniques have demonstrated a proficiency in presenting questionable cost-benefit analyses for questionable programs. Quantitative documentation is presented in full, but with a willing audience it appears subject to easy manipulation.

One glaring example is in water resources, for there Congress early required the responsible agencies to justify proposals in terms of cost-benefit calculations. But Congress displays a willingness to be persuaded, even when the calculations are only *pro forma*. In developing the case for the Marble Canyon dam, the Bureau of Reclamation calculated costs on the assumption that the load factor would be forty-six per cent. More recently, in response to certain criticism, the Bureau has indicated that the dam would be used for firming power — and the estimated load factor has slipped to thirty-six per cent. No one has insisted that the Bureau go back and recalculate its estimates of costs on the basis of the adjusted figure. When there is a willingness to be persuaded, fundamental changes in the data may be treated as minor perturbations.

It should come as no great surprise that government agencies, like other entrenched interests, will fight vigorously to preserve their activities.

The number of apprehensions that have been expressed might make it appear that I am indifferent, or even opposed, to the attempt to introduce systems analysis throughout the government. On the contrary, I am hopeful and even, within moderation, enthusiastic. This is a case of two and a half cheers for systems analysis. But before we begin to cheer we should be fully aware of what systems analysis cannot accomplish as well as what it can.

In the first place, systems analysis cannot achieve wonders: it cannot transmute the dross of politics into the fine gold of Platonic decision-making, which exists in the world of ideas rather than the world of reality. Political decisions in a democratic society can hardly be more "rational" than the public, the ultimate sovereign, is willing to tolerate. All of the old elements remain: the myths and ideologies, the pressure groups, the need for accommodation and compromise, the decision made under duress. Systems analysis may modify, but it cannot extirpate these elements. Analysis is not a substitute for any form of decisionmaking, but for political decisionmaking it will be an even less effective guide than in narrower decision contexts.

As long as the public displays an insatiable appetite for "constructive new ideas" (whether or not they have been systematically designed), democratic politics will inevitably revolve around the foot-in-the-door techniques that the analysts criticize. As long as interested clienteles will support inefficient or counterproductive government activities, obsolescent functions will be preserved. Democratic politics will remain unchanged: a combination of pie in the sky and a bird in the hand. Tokenism, catch-phrases, and cultivation of various interests will remain the guideposts.

What then can systems analysis accomplish? The question is perhaps most relevant for the long run, since we must recognize the problem of transition. The qualities that make for good analysis — detachment, breadth, interdisciplinary sympathies — do not appear like manna from heaven. It will take time to train an adequate supply of personnel and to produce good analysis. One cannot put new wine into old bottles. Even though the language of cost-effectiveness analysis is adopted by the agencies, one cannot expect a miraculous change of attitudes. At best, it will be years before analysis begins to have a significant influence in many agencies.

Nonetheless, even in the shorter run analysis will serve an educative function. In ways that may go unrecognized, analysis will begin to re-shape the way that agencies view their own problems. While the desire to preserve empires will not disappear, the concept of the agency's functions will undergo change. Perhaps this is the major accomplishment of analysis: it sharpens and educates the judgments and intuitions of those making decisions. Even when analytical drapings are employed consciously or unconsciously as a camouflage for prejudiced issues, the intuitions will have become sharper.

In the early stages, this educative function may be reinforced by the shock effect. The need to respond to probing questions will shake up many a stale mill pond. An advantage of all new techniques of managerial decisionmaking is that it forces management to think through its problems anew. In an environment so readily dominated by routine, this cannot help but have a favorable impact.

The other major function of analysis is to smoke out the ideologies and the hidden interests. By introducing numbers, systems analysis serves to move arguments from the level of ideology or syllogism to the level of quantitative calculation. Of course, numbers alone are not necessarily persuasive. The ideologies and the established interests may not be rooted out, but the whole character of the discussion is changed. There will be a far greater awareness of how much it costs to support programs revolving about particular interests or resources. The public may be willing to pay the price — at least temporarily — but such a program is put on the defensive. Ideology alone will no longer suffice. In the longer run less resources are likely to be committed to the program and less will be wasted than if the cost-effectiveness calculations had not been done.

Finally, we must remember that there is a certain amount of gross wastage in the government, which serves nobody's purpose. These situations reflect not differences of opinion, nor interests, nor ideologies, but simply the failure to perceive dominant solutions. It is in this realm that McNamara achieved his great savings within the Pentagon. With the elimination of these obvious sources of waste, analyses have had to become more subtle and recondite, but they are not necessarily as productive. Sources of gross waste may have been more common and certainly easier to get at in the Services than in the civilian programs. But within the civilian programs there does remain a margin which can be squeezed out — even without the modernization of the government's administrative structure.

IDA R. HOOS

When California System-Analyzed
the Welfare Problem

California's experience with systems analysis has been unfolding since 1964, when Governor Edmund G. Brown called upon the State's scientific and research community, especially its aerospace industry, to help find the weaknesses in existing government operations and to propose ways of improving operational achievement. The four specific areas of public concern designated originally were information handling, waste management, mass transportation, and criminal justice, with Lockheed Missiles & Space Corporation, Aerojet-General Corporation, North American Aviation Incorporated, and Space-General Corporation each the recipient of a $100,000 contract. Subsequently, a study of welfare operations was added, with Space-General Corporation awarded a $225,000 contract. It is on the Welfare Study that this paper will concentrate. Other states, as well as city and county units and Federal agencies, have espoused and are promoting systems studies in the form of cost-benefit analysis and program budgeting as a means to more efficient and effective government. A mere catalogue of the efforts now under way would serve no useful purpose in this context, especially since there has been very little systematic analysis of the analyses.

From Ida R. Hoos, "Systems Analysis, Information Handling, and the Research Function: Implications of the California Experience," a working paper produced for the Space Sciences Laboratory, Social Sciences Project, at the University of California, Berkeley, and supported by NASA grant NGL 05-003-012. Copyright © 1967 by Ida R. Hoos.
Mrs. Hoos is a staff member of the Space Sciences Laboratory, Social Sciences Project, at the University of California, Berkeley.

My research study of the California experience is intended to provide firsthand observations of the application of this technique so that the lessons to be derived will be available for all who will use them. The sustaining interest of the Space Sciences Laboratory at the University of California reflects the National Aeronautics and Space Administration's concern that the public derive maximum benefit from technological advance and that universities accept a responsible role in interpreting ongoing endeavors to provide an unbiased assessment of *all* aspects, positive and negative.

Initially, the State of California expected that the "powerful, methodological tool" of systems analysis would provide welfare administrators with alternative proposals to (a) maintain a decent quality of life for those who are dependent, and (b) reduce the welfare rolls by reducing dependency to the fullest extent possible. Space-General Corporation, in their winning proposal, specified the three following objectives, their focus throughout to be on the AFDC (Aid to Families with Dependent Children) group: (1) Definitions of the target population (i.e., those persons either at present or likely to become recipients) in quantitative terms and embracing the coalescence of handicapping factors, socioeconomic and such, contributing to dependency. (2) Functional and organizational description of the present welfare system, with a model simulating shifts and providing evaluative criteria with respect to program changes. Not only were such measurable criteria as cost to be taken into account, but also those specifically designated as nonmeasurable, such as, for example, family cohesiveness. (3) An integrated information system related to the target population data and the model; this was to be consistent with the statewide federated information system recommended by Lockheed Missiles & Space Company in an earlier study.

Although commendable, the first two objectives were unattainable. The description of a population at risk, for the purpose of designing a computer program capable of using information about present and potential welfare clients to make projections of future welfare aid loads, requires an understanding of the source materials as well as familiarity with sampling techniques and the rules of statistical analysis. The aerospace team had no meaningful, socially significant theoretical framework for formulating even an acceptable definition of a target population and could only grasp at isolated numbers and figures. Like many information technologists seeking new fields to conquer with their technique, they were wont to mistake their ignorance for objectivity. They tried, for example, to derive sweeping conclusions from one severely limited

410

sample, totally inadequate and inappropriate for this purpose, and were deterred only by persistent intervention by professionals. Here was a clear-cut instance of a phenomenon described by Robert Dorfman in an authoritative article.[1] He cited as common the situation where the gaps in knowledge are known to the client and not of a kind to be filled in by short-order research. From the point of view of the professional staff, the abortive attempt at a mathematically, but not substantively, contrived target population provided an irrefutable argument in favor of *research*. Conspicuously lacking was the kind of continuing population survey that would provide clues to size and growth trends, shifts in general composition, descriptive characteristics accessible to preventive and corrective programs, factors influencing entrance into or exit from dependent status, and the differentiating forces related to the necessity for some families to seek aid while others do not.

Lack of social research support is, apparently, an occupational handicap not limited to the California Department of Welfare. Mitchell I. Ginsberg, Welfare Commissioner of New York City, deplored this deficiency in an emphatic and dramatic statement: "Here we are with $900 million for welfare and nothing for research. What business that big would try to operate and not have research? We operate like a corner candy store." [2] Perhaps the prime value in California's $225,000 systems analysis was its highlighting of the areas still to be explored, the need for systematic research, the serious neglect of the research function in welfare.

The second objective, systems analysis with appropriate models, was never anything but a chimera. Perhaps the State hoped that the "powerful tools of technology" would accomplish something hitherto impossible — a clear understanding and delineation of the function and goals of welfare in modern society. There is little agreement on the subject. Some regard the services of welfare primarily as an aid to the recipient to achieve some kind of independence, financial preferably. Politicians, for example, are especially prone to cite as the legitimate objective of social welfare the reduction of dependency through various rehabilitation programs. This is probably the prevalent layman's view, if one may judge from the press and other media of communication. There is likely to be greater support for a policy of rehabilitation than for the improvement of the quality of life. Rehabilitation was apparently the orientation of

1. Robert Dorfman, "Operations Research," *American Economic Review* 5 (September 1960): 615.
2. Murray Schumach, "Ginsberg Decries Lack of Social Research Funds," *New York Times,* June 14, 1967.

the aerospace team, for they proposed cost/effectiveness criteria to be applied after dependency-producing factors had been ranged along with calculated average lifetime costs of persons in the target population. Such a limited conception obscured the long-term payoff of saturation of services, which may have entailed higher initial pay-out. If these result in improved standards, aspirations, and competitiveness, their ultimate impact would be better judged by the *next* generation — its health, its performance in school, its labor force participation, none of which is recognized in the simulation.

The limitations of cost-benefit analysis as a measure of welfare service were competently presented by Wilbur L. Parker in his discussion at the 1967 National Conference of Social Welfare.[3] Of his four major points, the one I should like to stress in this context has to do with the good and sufficient reason why this technique has not been used in social welfare programs. "The root of the problem," he said, "is precision — in definition of goals, in developing measuring devices for each criterion, in defining our intervention strategies, and in using experimental-control designs to discover which strategy or treatment model maximizes efficient reaching of objectives." The social benefit of services, a value judgment, is not amenable to mathematical manipulation, and there is no evidence yet to support the assumption that systems analysts can contrive precise evaluative measures.

There may be some who regard welfare as the dead end of the road, where society's rejects land. This would suggest that welfare is the result of the inadequate functioning of *other* social systems. Such a conception is not very far removed from the one discussed in the foregoing paragraphs, except that its emphasis is somewhat heavier on the institutional rather than the personal aspects. A proper systems analysis would perforce have to dwell on health services, educational facilities, training opportunities, housing conditions, and economic circumstances, prominent among which would be Social Security and Unemployment Benefits. But, in the absence of a great deal of substantive knowledge plus a sound theoretical framework, exercises in simulation, cost/benefit comparisons, and other technical manipulations are little else than a demonstration of sciolism, dangerous because of its "scientific" aura. The interrelationships between welfare and health, education, and the labor

3. Wilbur L. Parker, "Discussion of A. S. Levine Paper on Cost/Benefit Analysis and Social Welfare Program Evaluation," National Conference on Social Welfare, Dallas, Texas, May 22, 1967.

market are enormously complex. I have not yet seen them adequately expressed mathematically.

The welfare system might, as another possibility, be interpreted as an expression of a society's value system. It manifests itself in concern for the weak, the poor, and the underprivileged. On the assumption that human dignity and a decent living standard are not the prerogative of the few but the right of all, and, indeed, a prerequisite to a healthy democracy, welfare policy and programs should, perhaps, be categorically removed from the realm of the quantifiable. These rights, whose value is incalculable, are in greater danger than many of us may realize if they must be justified according to some economic scale of cost/benefit.

The dilemmas and dangers of submitting all public program planning to economic analysis are just beginning to become apparent as all federal government departments and many at state and local levels try to comply with a Presidential order (August, 1965) to adopt the Planning-Programming-Budgeting System (PPBS). The experience of the Department of Health, Education and Welfare is worth noting in this context, for it illustrates the arbitrariness of (1) the assumptions which must be made, (2) the data selected as significant, (3) the objectives which are defined, and (4) the values assigned. HEW had by the summer of 1967 completed four PPBS studies, of which the one on disease control seemed to provide decision makers with the most promising results.

In this, two criteria were used: cost per death averted and the ratio of cost to benefit. The cost per death figure was arrived at by estimating the cost of a given program over a period of five years, divided by the number of deaths presumed to be averted as a result of the program. Cost/benefit analysis was achieved by calculating the average lost lifetime earnings. Through the use of this technique, the "disease control study" came up with proof that public health dollars invested in "seat belt use" yielded by far the greatest return! [4] Occupying fifth place on the priority list was control of arthritis; "this disease cripples rather than kills," it seems. Syphilis eradication gets number seven priority, probably because it is a relatively minor cause of death today. And yet, if the focus were on the economic benefits of syphilis control programs, one would come to quite different conclusions. The findings of a study by Dr. Herbert E. Klarman suggest that early death on the highway would be preferable economically, in that this would be less costly than the hidden costs of

4. Elizabeth B. Drew, "HEW Grapples with PPBS," *The Public Interest* 8 (Summer 1967): 21.

413

syphilis, as well as the long term prevention, control, and cure programs necessary to counteract the rising incidence of the disease.[5] Depending on the criteria for measuring the worth (arbitrarily contrived) of a human life and the costs (conjectural) of preserving, protecting, and maintaining it, the analyst comes to absolute conclusions!

With the above described experiences with cost/benefit analysis in public health as background, one can better understand the failure of the aerospace team in California to provide an organizational functional model of the present welfare system, with both the measurable and non-measurable costs accounted for. Given the present state of the art, neither they nor anyone else could deliver such a product, and only great naivete or enormous presumptuousness could account for the request, on the one hand, and the response, on the other!

The third major item in the contract called for an information system study which was to cover the following questions:

(a) Given the current system, and the rehabilitative services which are the expressed goals of this system, what universal information is needed about recipients and potential recipients for diagnostic, prognostic, and administrative purposes? Conversely, what information is now being collected which is unnecessary? What duplications in information service exist?

(b) What information and information-gathering systems including computerization and use of personnel would seem to increase both administrative and functional efficiency?

(c) To put it another way, what models of both administrative and functional efficiency would drastically reduce the "paper blizzard" in the welfare services? [6]

In a state welfare system made up of some fifty county sub-systems, these questions were good and necessary. But they might better have been asked of research and statistics people experienced in welfare. Even among the professionals, there was no consensus about the factors which have real "diagnostic" and "prognostic" value. The engineers responded in characteristic fashion by assuming that *all* information was relevant unless proved otherwise. Every possible item, whatever its significance, was recorded just in case someone might some day call for it. For example, the system would not only provide the routine facts about age, marital status, etc., but it would also respond to special inquiries. It could tabu-

5. Herbert E. Klarman, "Syphillis Control Programs," in *Measuring Benefits of Government Investments,* ed. Robert Dorfman (Washington: The Brookings Institution, 1965), pp. 367–410.

6. California State Social Welfare Board, *Second Annual Report,* January 1966.

late the number of cases in which the unemployed father is a migrant fruit picker, with a bad heart condition, with two years of schooling and little English. And, like the sorcerer's apprentice, it could keep on pouring out information — that the area in which the family resides has x number of sub-standard dwellings, y number of unemployed bricklayers, and is z miles from the nearest police station.

From my observation of this and other attempts at information systems development, I am convinced that the handling of a system's information requires a thorough understanding of its theoretical and operational framework. This goes far deeper than the adoption of its jargon and implies a great deal more than simply replacing overflowing conventional files with busy-working computers. Larger quantities of institutionalized information have not yet demonstrated their value in the decision-making process; rather, there are beginning to appear signs that the information explosion may be contributing to a severe intelligence gap. A false sense of security can be generated by the flashy existence of an elaborate computer-based system, and masses of data can obscure imprecision and inaccuracy. That piles of data and powerful equipment do not necessarily good forecasts make has been shown in the experience of the federal administration's economic advisers. Their efforts to "fine tune" the economy have been based on imprecise data, according to the annual report of the National Bureau of Economic Research. Despite elaborate machinery and a wealth of information, the economists have been unable to make accurate predictions and frame appropriate policies. Observes the *New York Times* financial correspondent, the economic policy makers, like the Egyptian army, have often been caught by surprise.[7] "Too much trust in questionable information" has prevented realistic diagnosis and early corrective measures.

The lack of necessary knowledge should not be construed as a mandate to computerize every last bit of information flowing into Washington. That may, in fact, be the crux of the problem rather than a likely solution. Fundamental to the practical art of statistics is the gathering of the *relevant* facts. Moreover, technical skill in this profession lies not in the mere aggregation of data but in the ability "to devise methods for inferring from a comparatively small number of observations conclusions as to larger universes of which the observations in question form a part or a derivative."[8] Sensitivity to the meaning of the subject matter is a *sine*

7. M. J. Rossant, "The Intelligence Gap," *New York Times,* June 21, 1967.
8. Oskar N. Anderson, "Statistical Method," *Encyclopedia of the Social Sciences* (New York: Macmillan, 1935), 14:366–371.

qua non, stressed by Sir Isaiah Berlin among his prerequisites for adequate model-construction:

> The sense of what is characteristic and representative, of what is a true sample suitable for being generalized, and, above all, of how the generalizations fit in with each other — that is, the exercise of judgment, a qualitative, quasi-intuitive form of thinking dependent on wide experience, imagination, on the sense of 'reality,' of what goes with what, which may need control by, but is not at all identical with, the capacity for logical reasoning and the construction of laws and scientific models — the capacity for perceiving the relations of the particular case to law, instance to general rule, theorems to axioms.[9]

He makes the cogent point here that scientific techniques can aid, sharpen, and correct but never replace the practical judgment founded on observation, intelligence, imagination, and empirical insight.

The appropriate model, the significant frame of reference, is precisely what is lacking in the technological approach to information. The zeal of hardware manufacturers and software peddlers to merchandise their wares has made information a prized commodity, to be bought and sold. The capability of computerized systems to record, store, manipulate, and deliver quantities of data constitutes an enormous temptation. Although these tools of technology could, if handled properly, strengthen the research function, this, unfortunately, has not been the usual case. In succumbing to the oversell that accompanies acquisition of electronic data-processing systems, many administrators and executives have been drawn into a web of self-serving and self-perpetuating myths, viz.: (1) The more information, the better; (2) efficient handling of the great amounts of data requires the procuring of ever-faster, ever more powerful computers; (3) computer systems, being costly and elaborate, can be best understood, and therefore designed and managed, by specialists in technology.

This intertwining of technology and Madison Avenue could eventually remove information-handling, the heart of most government agencies, from the very professionals who understand best the purposes and uses of the data. Relying on the discretion and judgment of technologists for the design of an information system is really tantamount to inviting a fox into a henhouse. Implicit here is not only an abdication of responsibility but an insidious and invidious threat to carefully conceived research. The technically-oriented systems designer does not discriminate; he puts *everything* into the computer. Then, from the vast agglomera-

9. Isaiah Berlin, "History and Theory: The Concept of Scientific History," *History and Theory* 1 (1960): 17.

tion, he tries to "tease out" justification for almost any hypothesis he or someone else dreams up. This may be the place where juggling of costs and benefits comes in. But, from my observations, although the agency must bear heavy cost for the plethora of information and speed, the benefits have never been made clear. One is simply expected to accept as an article of faith the value of this cornucopia. So as to demonstrate the economies to be realized, the systems merchants extrapolate from today's high cost of clerical work, and warn that new orders of magnitude of cost will be reached.

This numbers game obscures fundamental issues: Who will use all these data? Whose purposes will best be served by the current information explosion? The welfare client appears to be on the front line of the constant and classic battle between the individual's claim to privacy and the community's need to know.[10] But the rest of us are not far behind. Technology is ranged formidably against him and against all of us, as has become clearly evident in the preliminary skirmishes over the National Data Bank. At present privacy is protected primarily by the inefficiency that this centralized concept is designed to overcome. But rapid progress is being made, all in the name of efficiency, to correct the fragmentation, gaps, and duplication — so righteously denounced by advocates of the federal statistical data center. What they apparently failed to recognize, in a fascinating and frightening display of trained incapacity, were the Orwellian dimensions of the proposed information system. This will provide an instant check on any American, with complete details on his birth, color, religious and political affiliation, school grades, employment, criminal or military record, credit rating, and medical history. Even if a man's past contained nothing like a mental illness or a conviction to render his present and future a Sisyphean struggle, he could be tabbed by the system as a potential member of some designated "risk" population, e.g., criminal or welfare, and as such become the object of unwarranted and unwelcome official attention. When we turn back the pages of history within our own time or shift the pointer on the map of even our own hemisphere, we cannot but sense the implications of such a federal facility.

10. Oscar Ruebhausen and Orville G. Brim, Jr., "Privacy and Behavioral Research," reprinted from *Columbia Law Review*, November 1965, in "Special Inquiry on Invasion of Privacy," Hearings before Subcommittee of the Committee on Government Operations, House of Representatives (89th Cong., 1st sess., June and September, 1965), p. 365.

417

Conclusion

The California experience with systems analysis has enormously important implications. The lessons to be learned have meaning for government administrators at all levels, from county to Congress, because of the growing ubiquity of the application of the tools of technology and the methods of management science. In view of the nationwide trend toward unquestioning acceptance of systems analysis as a nostrum for all societal ailments, there is urgent need for critical empirical observation. The Welfare Study, of most interest to us here, exemplified the fundamental problems that arise whenever data collection is attempted without a framework of socioecenomic theory. It also revealed serious deficiencies in current research and statistics practices. The persistence of archaic methods and reactionary resistance to innovation on the part of professionals will probably encourage continued incursions by "experts," armed with the tools and techniques of other disciplines. Reason would appear to dictate a strategy of, "If you can't lick 'em, join 'em," the first step of which would be enlightenment for self-interest!

The research needs of a complex society are great. Long-range planning calls for systems that are technologically logical, economically sensible, and socially, ethically, and morally desirable. This is a large order — requiring breadth of vision and sensitivity to the totality of human needs. Quality of human life is a precious goal, one which in the final analysis cannot be calculated by computer nor defined by technology.

ROBERT BOGUSLAW

Systems of Power and the Power of Systems

Computers are not found in nature. They have to be built. And they must take their places within a framework of existing social systems. A decision to place them within a framework redefines existing system arrangements in significant ways. Indeed, as computer complexes assume functions previously performed by bureaucratic hierarchies or disparate units or unorganized work groups, they almost invariably lead to the redesign of existing systems. Specifically, this means changes in information organization (with the aid of computers or other physical equipment), formalized work procedures (that is, customs, computer programs, organizational directives, and so forth), and people.

The credo of an engineer designing systems composed exclusively of physical or "hardware" components includes the assumption that all functions performed by the components will be *manifest* (that is, "intended and recognized" by the designer).[1] *Latent* functions (those that are neither intended nor recognized) are hopefully omitted. The same credo is held by designers of classical utopias.

The difficulties that arise when computerized systems are designed *without* deviating from this credo have become legend among sophisticates. Suppose, for example, you wish to "automate" the communication

From Robert Boguslaw, *The New Utopians: A Study of System Design and Social Change,* © 1965, by Prentice-Hall, Inc. Reprinted by permission of Prentice-Hall, Inc., Englewood Cliffs, New Jersey.

Mr. Boguslaw is Professor of Sociology at Washington University, St. Louis.

1. Robert K. Merton, *Social Theory and Social Structure,* rev. ed. (New York: Free Press of Glencoe, 1957), p. 51.

419

functions carried on within a large system. A preliminary step must consist of a detailed specification of the various classes of information currently being communicated. To obtain such a specification, one might examine messages transmitted in the past, and perhaps codify the information normally transmitted over telephone or telegraph lines, and so on. In the process of conducting such an examination, it is all too easy for the neophyte to overlook classes of information characteristically transmitted, let us say, during coffee breaks. Ignoring the latent communicative function of the coffee break can result in a highly complex computerized system that has no way of dealing with some of its most crucial categories of system information.

As Robert K. Merton expressed it many years ago, "Any attempt to eliminate an existing social structure without providing adequate alternative structures for fulfilling the functions previously fulfilled by the abolished organization is doomed to failure." [2]

Now one of the most pervasive characteristics of all social structures is the fact of social differentiation. This, in itself, does not seem very startling. We are accustomed to the notion that some people are old and some young, some female, some male, and so forth. Social differentiation becomes a matter for controversy only after it is used as a basis for social stratification: the distribution of unequal rewards among the various participants in a social system.

Many years ago, two sociologists (Kingsley Davis and Wilbert E. Moore) tried to explain these differences essentially on the basis that "*if* the more important, highly skilled, and physically and psychologically demanding positions in a complex division of labor are to be adequately filled both from the standpoint of numbers and of minimally efficient performance, *then* there must be *some* unequal rewards favoring these positions over others."

It seems clear that the particular scale of unequal rewards existing in a society tends to be self-perpetuating. People become accustomed to the allocation of certain differences in reward and tend to resist drastic changes. A president of an industrial firm makes more money than a charwoman — this is considered appropriate and fair; and anyone who suggested a reversal in the reward system for our society would encounter serious resistance, not only from presidents, but from most "reasonable" people — including charwomen.

In designing a computerized system on the site of a previously existing "manual" social structure, one inevitably must deal with the effects the

2. Ibid., p. 81.

new system will have on previously existing roles and their incumbents. When the role incumbents are unskilled or semiskilled workers whose more or less routinized jobs are assumed by the computer installation, this takes the form of concern with "technological displacement" and consideration of the consequences of "automation." The dialogue may proceed along lines of "these displaced workers must be trained for new skills — like computer programming; however, some people are untrainable and they constitute the core of the social problem accompanying automation. This is something like what happened when the automobile replaced the horse and buggy — new jobs will emerge for which people can be trained — the blacksmiths will simply have to face reality, and so forth."

In terms of social stratification, the human, low-skilled workers are simply eliminated. They are not just placed at the bottom of the status and economic-reward ladder; they are removed from it.

But this removal inevitably has direct consequences for those who remain. The middle-level bureaucrat whose value consisted primarily of the uncodified information in his desk, file, or head now finds that he has been asked to furnish all relevant information to a central repository. Much of the prior basis of his unequal reward has been removed. The second- or third-level executive whose value consisted of an ability to analyze large quantities of data and come up with significant policy recommendations now finds his data analysis can be done more effectively according to predetermined analytical schemes. The highly skilled and psychologically demanding positions become those relating to operations of the computer and the formulation of computer programs.

All this, of course, shakes the foundations of existing stratification realities. Former "key decision makers" begin to feel, and indeed are regarded, as anachronistic hangers-on. Experienced computer experts have many techniques for dealing with this problem. One approach is to point out that the locus of decision making still rests with the former executive or manager. This, of course, is not really true. Disbelievers see the light when they ask for a given set of figures or ask that a pet procedure be implemented.

The answer, all too frequently, becomes "but the program can't handle it." Or, "We can't do that just yet, but in about six months, after these immediate problems are ironed out, I'm sure we can get that for you." Or, "This set of figures will cover about 98 per cent of all the cases you could possibly be interested in; it just wouldn't be economical to try to get 100 per cent of all the cases," and so on.

To an executive accustomed to getting his own way from human employees, even if they have to work overtime or develop ulcers in the process, this may all sound like an unpardonable affront to managerial prerogatives. He is thus inexorably driven to the next step in the process — the "I want a computer course" step. The feeling seems to be: "If I could only learn a little about computer programming, I could keep those snotty kids from being in a position to tell me how to run my business."

But, unfortunately, computer courses for executives seldom provide enduring solutions. At best, the executive learns to deal with his frustrations by accepting the frame of reference of the computer expert and adjusting his sights accordingly. The exercise of power, which formerly was mediated through conventions of law, custom, "what the union will stand still for," or "principles of human relations" — now must be mediated through the current state of computer technology.

To proceed in this fashion (that is, through technology-screened power) is to adopt an orientation that is essentially formalist in nature (although the work of Newell, Simon, and Shaw in the area of heuristic programming provides the promise of creative alternatives). The specification of future and current system states within this orientation characteristically requires an insistence upon a uniformity of perspective, a standardization of language, and a consensus of values that is characteristic of highly authoritarian social structures. Nonconforming perspectives, language, and values can be and, indeed, must be excluded as system elements.

All this is a familiar pattern in classical utopias. Although the inhabitants of utopian societies were frequently prepared to deal with external threats, internal dissension was almost invariably taboo. The tradition of specifying functions within computer-based systems enhances the points of structural correspondence of these systems and classical utopias. In this connection, Ralf Dahrendorf's summary of the structural features of utopian societies provides some useful insights. He points out that: (1) Utopias do not grow out of familiar reality or follow realistic patterns of development. (2) Utopias characteristically have universal consensus on values and institutional arrangements; that is, they are highly uniform throughout. (3) Utopias are characterized by an absence of internal conflict; that is, they are characterized by social harmony, which helps to account for their stability. (4) All processes within utopian societies follow recurrent patterns and occur as part of the design of the whole. (5) Utopias are characteristically isolated in time and space from other parts of the world.

The simple fact of the matter seems to be that classically designed computer-based systems, like classical utopias, resolve problems of conflict, consensus, and reality by simple fiat. But these old problems do not thereby simply fade away. Environments change. Internal conditions change. Systems and utopias alike must be ready and able to change if they are to survive. But crucial types of change originate *within* systems — out of the contradictions and conflicts existing between two or more opposing sets of values, ideologies, roles, institutions, or groups.

To insist that social structures must always be shaped and controlled from "topside," is to reinforce maladaptive tendencies in systems and to help to insure their ultimate collapse. A façade of value homogeneity cannot resolve the internal stresses, conflicts, and dilemmas that arise in any system designed to cope effectively with the fact of change.

The problem of understanding what it is that makes human societies "stick together" or cohere has been studied by philosophers and social theorists for thousands of years. In general, two different kinds of explanation are offered. The first of these emphasizes the role of *consensus* — the existence of a general agreement on values within the society. The second explanation emphasizes the role of *coercion* — the use of force and constraint to hold a society together.[3]

One of the interesting limitations of traditional utopias is the relative lack of detailed concern they reflect about the composition of the glue used to hold things together.

In the *consensus* formula for social glue, people with common values voluntarily associate to help insure more effective cooperation. In the *coercion* formula, positions within the system are defined to insure effective application of force and constraints. To understand the operation of any system, it is crucial to understand the distribution of authority and power within it. Differences in system design may, in the last analysis, involve little more than different allocations of power and authority throughout the system. Indeed, alternate arguments about the merits of different system design formats may well involve little beyond implicit rationalizations for alternate modes of power distribution.

Each of these formulas is based upon a set of assumptions about the nature of society or social systems. The consensus formula assumes that society is a relatively stable and well-integrated structure of elements, each of which has a well-defined function. Throughout the system itself, there exists a consensus of values among its various members. The coercion formula assumes that every society is at every point subject to both

3. Ralf Dahrendorf, *Class and Class Conflict in Industrial Society* (Stanford: Stanford University Press, 1959), pp. 157–159.

processes of change and social conflict. It further assumes that every element in a society contributes to the system's disintegration and change. And finally, the coercion formula assumes that every society is based on the coercion of some of its members by others.

The point to be stressed here, however, is the importance of specifying the exact nature of the particular glue to be used in a specific system design. Perhaps the easiest error to make is the one that assumes that a consensus glue exists, when in point of fact the design either requires, or has surreptitiously imposed, a coercion formula.

To clarify this somewhat, it may be helpful to note how power, in the sociological sense, is differentiated from force on the one hand and authority on the other.

Force, in this context, refers to the reduction, limitation, closure, or total elimination of alternatives to the social action of one person or group by another person or group. For example, "Your money or your life," symbolizes a situation in which the alternatives have been reduced to two. Hanging a convicted criminal exemplifies the total elimination of alternatives. Dismissal or demotion of personnel in an organization illustrates the closure of alternatives. An army may successively place limitations upon the social action of its enemy until only two alternatives remain — to surrender or die.

Power refers to the ability to apply force, rather than to its actual application. It is the "predisposition or prior capacity which makes the application of force possible."

Authority refers to institutionalized power. In an idealized organization, power and authority become equivalent to each other. The right to use force is attached to certain statuses within the organization. "It is . . . authority in virtue of which persons in an association exercise command or control over other persons in the same association." [4] Examples of the use of authority include: the bishop who transfers a priest from his parish, the commanding officer who assigns a subordinate to a post of duty, a baseball team manager who changes a pitcher in the middle of an inning, and a factory superintendent who requires that an employee complete a task by a given time.

"Your money or your life," constitutes what in the computer trade would be called a binary choice. If the alternatives available were extended to include, let us say, "the twenty-dollar bill you now have in your pocket," "room and board at your home for two days," "a serviceable over-

4. Robert Bierstedt, "An Analysis of Social Power," *American Sociological Review* 15 (December 1950): 733.

coat," "the three bottles of scotch you have in your closet," or "a friendly chat over a good meal," then the intensity of the force being applied might be seen as somewhat diminished. This is simply another way of noting that the exercise of force is related to the range of action alternatives made possible. The person with the ability to specify the alternatives — in this case, the person with the gun — is the one who possesses power.

And so it is that a designer of systems, who has the de facto prerogative to specify the range of phenomena that his system will distinguish, clearly is in possession of enormous degrees of power (depending, of course, upon the nature of the system being designed). It is by no means necessary that this power be formalized through the allocation of specific authority to wield nightsticks or guns.

The strength of high-speed computers lies precisely in their capacity to process binary choice data rapidly. But to process these data, the world of reality must at some point in time be reduced to binary form. This occurs initially through operational specifications handed to a computer programmer. These specifications serve as the basis for more detailed reductions to binary choices. The range of possibilities is ultimately set by the circuitry of the computer, which places finite limits on alternatives for data storage and processing. The structure of the language used to communicate with the computer places additional restrictions on the range of alternatives. The programmer himself, through the specific sets of data he uses in his solution to a programming problem and the specific techniques he uses for his solution, places a final set of restrictions on action alternatives available within a computer-based system.

It is in this sense that computer programmers, the designers of computer equipment, and the developers of computer languages possess power. To the extent that decisions made by each of these participants in the design process serve to reduce, limit, or totally eliminate action alternatives, they are applying force and wielding power in the precise sociological meaning of these terms.

Indeed, a computer-based system in many ways represents the extreme of what Max Weber called a *monocratic bureaucracy*. For Weber, bureaucracy was "the most crucial phenomenon of the modern Western state." [5] He regarded it as completely indispensable for the requirements of contemporary mass administration. It possesses the advantages of precision, speed, unambiguity, knowledge of the files, continuity, discretion,

5. Max Weber, "The Essentials of Bureaucratic Organization," in *Reader in Bureaucracy*, ed. Robert K. Merton, Alisa P. Gray, Barbara Hockey, and Hannan C. Selvin (New York: Free Press of Glencoe, 1952), p. 24.

unity, strict subordination, and reduction of friction, material, and personal costs.[6]

The power position of a bureaucracy, Weber tells us, is normally overpowering. "The absolute monarch is powerless opposite the superior knowledge of the bureaucratic expert." [7]

One of the most powerful tools available to a bureaucracy is secrecy. To the extent that members of a bureaucracy can keep their knowledge and intentions secret, they increase the importance of "professional knowhow."

Perhaps the most significant implication of bureaucratic organization is the tendency to convert all political problems into administrative problems. Karl Mannheim explained this phenomenon by noting that the activity sphere of an official is bounded by the limits of laws already formulated. The genesis or development of new law lies beyond his scope. "As a result of his socially limited horizon, the functionary fails to see that behind every law that has been made there lie the socially fashioned interests and *Weltanschauungen* of a specific social group. . . . He does not understand that every rationalized order is only one of many forms in which socially conflicting irrational forces are reconciled." [8]

Mannheim's conception of "politics" and "political problems" was not, of course, confined to government situations. "Politics" in his definition includes all situations in which decisions cannot be made in accordance with clear precedent or according to the clear requirements of an existing rule. Under these conditions, a bureaucracy characteristically finds means for taking action or making "political" decisions by manipulating the rule structure within which it operates. To operate successfully, a bureaucracy must reach a high degree of reliability of response and conformity to prescribed rules. Under these conditions, the rules tend to be treated as absolutes rather than as relative to a given set of purposes. This, in turn, leads to difficulties in adaptation to new conditions that have not been anticipated clearly by those who drew up the rules. It thus seems to be an almost universal characteristic of bureaucratic structures that they result not only in dislocations in the patterns of power, but that in addition, "the very elements which conduce toward efficiency in general produce inefficiency in specific instances." [9]

6. H. H. Gerth and C. Wright Mills, eds., *From Max Weber: Essays in Sociology* (New York: Oxford University Press, 1958), p. 214.

7. Ibid., p. 234.

8. Karl Mannheim, *Ideology and Utopia* (New York: Harcourt, Brace and World, 1936), p. 105.

9. Merton, *Social Theory*, p. 200.

The place at which definitions are made of the precise meaning of the rules within which the bureaucracy must function is the point of maximum bureaucratic and political power. The simple fact of the matter is that whether your bureaucracy is composed entirely of the most intelligent human beings imaginable, or of the most intelligent machines available, it is the definition of the rule structure that becomes the central fact of significance in defining the structure of power relationships.

Replying to arguments about the possible superiority of computers over human beings can be an upsetting experience — if one happens to identify with the perspective of people.

So, it comes as a very small surprise indeed to those who believe that the crucial ingredient of the human condition is high-order intelligence that an argument such as Paul Armer's (purporting to demonstrate that computers are potentially just as smart as the rest of us) must be rejected out of hand. We all tend to be somewhat ethnocentric about the tribe of humanity. We *know* we have magic that Armer's cottonpickin' machine couldn't possibly have.

What precisely is it that we have in addition to that mechanistic kind of IQ which Armer implies is our last remaining talent?

As a minimum, we have a sense of values. Some things are important to us. Other things are not so important. As sophisticates of twentieth-century civilization rather than members of a nonliterate tribe, we can accept the possibility that Paul Armer's computer might not only be able to replicate our values. He might even dream up a set demonstrably better for us than our own. But they wouldn't be ours. And they wouldn't be the machine's. They would be Paul's. And that's the rub.

The point is simply that values are not derived either scientifically, logically, or intellectually. They are simply prime factors. And even if Armer's values were those of a saint, we might well wish to promote our own saint with a somewhat different set of values to be implemented. But, says the information processor, "I do only what the customer tells me to do. I implement the values of someone else, rather than my own. And in the absence of specific instructions, I use as a guide line the criterion of technical efficiency or cost, or speed or something similar."

Power in the design of large-scale computer-based systems resides to an increasing degree with (1) the customer — to the extent that he can specify in complete and rigorous detail exactly what decisions he wishes to see implemented by his bureaucracy under every conceivable set of conditions, or (2) the system designer and computer programmer, who insure that *some* decision is made in every case whether that case has

427

been clearly anticipated or not, and (3) the hardware manufacturer, whose technology and components determine what kind of data can be sensed and processed by computers, display equipment, and other system equipment.

To the extent that customers (and these may include government agencies or private industry) abdicate their power prerogatives because of ignorance of the details of system operation, de facto system decisions are made by equipment manufacturers or information-processing specialists. The customers may find it impossible to specify all future situations; they may be unable to devise foolproof heuristics; they may fail to specify detailed operating unit characteristics; they may be unable to devise appropriate ad hoc plans. Under each of these conditions, de facto decisions are again made for them by system designers or other technical specialists.

As computer-based systems become increasingly more significant in shaping the realistic terms of existence in contemporary society, it becomes increasingly more relevant to inquire about the implications contained for expression of individual values. The process of obtaining representation for individual values is one of the specific notions contained in popular conceptions of democracy. However, the central idea of democracy has been penetratingly described as "one particular way in which the authority to govern is acquired and held." [10] Thus, "A man may be said to hold authority democratically when he has been freely chosen to hold such authority by those who must live under it, when they have had, and will have, the alternative of choosing somebody else, and when he is accountable to them for the way in which he exercises this authority." [11]

It is, of course, clear that there are limits on the democratic principle and that legal and institutional safeguards must exist to protect values other than those of democracy itself. It is equally clear that at best the democratic principle can be only approximated. No one in our society seriously suggests that every person must be absolutely equal to every other person in power and influence. But, "the working touchstone of a 'democratic' system of authority is simply the degree to which it gives individuals legitimate instruments for reaching those who make the decisions that affect them, and for bringing influence to bear upon them. A system is more or less 'democratic' depending on the number, availability,

10. Charles Frankel, "Bureaucracy & Democracy in the New Europe," *Daedalus* 93 (Winter 1964): 476.
11. Ibid.

and effectiveness of these instruments, and on the proportion of the population entitled and able to use them." [12]

Now, whether the "masses" are denied legitimate access to decision makers by reason of despotism, bureaucratic deviousness, or simple technical obfuscation, the resultant erosion of democratic process can be much the same. To the extent that decisions made by equipment manufacturers, computer programmers, or system designers are enshrouded in the mystery of "technical" detail, the persons most affected by these decisions (including customers, publics, and employees) will be denied the opportunity to participate or react to the decision made. The spectrum of values represented in the new decision-making order can and is being increasingly more circumscribed by fiat disguised as technological necessity. The paramount issues to be raised in connection with the design of our new computerized utopias are not technological — they are issues of values and the power through which these values become translated into action.

A major difficulty is the lack of clarity involved in efforts to specify values in exact terms.

In short, value differences are sometimes nothing more than differences in ways of looking at reality. Sometimes they consist of honest differences in opinion about the most effective way to achieve mutually agreed-upon goals. Sometimes they reflect fundamental differences in primary orientation to the world we live in. These differences may be as simple as a preference for the Martins over the Coys; they can be as complex as the choice between egoism and humanitarianism.

Probably the most distinctive characteristic of classical utopian designs is the basic "humanitarian" bent of their value structures. In Sir Thomas More's *Utopia,* the inhabitants are more concerned with the welfare of their fellow men than with furthering their individual fortunes. The phalanstery designed by Charles Fourier provides environments and procedures calculated to undo the more undesirable human consequences of unbridled individualism. And even in Francis Bacon's *New Atlantis,* where the major emphasis is presumably placed upon scientific programs, the fundamental goal of scientific activity is seen as the solution of social problems and the welfare of human beings — rather than the advancement of science for its own sake.

And perhaps the most notable difference to be found between the classical system designers and their contemporary counterparts (system

12. Ibid., p. 477.

engineers, data processing specialists, computer manufacturers, and system designers) consists precisely in the fact that the humanitarian bent has disappeared. The dominant value orientation of the utopian renaissance can best be described as "efficiency" rather than "humanitarianism."

The powerful appeal of the efficiency concept is a well-known and well-documented feature of contemporary Western civilization. It is more efficient to ride in an automobile than it is to walk. It is more efficient to fly in an airplane than it is to ride in an automobile. It is more efficient to use a guided missile than it is to use a manned bomber, and so on. The fundamental challenge of efficiency arises in connection with the struggle for ascendancy over man's physical environment. This struggle may be rationalized as a necessity for the survival of man. More frequently these days it is simply attributed to the sport of satisfying man's insatiable curiosity about the universe in which he finds himself. For the American schoolboy, learning to exert mastery over the mysterious forces of nature has become every bit as much a challenge as the problem of overcoming rival princes ever was for Machiavelli's Lorenzo de Medici. But just as no de Medici could seriously be expected to learn his politics from pre-Machiavellian books, it is not reasonable to expect American schoolboys to learn the facts of the utopian renaissance exclusively from contemporary computer journals and works on system engineering. The strength of Machiavelli, as the first of the modern analysts of power, consisted of the fact that, "Where others looked at the figureheads, he kept his eyes glued behind the scenes. He wanted to know what made things tick; he wanted to take the clock of the world to pieces to find out how it worked." [13]

Information necessary to take apart the clock of the contemporary world is simply not underscored in contemporary computer journals and works on system engineering, which remain devoted to the idols of physical efficiency. The central consequences of the utopian renaissance involve fundamental changes not only in the value structure of Western people, but redistributions of power concentrations made possible through the use of system control mechanisms. The resurgence of intellectual and political orientations such as "conservative" and "liberal" must be re-examined in the light of these newly emerging, altered power relationships.

Classical utopias received their impetus from a dissatisfaction with existing reality. They represented attempts to design systems more con-

13. Max Lerner, "Introduction to Niccolo Machiavelli," in *The Prince and the Discourses* (New York: Random House, 1950), p. xxvi.

sistent with notions about what was really "good" for the mankinds they knew or dreamed about. They were unsuccessful largely because their designers, in attempting to transcend the limits of their own environmental realities, severed the threads between their brave new systems and the system control or power mechanisms of their times.

Our own utopian renaissance receives its impetus from a desire to extend the mastery of man over nature. Its greatest vigor stems from a dissatisfaction with the limitations of man's existing control over his physical environment. Its greatest threat consists precisely in its potential as a means for extending the control of man over man.

UNIVERSITY OF DENVER RESEARCH INSTITUTE

Defense Systems Approaches in the Civil Sector

By the early 1960's non-defense government agencies were faced with growing problems of increasing complexity. The urgency for solving some of these problems was increasing rapidly. Yet there were real difficulties in following the traditional and slow governmental approaches of cutting and trying and experimenting, or of relying on small incremental changes in existing systems. There were limited resources available, and these had to be apportioned among many claims. The conditions facing these civil government agencies were in certain ways quite similar to the conditions which had moved the defense establishment and the defense industry into evolving the systems approach a decade before.

In 1963 another pertinent factor affected this situation. A temporary end was in sight to the almost frantic development of major strategic weapons systems by the United States. The fear of the Russian threat began to abate and, as Cold War pressures decreased, defense hardware procurement expenditures leveled off. By 1964 there was the prospect that defense spending might decline. Defense industry, and particularly that part of it with important systems capabilities, began to worry about future demand for its services and products.

From "Defense Systems Resources in the Civil Sector: An Evolving Approach, An Uncertain Market," a report prepared for the U.S. Arms Control and Disarmament Agency, July 1967; authors: John S. Gilmore, John J. Ryan, and William S. Gould, University of Denver Research Institute.

The California Experience

The State of California was uniquely susceptible to all of these concerns. Its rapid growth posed major financial and administrative problems for the State government; and the economic threat to its leading industry — the defense firms with substantial systems capability — was direct. It was logical, therefore, that the State would experiment with the application of this defense systems capability to solving its own complex problems.

Background and history. During much of 1964, staff people from several California aerospace firms discussed with representatives of the executive branch of California's state government (largely personnel in the Economic Development Agency and the Department of Finance) the possibility of applying systems approaches to State problems. As a result, the California aerospace study program was announced in November of 1964 by Governor Edmund G. Brown. Requests for proposals (RFP's) were quickly issued, and four $100,000 contracts were let by February of 1965 for four nine month systems studies. The projects covered and the aerospace contractors were:

1. The Lockheed Missiles & Space Company undertook to design a statewide information handling system, and to develop a plan for its implementation.
2. Space-General Corporation (a subsidiary of Aerojet-General Corporation) set out to explore the feasibility of applying systems engineering and operations analysis techniques to social problems, and to recommend a program for prevention and control of crime and delinquency.
3. The Aerojet-General Corporation contracted to assess the suitability of systems analysis and systems engineering as tools for solving California's waste management problem, and to define research and development activities to be undertaken as the first step of an over-all program.
4. North American Aviation, Inc. developed a work program indicating the content and specifications for a systems approach to solving basic transportation problems.

Two primary motivations pushed the program: (1) Both State and defense industry personnel were concerned over the possibility of lagging defense expenditures, and were looking for ways to ease the impact of possible defense cutbacks. Civil sector studies by the aerospace industry seemed to offer one possible approach. (2) Some administrators in the

State were convinced of a need for drastic changes and improvements in governmental organization, management, and administration, but did not know how to cope with the problems in view of institutionalized inertia and the existing power structure. This was aggravated by the lack of uncommitted discretionary funds for studying these problems and for evolving new solutions in-house. Thus the administrators hoped that aerospace industry talent might not only provide fresh insights and useful technical solutions, but also serve as an outside authority and hence believable mechanism for initiating needed change.

This last consideration accounted in part for the somewhat "sub rosa" approach taken in the planning and financing of the four initial California studies. Only after the preliminary RFP's had been written were the affected agencies involved (with the exception of the Division of Highways which did participate in preparing the transportation RFP). The ideas were not submitted to the Legislature for approval and financing. Instead, financing was arranged by tapping agency budgets. The program thus was labeled as an effort inaugurated and executed exclusively by Governor Brown's administration.

Initially, the State agencies and personnel were unfamiliar with the systems approach — its potential and limitations, and how to communicate effectively with its practitioners in the defense firms. The few relatively knowledgeable people in the State were apparently all in the Department of Finance or a part of the Governor's staff, and they leaned heavily on the aerospace personnel (a group formalized by establishing the Governor's Advisory Panel on the Aerospace and Electronics Industry) to prepare the initial RFP's. Only in the transportation RFP did the affected agency have any say in its scope and wording (this is why the transportation RFP was different from the other three in that it asked for the design of a study — a task the Division of Highways felt the contractor could realistically perform and which would result in a useful product).

The State appointed ad hoc evaluation panels for each of the study areas to evaluate the 50 proposals received. However, System Development Corporation was hired to assist in the over-all proposal evaluation process and the technical monitoring of the four contracts because the State personnel felt unqualified for these tasks.

Assessment of the four studies — from the customers' standpoint. The four initial California studies certainly achieved the objective of creating local and national publicity — in fact, they stirred international interest. Outside of negative (but not well publicized) criticisms within the professional and academic communities, most of the publicity was favorable. From this standpoint, the studies were successful.

From the standpoint of providing technically sound and politically implementable solutions and recommendations, the studies were less successful. Considering the scope of the problems tackled, and the limited time and money available for each contractor, this was an understandable result.

It is too early to determine how effective the studies were in enabling or hastening hoped-for administrative and organizational reforms within the State government. Prior to the 1966 California gubernatorial elections, indications were that the studies helped and certainly had not impeded this movement.

The recent switch in California administration from Democratic under Governor Brown to Republican under Governor Reagan has introduced so many changes in personnel, policies, and basic administrative philosophy that it is impossible to isolate change resulting primarily from the experiment with the four initial systems studies. Governor Brown had repeatedly spoken of the studies program as a prime example of governmental innovation by his administration. His successor has not yet expressed particular interest in the Brown program, nor in any more generically labeled program of systems studies. However, several defense industry personnel voice confidence that the State of California still represents a good potential market for their civil systems capabilities.

Assessment of the four studies — from the contractors' standpoint. For the four contractors who performed the studies, it is unclear whether the studies were beneficial or not. Each spent far more than $100,000 on the studies (estimates of the out-of-pocket costs to each company vary from $50,000 to $200,000), and, to date, there have been no obviously profitable follow-on studies with which losses could be recouped. But most of the aerospace firms realized and accepted the fact that it might take four to five years before this kind of work became profitable, and that they were generating presumably valuable experience.

Each of the four initial studies recommended follow-on programs to cost at least $1 million a year. To date, none of these follow-on programs have been implemented. In early 1966, Frank Lehan, President of Space-General, was discouraged enough to say, "Perhaps the world is not ready yet for systems engineering." [1] (Space-General later received another sys-

1. Harold D. Watkins, "California Effort is Key to Growth Area; 'Socio-Economic' Aerospace Market — Part 2," *Aviation Week & Space Technology* 84 (February 7, 1966): 79.

tems study contract from California.) Nonetheless, many of the aerospace firms apparently underestimated the problems of developing the market.

Two of the firms (Space-General and Aerojet-General) have received second contracts from the State of California, and neither was a direct follow-on to their earlier work. But all of the four original contractors, plus other defense firms, have expanded their civil sector systems activity, and most are performing work for a variety of state, local, and Federal governments.

Personnel of the systems teams carrying out the studies were mildly disgruntled at the introduction of a third party, System Development Corporation (SDC), to assist the State in monitoring and evaluating the study projects.[2] This was somewhat similar to the defense systems contractors' early complaints about the introduction of separate program management contractors (e.g., Space Technology Laboratory or the Aerospace Corporation) into their relations with the defense customer.

Specific criticisms of the four initial California studies. Some severe early criticism of the studies came from the California State Legislature. Substantial criticism arose in the Legislature because: (1) the Legislature had never been asked to approve the programs; (2) the programs were instituted with no consultation with the Legislature, even though it was in session when the contracts were let; and (3) a substantial amount of the funding for the program came from appropriations passed by the Legislature for specifically different purposes. An outside consultant was employed by the Legislature to do a critical evaluation of the project reports. It seems unlikely that the Legislature was favorably conditioned for its necessary participation in later efforts to implement these programs or to fund others like them.[3]

The most frequently voiced criticisms of the studies themselves encountered during the research reported here included:

- The four reports were sometimes weak in their knowledge of the subject area, as evidenced by incomplete, inadequate, or incorrect data, and incomplete knowledge of the literature and state-of-the-art.
- Some recommendations were politically naive and impractical to implement; the implementation or integration phases were often underemphasized.

2. Elliot Fugate Beideman, "State Sponsorship of the Application of Aerospace Industry Systems Analysis for the Solution of Major Public Problems of California," Ph.D. dissertation for the School of Business Administration, University of Southern California, 1966, pp. 426–435.

3. Much of the information concerning the California studies comes from Beideman, ibid.

- There was too much emphasis on engineering and not enough attention paid to social and institutional aspects.
- The four studies tried to accomplish too much. They should have focused on identifying problem areas amenable to solution and developed viable strategies and research methodologies for tackling these problems, instead of trying to solve the complex problems in the initial study period.
- The contractors failed to adequately identify and analyze a sufficient number of alternative approaches or solutions. At most, the contractors talked about two or three different programs, but these generally represented different levels of funding rather than alternative methods, and they generally devoted most of their analysis and justification to one solution.

Regardless of the merits of these criticisms, they represent the perceptions of many potential customers (or their advisors) at state and Federal levels for civil systems services.

On the positive side, perhaps the two most praised characteristics of the four studies were: (1) the comprehensive scope with which the contractors tackled the problem areas, and (2) the freshness of their thinking and recommendations compared to the more traditional efforts to tackle similar problems.

Administrative developments in California after the four initial studies. Based on the lessons learned during the four initial studies, California took steps to improve its in-house understanding of and ability to deal with systems studies. Some of these include:

1. Establishment of a new civil service classification for operations analysts.
2. Hiring of a defense industry information systems expert to serve as coordinator of the State's systems and data processing activities.
3. Setting up a Governor's Advisory Commission on Ocean Resources to explore in a systematic fashion the State's potential to develop an active ocean resource development program.

As mentioned before, the Brown administration maintained extensive discussion about the systems approach. For example, California had a very active planning effort within the Department of Finance to initiate research projects aimed at identifying and defining key problems and future needs within the State. This extensive planning effort facilitated the awarding of systems contracts in California.

There has been interest in establishing a non-profit policy research organization to apply the systems approach to the State's problems, functioning similarly to the way The RAND Corporation serves the Air Force. State House Speaker Jesse Unruh has been a proponent and spokesman for such a California-RAND concept. In addition, the University of California at Irvine has established an organization called the Public Policy Research Organization whose purpose is to conduct policy research for State and Federal government agencies.

As a result of the $440,000 expenditure by the State for the four initial studies and consulting work by SDC, California has received roughly $1 million in Federal funds to support five additional systems studies. These include:

1. $350,000 for a study of the criminal justice information system needs.
2. $190,000 for a statewide systems study aimed at inventorying and providing planning information relative to solid waste disposal.
3. $175,000 for a solid waste management study in the Fresno area (awarded to Aerojet-General).
4. $220,000 for a land use information study in Santa Clara County (awarded to TRW Systems, Inc.)
5. $225,000 for an examination of the AFDC program in the California social welfare systems (awarded to Space-General Corporation).

Some of this Federal money was used for research performed by State employees, but most went to aerospace firms. In the case of Space-General's welfare study, the State added $55,000.

In addition, the State has inaugurated a program to develop a Statewide Federated Information System (SFIS). While most of this effort is presently being performed by State employees, it has resulted in three small consulting contracts for Lockheed Missiles & Space Company, and offers the promise of additional contracts at a point in time when it becomes feasible to develop and implement the SFIS program.

In recent years the California Department of Water Resources (DWR) has also utilized the services of defense firms. Both Aerojet-General and Philco-Ford have won sizable contracts with DWR to design and produce control systems and control centers for DWR's State Water Project. This highly hardware-oriented control center work has benefited in part from the capabilities these two defense firms developed in designing control systems for the military.

Yet defense firms in California have been faced with difficult problems in keeping civil sector systems teams together and self-supporting. While the State has awarded systems contracts to defense firms since completion of the four initial studies in 1965, the number and dollar volume of contracts awarded has not been as large as the multi-million dollar effort recommended by the original contractors. And the State has chosen to explore subject areas other than the four originally studied. The total level of effort for all subject areas is presently averaging approximately $500,000 a year. Furthermore, there was a gap of roughly a year between the completion of the four initial studies and award of the next systems contract (the welfare study) by the State.

Most of the firms have actively attempted to generate work with other states and with various Federal agencies, as well as with private organizations. This has meant establishing new contacts, opening up new lines of communication, and going through another joint educational process between civil servants in other states and Federal agencies and the defense firm personnel. The firms have found this a rather long, drawn out process.

It has become apparent that completion of one study does not automatically lead to follow-on work with either the same government agency or agencies in other states. None of the original four contractors was able to establish a clear advantage in any growing, specialized field as a result of its earlier work.

The Subsequent Civil Sector Systems Experience

Presently (April 1967), the uncertain nature of the civil sector market for systems work makes it difficult to identify meaningful patterns or trends for either defense firms or their non-defense competitors.

The defense and aerospace firms. Because of the uncertainty of the market, most of the large firms appear to be exploring many civil sector areas simultaneously. For example, Lockheed Missiles & Space Company is applying its systems capabilities in three broad civil sector areas: government information systems, medical information systems, and education information systems.

Besides their information systems work for California, Lockheed has small contracts with Alaska and Massachusetts. In the medical area, 16 Lockheed engineers are working with personnel of the Mayo Clinic in Rochester, Minnesota, in the design and development of an over-all medical services system. They are also developing information systems for blood banks in Sacramento and Los Angeles, have a disaster casualty management information program in progress with a Texas hospital association, and are developing information systems for small community hospitals. This same group of roughly 30 people in Lockheed also recently bid on a criminal justice information system about to be awarded by California.

Lockheed is also interested in systems work in other areas. The firm has an $88,000 contract from the U.S. Office of Education in connection with a regional education technology laboratory. One sizable operation within Lockheed which has some relevance to civil sector areas is their oceanology program, much of which is connected with military oceanology. In addition, Lockheed International performed a 32-month systems study of the transportation needs in the Sudan in a contract sponsored by the Agency for International Development.

Most of the other large aerospace firms show a similar diversity of subject areas being tackled in the civil sector.

Aerojet-General has performed on contracts dealing with waste management, the development of an aqueduct control model, and a management information system for community action programs. In addition, the Industrial Systems Division of Aerojet-General has had several contracts for multi-million dollar sack and parcel sorters and mail handling systems for the U.S. Post Office. Space-General Corporation, an Aerojet subsidiary, is involved in a systems analysis of the welfare program in the State of California, and earlier performed the initial crime and delinquency study for that state.

TRW Systems, Inc. currently has civil sector work under way in areas of high speed ground transportation, land use information systems, and medical services. In the medical area, TRW has a $650,000 contract for a 9–12 month study of consulting services to assist in the planning of an $88 million Health Sciences Center in Edmonton, Alberta. The work involves logistical and communications planning to promote efficient flows of information, people, and material within the center. A smaller planning study is being done for a regional medical information system in Vermont. In the transportation field, TRW received a $2.9 million contract for systems engineering from the Office of High Speed Ground Transportation, U.S. Department of Commerce, which will involve analysis of methods proposed to move masses of people and materials from city to city. The firm is also doing the Santa Clara County, California, Land Use Information study mentioned earlier.

United Aircraft Corporation (UAC) is working in the area of high speed ground transportation. Their high speed passenger train was designed and engineered in UAC's Corporate Systems Center. The trains are being built by the Pullman Company and (in Canada) by the Montreal Locomotive Works. They embody turbines from Pratt & Whitney and air conditioning by Hamilton Standard, both divisions of United Aircraft. Other subcontractors are drawn from non-defense industry. Two trains are being leased to the U.S. Department of Commerce for $2 million, and the Canadian National Railways system is taking two larger trains on a lease-purchase arrangement which railroad officials have hinted is in the $5–10 million range. The present turbine train program is the culmination of research, development, and marketing efforts dating back to the early 1960's, first carried out by the Turbo-Power and Marine Department of UAC's Pratt & Whitney Division.

A contract for design and development of a passenger and automobile carrying train by UAC for the U.S. Department of Transportation was announced April 28, 1967. UAC's Hamilton Standard Division has applied a systems approach to designing a proposed organ implant program for the Department of Health, Education and Welfare.

Diversity or specialization? Most of the aerospace and defense firms are involved in a variety of subject areas, and are dealing with a mixture of state and Federal agencies in their civil sector systems work. At this point, it is unclear whether particular companies will focus on one or more general subject areas, and, if so, which companies will capture which area. Based on past experience with military systems, it seems likely that no one firm will long maintain a competitive advantage in any one area. Because of the high mobility of systems talent within defense industry, it seems possible that, at least for the next five or ten years, there will be a continuing competitive struggle for many areas of civil systems work, with few individual firms achieving ascendency in particular areas.

Some major problems facing civil systems contractors. One of the difficulties in doing systems work in the civil sector comes from multiple agency jurisdiction. This is a problem in market development, and the diffusion of authority also makes reporting and implementation difficult. The first problem can be illustrated by the experience of one defense firm which attempted, in the middle 1960's, to conduct systems work in the area of water resource management. The firm experienced great difficulty in convincing the many customers involved of the utility of a system-wide study. It was extremely difficult to get organizations such as the Bureau of Reclamation, Bureau of Land Management, Corps of Engineers, Soil Conservation Service, power agencies, and the U.S. Geological Survey all together to agree on the need for a joint systems effort. In fact, it was impossible.

In the end, the firm tried to sell each individual agency on the idea of conducting one small portion of the total systems study. Yet this was inefficient and not the most desirable strategy to follow. This kind of problem, resulting from multi-agency jurisdiction, occurs in many other

441

civil sector areas, and must be faced realistically by both customer and potential contractor.

Another problem occurs in identifying the audiences to whom study results must be addressed. For example, an aerospace firm executive who headed one of the four initial California studies said he felt constrained to address five different audiences: (1) the technical person within the affected State administrative agency; (2) the political type within the States; (3) the professional public relations individual working for the State administration; (4) the professional technical people outside the State agencies in universities, industries, etc.; and (5) the management and professional people within the aerospace firm itself.

This problem of identifying and determining how most effectively to address each audience is much more severe in the civil sector than it is in the military environment. The hierarchical and authoritarian structure, as well as the often classified nature of military systems contracts, precludes much public debate and minimizes the number and variety of audiences for the report. Yet, almost all civil systems work must be responsive to many sets of requirements and many audiences — a problem which constitutes much of the so-called communications gap between defense systems people and civil servants.

Not only must the aerospace firms' marketing efforts be addressed to several levels, but often the decision to go ahead with a systems contract must come from both executive and legislative branches and, frequently, the people themselves through an election. Similarly, the systems contractor must explain the findings of his study to many levels and types of people within the civil sector, and must convince each of the need to implement recommendations.

The civil systems experience described in this chapter is current. Most of the projects have not been completed, much less evaluated.

The projects are extremely varied, representing diverse points on a scale ranging from system to subsystem. They each embody different mixtures of management systems (to assist decision-making) and response systems (to carry out decisions or programs). The United Aircraft turbine train is a major subsystem for a transportation system, and would be considered a response system. The medical information systems (and most other information systems) are obviously on the management side.

Most of the projects are small, particularly if compared with typical defense projects. However, they are generating experience in marketing, and executing systems work in new market and subject areas. They are more or less tentative efforts at diversification. None of them demonstrate the feasibility of overnight conversion from effective large-scale defense and space systems work to effective large-scale civil systems projects (excluding space projects).

The experience thus far suggests that this diversification faces many obstacles — but that it is possible.

IDA R. HOOS

Systems Experts: Foxes in the Henhouse

An era characterized by bigness — big budgets, big business, big government, big explosions — of population, information, and technology — provides an environment hospitable to the growth and development of the big, total approach. Such is systems analysis, with its components and companions, cost/effectiveness measures and program planning/budgeting. These methods, utilized and refined in military and space missions, have gained favor for the apparent tidiness with which they have achieved management marvels. For this and other reasons to be mentioned later, systems analysis has come to be accepted as a nostrum for all manner of social ailments, and the market for socio-economic systems is booming. At present receiving one dollar out of every five in the U.S. Budget, socio-economic programs, by 1975, will acount for one or perhaps two out of every four dollars. With the federal investment in urban renewal for 1968–78 amounting to $250 billion, predictions that the market for urban civil systems will reach somewhere between $210 and $298 billion by 1980 may prove accurate.[1]

The prospect of so bountiful a market is enticing, and prospectors of

From Ida R. Hoos, "A Realistic Look at the Systems Approach to Social Problems," *Datamation* 15 (February 1969): 223–228. Reprinted with permission from *Datamation®*, February, copyrighted 1969 by F. D. Thompson Publications, Inc., 35 Mason Street, Greenwich, Conn. 06830.

Mrs. Hoos is a staff member of the Space Sciences Laboratory, Social Science Project, at the University of California, Berkeley.

1. *Finance Magazine,* January 1968. Staff, V-P Marketing, North American Aviation, *The Economic Business Spectrum as Related to National Goals — Identification of New Business Opportunities,* 1967.

remarkable diversity as to discipline, background, and competence are converging on it. There are aerospace and aviation firms, computer manufacturers and their multifarious subsidiaries, electronics companies, management consultants, appliance makers, directory publishers, and university-based entrepreneurs. Prominent among the contenders for contracts are the non-profit but highly profitable "think tanks," with their in-house experts and on-tap consultants and their proliferating satellites with unpronounceable acronyms. They are all competing energetically to bring what journalists enthusiastically hail as "the powerful tools of technology" to bear on matters concerning the commonweal.

The forensic is familiar: A nation that can send men to the moon should be capable of closer-to-home accomplishments. All we need to do is to apply our scientific know-how to the analysis and solution of social problems with the same creativity we have applied to space problems.[2] This type of argument is persuasive on several counts: first, the prestigious origin and logical, scientific aura of systems analysis, and second, the growing recognition of the need for better planning, organization, and management of social affairs. A brief review of the genealogy and current conception of the systems approach will adequately illustrate the first point. Charles J. Hitch, whose imprint on this methodology is so great that it is sometimes called "Hitchcraft," described systems analysis as a direct lineal descendant of World War II operations research.[3] O.R. was used to solve tactical and strategic problems of a military nature; systems analysis uses the same principles but has wider range and scope. It encompasses (1) a more distant future environment, (2) more interdependent variables, (3) greater uncertainties, (4) less obvious objectives and rules of choice.[4] Impressive as to historical background, systems analysis, with its heavy reliance on models and mathematical computations and manipulations, has special appeal in an era characterized by a universal craving for certainty and orderliness.

This yearning underlies the present impatience with traditional approaches. Juxtaposing the duplication, confusion, and disarray of current public administration with the rationality and neatness of program management to be realized from application of the "revolutionary concepts," proponents of systems analysis make a strong case for their wares.

2. Statement by Senator Gaylord P. Nelson, *Congressional Record.* Proceedings and Debates of the 89th Congress, First Session, Oct. 18, 1965, No. 194.

3. Charles J. Hitch, Royal Society Nuffield Lecture, London, Oct. 25, 1966.

4. This comparison was made by Albert Wohlstetter in "Scientists, Seers, and Strategy," Columbia University, Council for Atomic Age Studies, 1962, pp. 36-7 (unpublished paper).

And there is no gainsaying the fact that social problems beset us: urban blight deepens and spreads; pollution of air, water, and land proceed at an awesome pace; crime rates soar; arteries and facilities for air and ground travel are dangerously clogged. In one way or another, these problems ultimately become the business of government, already regarded by many as too big to be potent and too trapped in a bureaucratic maze to respond effectively.

Since 1964, when the state of California pioneered by hiring aerospace engineers to help solve problems of public concern through systems analysis, many public officials, from county to Congress, have chosen the same vehicle on the high road to grants and contracts.

Can we assume from the vast expenditure of public funds and mobilization of motley systems experts that we will now witness a diminution of the inefficiency, ineptness, and uncertainty that plague planners of public programs? The question deserves serious consideration, for there are signs that the incoming administration in Washington will be especially receptive to further involvement of the private sector in public affairs. Its managerial techniques will be given full play. We may find it useful, therefore, to note the factors surrounding the adoption of systems analysis in the social arena. Four are especially important: historical antecedents and scientific attributes, already mentioned briefly, and political and economic circumstances. Because of the admirable escutcheon derived from its association with defense and space achievements, systems analysis has enjoyed almost total immunity from the critical evaluation to which some other methodology might have been subjected. And yet, to judge from recent discussion,[5] the DOD model may not be optimal for military, let alone other kinds of decisions. Government officials struggling with program budgeting as decreed by President Johnson are learning, the hard way, that the circumstances governing and the criteria for judging effectiveness in the DOD resemble not remotely those prevailing in matters for social accounting.

Since, however, the same assumptions, rules, and courses of action that appeared so logical and scientific in their earlier context are being transplanted bodily, they deserve scrutiny. First and foremost, there is the assumption that because the word *system* can be used for everything from atomic weapons delivery to anthropotomy, the same analytic tools can aid in understanding all of them and the same type of remedies can be

---

5. James R. Schlesinger, *Systems Analysis and the Political Process*, RAND Paper P-3464, June, 1967, pp. 14 ff. See also Hearings before the Committee on Foreign Relations, U.S. Senate, 90th Congress, Second Session, Part 2, May 28, 1968.

applied to their malfunctioning. There is the related assumption that since large scale, complex systems have been "managed" by use of certain techniques, then social systems, which are often large and always complex, can be "managed" in like fashion. This presupposes similarity of structure, with social systems reducible to measurable, controllable components, all of whose relationships are fully recognized, appreciated, and amenable to manipulation. To the extent that these are fallacies, they must be attributed to semantic impoverishment. Moreover, the very characteristics which distinguish social from other species of systems render them resistant to treatment that tries to force them into analytically tractable shape:

1. They defy definition as to objective, philosophy, and scope. For example, what kind of definition of a welfare system can be regarded as valid — that which encompasses the shortcomings of *other* systems, such as health, education, employment, or the one which focuses on individual inadequacy? A definition depends on the point of view and the ideological posture. The system looks very different to the administrator, the recipient, the black power-monger, the social critic, and the politician.

2. "Solution" of social problems is never achieved. You do not "solve" the problems of health or transportation. Consequently, where you start and where you stop is purely arbitrary, usually a reflection of the amount of money the government has to fund the particular analysis.

3. Despite the semblance of precision, there are no right or wrong, true or false solutions. Consequently, it is presumptuous to label as *wrong* anything being done now and *right* that which looks good on paper. By concentrating on minuscule portions or isolated variables simply because they are quantifiable, the technique may actually lead to results which are irrelevant and inappropriate. Assignment of social costs and social benefits is an arbitrary matter, and even dollar cost/benefit comparison is a matter of interpretation. There are no ground rules for identifying the Peter being robbed and the Paul getting paid. It should here be noted that anyone can join the popular sport of knocking bureaucracy; playing utopian games is easy.

Corollary to the assumption that systems analysis can improve the state of the art of public program planning is the notion that the "systems expert" is a past master of advanced concepts on all fronts. He often ascribes to himself a clairvoyance denied specialists in the subject area, for, with the greatest of ease, he hurdles 1984 and designs year 2000 plans. As though by his own original discovery, he brands present practices as fragmentary and duplicatory. This situation he corrects by an unfurling of flip charts, a dubbing of labels in blank boxes, and an affixing of arrows on the flow diagrams. He deplores the lack of information and proposes a data bank to capture every last bit. After an exercise in present-day serendipity now known as "playing around with some models" and a series of optimistically called "progress reports," time and money will have run out. The air may be no safer to breathe, urban ills no less crucial, but conclusions and recommendations, like campaign speeches, will ring with truisms and promises: (1) Present planning is wasteful and ineffective; (2) the prescribed course of action is more systems studies which will harness huge reservoirs of talent and put to use the "powerful tools of technology" and produce knowledge and understanding. Anyone who has reviewed systems reports cannot fail to recognize the pervasiveness of the "Perils of Pauline" feature, which may be intrinsic to the nature of the technique.

This hard look has fallen on the technicians as much as the technique and necessarily so, for the two are inextricably intertwined. What the analyst conceives as the system is reflected in its definition, its objectives, its interfaces, its significant variables, its relevant data. The methodology of systems analysis supplies the form; the analyst, the content. The inputs which he selects become determinative. That he chooses to omit certain phenomena because of his own bias or because they resist quantitative treatment may be far more crucial to society than his model, but neither the technique nor the technician has use for them. It is precisely because of the centrality of his role that the analyst should possess a deep and sensitive understanding of the social matter with which he is engaged. Unfortunately, this is seldom the case. On the contrary, "expertness" is an ad hoc affair, with titles bestowed to suit the contract in hand. The casting of characters reminds one rather uncomfortably of the Puritan who marched around the fort in a succession of hats to fool the Indians. Lacking in orientation and without an appropriate frame of reference, such an analyst substitutes ignorance for objectivity and banal generalization for total system comprehension.

If anyone is surprised at the discovery that the emperor, for all his multi-million-dollar wardrobe, goes naked, that may well be because oversell dominates every stage of the system analysis, from proposal to final report. The "expert" appears in many forms — as undersecretary of a government agency, as think tanker, as advisor to contracting agencies — but always as a salesman in disguise. He testifies at Congressional hearings; he delivers keynote addresses at meetings of all kinds of professional groups. His presence at the latter is strictly that of the fox in the henhouse, for he invariably predicts growing complexity ahead and promulgates the notion that nothing short of the powerful tools of his technology will suffice to handle the problems. He may occasionally offer the modest disclaimer that systems analysis cannot solve every problem, but he earnestly implores his listeners not to throw out the baby with the bathwater, or the egg with the eggshells. The rules of his game are simple: one for the money, two for the show. The name of the game is self-perpetuation, the stakes are high, for systems business is booming, here and abroad.[6]

Economic considerations on the part of all participants keep the game going. The prosperous and growing community of problem solvers is apparently more concerned with obtaining more contracts than with improving the state of the art or of the nation. There is a serious dearth, among practitioners, of critical evaluation. Apparently, no one with sufficient claim to systems expertness to preach or practice the technique would be so rash as to shoot down the goose that lays the eggs, especially when they are golden! The moral problem of the profession as expressed by C. West Churchman[7] has been delicately sidestepped in pursuit of the objective not to do better, but to do more. The political arena in which the game is played discourages rigorous review, since large sums of public money are involved. In their expenditure, everyone must look good. No official is so possessed of the death wish as to admit that the venture was anything but successful. Consequently, every aspect of the transaction, quite irrespective of its true color, comes through tinted with a glow of success.

The mixture of salesmanship and politics may, ultimately, undermine the state of the art, for short-run, pervasive zeal for self-perpetuation practically guarantees stagnation. With little benefit of feedback from earlier experience, the same level of sophistication remains, with the same shortcomings, the same deficiencies, the same old excuses. Conceptual and methodological mutations are needed in order to create a tool useful in social planning, but these cannot occur unless there are open channels of inquiry and assessment free from public relations embellishments.

Such evaluations are not the private preserve of any one professor or any particular discipline. Nor need they be considered the bailiwick of any one sector. There is an important role in the process of social account-

6. Daniel S. Greenberg, "Consulting: U.S. Firms Thrive on Jobs for European Clients," *Science* 162 (Nov. 21, 1968): 986–7.

7. C. West Churchman, "Wicked Problems," *Management Science*, vol. 14, no. 4 (December, 1967), pp. B-141-2.

ing and planning to be played by professional persons, whether in the employ of government, industry, universities, or elsewhere. In every system study, the close and constant involvement of individuals expert in the relevant disciplines is absolutely essential. Every major problem facing urban society today is multifaceted in nature. Economic, political, and social rationality must all contribute to developing a viable model, for human and social values are at stake as old problem areas are subjected to new modes of treatment. Understanding calls for knowledge on many fronts. Highly desirable, indeed, would be a creative synthesis achieved through a genuine multidisciplined approach. It is interesting to speculate on the extent to which systems analysis will be the means to an end of such a synthesis.

WILLIAM H. MITCHEL

The Cities Can't Pay for Aerospace Work

The engraved invitation announced the presentation of an "Urban Systems Workshop." The RSVP and "by invitation only" suggested that the series of programmed sessions were to be only for the privileged and relevant. The host was McDonnell Douglas and within *that* complex, the Information Technology Department of its Information Systems Subdivision. The well-ordered agenda indicated it was to be an all day affair attended by academicians and practitioners involved in and beneficiaries of information processing technology. About 200 people from universities, colleges, and cities found both the interest in and the time for the workshop to attend. The proposed undertaking was performed as planned and on schedule. The presentation site was the M-D Advanced Research Laboratory and the mini-skirts of the registration clerks really couldn't be much more advanced. Lunch was on the house and a tour of the Space Systems Center facilities at Huntington Beach followed.

The purpose of the workshop was not so clearly defined. The program included academicians deeply engaged in the study of urban data processing and information systems, both as total systems and as functioning subsystems. Dr. B. G. Schumacher and Dr. William Mitchel played the

From William H. Mitchel, "Aerospace Technology and Urban Systems," *Datamation* 14 (April 1968): 85–90. Reprinted with permission from *Datamation®*, April, published and copyrighted 1968 by F. D. Thompson Publications, Inc., 35 Mason Street, Greenwich, Conn. 06830.

Mr. Mitchel is Deputy Assistant Secretary for Management Systems, United States Department of Health, Education and Welfare.

general systems theme. Dr. Paul Whisenand of Long Beach State discussed the functional area of automated police information systems.

. The practitioner's viewpoint was well carried by D. Riesau, Los Angeles Sheriff's Office (court and law enforcement); J. P. Mumau, communications engineers, City of Los Angeles (command and control functions in fire prevention and suppression); R. E. Kirten, FBI (National Crime and Information Center); and R. A. Oman, finance director of Costa Mesa (municipal integrated data processing).

The urban systems beneficiary point of view was presented by N. Goedhard of Covina (the San Gabriel Valley Joint Powers, a time-shared municipal data system). The private sector got its innings with Dr. M. W. Ladato, manager of Information Technology for McDonnell-Douglas (systems analysis and its applicability to municipal systems problems); G. E. Cash, branch manager, Planning Technology of M-D (data organizing and structuring applications in municipal and urban information systems); and V. Azgapetian, director of M-D Information Sciences (panel review and conclusions).

Behind the agenda and the schedule of presentations there also appeared to be a hidden agenda of equal if not greater significance. S. C. Perry, v.p. for McDonnell-Douglas Information Systems, in his welcoming address provided the framework for the agenda, and Dr. Ladato, in his role of moderator, added the detail. Basically, this second agenda related to the recent exhortations of the Federal Government for aerospace industry help to solve the problems of our urban society and its governing cities through use of their know-how in systems analysis and information technology. It would appear that the M-D people in St. Louis had already been investigating this field of possible expansion. Dr. Schumacher, for example, was listed on the agenda as a consultant to the McDonnell Automation Corporation although he finds acadamic status as a professor of political science at the Univ. of Missouri, as director of their Urban Studies group, and as a specialist in public administration and related computer dynamics. The Douglas Information Systems people at Huntington Beach, encouraged perhaps by McDonnell-St. Louis people, were taking the Federal suggestion at its face: what were the informational problems of an urban society and its governments? What particular skills, know-how, and capability in information processing which have grown out of the aerospace efforts were, or could be made, applicable to the urban sector? More germane perhaps, the Douglas people were asking what areas of the urban picture appear to have an exploitation potential for new business and a promise of future profitability? Answers or insights to these questions constituted the carrots for the host and formed the basis of his hidden agenda.

The presentations by the speakers of the workshop and the discussion which they engendered served well the purposes of the host and equally well the invited guests with their program expectations. The total performance provided an excellent over-view of what is happening in the urban information systems field. It also covered most of the major problem areas.

The Problems

Certainly these relevant points were made:

1. Relatively little research, by aerospace standards, on general urban systems or their informational component is occurring. Most of the research which does exist with reference to the urban environment and its governments is either woefully under-financed and/or concentrated in limited functional areas such as law enforcement, fire, or urban planning. USC's broadly construed municipal systems research project is an apparent exception. Its findings were outlined for the group. This half-million dollar effort was reported having completed work on the development of a conceptual structure to guide urban municipalities in the use of the computer and the design of an automated information system which will serve the data processing needs both for operations and planning and analysis. Termination of the research project due to lack of interest in moving the project from a conceptual effort into a development and test phase was also noted. The $3 million price tag on such an effort may have represented a relatively small venture in the aerospace world, but was of overwhelming proportions to the urban problems people who control where the available funds will go.

2. The viability of urban governments rests to a considerable degree on their ability to develop the necessary framework of computer applications and to effect the organizational changes which such an acceptance of information systems technology requires. Dr. Schumacher expressed it succinctly and strongly as a caveat to the cities: "automate or die."

3. The social problems of a city are reflective of and interactive with the economic function and posture of the city. Public administration in the average city has not internalized the perspectives and values of computer-driven information technology or the rationalizing mechanisms of systems analysis for problem solving. V. P. Perry suggested that the situation was one of the need to join the "problem havers" with the "problem

453

solvers." Systems analysis, "a way to structure a problem rationally," is still in the ad hoc stages for urban governments with a known evolution yet to come from preventive systems to predictive systems. Compared to aerospace managerial criteria, local governments have a long, long way to go and not much time to do it in.

4. The informational base required for the administrative cycle (plan, operate, and evaluate) and its research cycle interface (basic research, development, and test application), which characterizes the aerospace effort, does not exist for the cities. The contrast in information handling capability was starkly reflected in Dr. Schumacher's inventory of McDonnell Automation's stall of computers: 50 third-generation computers — perhaps as much capacity as the total for all municipal government installations in the United States! The critical issue here, however, was left unarticulated by the conference members. This is whether the conclusion to be reached by this contrast is that of having our nation of cities turn to such computer institutions for their systems and computational capability and know-how or to generate an equal capability within the framework of local government. It would appear that in the event of a cessation of hostilities this question may become one of major importance to both the current major users and manufacturers of computers and the cities that presumably will have the resources and needs for such capability. At this stage it isn't clear who is Mohammed and who is the mountain.

5. There exist throughout the nation, islands of commendable, if not inspirational, effort on the part of cities to improve their level of institutional capability through use of computers. Most of this work rests in the functional areas (police, finance, planning, etc.), and is relatively uncoordinated (how many times do we have to "invent" a municipal payroll application?), under-financed, and characterized by an almost total unconcern on the part of federal agencies (HUD is no exception) for use of the computer, automated information processing techniques, and systems analysis to upgrade the urban city as a single, integrated unit of general government.

6. Viewed from the perspective of where the average city stands in the use of computers, some very interesting applications are developing. An example is the San Gabriel Valley proposal which includes a single, central computer facility with remote inputs to serve a series of small cities. Financing, however, is still unresolved. The Los Angeles fire command-control system is another example of local effort. However, when these projects are contrasted to the sophistication level achieved by the space

people, it is no surprise that we can make probes into space but can't get city garbage off of front porches. The data processing sophistication levels are so far apart as to raise a serious question about the utility of the aerospace industry in urban systems without first an orientation program to develop mutual understanding, if not sympathy. This contrast was strikingly evident in the perceptions of potential systems and computer projects suggested for the urban society by the M-D people: the use of infrared techniques, automation of all routine decisions, integrated and computer-directed traffic control, systems analysis for social disorders, etc. In contrast, the urban government people were concerned with getting a computer-driven accounting subsystem to provide current, unexpended balances and timely payrolls. The sociologist may talk about a nation split into two racial parts. But in the aerospace and urban government activities, we also have two worlds separated by values, infrastructure, language, skills, and economic resources. The common denominator for our two sets of split worlds may well be the same: the haves and the have nots.

7. Finally, there was evidence throughout each presentation and its subsequent discussion, that the critical element in any aerospace information systems contribution to urban problems would be the financial resources available to fund their efforts. The magnitude of funds which have been available for space research and development in information systems have no equivalent or promise in the urban environment or Federal budgets. Information systems work is costly and capability is slowly developed from resources, vision, and the encouragement of relative advantage. Computer hardware and software have not been characterized by bargain basement prices. Yet any private corporation contemplating the investment of risk capital in urban problems must evaluate the potential profitability of other choices available to it. Exhortations to bring the skills and problem solving techniques of the aerospace industry to our urban environment and governments will remain just that: exhortations, unless there is more reassuring evidence that such an emphasis can be rewarding to the relevant corporations. The urban cupboard unfortunately is bare. Exit aerospace.

THOMAS M. CONRAD

Systems Analysis and the Liberal Establishment

U.S. society, and to a growing extent, Soviet society — the two post-modern societies in the world today — are beset with a disastrous separation between value and analysis, meaning and means. We have a growing group of technocratic "experts" whose personalities are so warped as to make them very effective at devising methods for accomplishing given results, but almost totally illiterate concerning basic values; and we have, in reaction, a growing group of "obstructionists" who cultivate an exquisite moral sensitivity together with an almost total ignorance and disdain for methods of realizing values in practice.

The "experts," the "professionals," concentrate upon the factual ignorance of their opponents and offer that ignorance as a reason for rule by elites, while the "obstructionists" play their own games of personal purity on the basis of a "demonic principle": that only the morally vicious can rule, and conversely, that political victory is evidence of moral impurity.

In the case of the high-technology corporations, we have a particularly clear example of the general problem of tools in search of a problem. Having built up a whole social subsystem for the military defense of the society, we must now worry about the ramifications of not simply a *reduction* in demand for its original functions, but even a *leveling-off* of demand, ramifications which go much further than narrow "economic"

From Thomas M. Conrad, "Systems Analysis, the Liberal Establishment, and Totalitarian Dystopias," *Commonweal* 90 (May 30, 1969): 321–323. Copyright © 1969 by Commonweal Publishing Co., Inc.

Mr. Conrad is a physicist and political scientist specializing in defense analysis.

considerations. Bluntly put, we have several million workers whose skills are not really relevant to the kinds of productive activities involved in consumer goods, where cost is not secondary to performance; these workers are used to an unusually high standard of living; and they are not likely to be emotionally prepared — by desperation and years of attacks on self-image and status, like the chronically poor — to be displaced and forced to undergo job retraining and loss of income and status. Even aside from the large investors in the high-technology industries, the technical workers themselves have major potential political muscle; they are quite formidable enough to force the rest of the society to provide income and status supports to offset any potential losses due to a stagnation of military and space projects.

With these considerations in mind, we can already see reasons for viewing arguments like Dr. Ramo's[1] with some cynicism. Given the economic and political pressures to "make-work" in systems syntheses, for domestic programs in lieu of continued growth in military programs, it would be naive to assume that the only, or even the primary, criterion for use of systems analysis in domestic programs would be its demonstrable utility. In fact, many of the proposed deflections of expertise into domestic programs so far suggested seem precisely wrong. It is an article of faith, for example, that the right kind of planning and action, with suitable amounts of investment, can rescue the major cities. Let us ask a naive question: are the cities worth "saving," in the sense of salvation likely to emerge from current assumptions of planning? There is massive evidence that even the most sophisticated systems approach to the cities merely extends, for a short period, the viability of urban systems which are basically headed for collapse, and that further investments will very soon reach drastically diminishing returns.

A really free systems analysis does something which Dr. Ramo, quite shockingly, does not go into in his little "primer" for laymen: it asks whether the initial goals of the project make sense. What Ramo is describing in his book is not really systems analysis; it is operations research. The difference is not academic, and in consideration of the likely motivation for writing this book, it is of central political interest: operations research, unlike systems analysis, takes the basic goals as *given,* given by the sponsor of the project. In a case such as that of the cities, the first step in a systems analysis is to challenge the idea that we need great cities at all in the historical definition, given on the one hand the technical changes which have rendered most of the positive functions of large

1. Simon Ramo, *Cure for Chaos* (New York: McKay, 1969).

population concentrations obsolete, and given on the other hand the technical changes which have made such concentrations increasingly dangerous to life and otherwise damaging.

Another example: much is made of the possibility of a new high-speed transportation system in the Boston-Washington strip. What for? I have seen virtually no interest in the amount of time wasted by executives in jet-set meetings; no study of the physiological and psychological damage produced by such constant meeting-hopping, and the cost in lives and ulcers to key personnel. Why is there not more interest in an alternative in which fancier electronic communications (say, closed circuit TV conference lines, with coding for security) would replace travel? After all, since our ancestors began visiting each other two million years ago, the method has always been to physically travel to a meeting place; this seems a little primitive, given the presently available alternatives. It is, in fact, an illustration of one of the very common features of "social technology" as it has been touted in the past few years: extraordinarily expensive, complex, humanly-stressing "solutions" to the problem of maintaining peculiarly favored historical habits or atavisms; means of maintaining some past patterns of behavior at the expense of extreme distortion of others. It is natural to expect humans facing frightening social and technical change to cling to some continuities with the past; the anomaly lies in the genius of our society to choose, almost unerringly, all the most destructive remnants to cling to, while embracing — out of the alternatives which open up — those new technologies and other changes which will exact the most wrenching of human scale and personality for a given benefit.

Systems analysis, at the service of the Liberal Establishment, can be a powerful tool for the construction of closed systems of social control: systems analysis, unlike the sciences which developed in the past, *is* really capable, in principle, of drawing together the factors necessary to create totalitarian dystopias. So far, however, the Establishment's mass irrationalism and self-deceit have blocked the realization of this potential; systems analysis, with a few exceptions, has been used by the Establishment to carry out their propensity for the exhaustive and compulsive answering of the wrong questions, in a way more technical than the usual.

There is nothing inherent in systems analysis which makes it useful only for elitists or totalitarians. To the contrary, there are basic intellectual and ethical strains in systems analysis which are of vital usefulness to radical social critics. There is the questioning of basic goals, and the demand that instrumental values be derived from final values and from an understanding of the world, through empirical reason rather than received dogma from the past: this orientation toward the synthesis of value and analysis is in the radical tradition, and can also be understood as having common features with what is recently called situation ethics or the ethics of specific consequences.

There is also a demand in systems analysis for understanding the world, and Man in it, in terms of interdependences rather than in the atomistic views of the past. This search for higher-level coherences is an obvious echo of the drive toward personal integration of all the human possibilities which makes up such a large part of radical thought and action today; and the attempt to see a society as "a system" constitutes a major part of the young radical movement today. So far, the attempts of the New Left to understand the possibilities of a post-modern society have not been very successful; but these attempts at understanding and guiding social change, while they may be *poor* (ignorant, oversimplified) systems analyses of U.S. society, are nevertheless quite perfect examples of the essential features of systems analyses.

Radical critics of the Establishment's "business as usual" need every modern weapon if they are to head off disaster; and the most basic weapon is relevant knowledge, including the kinds of broad knowledge involved in systems analysis. Aside from the direct uses of knowledge for radicals, it is of the utmost importance for the emotional support of radical dissenters that they have solid, detailed reasons for refuting, in their own minds and for the benefit of others, the liberal charges that the radicals have become historically irrelevant Luddites. The only adequate refutation of the "Luddite — obstructionist — romanticist" argument, and the only refutation which offers positive political opportunities for radicals aside from "debating points," requires personal knowledge and competence, and the self-discipline and integrity to seek and use them: the knowledge and competence which will permit radicals to compete equally with the "professionals" of the Establishment on matters of technique while surpassing them on matters of values and vision.

Bibliography

Index

Bibliography

This bibliography presents a selection of important and representative items and has been organized to follow the main themes of *Information Technology in a Democracy*. Part I collects references on the "Routes to the New Information Technology," with Section A focusing on "Databanks" and Section B on "Management Science Techniques" (organized under two headings: Programming-Planning-Budgeting, and Systems Analysis and Operations Research). Part II contains items on "Information Techniques and Decision-Making." Broad ideological discussions of computerized information systems and management science methods are listed together in Part II.

Following the rapidly changing field of information technology requires an analyst to pay more than ordinary attention to the periodical literature, as well as to the papers delivered at professional conferences in a wide spectrum of fields. For this reason, an overview of these areas may be of help to the reader.

Much of the literature is highly technical, but relevant articles on developments in information systems appear regularly in *Datamation, Computerworld, Computers and Automation, Data Processing Magazine, Information Week,* and *Data Systems News.* The *Annual Review of Information Science and Technology,* published by Interscience Publishers, a division of John Wiley and Sons, in collaboration with the American Documentation Institute, is a useful summary of yearly developments in the field. Also valuable to indicate current thinking by information system specialists are the proceedings of the annual meetings of such key organizations as the Institute of Electrical Engineers and the International Federation for Documentation, which are issued in book form by those organizations.

The literature of public administration has paid increasing attention to information technology in recent years. Of special value are *Public Administration Review, Public Automation, Public Management, Computers and Management, Planning,* and the *Journal of the American Institute of Planners.* Paralleling this is the periodical literature specializing in state and local government. Here, useful publications are *City, Nation's Cities, State Government, Urban Research News,* and *Urban Affairs Quarterly.* In various subject-areas of government, key periodicals have begun to give increasing attention to information technology developments. For example, in law enforcement and criminal justice, *Police* and *Law and Order* regularly contain articles on information technology. In education, the Association for Educational Data Systems' *Journal* and *Monitor* are essential. Similar attention should be given to periodicals for health, welfare, public finance, housing, fire and sanitation, and the like.

Helpful periodicals on the subject of technology itself include *Science and Technology, Technology and Culture, Technology Review,* and *Technology and Society. Scientific American* and *Science* are also important. Several "house organs" by leading computer manufacturers or systems consultants contain a flow of important articles, not only by organizational spokesmen but often by invited experts; see, for example, the IBM magazine, *Think,* and the magazine of System Development Corporation, *SDC News.* Lists of major firms in the hardware and software fields are compiled and published by *Computers and Automation,* and writing directly to some of these companies for brochures on their "Public Systems" activities will supply important coverage of trends. Among scholarly journals, articles of importance appear from time to time in various magazines of the social and behavioral sciences, but the *American Behavioral Scientist, The Public Interest,* and the *Harvard Business Review* deserve special attention for the frequency and quality of their discussion of information technology developments.

Finally, the annual meetings of groups such as the Association for Computing Machinery, Institute for Electrical Engineers, American Society for Information Science, American Society for Public Administration, Association for Educational Data Systems, American Association for the Advancement of Science, the Fall and Spring Joint Computer Conferences, and American Orthopsychiatric Association provide both leading commentaries and early reports of specific developments. Examples of special conferences that are of continuing value are the Annual Conference on ADP Systems in Local Government, held by New York University, and the Annual Symposium on Application of Computers to Problems of Urban Society.

Several of the computer magazines, such as *Datamation* and *Computers and Automation,* publish in each issue an agenda of professional and special conferences, many of which deal with aspects of information technology; these magazines also include lists of awards by government agencies to computer firms and systems developers for work on information systems. An extensive calendar of conferences and seminars also appears in *Public Automation.* Two discount book clubs, the Library of Computer and Automation Service and the Library of Urban Affairs, feature important books relating to the use of technology for dealing with social problems.

I. Routes to the New Information Technology

A. DATABANKS

Almendinger, Vladimir V. "SPAN: A System for Urban Data Management." *Computer Yearbook and Directory,* 1966, pp. 175–182. Detroit: Frank H. Gille.

Auerbach, Isaac L. "Information Technology in the United States." *Computer Yearbook and Directory,* 1966, pp. 49–55. Detroit: Frank H. Gille.

Automated Management Information System for the State of California Department of Motor Vehicles, An. Sacramento: Transportation Agency, Department of Motor Vehicles, January 1966.

Baran, Paul. *Remarks on the Question of Privacy Raised by the Automation of Mental Health Records.* Santa Monica, California: The RAND Corporation, April 1967.

Behrens, Carl. "Computers and Security." *Science News* 91 (June 3, 1967): 532–533.

Berkeley, Edmund C. "Individual Privacy and Central Computerized Files." *Computers and Automation* 15 (October 1966): 7.

Bigelow, Robert P. "Legal and Security Issues Posed by Computer Utilities." *Harvard Business Review* 45 (September/October 1967): 150–161.

Bisco, Ralph L. "Social Science Data Archives: A Review of Developments." *American Political Science Review* 60 (March 1966): 93–109.

——— *Urban Study Data Banks: A Preliminary Report.* New York: Council of Social Science Data Archives, October 1966.

Black, Harold, and Edward Shaw. "Detroit's Data Banks." *Datamation* 13 (March 1967): 25–27.

Brooks, Edward M. "The Role of the Data Bank in the UPO." Paper prepared by the Research Division of the United Planning Organization, Washington, D.C., May 25, 1967, revised July 17, 1969.

"California Statewide Federated Information Systems (SFIS) Status Report." Sacramento: Systems Analysis Office, Department of General Services, December 31, 1968.

Cattani, Jim. "Calls Data Banks Inefficient in Serving Statistics Users." *Electronic News* (November 17, 1969), Sec. 1, p. 32.

"Census Bureau Tackles Information Revolution." *Public Management* 50 (February 1968): 48–49.

Comber, E. V. "Management of Confidential Information." From the proceedings of the Fall Joint Computer Conference, Las Vegas, Nevada, November 1969.

Computer and Invasion of Privacy, The. U.S. House of Representatives, Special Subcommittee on Invasion of Privacy, Committee on Government Operations, 89th Congress, 2nd Session, July 26–28, 1966.

"Computer-Based Justice Identification and Intelligence System." *Digital Computer Newsletter* 17 (April 1965): 52–53.

Computer Privacy, U.S. Senate, Subcommittee on Administrative Practice and Procedure, Committee on the Judiciary, 90th Congress, 1st Session, March 14–15, 1967.

"Computer Systems for Welfare." *Public Automation,* December 1969, p. 5.

"Computerization of Government Files, The: What Impact on the Individual?" *U.C.L.A. Law Review* 15 (1968): 1371–1409.

Coon, Thomas F. "Technological Law Enforcement—Victories and Voids." *Police* 12 (January/February 1968): 19–22.

Cunningham, Joseph F. "The Need for ADP Standards in the Federal Government." *Datamation* 15 (February 1969): 26–28.

Curran, William J., Barbara Stearns, and Honora Kaplan. *Legal Considerations in the Establishment of a Health Information System in Greater Boston and the State of Massachusetts.* A Report to the Project for the Preliminary Design of a Health Information System for Boston. Cambridge, Mass.: Joint Center for Urban Studies of M.I.T. and Harvard University, December 1, 1968.

Darby, Ralph L. "Information Analysis Centers as a Source for Information and Data." *Special Libraries* 59 (February 1968): 91–97.

Data Processing Management in the Federal Government. U.S. House of Representatives, Subcommittee on Government Activities, Committee on Government Operations, 90th Congress, 1st Session, July 18–20, 1967.

"Debate Will Rage and Confuse the Issues, but a National Data Center will Become Reality." *Business Automation* 17 (January 1970): 62–63.

Design of a Federal Statistical Data Center, The. U.S. House of Representatives, Special Subcommittee on Invasion of Privacy, Committee on Government Operations, 89th Congress, 2nd Session, July 26–28, 1966.

Doyle, J. "California First: A Computerized Welfare System." *San Francisco Chronicle,* September 15, 1969.

Dunn, Edgar. "The Idea of a National Data Center and the Issue of Privacy." *The American Statistician* 21 (February 1967): 21–27.

—— *Review of Proposal for a National Data Center,* Statistical Evaluation Report No. 6. Washington, D.C.: Office of Statistical Standards, Bureau of the Budget, December 1965.

Dyba, Jerome E. "Law Enforcement Management in Anne Arundel County, Maryland." *Law and Computer Technology* 2 (May 1969): 16–25.

Evans, J. A. *A Framework for the Evolutionary Development of an Executive Information System.* Bedford, Mass.: The Mitre Corporation, June 1968.

"Everything's Up-to-Date in Kansas City." *Journal of Data Management* 5 (October 1967): 30–32, 34.

Fanwick, Charles. *Maintaining Privacy of Computerized Data.* Santa Monica, California: System Development Corporation, December 1, 1966.

Feige, Edgar L., and Harold Watts. "Protection of Privacy through Micro-Aggregation." Social Science Research Institute, University of Wisconsin, June 1967. Presented to the Fourth Annual Conference on the Council of Social Science Data Archives, Los Angeles, California, June 1967.

Finke, Walter. "Information: Dilemma or Deliverance?" *Computers and Automation* 15 (August 1966): 22–25.

First Ten Years, The: A Proposed Government Information System for Dade County, Florida. Miami, Florida: Data Processing Division, Office of the County Manager, 1969.

Gallagher, Cornelius E. "Databanks and Civil Liberties." *Congressional Record,* August 8, 1968.

——— "Efficiency — Purchased at the Price of Privacy." *Banking* 60 (April 1968): 38–39.

Glaser, E., D. Rosenblatt, and M. K. Wood. "The Design of a Federal Statistical Data Center." *The American Statistician* 21 (February 1967): 12–20.

Goodlad, John I., John F. O'Toole, Jr., and Louise L. Tyler. *Computers and Information Systems in Education.* New York: Harcourt, Brace and World, 1966.

Government Dossier (Survey of Information Contained in Government Files). U.S. Senate, Subcommittee on Administrative Practice and Procedure, Committee on the Judiciary, 90th Congress, 1st Session, November 1967.

Graetz, Robert E. "Integrated Information Systems: A Problem in Psychology." In *Threshold of Planning Information Systems.* Chicago: American Society of Planning Officials, 1967. First presented at the ADP workshops conducted at the ASPO National Planning Conference, Houston, April 1967.

Grossman, Alvin. "The California Educational Information System, with Regional Centers." *Datamation* 13 (March 1967): 32–37.

Haak, Harold H. "The Evolution of a Metropolitan Data System." *Urban Affairs Quarterly* 3 (December 1967): 3–13.

Hair, A. M., Jr. "Municipal Decision Making by 'Databank.'" *Western City,* May 1965.

Halloran, Norbert A. "Judicial Data Centers." *Law and Computer Technology* 2 (April 1969): 9–15.

Hearle, Edward F. R., and Raymond J. Mason. *A Data Processing System for State and Local Governments,* A RAND Corporation Research Study. Englewood Cliffs, N.J.: Prentice-Hall, Inc., 1963.

Hermann, W. W., and H. H. Isaacs. *Advanced Computer Technology and Crime Information Retrieval.* Santa Monica, California: System Development Corporation, January 1965.

Hoffman, J. "Computers and Privacy: A Survey." *Computing Surveys,* vol. 1, no. 2 (June 1969).

INFO: Information Network and File Organization. Miami, Florida: Dade County Computer Center, 1967.

Joint Center for Urban Studies. Project for the Preliminary Design of a Health Information System for Boston for the Period July 1 through September 30, 1967: *Report.* Cambridge, Mass.: Joint Center for Urban Studies of M.I.T. and Harvard University, 1967.

Kennedy, John P. "The California Integrated Law Enforcement Information Systems." *Police* 12 (September/October 1967): 10–15.

Kraemer, Kenneth L., and William H. Mitchel. "Urban Data Processing." *Datamation* 13 (August 1967): 66–68.

Kraemer, Kenneth L., and Paul M. Whisenand. "Status of Automatic Data Processing in Los Angeles and Orange Counties." *Data Processing Magazine* 8 (June 1966): 28–33.

"Logic" Information System, The. Sacramento: Data Processing Center, General Services Agency, County of Santa Clara, California, August 1969.

"Long Range Master Plan for the Utilization of Electronic Data Processing in the State of California." Sacramento: Office of Management Services, State of California. Draft, 1969.

Lottes, James F. "The Georgia Urban Information System." *Law and Computer Technology* 2 (August 1969): 10–13.

Loughary, John W., and Murray Tondow, eds. *Educational Information System Requirements: The Next Two Decades.* Eugene: University of Oregon, College of Education, 1967. Papers from a Conference held at the University of Oregon, at Eugene, Oregon, August 1967.

Lundberg, Fred J. "Urban Information Systems and Data Banks: Better Prospects With an Environmental Model." In *Threshold of Planning Information Systems.* Chicago: American Society of Planning Officials, 1967. First presented at the ADP workshops conducted at the ASPO National Planning Conference, Houston, April 1967.

Mallinson, C. W. "The Use of Computers in Local Government in Great Britain." *Law and Computer Technology* 2 (August 1969): 16–23.

Maron, M. E. "Large-Scale Data Banks." *Law and Computer Technology* 2 (October 1969): 12–19.

Miller, Robert J. "Can EDP Win the War on Crime?" *Datamation* 14 (June 1968): 81–84.

Milliman, Gordon. "Alameda County's People Information System." *Datamation* 13 (March 1967): 28–31.

Mitchel, William H. "Tooling Computers to the Medium-Sized City." *Public Management* 59 (March 1967): 63–73.

Modernizing the Management Information System for Federal Civilian Manpower (Complete Report). U.S. Civil Service Commission, Policy Development Division, Bureau of Policies and Standards, March 31, 1966.

Montijo, Robert E., Jr. "California DMV Goes On-Line." *Datamation* 13 (May 1967): 31–36.

Morgan, Dan. "The District Government on Tape." *Potomac Magazine* (The Sunday Magazine of the Washington *Post*), January 1, 1967, pp. 12–15.

Moss, Judith. "Approaches to Municipal Information Systems." *Output of Public Automation,* vol. 5, July 1969.

National Commission on Technology, Automation, and Economic Progress. *Educational Implications of Technological Change,* Appendix Volume IV, Report of the Commission on Technology and the American Economy. Washington, D.C., February 1966.

"National Crime Information Center, A." *F.B.I. Law and Enforcement Bulletin,* May 1966.

"New Job Banks Called Success by U.S. Official." *Computerworld,* November 26, 1969, p. 14.

Nixon, Julian. "Federal Data Centers — Present and Proposed." Presented at Hearings on Computer Privacy, before the Subcommittee on Administrative Practice and Procedure, Committee on the Judiciary, U.S. Senate, 90th Congress, 1st Session, March 14–15, 1968.

Norrgard, David L. *Regional Law Enforcement.* Chicago, Illinois: Public Administration Service, 1969.

Orchanian, Paul L. "Data Processing Techniques for Computers and Local Law Enforcement." *Law and Computer Technology* 2 (May 1969): 11–15.

O'Toole, John F., Jr. *Applications of Computers and Information Processing Systems in Education.* Santa Monica, California: System Development Corporation, March 12, 1965.

Parker, J. K. "The Comprehensive Municipal Data System of Alexandria, Virginia." Paper delivered at the Census Tract Conference, Bureau of the Census, Philadelphia, 1965.

———— "Operating a City Databank." *Public Automation,* vol. 1, June 1965.

Parkoff, Stephen B. "The Form and Function of National Educational Data Center." *Data Processing Magazine* 10 (February 1968): 34–37.

Petersen, H. E., and R. Turn. 'System Implications of Information Privacy." Paper presented for Spring Joint Computer Conference, April 17–19, 1967, Atlantic City, N.J.

"Plans for Congressional EDP System Again Revived." *Datamation* 15 (November 1969): 375, 377.

Price, Dennis G. "Automation in State and Local Governments." *Datamation* 13 (March 1967): 22–25.

Prisendorf, Anthony. "The Computer vs. the Bill of Rights." *The Nation,* October 31, 1966, pp. 449–452.

"Privacy." *Law and Contemporary Problems,* vol. 31, no. 2 (Spring 1966).

"Proposals for Municipal Information Systems Asked." *Datamation* 15 (November 1969): 383.

"Proposed Registrar Would Keep Track of Data Banks." *Computerworld,* August 6, 1969.

Remy, Raymond. "Survey Discloses Tremendous Growth of Data Processing in California Cities." *Western City,* July 1969, pp. 13–14, 31.

Riesan, Victor D. "An Integrated Justice System." *Law and Computer Technology* 2 (September 1969): 15–22.

Rogers, C. D. "AIP Survey of Automated Information Systems for Urban Planning." Unpublished report for American Institute of Planners. 1967.

Rosove, Perry E. *Developing Computer-Based Information Systems.* New York: John Wiley and Sons, Inc., 1968.

Ross, Charles U. "Data Banks for Crime Detection." *Output of Public Automation,* vol. 6, no. 1 (January 1970).

Rothman, Stanley. "Centralized Government Information Systems and Privacy." Paper presented to the President's Commission on Law Enforcement and Administration of Justice, September 22, 1966.

Rubinoff, Morris, ed. *Toward a National Information System.* Washington, D.C.: Spartan Books, 1965. Proceedings of the Second National Colloquium on Information Retrieval, Philadelphia, 1965.

Sable, Robert W. "Law Enforcement Data Processing." *Communications of the ACM* (Association for Computing Machinery) 8 (April 1965): 248.

"San Mateo County to Install Electronic Records System." *National Civic Review* 52 (July 1963): 388–389.

" 'Scope' Completes First Year of Fighting Crime in Nevada." *Computerworld,* December 11, 1968, p. 8.

Selecting a Computer System. Occasional Paper No. 1. Chicago: Public Automated Systems Service, 1969.

Semling, Harold V., Jr. "Congress and the Computer." *Law and Computer Technology* 2 (November 1969): 7–13.

"Short-Range Master Plan for the Utilization of Electronic Data Processing (EDP) in the State of California." Sacramento: Office of Management Services, December 30, 1968.

Singer, J. Peter. "Computer-Based Hospital Information Systems." *Datamation* 15 (May 1969): 38–45.

Soper, L. G. "Regional Cooperation Initiates San Gabriel Valley Municipal Data System." *Western City,* July 1969, pp. 16, 31.

Steinberg, Joseph, and Heyman C. Cooper. "Social Security Statistical Data, Social Science Research, and Confidentiality." *Social Security Bulletin* 30 (October 1967): 3–15.

Survey of City Data Processing. Sacramento: League of California Cities, June 26, 1969.

System for Processing Educational Data Electronically. Tallahassee, Florida: State Department of Education, 1967.

Tamaru, Takuji. "Prospects in Municipal Information Systems: The Example of Los Angeles." *Computers and Automation* 17 (January 1968): 15–18.

Tondow, M. "Computers in the Schools: Palo Alto." *Datamation* 14 (June 1968): 57–62.

"Toward California Intergovernment Information Systems." *Public Automation* 5 (September 1969): 1–2.

"Traffic Safety — A National Data Center." *SDC Magazine* 11 (May 1969): 19.

"Urban and Regional Information Systems for Social Programs," Conference Proceedings. Mineola, N.Y.: Urban Regional Information Systems Association, 1967.

Urban and Regional Information Systems: Support for Planning in Metropolitan Areas. U.S. Department of Housing and Urban Development. Washington, D.C., October 1968.

Wagner, Robert C. "Jury Selection by Computer." *Law and Computer Technology* 2 (October 1969): 6–11.

Ware, Willis H. "Security and Privacy in Computer Systems." Paper presented at Spring Joint Computer Conference, April 17–19, 1967, Atlantic City, N.J.
——— "Security and Privacy: Similarities and Differences." *AFIPS* 30:287–290. Proceedings of Spring Joint Computer Conference. Washington, D.C.: Thompson Books, 1967.

Warren, David G. "Computers at Work in State Legislatures." *Law and Computer Technology* 2 (August 1969): 3–9.

Westin, Alan F. "Computers and the Protection of Privacy." *Technology Review* 71 (April 1969): 32–37.
——— "Legal Safeguards to Insure Privacy in a Computer Society." *Communications of the ACM* 10 (September 1967): 533–537.
——— *Privacy and Freedom.* New York: Atheneum, 1967.

Whisenand, Paul M. "California State EDP." *Datamation* 14 (March 1968): 96–97.

Whisenand, Paul M., and John D. Hodges, Jr. "Automated Police Information Systems: A Survey." *Datamation* 15 (May 1969): 91–96.

Yarbrough, L. Everett. "The Florida Project: A System for Processing Educational Data Electronically." *Journal of Educational Data Processing* 3 (Spring 1966): 58–66.

B. Management Science Techniques

Planning-Programming-Budgeting

"Administrative Framework for Establishing Planning-Programming-Budgeting Systems in States, Cities and Counties: Some Considerations and Suggested Possibilities (January 1967): PPB Note 2." In *Planning, Programming, Budgeting for City, State, County Objectives: PPB Notes 1–8*. Washington, D.C.: George Washington University, State-Local Finances Project, June 1968.

Alesch, Daniel J. "Government in Evolution: A Real World Focus for State Planning." *Public Administration Review* 28 (May/June 1968): 264–267.

Cananese, Anthony George, and Alan Walter Steiss. "Programming for Governmental Operations: The Critical Path Approach." *Public Administration Review* 28 (March/April 1968): 155–167.

Capron, William M. "PPB and State Budgeting." *Public Administration Review* 29 (March/April 1969): 155–159.

Churchman, C. W., and A. H. Schainblatt. "PPB: How Can It Be Implemented?" *Public Administration Review* 29 (March/April 1969): 178–188.

Diebold, John. "Computers, Program Management, and Foreign Affairs." *Foreign Affairs* 45 (October 1966): 125–134.

Downs, Anthony. "PPBS And The Evolution of Planning." In *Threshold of Planning Information Systems*. Chicago: American Society of Planning Officials, 1967. First presented at the ADP workshops conducted at the ASPO National Planning Conference, Houston, April 1967.

Drew, Elizabeth. "HEW Grapples with PPBS." *Public Interest* 8 (Summer 1967): 9–29.

Dror, Yehezkel. "PPB and the Public Policy-Making System: Some Reflections on the Papers by Bertram Gross and Allen Schick." *Public Administration Review* 29 (March/April 1969): 152–154.

Gorham, William. "Notes of a Practitioner." *Public Interest* 8 (Summer 1967): 4–8.

Governmental ADP: The Practitioners Speak. Compiled by the Public Automated Systems Service. Chicago: Public Automated Systems Service and Public Administration Service, 1968.

Gross, Bertram M. "The New Systems Budgeting." *Public Administration Review* 29 (March–April 1969): 113–132.

Harper, Edwin L., Fred A. Kramer, and Andrew M. Rouse. "Implementation and Use of PPB in Sixteen Federal Agencies." *Public Administration Review* 29 (November–December 1969): 623–632.

Held, Virginia. "PPBS Comes to Washington." *Public Interest* 4 (Summer 1966): 102–115.

Hovey, Harold A. *The Planning-Programming-Budgeting Approach to Government Decision-Making.* New York: Praeger, 1968.

Lauber, John G. "PPBS in State Government — Maryland's Approach." *State Government* 42 (Winter 1969): 31–37.

Lyden, Fremont J., and Ernest G. Miller. *Planning, Programming, Budgeting: A Systems Approach to Management.* Chicago: Markham Publishing Co., 1968.

McKean, Roland N., and Melvin Anshen. "Limitations, Risks, and Problems." In *Program Budgeting: Program Analysis and the Federal Government,* ed. David Novick, 2nd ed., pp. 285–307. Cambridge, Mass.: Harvard University Press, 1967.

Millward, Robert E. "PPBS: Problems of Implementation." *Journal of the AIP* 34 (March 1968): 88–94.

Mitchell, James. "A Series of Comment . . . PPBS: Panacea or Pestilence?" *AEDS Monitor,* January 1970, pp. 6, 7, 10, 13.

Mosher, Frederick C. "Limitations and Problems of PPBS in the States." *Public Administration Review* 29 (March/April 1969): 160–166.

Mosher, Frederick C., and John E. Harr. *Program Budgeting Visits Foreign Affairs.* Syracuse, N.Y.: Inter-University Case Program, Inc., 1969.

Mushkin, Selma J. "PPB in Cities." *Public Administration Review* 29 (March/April 1969): 167–177.

Mushkin, Selma J., and Marjorie Wilcox. *An Operative PPB System: A Collaborative Undertaking in the States.* Washington, D.C.: George Washington University, State-Local Finances Project, 1968.

Novick, David. *Program Budgeting: Program Analysis and the Federal Budget.* Cambridge, Mass.: Harvard University Press, 1965. 2nd ed., 1967.

Planning-Programming and Budgeting — Interim Observations. U.S. Senate, Subcommittee on National Security and International Operations (Jackson Subcommittee), Committee on Government Operations, December 2, 1968.

Planning-Programming-Budgeting, Hearings, Part I. U.S. Senate, Subcommittee on National Security and International Operations, Committee on Government Operations, 90th Congress, 1st Session, August 23, 1967.

Planning-Programming-Budgeting, Hearings, Part II. U.S. Senate, Subcommittee on National Security and International Operations, Committee on Government Operations, 90th Congress, 1st Session, September 27 and October 18, 1967.

Planning-Programming-Budgeting: PPBS and Foreign Affairs, Memorandum. U.S. Senate, Subcommittee on National Security and International Operations, Committee on Government Operations, 90th Congress, 1st Session, January 5, 1968.

Planning-Programming-Budgeting: Selected Comment. U.S. Senate Subcommittee on National Security and International Operations, Committee on Government Operations, 90th Congress, 1st Session, July 26, 1967.

"Program Budgeting for Police Departments." *Yale Law Journal* 76 (March 1967): 822–838.

"The Role and Nature of Cost Analysis in a PPB System: PPB Note 6 (April 1967)." In *Planning, Programming, Budgeting for City, State, County*

Objectives: PPB Notes 1–8. Washington, D.C.: George Washington University, State-Local Finances Project, June 1968.

Schelling, Thomas. "PPBS and Foreign Affairs." *Public Interest* 11 (Spring 1968): 26–36.

Tunney, John V. "PPBS and the Congress." *Congressional Record — House of Representatives,* June 18, 1969, p. E5041.

Wildavsky, Aaron. "The Political Economy of Efficiency: Cost Benefit Analysis, Systems Analysis, and Program Budgeting." *Public Administration Review* 26 (December 1966): 292–310.

——— "Rescuing Policy Analysis from PPBS." *Public Administration Review* 29 (March/April 1969): 189–202.

Systems Analysis and Operations Research

Abt, Clark C. "Computer Applications to Social and Economic Problem Solving." *Nerem Report*: Proceedings of the 1968 Northeast Electronics Research and Engineering Meeting, sponsored by Institute of Electrical and Electronics Engineers, Newton, Mass., 1968, p. 46.

"Aerospace Aims to Link Talent with Problems." *Aviation Week & Space Technology* 89 (July 1, 1968): 40.

Anstutz, Arnold E. "City Management — A Problem in Systems Analysis." *Technology Review* 71 (Oct.–Nov. 1968): 47–52.

Anthony, Robert N. *Planning and Control Systems: A Framework for Analysis.* Boston: Graduate School of Business Administration, Harvard University, 1965.

Beshers, James M., ed. *Computer Methods in the Analysis of Large-Scale Social Systems.* Cambridge, Mass.: Joint Center for Urban Studies of M.I.T. and Harvard University, 1965.

Black, Guy. *The Application of Systems Analysis to Government Operations.* New York: Praeger, 1968.

Boffey, Philip M. "Systems Analysis: No Panacea for Nation's Domestic Problems." *Science* 158 (November 24, 1967): 1028–1030.

Bower, Joseph L. "Systems Analysis for Social Decisions." *Operations Research* 17 (November–December 1969): 927–940.

Branch, Melville C. "Simulation, Mathematical Models, and Comprehensive City Planning." *Urban Affairs Quarterly* 1 (March 1966): 15–38.

Brown, Edmund. "Aerospace Studies for the Problems of Men." *State Government* 39 (Winter 1966): 2–7.

Bushnell, Don D. "Education: Future Computer Applications." *Data Processing Yearbook,* 1965, pp. 207–212.

"California Integrated Transportation Study." El Segundo, California: North American Aviation, Inc., 1965.

"California Statewide Information Systems Study" (Final Report). Burbank, California: Lockheed Missiles and Space Company, 1965.

California Waste Management Study. A Report to the State of California Department of Public Health. Aguza, California: Aerojet-General Corporation, 1965.

Chartrand, Robert L. "Congress Seeks a Systems Approach," *Datamation* 14 (May 1968): 46–49.

Churchman, C. West. *The Systems Approach.* New York: Dell Publishing Company, 1968.

"Cities and Systems Management," *Aviation Week & Space Technology* 89 (July 1, 1968): 11.

Clark, Evert. "Systems Analysts Are Baffled By Problems of Social Change," *The New York Times,* March 24, 1968, p. 28.

Cleland, David I. and William R. King. *Systems Analysis and Project Management.* New York: McGraw-Hill Company, 1968.

Collins, Frederic W. "Computers in Public Service: Down to Earth Systems Analysis," *Round Table* 223 (July 1966): 274–278.

Conlisk, G. Michael. "Systems Analysis — How It Works in East Lansing," *Public Management* 51 (February 1969): 6–8.

"COSPUP Suggests Restraint In Application of Systems Analysis Techniques to Research," *NAS/NRC/NAE News Report* 17 (October 1967): 5.

Crecine, John P. "Computer Simulation in Urban Research," *Public Administration Review* 28 (January/February 1968): 66–77.

Forrester, Jay W. "A Deeper Knowledge of Social Systems," *Technology Review* 71 (April 1969): 21–31.

Frieden, Bernard J. "The Governmental Maze: National Goals and Local Barriers," *Technology Review* 70 (January 1968): 31–35.

Genensky, S. M. "Some Comments on Urban Research." Paper presented at the IEEE Meeting at the Space Technology Laboratories, Los Angeles, California, March 19, 1968, and issued as RAND Paper P-3827. Santa Monica, Calif.: RAND Corporation, April 1968.

Gilmore, John S., John J. Ryan, and William Gould. "Defense Systems Resources in the Civil Sector: An Evolving Approach An Uncertain Market." University of Denver Research Institute. Report prepared for the U.S. Arms Control and Disarmament Agency, July 1967.

Gross, Bertram M. "The New Systems Budgeting." *Public Administration Review* 29 (March/April 1969): 113–137.

Hemmens, George C. "Planning Agency Experience with Urban Development Models and Data Processing." *Journal of the American Institute of Planners* 34 (September 1968): 323–327.

Hermann, William. *A Systems Approach to Command and Control in Crime Prevention and Control.* SDC Publication. Santa Monica, California: System Development Corporation, 1968.

Hitch, Charles J. *Decision-Making for Defense.* Berkeley and Los Angeles: University of California Press, 1965.

Hoos, Ida R. "Automation, Systems Engineering, and Public Administration: Observations and Reflections on the California Experience." *Public Administration Review* 26 (December 1966): 311–319.

——— "A Realistic Look at the Systems Approach to Social Problems." *Datamation* 15 (February 1969): 233–238.

"Industry Concern Grows but Solutions to Problems Arrive Slowly Due to Lack of Public Pressure." *Business Automation* 17 (January 1970): 60–62.

Kalish, James A. "Flim-Flam, Double-Talk, and Hustle: The Urban Problems Industry." *Washington Monthly* 1 (November 1969): 6–16.

Menkhaus, Edward J. "Systems in the 70's." *Business Automation* 16 (January 1969): 46–56.

Mitchel, William H. "Aerospace Technology and Urban Systems." *Datamation* 14 (April 1968): 85–90.

————— "Urban Planners and Information." *Datamation* 12 (October 1966): 82–84, 86.

Morse, Philip, and Laura Bacon, eds. *Operations Research for Public Systems.* Cambridge: The M.I.T. Press, 1967.

Navarro, Joseph A., and Jean G. Taylor. "An Application of Systems Analysis to Aid in the Efficient Administration of Justice." *Judicature* 51 (August/ September 1967): 47–52.

Nelson, F. Barry. "ACM Symposium Tackles Urban Ills." *Datamation* 14 (December 1968): 74–75, 78.

O'Meara, Francis E. "The Challenge of Operations Review." *California Management Review* 7 (Summer 1965): 19–26.

Overly, Don H. "An Application of Systems Analysis to Decision-Making in Local Government." Paper presented to the Third Annual Conference on ADP Systems in Local Government, New York, New York, June 19–21, 1967.

Ramo, Simon. *Cure for Chaos.* New York: David McKay, 1968.

————— "The Systems Approach: Automated Common Sense." *Nation's Cities* 6 (March 1968): 14–19.

Rogers, W. L. "Aerospace Systems Technology and the Creation of Environment." In *Environment for Man: The Next Fifty Years,* ed. William R. Ewald, Jr., pp. 260–274. Bloomington, Indiana: Indiana University Press, 1967.

Saloma, John S. "Systems Politics: The Presidency and Congress in the Future." *Technology Review* 71 (December 1968): 23–33.

Schick, Allen. "Systems Politics and Systems Budgeting." *Public Administration Review* 29 (March/April 1969): 137–151.

Schriever, Bernard A. "Systems Analysis, An Evolving Tool of Defense Management," with comments by Fred S. Hoffman. Presented to the AIAA-ORSA Forum on Systems Analysis and Social Change, Washington, D.C., March 18–20, 1968.

Smith, Bruce L. R. *The RAND Corporation: Case Study of a Nonprofit Advisory Corporation.* Cambridge, Mass.: Harvard University Press, 1966.

Systems Concepts. Report No. 1 of IBM–City of New Haven Joint Information Study. New Haven, Conn., 1967.

"Systems Technology Applied to Social and Community Problems." A Report Prepared for the Subcommittee on Employment, Manpower, and Poverty of the Committee on Labor and Public Welfare, U.S. Senate, June 1969.

"Technological Transfer Faces 'Real World' Test." *Aviation Week and Space Technology* 89 (July 1, 1968): 51.

Teitz, Michael B. "Cost Effectiveness: A Systems Approach to Analysis of Urban Services." *Journal of the American Institute of Planners* 34 (September 1968): 303.

Tomlinson, R. C. "Decision-Making, Operational Research and the Systems Approach." *Operational Research Quarterly* 19 (Special Issue, April 1968): 1–4.

Tunney, John V. "Congress Views the Application of the Systems Approach to Public Problems." *Congressional Record,* February 8, 1968, E643–645.

"Use of Computers Challenges Cities." *Nation's Cities,* vol. 6, no. 9 (September 1968).

II. Information Techniques and Decision-Making

Abt, Clark C. "Public Participation in Future Forecasting and Planning." Remarks to World Future Society, Washington, D.C., June 14, 1967.

Ackoff, Russell. "Management Misinformation Systems." *Management Science* 14 (December 1967): B-147–B-156.

Adams, Sexton. "EDP Effects on Organization Structure." *Business Review* (University of Houston) 14 (Winter 1966/1967): 16–27.

Alexander, Tom. "Computers Can't Solve Everything." *Fortune* 80 (October 1969): 126–129, 168, 171.

Armer, Paul. *Social Implications of the Computer Utility.* Santa Monica, California: The RAND Corporation, August 1967.

Baran, Paul. *Communications, Computers and People.* Santa Monica, California: The RAND Corporation, November 1965.

Barnett, C. C. *The Future of the Computer Utility.* New York: American Management Association, 1967.

Bell, Daniel, "The Post-Industrial Society." In *Technology and Social Change,* ed. Eli Ginzberg, pp. 45–59. New York: Columbia University Press, 1964.

Bennis, Warren G. "Post-Bureaucratic Leadership." *Trans-action* 6 (July–August 1969): 44–51, 61.

Blatt, Donald H. "In Nassau County: Organizing for Information." *Public Management* 49 (October 1967): 292–293.

Boguslaw, Robert. *The New Utopians: A Study of System Design and Social Change.* Englewood Cliffs, N.J.: Prentice-Hall, Inc., 1965.

Brady, Rodney H. "Computers in Top-Level Decision-Making." *Harvard Business Review* 45 (July/August 1967): 67–76.

Brzezinski, Zbigniew. "The American Transition," *New Republic* 157 (December 23, 1967), 18–21.

Burlingame, J. F. "Information Technology and Decentralization." *Harvard Business Review* 39 (November/December 1961): 121–126.

Calder, Nigel. "Brains Versus Computers: How Much Decision-Making Can We Leave to the Machine?" *New Statesman* 75 (May 17, 1968): 645–648.

Carlson, Walter M. "A Management Information System Designed by Managers." *Datamation* 13 (May 1967): 37–43.

"Centralized Management Information System, A: The Experience of the 'Largest Organization in the Free World.'" *SDC Magazine* 11 (October 1968): 2–16.

Chamis, Alice Yanosko. "The Design of Information Systems." *Law and Computer Technology* 2 (September 1969): 2–14.

Cheng, Kenneth. "Statistics and General Purpose Information System for the Provincial Government of Ontario, Canada." Paper presented at the Conference on "The Large-Scale Public System: Its Problems and Prospects," New York University, April 1–2, 1966.

Conrad, Thomas M. "Systems Analysis, the Liberal Establishment, and Totalitarian Dystopias." *Commonweal* 90 (May 30, 1969): 321–323.

Cornog, Geoffrey Y., et al., eds. *EDP Systems in Public Management*. Chicago: Rand McNally and Co., 1968.

Criteria for Evaluation in Planning State and Local Programs. U.S. Senate, Subcommittee on Intergovernmental Relations, Committee on Government Operations, 90th Congress, 1st Session, July 21, 1967.

Dean, Neal J. "The Computer Comes of Age." *Harvard Business Review* 46 (January/February 1968): 83–91.

Dearden, John. "Myth of Real-Time Management Information." *Harvard Business Review* 44 (May/June 1966): 123–132.

Dial, O. E. "Urban Information Systems: A Bibliographic Essay." Paper presented for The Summer Studies Group on Urban Information Systems, June 24–August 31, 1968. Published by the Urban Systems Laboratory, Massachusetts Institute of Technology, Cambridge, Massachusetts.

Diebold, John. "Bad Decisions on Computer Use." *Harvard Business Review*, 47 (January/February 1969): 14–16, 27–28, 176.

——— *Man and the Computer: Technology as an Agent of Social Change*. New York: Frederick A. Praeger, 1969.

——— "What's Ahead for Computer Technology?" *Management Review* 56 (December 1967): 28–31.

Donald, A. G. *Management Information and Systems*. Oxford: Pergamon Press, 1967.

Downs, Anthony. "A Realistic Look at the Final Payoffs from Urban Data Systems." *Public Administration Review* 27 (September 1967): 204–210.

Drucker, Peter F. *The Age of Discontinuity: Guidelines to Our Changing Society*. New York: Harper and Row, 1969.

Edwards, W., H. Lindman, and L. Phillips. *Emerging Technologies for Making Decisions*. New York: Holt, Rinehart, and Winston, 1965.

Ehrle, Raymond A. "Decision-Making in an Automated Age." *Personnel Journal* 42 (November 1963): 492–494.

Eilon, Samuel. "Some Notes on Information Processing." *The Journal of Management Studies* 5 (May 1968): 139–153.

"Electronic Data Processing in Public Administration" (Symposium). *Public Administration Review* 22 (September 1962): 129–152.

Emery, James C. "The Impact of Information Technology on Organizations." In *Evolving Concepts of Management,* ed. Edwin B. Flippo. Proceedings of the 24th Annual Meeting of the Academy of Management, Chicago, 1964. Available from Dept. of Management, Bowling Green State University, Bowling Green, Ohio.

Ewing, David W. *The Practice of Planning*. New York: Harper and Row, 1968.

Federal Research and Development Programs, The: The Decision-Making Process, Hearings. U.S. House of Representatives, Subcommittee on Research and Technical Problems, Committee on Government Operations, 89th Congress, 2nd Session, January 7, 10, 11, 1966.

Ferkiss, Victor C. *Technological Man: The Myth and the Reality.* New York: George Braziller, 1969.

Ferry, W. H. "Must We Rewrite the Constitution to Control Technology?" *Saturday Review* 51 (March 2, 1968): 50–54.

Friedland, Edward I. "Technology as a Resource in Public Administration." Prepared for delivery at the Sixty-Fifth Annual Meeting of the American Political Science Association, Commodore Hotel, New York City, September 2–6, 1969.

Friedmann, John. "An Information Model of Urbanization." *Urban Affairs Quarterly* 4 (December 1968): 235–244.

Fromm, Erich. *The Revolution of Hope: Toward a Humanized Technology.* New York: Harper and Row, 1968.

Gallagher, Cornelius E. "Computing in Real Time." Speech before the Association for Computing Machinery Technical Symposium, June 19, 1969.

Gardner, John W. "Toward a Humane Technology." *Science and Technology,* no. 73 (January 1968), pp. 56–60.

Gill, William A. "Sound Management and Effective Use of Computers in the Federal Government." *Computers and Automation* 14 (April 1965): 14–17.

Ginsburg, Sigmund G. "Municipal Management Innovations." *Nation's Cities* 7 (February 1969): 26–29.

Green, Harold P. "The New Technological Era: A View from the Law." *Bulletin of the Atomic Scientists* 23 (November 1967): 12–18.

Grundstein, Nathan D. "Urban Information Systems and Urban Management Decisions and Control." *Urban Affairs Quarterly* 1 (June 1966): 20–32.

Hambleton, Glen W. "The Computer's Role in Decision-Making." *Automation* 15 (January 1968): 141–143.

Harrington, Michael. *The Accidental Century.* New York: Macmillan, 1965.

———— *Toward a Democratic Left: A Radical Program for a New Majority.* New York: The Macmillan Company, 1968.

Harris, Britton. "The New Technology and Urban Planning." *Urban Affairs Quarterly* 3 (December 1967): 14–40.

Hattery, Lowell H. "EDP: Implications for Public Administration." *Public Administration Review* 22 (September 1962): 129–130.

Heit, Marvin. "Computers and the City." *Computer Usage,* vol. 3, no. 1 (Winter 1968).

Holmer, Freeman. "Alterations in the Management Environment: The Separation of Duties and Responsibilities Resulting from Installation of ADP." Paper presented to the 3rd Annual Conference on ADP Systems in Local Government, New York University, New York, New York, June 19, 1967.

Hoos, Ida R. "Systems Analysis, Information Handling, and the Research Function: Implication of the California Experience." Berkeley, California: University of California, Space Sciences Laboratory, Social Sciences Project, Internal Working Paper No. 68, November 1967.

Information, See Scientific American.

Institute for Defense Analysis. *Science and Technology: Task Force Report.*

Report to the President's Commission on Law Enforcement and Administration of Justice. Washington, D.C.: Government Printing Office, 1967.

Isaacs, Herbert H. *Time-Sharing and User-Oriented Computer Systems: Some Implications for Public Administration.* Santa Monica, California: System Development Corporation, September 30, 1964.

—— *User-Oriented Systems for State and Local Government.* Santa Monica, California: System Development Corporation, March 5, 1965.

—— "User-Oriented Computer Systems: Some Implications for Public Administration." *Data Processing Magazine* 7 (February 1965): 16–18.

Kibbee, J. M. *SDC Documents Applicable to State and Local Government Problems.* Santa Monica, California: System Development Corporation, February 16, 1965.

Kraemer, Kenneth L. "The Evolution of Information Systems for Urban Administration." *Public Administration Review* 29 (July–August 1969): 389–402.

Kraemer, Kenneth L., and William H. Mitchel. "Urban Data Processing." *Datamation* 13 (August 1967): 66–68.

Kranzberg, Melvin. "Computers: New Values for Society." *Management Review* 56 (February 1967): 30–33.

Lane, Robert E. "The Decline of Politics and Ideology in a Knowledgeable Society." *American Sociological Review* 31 (October 1966): 649–662.

La Porte, Todd R. "Politics and 'Inventing the Future': Perspectives in Science and Government." *Public Administration Review* 27 (June 1967): 117–127.

Lasswell, Harold. "Policy Problems of a Data-Rich Civilization." *International Federation for Documentation, 31st Meeting, and Congress, Proceedings of the 1965 Congress,* Washington, D.C., October 7–16, 1965. In cooperation with the American Documentation Institute. Washington, D.C.: Spartan Books, and London: Macmillan and Company, Ltd., 1965.

MacBride, Robert O. *The Automated State: Computer Systems As a New Force in Society.* Philadelphia: Chilton Book Co., 1967.

McDermott, John. "Technology: The Opiate of the Intellectuals." *New York Review of Books* 13 (July 31, 1969): 25–35.

McLaughlin, John. *Information Technology and the Survival of the Firm.* Homewood, Ill.: Dow Jones-Irwin, Inc., 1966.

Mendel, Arthur P. "Robots and Rebels." *The New Republic* 160 (January 11, 1969): 16–19.

Mesthene, Emmanuel G. "How Technology Will Shape the Future." *Science* 161 (July 12, 1968): 135–143.

—— *Technological Change: Its Impact on Man and Society.* Cambridge, Mass.: Harvard University Press, 1970.

Michael, Donald N. "Planning and Politics." *Daedalus* 97 (Fall 1968): 1179–1193.

—— "Social Engineering and the Future Environment." *American Psychologist* 22 (November 1967): 588–592.

—— "Some Long-Range Implications of Computer Technology for Human Behavior in Organizations." *American Behavioral Scientist* 9 (April 1966): 29–35.

479

———— *The Unprepared Society: Planning for a Precarious Future.* New York: Basic Books, Inc., 1968.

Michaelis, Michael. "Private Enterprise and Public Needs." *Congressional Record,* January 29, 1968, pp. S557–560.

Millikan, Max F. "Inquiry and Policy: The Relation of Knowledge to Action." In *The Human Meaning of the Social Sciences,* ed. Daniel Lerner, pp. 158–182. New York: World Publishing Company, 1959.

Mitchel, William H. "The Anatomy of a Municipal Information and Decision System." In *Threshold of Planning Information Systems.* Chicago: American Society of Planning Officials, 1967. First presented at the ADP workshops conducted at the ASPO National Planning Conference, Houston, April 1967.

———— "The Information Explosion Touches the City Manager." Paper presented for the Executive and the Information Explosion Panel, 1967 ASPA Conference, San Francisco, California, March 29, 1967.

Myers, Charles A., ed. *The Impact of Computers on Management.* Cambridge, Mass.: The M.I.T. Press, 1967.

National Commission on Technology, Automation, and Economic Progress. *Applying Technology to Unmet Needs.* Washington D.C.: Government Printing Office, 1966.

Negroponte, Nicholas. "Towards a Humanism through Machines." *Technology Review* 71 (April 1969): 44–53.

Nickerson, Eugene H. *Management Information System.* Nassau County, New York. Revised edition, March 1968.

Oettinger, Anthony G. "A Bull's Eye View of Management and Engineering Information Systems." Proceedings of the Association for Computing Machinery, 19th National Conference, Philadelphia, August 25–27, 1964.

———— "Communications in the National Decision-Making Process." In Martin Greenberger, ed., *Computers, Communications and the Public Interest.* Baltimore, Md.: The Johns Hopkins Press, 1970. A series of lectures sponsored by the Johns Hopkins University and the Brookings Institution, 1969.

Oettinger, Anthony G., with Sema Marks. *Run, Computer, Run: The Mythology of Educational Innovation.* Cambridge, Mass.: Harvard University Press, 1969.

Parker, John K. "Decisions, Data Needs and Rationality." In *Threshold of Planning Information Systems.* Chicago: American Society of Planning Officials, 1967. First presented at the ADP workshop conducted at the ASPO National Planning Conference, Houston, April 1967.

Parsons, William W. "The Implications of the Information Sciences for Intergovernmental Cooperation in Communications and Exchange of Information." *Computers and Automation,* 18 April 1969, pp. 34–37.

Patrick, R. L. "Computing in the 1970's." *Datamation* 13 (January 1967): 27–30.

Pool, Ithiel de Sola, Stuart McIntosh, and David Griffel. "On the Design of Computer-Based Information Systems." Paper issued by the Massachusetts Institute of Technology, Cambridge, Massachusetts, 1968.

Price, Dennis G. "Automation in State and Local Governments." *Datamation* 13 (March 1967): 22–25.

Price, Dennis G., and Dennis E. Mulvihill. "The Present and Future Use of Computers in State Government." *Public Administration Review* 25 (June 1965): 142–150.

Reilly, Frank H. "Policy Decisions and EDP Systems in the Federal Government." *Public Administration Review* 22 (September 1962): 130–133.

"Report to the President on the Management of Automatic Data Processing in the Federal Government." Report prepared for the Senate Committee on Government Operations, 89th Congress, 1st Session, March 4, 1965, by the Bureau of the Budget.

Rickover, Hyman G. "Humanistic Technology." *American Behavioral Scientist* 9 (January 1965): 3–8.

Rogers, Clark D., ed. *Urban Information and Policy Decisions: Second Annual Conference on Urban Planning Information Systems and Programs, September 24–26, 1964.* Pittsburgh: University of Pittsburgh Institute of Local Government, 1964.

Rowan, Thomas C. "Cybernation and Society: An Overview." *SDC Magazine,* vol. 8, no. 9 (September 1965).

Sage, David M. "Information Systems: A Brief Look into History." *Datamation* 14 (November 1968): 63–69.

Schlesinger, James. "Systems Analysis and the Political Process." *Journal of Law and Economics* 11 (October 1968): 281–298.

Schumacher, B. G. *Computer Dynamics in Public Administration.* Washington, D.C.: Spartan Books, 1967.

Science and Technology, see Institute for Defense Analysis.

Scientific American. *Information.* San Francisco: W. H. Freeman, 1966.

"Second Annual Management Meet Examines the Milieu of MIS." *Datamation* 15 (February 1969): 106–107.

Sherman, Harvey. "Methodology in the Practice of Public Administration." In *The American Academy of Political and Social Science Monograph 8: Theory and Practice of Public Administration: Scope, Objectives, and Methods,* ed. James C. Charlesworth, pp. 254–290. Philadelphia: American Academy of Political and Social Sciences, 1968.

Shubik, Martin. "Information, Rationality, and Free Choice in a Future Democratic Society." *Daedalus* 96 (Summer 1967): 771–778.

Siffin, William J. "Information Technology and Training for Public Administration." In *Management Information Technology: Recent Advance and Implications for Public Administration,* ed. Martin Landau. Symposium, 1964 National Conference on Public Administration, New York, April 17, 1964. Philadelphia: University of Pennsylvania, Fels Institute of Local and State Government, 1965.

Simon, Herbert A. "Designing Organizations for an Information-Rich World." In Martin Greenberger, ed., *Computers, Communications and the Public Interest.* Baltimore, Md.: The Johns Hopkins Press, 1970. A series of lectures sponsored by the Johns Hopkins University and the Brookings Institution, 1969.

Smith, Lloyd P. "Management Problems in a Changing Technological Environment." *Computers and Automation* 14 (April 1965): 18–22.

Staats, Elmer B. "The Government Manager in 2000 A.D." *Wilson Library Bulletin* 42 (March 1968): 701–710.

—— "Information Systems in an Era of Change." *Financial Executive* 35 (December 1967): 37–41.

Stover, Carl F. "Industry, Technology, and Metropolitan Problems." *Public Administration Review* 27 (June 1967): 112–117.

Strausz-Hupé, Robert. "The Uninvited Guests." *Review of Politics* 30 (January 1968): 59–78.

"Toward the Year 2000: Work in Progress." *Daedalus,* vol. 96, no. 3 (Summer 1967).

Tugend, Tom. "Los Angeles' Plunge into Technology." *Nation's Cities* 6 (June 1968): 16–18.

United States, Department of Health, Education, and Welfare. *Toward a Social Report.* Washington: Government Printing Office, 1969.

"Urban Development Models: New Tools for Planning." Special Issue, *Journal of the American Institute of Planners,* May 1965.

Warburton, Peter. "Human Protests and Objections to the Computer, and the Philosophical Sources of Them." *Computers and Automation* 16 (October 1967): 12–13.

Ware, Willis H. *Future Computer Technology and Its Impact.* RAND Paper P-3279. Santa Monica, California: The RAND Corporation, March 1966.

Webber, Melvin H. "The Policy Sciences and the Role of Information in Urban-Systems Planning." In *Urban Information and Policy Decisions: Second Annual Conference on Urban Planning Information and Systems and Programs, September 24–26, 1964,* ed. Clark D. Rogers. Pittsburgh: University of Pittsburgh Institute of Local Government, 1964.

Weiner, Myron E. *Information, Technology, and Municipal Government.* Storrs, Conn.: Institute of Public Service, University of Connecticut, 1967.

Weizenbaum, Joseph. "The Two Cultures of the Computer Age." *Technology Review* 71 (April 1969): 54–57.

Wheaton, William L. C. "Operations Research for Metropolitan Planning." *Journal of the American Institute of Planners* 29 (November 1963): 250–259.

Whisler, Thomas L., and Harold H. Leavitt. "Management in the 1980's." *Harvard Business Review* 36 (November/December 1958): 41–48.

Wilensky, Harold L. *Organizational Intelligence: Knowledge and Policy in Government and Industry.* New York: Basic Books, Inc., 1967.

Withington, Frederic G. "Data Processing's Evolving Place in the Organization." *Datamation* 15 (June 1969): 58, 65–68.

Zannetos, Zenon S. "New Directions for Management Information Systems." *Technology Review* 71 (October–November 1968): 35–39.

Index